SEASONAL GUIDE TO THE NATURAL YEAR

A Month by Month Guide to Natural Events

Oregon, Washington and British Columbia

James Luther Davis

Fulcrum Publishing
Golden, Colorado

Dedicated to my wife, Lani, and my daughter, Risa,
who gave me encouragement and support throughout the project;
and to my parents, Natalie and Luther Davis,
who provided me with so many opportunities

Copyright © 1996 James Luther Davis
Cover photograph copyright © 1996 John Greim/Stock Imagery
Interior photographs by James Luther Davis
Book design by Deborah Rich

Maps included in this book are for general reference only. For more detailed maps and additional information, contact the agencies or specific sites listed in the appendix.

Library of Congress Cataloging-in-Publication Data

Davis, James L. (James Luther).
    Seasonal guide to the natural year : a month by month guide to natural events. Oregon, Washington, and British Columbia / James L. Davis.
        p.   cm.
    Includes bibliographical references and index.
    ISBN 1-55591-197-8 (pbk.)
    1. Natural history—Oregon—Guidebooks. 2. Natural history—Washington (State)—Guidebooks. 3. Natural history—British Columbia—Guidebooks. 4. Seasons—Oregon—Guidebooks. 5. Seasons—Washington (State)—Guidebooks. 6. Seasons—British Columbia—Guidebooks. 7. Oregon—Guidebooks. 8. Washington (State)—Guidebooks. 9. British Columbia—Guidebooks. I. Title.
QH104.5.N6D38 1996
508.795—dc20
                                                                                96-5271
                                                                                CIP

Printed in the United States of America

0 9 8 7 6 5 4 3 2 1

Fulcrum Publishing
350 Indiana Street, Suite 350
Golden, Colorado 80401-5093
(800) 992-2908
(303) 277-1623

The Seasonal Guide to the Natural Year Series

Pennsylvania, New Jersey, Maryland, Delaware, Virginia, West Virginia and Washington, D.C., Scott Weidensaul

New England and New York, Scott Weidensaul

Illinois, Missouri and Arkansas, Barbara Perry Lawton

Colorado, New Mexico, Arizona and Utah, Ben Guterson

Northern California, Bill McMillon

Oregon, Washington and British Columbia, James Luther Davis

Texas, Steve Price

Forthcoming Titles

North Carolina, South Carolina and Tennessee, John Rucker

Florida with Georgia and Alabama Coasts, M. Timothy O'Keefe

Minnesota, Michigan and Wisconsin, John Bates

Southern California, Judy Wade

OREGON HOTSPOTS

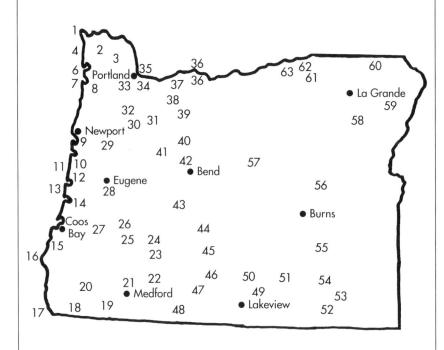

1
4
2
3
6
7 Portland
8 33 34
35
36
36
37
38
63 62
61
60
La Grande
59
58
32
30 31
39
Newport
9 29
40
41
11 10
12
13
42
Bend
57
56
Eugene
28
43
55
14
Coos
Bay 27
26
25 24
23
44
45
Burns
15
16
20
21 22
Medford
46
47
50
49
51
48
54
53
52
Lakeview
18 19
17

Seasonal Guide to
the Natural Year

SITE LOCATOR MAP

N

LIST OF SITES
Oregon

WASHINGTON HOTSPOTS

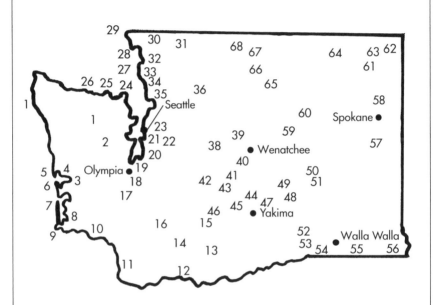

29
30 31   68 67   64   63 62
28   32   61
27   33   66
26 25 24 34   36   65
1   58
        35
        Seattle   60   Spokane ●
1   59
        23
2   21 22   39   57
        20   38   Wenatchee
5 4   40
6   3 Olympia ● 19   50
        18   41   51
7   42 43   49
8   44 47 48
10   45
9   46   15   Yakima
        16
        14 13   52   Walla Walla ●
                        53 54   55   56
11
    12

Seasonal Guide to
the Natural Year

N

SITE LOCATOR MAP

List of Sites
Washington

1. Olympic National Park
2. Brown Creek Beaver Pond
3. Aberdeen Fish Hatchery
4. Bowerman Basin/Grays Harbor
5. Ocean Shores Peninsula
6. Westport
7. Leadbetter Point
8. Willapa Bay National Wildlife Refuge
9. Fort Canby State Park
10. J.B. Hansen National Wildlife Refuge
11. Ridgefield National Wildlife Refuge/ Shillapoo Wildlife Area
12. Little White Salmon National Fish Hatchery
13. Klickitat Wildlife Area
14. Gifford Pinchot National Forest
15. Mount Adams/Bird Creek Meadows
16. Mount Saint Helens National Volcanic Monument
17. Mima Mounds Natural Area Preserve
18. Tumwater Falls
19. Nature Center at Snake Lake
20. Auburn Heron Rookery
21. Bellevue City Parks
22. Issaquah Salmon Hatchery
23. Seattle sites (Discovery Park, Montlake Fill, Lake Washington Locks, etc.)
24. Port Townsend
25. Dungeness National Wildlife Refuge/ Ediz Hook
26. Salt Creek County Park
27. Deception Pass State Park/Washington Park-Anacortes
28. San Juan Islands
29. Birch Bay State Park
30. Sumas
31. Mount Baker
32. Chuckanut Drive
33. Padilla Bay
34. Skagit Wildlife Area and Skagit Flats
35. Kayak Point Regional Park
36. Darrington
37. Mount Baker–Snoqualmie National Forest
38. Gold Creek Pond
39. Leavenworth National Fish Hatchery/ Wenatchee River
40. Red Top Mountain
41. Heart K Ranch
42. Mount Rainier National Park
43. Wenas Creek
44. Yakima River Canyon
45. Oak Creek Wildlife Area
46. Timberwolf Mountain/Rimrock Lake
47. Yakima Training Center
48. Wanapum Dam
49. Ginkgo Petrified Forest State Park
50. Potholes Reservoir
51. Columbia National Wildlife Refuge
52. McNary National Wildlife Refuge
53. Wallula Habitat Management Unit
54. Walla Walla Valley/Touchet
55. Coppei Creek
56. Fields Spring State Park
57. Turnbull National Wildlife Refuge
58. Riverside State Park/Little Spokane River Natural Area
59. Saint Andrews/Banks Lake
60. Steamboat Rock State Park
61. Little Pend Oreille National Wildlife Refuge
62. Sullivan Lake
63. Big Meadow Lake
64. Sherman Pass
65. Loup Loup Campground
66. Methow Valley
67. Hart's Pass
68. North Cascades National Park

SW British Columbia Hotspots

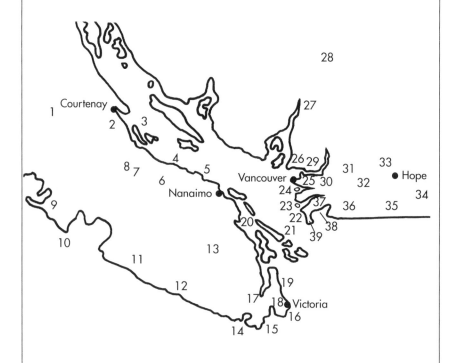

28

Courtenay

1

2

3

27

26 29

4

5

31 33

8 7

6

Vancouver 25 30

32 Hope

Nanaimo

24

9

23 37 36 35 34

10

20 22

13

21 38

39

11

19

12

17

18 Victoria

16

14 15

Seasonal Guide to
the Natural Year

Site Locator Map

N

LIST OF SITES
SW British Columbia

1. Strathcona Provincial Park
2. Comox Harbor
3. Denman and Hornby Islands
4. Qualicum Beach
5. Parksville/Rathtrevor Beach Provincial Park
6. MacMillian Provincial Park
7. Stamp Falls Provincial Park
8. Robertson Creek Fish Hatchery
9. Pacific Rim National Park
10. Amphitrite Point
11. Carmanah Pacific Provincial Park
12. Botanical Beach Provincial Park
13. Honeymoon Bay Preserve
14. East Sooke Regional Park
15. Esquimalt and Witty's Lagoons
16. Victoria breakwater (Cattle Pt., Clover Pt., etc.)
17. Goldstream Provincial Park
18. Victoria parks (Mt. Douglas, Mill Hill, Swan Lake, etc.)
19. Martindale Flats
20. Yellow Point
21. Active Pass
22. Roberts Bank Superport
23. Reifel Migratory Bird Sanctuary
24. Iona Island
25. Vancouver Parks/Capilano Fish Hatchery
26. Cypress Provincial Park
27. Squamish
28. Garibaldi Provincial Park
29. Mount Seymour Provincial Park
30. Burnaby Lake Regional Park
31. Pitt Wildlife Area
32. Kanaka Creek Regional Park/Bell-Irving Fish Hatchery
33. Chehalis Fish Hatchery/Weaver Creek
34. Manning Provincial Park
35. Chilliwack Fish Hatchery
36. Campbell Valley Regional Park
37. Delta
38. Boundary Bay
39. Point Roberts

Contents

Acknowledgments

It would be impossible to write a book like this without the help of many people. There isn't room here to thank them all but I want to express my sincerest gratitude to *everyone* who provided information. My apologizes to anyone I've missed or whose name I've misspelled. I'll break with the tradition of sticking her on the end and thank first and foremost my wife, Lani. Her encouragement and advice were very important, and she reviewed more of the text than anyone else. I am very grateful to my editor Carmel Huestis and Fulcrum Publishing for giving me the opportunity to do this book and showing confidence in my work.

Harry Nehls was a great help in the initial selection of monthly topics. Portland writers Judy Jewell and Phil Jones gave sound advice on business matters as well as encouragement. Thanks to the following who reviewed various chapters and provided additional advice as well: Rick Brown, Evelyn Bull, Sue Foster, Larry Hanson, Mike Houck, George Jett, Dave Marshall, Judy Maule, Margaret Pounds, Maurita Smyth, Alan St. John, Walt Van Dyke and my parents. Scott Bowler wins the prize for returning my questionnaire jammed with the most information. Special thanks to my sister Peg and her family for letting me use their home as my Seattle base.

Six books that were major sources of information deserve special recognition—the *Oregon Wildlife Viewing Guide* by James Yuskavitch, the *Washington Wildlife Viewing Guide* by Joe La Tourette and the *British Columbia Wildlife Viewing Guide* by Bill Wareham. Birding information is the easiest to find since there are guides for almost every state. *The Birder's Guide to Oregon* by Joseph Evanich, Jr., *A Guide to Bird Finding in Washington* by Terry Wahl and Dennis Paulson and *A Birder's Guide to British Columbia* and *A Birder's Guide to Vancouver Island* by Keith Taylor are all essential for birding in their respective areas. I am fortunate to live in a community with a great public library system and express my sincerest appreciation to the staff of the Multnomah County Library.

In my research I spoke with hundreds of people working in federal, state, provincial, municipal and other public agencies involved in managing natural resources and I found the vast majority to be knowledgeable, helpful and dedicated to protecting the resources under their care. Sure, it can be really frustrating winding your way through labyrinthine agencies or wading through voice-mail systems trying to reach the right person "at their desk," but that's reality these days with any big organization. Many of these agencies are getting budget and personnel cuts while their responsibilities and workloads are increasing. There are lots of good folks out there who are doing their best to properly manage and protect *our* resources. They need our understanding and support and welcome our involvement. How about a new bumper sticker—"Support Your Local Natural Resource Management Agency Professional."

I wish to express my thanks to the following people. In the U.S. National Park Service: Paul Crawford, Ron Holms, Molly Juilleiat, Bob Kuntz, Rod Norvell and Ron Warfield. In the U.S. Fish and Wildlife Service: Dan Alonso, Corky Broaddus, Marguerite Hills, Randy Hill, David Klinger, Roy Lowe, Ed Murczek, Bill Pyle, Mike Rule and Susan Saul. In the U.S. National Forest Service: Cathy Ahlenslager, Mariann Armijo, Tom Bertram, Sally Claggett, Bob Diebel, Jeff Dose, Pete Forbes, Mike Gerdes, Martha Jensen, Virginia Kelly, Tom Kogut, Dean Longrie, Laura Potash, Jo Ellen Richards, Sharon Selvaggio, David Sotnik, Marty Stein, George Wooten and Asia Young. In the Bureau of Land Management: Pam Camp, Dave Ericson, Jeanne Klein, Bob Ratcliff and Fred Taylor. Jim Ruff with the Northwest Power Planning Council and Dave Cantillen at the National Marine Fisheries Service provided information regarding the Northwest's salmon.

At the Oregon Department of Fish and Wildlife: Robin Brown, Mike Burner, Vic Coggins, Larry Cooper, Dan Edwards, Dave Fox, Cliff Hamilton (one of the original "watchable wildlife guys"), Dave Harcombe, Bill Hastie, Mark Henjum, George Keister, Dave Loomis, Steve Pribyl, Dan Renolds, Marty St. Louis, John Yaskovic and my former colleague at Audubon, Claire Puchy. Other helpful folks at various agencies in Oregon were Bev Lund and Carol Walker at the Hatfield Marine Science Center, Deb Scrivens and Ron Klein at Metro, Jim Sjulin at Portland Parks, Monte Turner at State Parks and Pat Willis and Neil Bjorklund with the cities of Hillsboro and Eugene.

With the Washington Department of Fish and Wildlife: Kelly McAllister, David Anderson, Brian Calkins, John Garrett, Chuck Gibilisco, Steve Jenks, Rolf Johnson, Robert Kent, Diane Ludwig, John McGowan, Roger McKeel, Woody Myers, John Pierce, Steve Pozzanghera, Mark Quinn, Elizabeth Roderick and Lee Van Tussenbrook. Debbie Hall, James Horan and Terry Patton with Washington State Parks were helpful as were Mark Olsen at Padilla Bay and Darrel Barnes with U.S. Customs in Sumas.

Those associated with private nonprofit conservation organizations are Bob Barnes, Bonnie Brunkow, Sarah Gage, Jeff Gottfried, Linda Hardie, Steve Hoffman, Ruthie Johns, Geoff LeBaron, Tom LoCascio, Jim Myron, Bob Straub and Wendell Wood. Some of the "non-agency naturalists" that provided much specialized knowledge are: Don Baccus, Bill Bakke, Nelsa Buckingham, Mike Fahey, John Hinchleff, Jerry Igo, Russ Jolly, Brian McNett, Bill Neill, Barbara Robertson, Maggie Rogers, Steve Yates and Peggy Goldie who gave me lots of initial information on British Columbia. Wildlife photographer Scott Price showed me some of the wonders of northeast Washington. Thanks to my friends and colleagues at Portland Audubon who discussed the book with me for two years.

A flock of Washington birders provided lots of good information for their state: Michael Carmody, Glen Hoge, Eugene Hunn, Andy Mlodinow, Bob Morse, Dennis Paulson, Russell Rogers, Andy Stepniewski, Terry Wahl, and Bob Woodley. Also, my thanks to Ken Knittle and Mike Denny, who really filled me in on the Walla Walla area. Oregon birders included Jeff Gilligan, Rick Krabbe, Tom Mickel and Owen Schmidt in addition to those already mentioned elsewhere.

I needed the most help finding information on British Columbia but didn't need to worry given the enthusiastic helpfulness of the Canadians I encountered. In federal agencies were Don Buxton, Joanne Day, Doug Hay, Mark Johnson and Brian Pearce with the Department of Fisheries and Oceans; Bill McIntyre with Parks Canada and Neal Dawe with the Canadian Wildlife Service. In the provincial Ministry of Environment, Land, and Parks, B.C. Parks branch: Jim Cuthbert, Debbie Funk, Rick Howie, Bill Merilees, Jill Ryan and especially Al Grass who broke all records for printed information sent. Also in MELP, in the wildlife branch: Syd Cannings, Don Doyle, Tom Plath, Elizabeth Stanlake and Betsy Terpsma. With regional park districts: Jude Grass, John Heaven and Deb Thiessen.

Other Canadian naturalists and birders (not necessarily with an agency) were Robert Adam, David Allinson, Barbara Begg, Dick Cannings, Michael Force, Brian Gates, Richard Hebda, John Ireland, Hue and Jo Ann MacKenzie, Eric McBean, Hans Roemer, Daphne Solecki, David Stirling, Keith Taylor, Hank Vander Pol and Beth Whittaker. Special thanks to FBCN manager Frieda Davidson for many answers and to Sandy Bell and Michael Jansen-Reynaud for that great day at Botanical Beach.

Introduction

Ah, another day in paradise! If you've lived in the Pacific Northwest for long you've undoubtedly recognized that it's one of the greatest places on earth. Yet like many urbanites we northwesterners spend so much of our time in artificial environments of our own creation and on schedules of our own design that we are out of touch with the natural world and its rhythms.

Interest in outdoor activities, wildlife and environmental issues is high in the Northwest, and the purpose of this book is to help you discover opportunities to experience the natural world. Most of these opportunities involve observing native animals in their natural habitats, but some focus on plants, and a few deal with physical elements of the earth. I hope that by using this book you will have outdoor adventures that leave you feeling revitalized and inspired, with a renewed sense of wonder and appreciation for nature. Ultimately, I hope that those who use this book are moved to do all they can to protect our earth and its awesome diversity of life.

Wildlife watching is becoming an increasingly popular activity in North America. In the United States the National Watchable Wildlife Program was initiated to develop wildlife viewing sites throughout the nation, produce wildlife viewing guides for every state and establish new sources of funding for wildlife habitat protection in the face of decreasing revenue from traditional hunting and fishing fees. The program is coordinated by the conservation organization Defenders of Wildlife and has made much progress. Standardized brown-and-white watchable wildlife signs with the binocular logo are popping up all over the country. Wildlife viewing guides have been produced for many states, and they are excellent resources. British Columbia is developing a similar system through the Wildlife Branch of the Ministry of Environment.

This book focuses on Oregon, Washington and southwestern British Columbia. Although the southwest represents a small part of the vast Canadian province of British Columbia, it includes some of that country's richest wildlife habitats and a large portion of the province's human population. The inclusion of southwestern British Columbia makes sense biologically—and the plants and animals certainly don't recognize any political boundaries. Throughout this book, "our region" means Oregon, Washington and southwest British Columbia, and "we" means residents of this region.

Since timing is so important in natural events, all the books in the *Seasonal Guide* series take readers through the year month by month. The sections covering each month highlight four main wildlife attractions or natural events. Included are detailed directions to specific hotspots throughout the region for observing each event, in addition to background information on featured wildlife. For each month there is also a shorttakes chapter mentioning other natural happenings in brief, and an additional chapter, "A Closer Look," about a general topic pertinent to the month.

Although many natural events do occur with surprising regularity, keep in mind that wildlife is unpredictable. There is never a guarantee that you will see a particular animal in a particular place, but if you follow the suggestions in this guide your chances will be very good. The sites included here were chosen not only because they are fairly predictable for wildlife viewing but also because they are great places to visit. Most sites are beautiful, and many have interesting historical and cultural features. An effort was made to represent the major habitats of our region. If you happen to miss some of the things you want to see, you can still enjoy your time in the environment. Be patient, flexible and observant and you will probably see things you didn't expect. And remember that change is fundamental to the natural world: An area's natural character may be altered by natural processes or human intervention; roads and signs may change at any time.

The Salish Sea

One of the major physical features in our region is the vast, complex inland sea consisting of Puget Sound, the Strait of Georgia, the Strait of Juan de Fuca and numerous interconnected inlets, channels, passages, straits and bays. Unfortunately, there is no simple inclusive name for this ecosystem, making it very awkward to refer to it in its entirety. The phrase "Puget Sound, the Straits of Georgia and Juan de Fuca and adjacent waters" is often used. There is confusion about the boundaries of Puget Sound itself, and many people who don't live on Puget Sound resent the name being used for the wider area. It would be great to have a good, simple name that could be used for the entire "greater Puget Sound and adjacent waters superestuary ecosystem."

Were there names for this ecosystem before the Europeans came? Some historians state that the original Native American name for this inland sea was *Whulge* or *Whulch*. Others believe that these names only referred to a specific bay or channel, and that the first human inhabitants did not have one name for the whole sea. Although there doesn't seem to be a popular movement to establish the name *Whulge,* another term that has received some attention and support is "Salish Sea." The majority of Native Americans living adjacent to these waters belonged to the linguistic group called Coast Salish. This has led to the proposal advocated by Steve Yates in his natural history of the area, *Orcas, Eagles and Kings,* that this saltwater ecosystem be called the Salish Sea. I like this name because it stems from the well-established name for the native inhabitants of the area and it acknowledges the significance of this body of water by calling it a sea. I will use the term Salish Sea throughout this book.

Wildlife Watching Tips

Time of day is a very important factor in seeing animals. Dawn and dusk are the best times, for many animals are active then (they are *crepuscular,* or active in twilight), and these are virtually the only times you have a chance of seeing animals that are nocturnal. The time of year is, of course, equally important, and that's what this book is all about!

Know the habitat and habits of the animals you seek. Each species is usually found in its preferred habitat, and knowing what that habitat is will allow you to concentrate your efforts in the right places. An animal's habits, such as when and how it feeds, where it nests or roosts and how it moves, are clues that will help you find the animal and that can often be useful for identification.

The best way to see wildlife is to go alone, but most people enjoy going on outings with their family or friends. Just remember that the smaller the group, the better the chances for seeing wildlife. Move slowly, be quiet, have patience and try to blend with the surroundings.

As incongruous as it may seem, cars often make excellent wildlife observation blinds. Many animals are not frightened by the shape of a car. Car blinds work especially well on the roads on dikes in a typical national wildlife refuge. In some cases—watching sage grouse, for example—it is critical that you do not get out of your car at all, or the animals will be frightened away.

Binoculars and spotting scopes are two pieces of equipment that greatly improve the wildlife viewing experience and expand its opportunities. Many quality instruments are available at reasonable prices, and good advice on selection can be found in books, magazines and in outdoor recreation stores. If you go wildlife watching with a group, ask others what they have and would recommend. You can often get lots of good advice and the opportunity to try many different kinds of scopes and "binos" in situations like this.

There are many good books on the wildlife and general natural history of the Northwest, and some are included in the bibliography. Field guides are essential for identification unless you are lucky enough to by accompanied by someone who knows the local wildlife. This is the great advantage of going on guided nature walks in parks or on organized field trips with groups like an Audubon Society chapter or, in Canada, with a field naturalist club (suggestions for finding these are in the appendix).

Don't hesitate to ask others for advice or help. If you see someone prowling around the headquarters at Malheur National Wildlife Refuge with binoculars, chances are pretty good that he or she will be more than delighted to tell you about what he or she has seen and where. Be sure to ask the staff at national parks, state or provincial parks, national forests and wildlife refuges about good wildlife-watching opportunities—you might get a hot new viewing tip!

Good maps are essential for finding your way. Outstanding maps that have become almost de rigueur among U.S. naturalists and wildlife agency personnel are the DeLorme atlases for each state. These are excellent maps for all areas outside of cities and are invaluable for finding the sites in Oregon and Washington recommended in this book. An atlas for British Columbia that is not as detailed but that is very useful, with many wildlife viewing sites, is *Southwestern British Columbia Recreational Atlas,* published by PTC Phototype Composing,

Ltd. of Victoria in conjunction with British Columbia Environment. It is sometimes hard to find good maps of British Columbia in the United States. I have found Davenport Maps (from Custom Drafting, Ltd.) and the BCAA maps (from Canadian Cartographics, Ltd.) to be excellent.

Wildlife Watching Etiquette and Personal Safety

It is important to be an ethical wildlife watcher and not harm or harass the animals we enjoy seeing. The basic rule is that if you can tell you are affecting an animal's behavior, back off—you're getting too close. Ideally, you should not frighten an animal so much that it flees. Bird nests are especially sensitive, and you should stay well away from any known or suspected nesting areas.

Remember that wild animals are indeed *wild,* and do not try to pet or handle anything unless you know that neither you nor the animal can be hurt (touching sea stars in a tide pool or picking up sow bugs, for example). If you are in any doubt—hands off! Do not feed wildlife except in those situations that are widely accepted as not harmful—such as feeding backyard birds at a feeder. In particular, and despite temptation and the behavior of others, do not feed human food to mammals, especially in parks that ask visitors not to do so. This rule is for human safety as well as for the animals' welfare. Every year people are injured, some seriously, as a result of feeding deer in state parks.

It is very important to respect private property. All the sites in this book are on public land or on private land where visitation is allowed, if not encouraged. When on public lands follow all appropriate rules and regulations and leave every place you visit cleaner than when you found it. Stay on roads and trails designated for public use and be aware that many wildlife refuges close some areas seasonally.

Wildlife watchers need to be aware of hunting seasons for personal safety and also for the best viewing opportunities. Hunting seasons generally take place between September and January, but this can vary from place to place, species to species and year to year, so it requires a bit of research to be sure there is no hunting in a particular area at the time you want to visit. Hunting regulations and schedules are usually available in sporting goods stores by August; they are also found at your nearest state wildlife agency office. Hunting is not necessarily incompatible with wildlife viewing—you could be on top of a mountain watching migrating raptors while a hunter is combing the forest below for grouse, and neither of you will have much, if any, affect on the other's activity.

Many of the hotspots are in remote rural country, so be well prepared for travel in these areas. This is especially true for traveling in winter, an excellent time for much wildlife viewing but also potentially hazardous for the wildlife viewer. Check on road conditions, take plenty of appropriate clothing (always assume the weather will change for the worse in the Northwest) and have food and water in your vehicle. All sites in this book are normally accessible by regular passenger car or by foot, but mention is made of those roads where high clearance is desirable. In warm months always have insect repellent with you—northwestern mosquitoes can hold their own against Alaskan brutes any time.

International Travel

The United States and Canada are famous for having the longest undefended international boundary in the world, and most Canadians and Americans seem to have a lot of mutual respect and admiration for one another. Most Americans find British Columbians exceptionally friendly, helpful and polite. Most Canadians I've met also consider Americans very friendly and enjoy our exuberance.

Traveling between the two countries is easy, but you must have proof of citizenship with you at all border crossings (although sometimes when crossing by car you won't be asked to show your papers). The best documentation by far is a passport, which is especially helpful when traveling by air. If you don't have a passport, have either a voter registration card *or* a certified copy of your birth certificate *and,* in either case, some photo identification, which for most people is their driver's license.

Good news for American travelers to Canada. The Canadian federal GST (Goods and Services Tax), which you will pay on just about everything, will be refunded for many items, particularly durable goods and lodging. All you have to do is save your receipts (make sure they show the GST has been paid) and mail them in with a simple form. Some duty-free shops give GST refunds on the spot. What's even better is that you can accumulate your receipts for a year and send them in all at once. A few nights' lodging in a fancy hotel and some intense shopping can make applying for a refund worthwhile. You can usually get information and forms at any border crossing, airport, customs desk or tourist information center in Canada. Unfortunately, Canadian visitors to the U.S. do not get a similar refund, but taxes are much lower in the United States.

Request for Help

Although every effort has been made to be sure all information is correct and up to date, things are bound to slip through the cracks, and addresses, phone numbers, even street names, can start changing as soon as they are printed. The responsibility for errors herein is mine, and I want to correct all that exist before any future printings or editions. Please send any corrections, suggestions for additional material or other ideas to: James Davis, c/o Fulcrum Publishing, 350 Indiana Street, Suite 350, Golden, CO 80401.

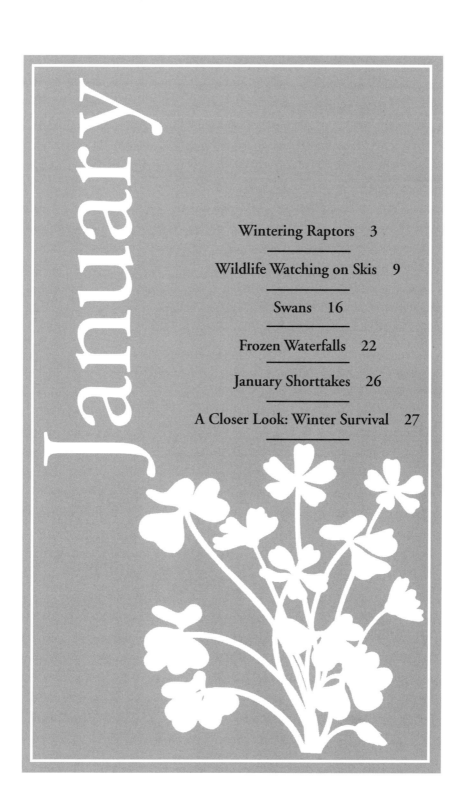

January

Notes

1

Wintering Raptors

When most people think of winter, images of bare trees, snowy lifeless land-scapes and a pervading stillness come to mind. Many are surprised to find that the dead of winter is actually the liveliest time of the year for some kinds of wildlife. At least that's the case in the Pacific Northwest, which experiences mild winters because of the climate-moderating influence of the Pacific Ocean. We do have our cold spells, especially east of the Cascades, but we are downright balmy compared to the Midwest or the Canadian or Alaskan tundra. It was hard for me to believe when I first moved here from warmer climates, but for many animals, *this* is the south they come to for the winter.

Two major groups of birds that are more numerous and conspicuous here in the winter are waterfowl and raptors. Waterfowl are the subject of several other chapters, and here we will focus on wintering raptors. *Raptor* is synonymous with the term "bird of prey," which has a very precise meaning to biologists, birders and other naturalists. Birds of prey, or raptors, are all predators, which simply means that they eat other animals for their food. But not all predators are birds of prey, a confusing state of affairs. To be a bird of prey, a bird must be a member of one of two orders: the owls or the hawks. Owls are a very homoge-neous group; all owls are called owls and look unmistakably like owls, a very distinctive look indeed. The hawk order, however, is much more diverse (and confusing) and includes birds called hawks, eagles, falcons, vultures, kites and harriers, as well as a few others. (Vultures are considered birds of prey even though they are scavengers.) When it comes to bird classification, family ties are more important than eating habits.

Raptors are easily recognized by their talons, big claws for catching and kill-ing prey, and their sharp, distinctively hooked beaks, used for tearing prey apart. What is interesting about owls and hawks is that, biologically, they are not closely related. They have evolved independently with similar adaptations because they behave similarly, not because one group has inherited characteristics from the other. Owls and hawks are an excellent example of what is called *convergent evolution:* two unrelated types of animals converge on a similar body style be-cause of similar lifestyles and selective pressures.

Most birds of prey eat rodents and thereby play an important ecological role in helping regulate the numbers of these prolific mammals. Until recently, this clear benefit to humans went ignored and raptors were relentlessly persecuted by people who saw them as vicious killers competing for game or threatening domestic animals. Fortunately, all raptors are heavily protected today by state and federal laws, and there has been a dramatic emphasis on the enforcement of these laws.

Fourteen owls and eighteen hawks reside in or visit our region. Of these, four species are almost never seen except during the winter: the rough-legged hawk, the merlin, the gyrfalcon and the snowy owl. The merlin and rough-legged hawk may arrive fairly early in the fall and stay late in the spring. A few merlin even stay and nest. But the gyrfalcon and snowy owl are truly birds of the Far North and come this far south only when driven by severe winter weather or a decline in their prey populations. Because their movements vary, they are not predictable winter visitors every year. When one does show up in a particular place, however, it is hot news and will be on the nearest rare-bird-alert tape.

Most of our raptors, especially the owls, are residents year-round and can be seen any time of year. However, many of them are much more conspicuous in the winter, for several reasons. Some, such as bald eagles and peregrine falcons, are actually more abundant in the winter, when there is a significant influx of winter visitors to add to the permanent residents. Others are easier to see because of their behavior: sharp-shinned and Cooper's hawks may stalk bird feeders, for example. Still others move closer to human settlements, such as when goshawks get pushed down out of the mountains by severe weather. And all are easier to see because the deciduous trees have lost their leaves! This means that even common permanent residents like red-tailed hawks and kestrels become more conspicuous in the winter.

Looking for owls always presents a challenge, and winter doesn't improve the chances very much. The one advantage in the winter is that you have a much better chance of spotting an owl roosting during the day in a bare deciduous tree. Your most likely winter owl sighting will be a great horned owl hunkered down in a tree. In some areas west of the Cascades, short-eared owls are more conspicuous during the winter. The one owl that is a winter specialty is the snowy owl, and some of the hotspots described later in this chapter are places to try and look for these visitors from the Arctic.

Seeing wintering hawks can be as simple as driving through farmland. A trip down I-5 in the Willamette Valley in January can easily produce sightings of a dozen red-tailed hawks and a few rough-legged hawks in less than an hour. Anywhere in the region where there are pastures, farm fields or grasslands, and plenty of perches in the form of power poles, fence poles and trees, is potentially good habitat for birds of prey. Weather will not have a big effect on your chances of seeing raptors unless it is really windy or storming. A typical Northwest winter day that is overcast with intermittent drizzle and temperatures in the thirties or forties on the Fahrenheit scale is just fine for raptor finding.

The target birds for the hotspots to follow are four winter specialties—rough-legged hawk, merlin, gyrfalcon and snowy owl. When looking for these, expect to see plenty of the common year-round hawks—red-tailed hawk, sharp-shinned and Cooper's hawks, northern harrier, American kestrel and, east of the Cascades, the golden eagle. Not as common but likely in small numbers in the right place are peregrine and prairie falcons and the black-shouldered kite. Hardest of all to see is the goshawk; consider any sighting of this bird a lucky gift. (What many consider the most spectacular raptor, the bald eagle, is discussed in chapter 7.)

Oregon

The **Klamath Basin** is one of Oregon's best birding areas almost any time of year, but winter is the peak time for bald eagles and rough-legged hawks. There are also plenty of red-tailed hawks, kestrels and northern harriers around, plus a few golden eagles, prairie falcons, merlins and an accipiter or two (the *accipiters* are a genus of the hawks that includes the Cooper's and sharp-shinned). This is a good place to practice distinguishing the two *buteos,* the red-tails and the roughlegs. Buteos are large soaring hawks, and the individual variations within each species can make telling them apart a real challenge. (The Klamath Basin is described in more detail in chapter 7.)

Where Oregon's coastal rivers come down out of the Coast Range and meet the sea there are often broad floodplains that are used mainly as pastures today. These pastures are full of rodents and are attractive to raptors. The most famous for birds is the **Nehalem Meadows.** From the small town of Nehalem drive south on U.S. Highway 101 and cross the Nehalem River. As soon as you cross the river, turn right onto Tideland Road. Follow it as it turns and takes you back under the bridge. Tideland Road winds through Nehalem Meadows until it intersects State Highway 53, which can be taken back to U.S. 101 (turn right), making a loop trip.

Search all the trees, the power and fence poles and, of course, keep your eyes on the sky as you drive through the meadows. (This is the kind of birder's driving that turns passengers' knuckles white, so try to make it look like you're keeping your eye on the road also.) These pastures are the most reliable spot in the state for seeing black-shouldered kites, a "California bird" that just barely makes it into the Northwest. Other noteworthy species include merlin, peregrine falcons and a few gyrfalcons. Regardless of the raptor action, be sure to stop at the sewage treatment plant on Tideland Road to check out the waterfowl, gulls and shorebirds—birders are welcome on the plant grounds when the gate is open on weekdays.

Snowy owls are unpredictable, but the one place they have shown up the most regularly in Oregon has been **Clatsop Spit,** site of the south jetty of the Columbia River (which is often just referred to as *the* "south jetty" by Oregon birders). This area is part of **Fort Stevens State Park,** about halfway between Seaside and Astoria. From Hwy. 101 turn west onto Ridge Road into the park, drive past the main camping area and follow signs to the south jetty. Parking area C is the closest to the jetty itself and has an observation tower. Parking lot D is at the end of the road and is the area where snowy owls, and a few gyrfalcons, have been seen in past years. If either bird is at the jetty, information about it will likely be on the Portland Audubon rare-bird-alert tape (see appendix). In both places you must park and do your searching on foot.

Washington

There doesn't seem to be any question among Washington birders that the hotspot for winter raptors in their state is western Skagit County, especially the two areas known as the **Skagit Flats** and the **Samish Flats**. The Washington Department of Wildlife produces a great brochure, "Skagit County Bird Watching Guide," which covers these and other bird-watching areas. Write the Olympia office for a copy (see the appendix for address).

The Skagit Flats are sometimes defined differently, but in the broadest terms the area encompasses Fir Island and the farm fields north of Fir Island and south of State Highway 20, west of the town of Mount Vernon and I-5. Part of Fir Island is the **Skagit Wildlife Area,** famous for snow geese, which is described in chapter 56. To get to the Skagit Flats, take the Conway Exit (221) from I-5 and go west on Fir Island Road. After visiting the Skagit Wildlife Area, wander the roads on Fir Island, then take Chilberg Road to the fields north of Fir Island. The roads in this area form a basic grid and you can cruise around looking for raptors. The main roads are Calhoun, Bradshaw and Beaver Marsh. Chilberg turns into Best Road, which is the most direct way north to the Samish Flats.

The Samish Flats is the area around the Samish River between the Bayview-Edison Road and State Highway 11. From the Skagit Flats, drive north on Best Road, which turns into State Highway 237, and it will take you right to the heart of the Samish Flats. Again, there is a basic grid of roads to explore. Some of the main roads to drive are Bayview-Edison Road, Sunset Road, Field Road and Thomas Road.

The most common raptors in both areas are red-tailed and rough-legged hawks, bald eagles and northern harriers. Other regulars, in smaller numbers, are peregrine falcons, kestrels, merlin, Cooper's hawks and barn owls. Unpredictable but possible species are golden eagles, prairie falcons, great horned and short-eared owls, the much sought after gyrfalcon and an occasional snowy owl. The Seattle Audubon rare-bird-alert tape (see appendix) will have information about gyrfalcons and snowy owls if they are in the area.

Two areas in eastern Washington are noted for winter raptors. The **Walla Walla Valley** south of State Highway 12, between Walla Walla and the little town of **Touchet,** is mainly alfalfa fields with the Walla Walla River winding through them. The alfalfa fields provide lots of rodents, and the cottonwoods along the river provide nesting and roosting sites for plenty of raptors. You can wander around on any of the roads in the area, but here is one route that provides a "raptor alternative" to driving Hwy. 12 to Walla Walla. Starting at the Columbia River on Hwy. 12, head east toward Walla Walla. You will drive by the Wallula Habitat Management Unit, good for observing waterfowl, and discussed in chapter 8. In about six miles turn south onto Byrnes Road. This junction is at Milepost 314, across from the Nine Mile Ranch, and is well marked. Stay on Byrnes, which is part gravel, until it rejoins Hwy. 12 just west of Touchet. Just after you pass the Entering Touchet sign and a

Skagit and Samish Flats

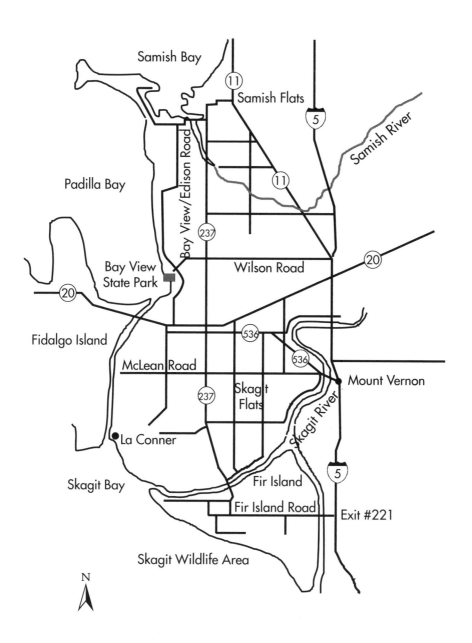

grain elevator, turn south (right) onto Balm Road. Take Balm until it and you have to turn left, and go to the stop sign on the Touchet-Gardena Road, which is marked Tou. Gard. Rd. Turn right and go south until you come to Gardena Road, then turn left and take Gardena east. It will twist and turn a bit, but stay on the main road and it will become Frog Hollow Road.

You can take Frog Hollow (what a great name—I wish I lived on a Frog Hollow Road) all the way into Walla Walla, or you can turn north on McDonald Road and take it north to Detour Road to see the heron rookery described in chapter 16. The rookery is in the cottonwoods along the river just east of McDonald and can be seen from Detour Road. If you go east on Detour Road, you'll also eventually find your way into Walla Walla. The older, central part of Walla Walla is very charming and picturesque. All along this route watch for raptors; the most common will be the typical red-tail-roughleg-northern harrier trio. I've never seen as many harriers at one time as I've seen on Byrnes Road.

For snowy owls, try the irrigated fields east of **Potholes Reservoir.** The Potholes region is excellent for waterfowl and is discussed in chapter 15, but here's the deal on the owls. State Highway 17 goes southeast from the town of Moses Lake. The east-west roads are numbered, and the north-south roads are lettered. Drive the roads between 2 SE and 5 SE a couple of miles on either side of Hwy. 17, but particularly near road M SE. The owls usually perch on the sides of the cement irrigation ditches. Special thanks to birder Mike Denny for the tip on this one. If snowy owls are in the area, it will be reported on southeastern Washington's rare-bird-alert tape.

British Columbia

In the farmlands north of **Boundary Bay,** an extraordinary area just north of the U.S.-Canada border, is the highest density of wintering birds of prey in Canada. Provincial Highway 99, the main freeway to Vancouver, goes through the area. South of Hwy. 99, and basically parallel to it, is the Ladner Trunk Road, which is also Provincial Highway 10. Exit 20 off Hwy. 99 will put you on Ladner Trunk Road. Note that at this interchange, Hwy. 10 crosses to the north side of Hwy. 99. To stay south of Hwy. 99 and continue east, Ladner Trunk Road changes and becomes Hornby Drive. Be sure to stay on Hornby and Ladner Trunk south of Hwy. 99 as you travel east and west through the area.

There are six numbered streets whose numbers increase as you go east, and they all go south from Ladner Trunk Road (or Hornby) and end at the dike at the northern shore of Boundary Bay. Their numbers are 64, 72, 88, 96, 104 and 112. All of them are worth driving through the farmlands to look for raptors. Birder Terry Wahl says that there have been dozens of snowy owls in the area in some years! This area is also great for gulls, waterfowl and shorebirds. The dike at the ends of 88th to 112th Streets provides the best views of waterfowl and shorebirds. To see all birds except the raptors, it is important to come during high tide.

2

Wildlife Watching on Skis

It used to be that when winter and heavy snows came to the mountains, the number of humans out and about was pretty small. Boy, have things changed! In my lifetime two recreational activities have totally changed the face of winter in most mountain areas that have reliable snowfall—skiing and snowmobiling. Many people probably wouldn't consider these part of any natural cycle, but here in the Northwest, winter brings these activities as surely as it brings waterfowl and bald eagles. Such winter recreation brings a lot of people into the mountains in winter and presents new opportunities for seeing wildlife and experiencing nature.

I can't think of a better way *not* to see wildlife than to ride a snowmobile, so I consider wildlife viewing and snowmobiling as basically incompatible. And downhill skiers remain restricted to developed downhill ski areas, so their opportunities for seeing wildlife also are limited. To see wildlife and evidence of wildlife, the way to travel in the snow is to cross-country ski or snowshoe. Cross-country skiing and snowshoeing are the winter equivalents of hiking and provide unique opportunities for seeing wildlife activity. This chapter describes the most common wildlife and wildlife sign that people see when cross-country skiing or snowshoeing in our region's mountains, although downhill skiers and even snowmobilers will see some of these animals.

Most cross-country skiing takes place in coniferous forests above about 4,000 feet, and the wildlife in these forests is very similar throughout our region. Because we're concerned with wildlife that is active in the winter, we are pretty much limited to the *endotherms*—warm-blooded animals. Birds we often see, but the mammals are more often known by the sign they leave. In general, the lower one is in elevation and the more forested the area one is skiing in, the more wildlife and wildlife sign one will see. Of course, the farther you get from snowmobiles, roads and other humans, the better your chances are of seeing wildlife. The best time for cross-country skiing in the Northwest is January and February, although December and March may be sporadically excellent.

A group of birds that is very conspicuous almost any time of year is the *corvids*, the jays and crows. Corvids are intelligent, aggressive, noisy and bold. Being generalists, they will eat a wide variety of foods and can adapt quickly to new food sources. They have learned that humans often leave edible waste behind them and will carefully check spots where skiers have stopped to eat or where there is human garbage. In our northwestern mountains four members of this family are regularly seen in winter—Steller's jay, gray jay, Clark's nutcracker and the common raven.

The blue-and-black Steller's jay is probably the most conspicuous bird of western coniferous forests and readily makes its presence know with its loud, raucous calls. These crested jays range from sea level all the way to timberline but generally are seen less higher in the mountains. At higher elevations the Steller's jay is replaced by its relatives, the gray jay and the Clark's nutcracker. These two high-mountain jays are similar to each other and thus often confused. Both are very bold and are commonly called "camp robbers" because they will readily snatch food from snacking humans. The gray jay is particularly amazing and will grab food from picnic tables, packs, tents, people's hands and pans on a stove. I've even seen one perch on a person's shoulder and pull a cracker from his mouth! Gray jays usually travel in flocks and have certainly figured out where the skiers eat. I have never stopped to eat lunch while cross-country skiing in Oregon without a flock of gray jays showing up to join in the meal.

The Clark's nutcracker is named after William Clark of the Lewis and Clark Expedition, who was the first to describe the bird scientifically. This bird is not as common as the gray jay and is a bit more reserved in its camp robbing. Clark's nutcrackers store tremendous numbers of seeds for the winter by burying them, and this behavior is important in the distribution of some conifers, especially the whitebark pine.

The common raven remains the most wary of the corvids you'll see while skiing. Ravens will not come and snatch food from your hand, but they will keep track of your comings and goings and may check out places where food scraps might be. Ravens are really big-time scavengers and will usually be out looking for carrion. But you will see them regularly and often hear their deep, raspy croaking call.

Chickadees announce their presence with the distinctive *chick-a-dee-dee* call, one of the most common sounds in the woods in winter. We have three types of chickadees in the Northwest, and depending on your elevation you could see any of them. But the chickadee that is a common companion in the mountains is, of course, the mountain chickadee. (I wish all bird names were so sensible.) Mountain chickadees can be distinguished from other chickadees by the white line above the eyes that runs into the black cap. But look carefully, for the line is sometimes narrow and hard to see. Chickadees are very active as they search for insects, spiders, and insect eggs, larvae or pupae, and they are not shy. It is often easy to get quite close to chickadees and to attract them by imitating their calls or making sibilant "pishing" noises.

Close relatives of the chickadees are the nuthatches. There are three types of nuthatches, and all may be observed, but the red-breasted nuthatch is more commonly seen and heard than the others. The high nasal *beep-beep-beep* of the red-breasted nuthatch sounds like a little electric bicycle horn in the distance and is another familiar sound in northwestern coniferous forests. It is quite common to find chickadees and nuthatches flocking together, often with kinglets and sometimes with warblers and downy woodpeckers. Nuthatches are well known for their tendency to descend tree trunks upside down as they search for bugs, and this behavior is a good clue for identification.

Woodpeckers eat insect larvae that are living under the bark of dead and dying trees. Because woodpeckers have a year-round food source and don't have to migrate, they are another family of common winter birds. Species do vary, however, and some woodpeckers migrate regularly while others make seasonal movements depending on local weather conditions and food supply. Woodpeckers you can expect to see in winter are the downy and its larger look-alike, the hairy woodpecker, and the northern flicker. In lodgepole pine forests one sometimes encounters the black-backed woodpecker, and in ponderosa pine forests the white-headed woodpecker. As you go farther north into British Columbia, your chances of seeing the less-common three-toed woodpecker get better. You may see sapsuckers and the big pileated woodpecker (the largest woodpecker in North America), but these birds are more common at lower elevations.

Several finches and sparrows are common breeders in the mountains and are often present in the winter, although they ususally descend to lower elevations if conditions are harsh. Red crossbills, evening grosbeaks, dark-eyed juncos and pine siskins are all common seedeaters of the mountains, although the crossbill is somewhat unpredictable and localized. A flock of juncos, flying away from you and flashing their white tail feathers, is a common winter sight.

Seeing mammals is usually much harder than seeing birds. It is much more likely that you will see mammal tracks, or sign like scat, than the animals themselves. Identifying animal tracks and sign has increased in popularity in the last few years, and there are now many books available on this outdoor skill. Several common field guides to mammals also have small sections on tracks.

One of the most common tracks seen is that of the snowshoe hare, so named because of its huge hind feet that are heavily furred for easier travel over snow. The distinctive tracks, with two large snowshoe-shaped prints in front and two smaller round prints just behind, are easy to recognize with practice. This hare is sometimes called the "varying hare" because in most of its range its coat changes color from brown in the summer to white in the winter. Rabbits and hares never hibernate, so they are active all winter searching for food.

The tracks of hoofed mammals are easy to spot, and most people can recognize the familiar tracks of deer with their two side-by-side, curved prints for each hoof. Unfortunately, all of our hoofed mammals have tracks that look very similar to deer tracks, so you can't usually tell, even armed with a field guide, whether your animal is a deer, bighorn sheep or pronghorn. Of course, this is where knowing the habits and habitats of the different animals helps. In most places you will be skiing, any tracks that look like deer will be deer, unless they are really big, and then you have elk. And if you're skiing in the Selkirk Mountains of northeastern Washington, really big deerlike tracks could belong to a moose!

At the other size extreme are the tiny footprints of mice and shrews, which are both quite active in the winter. You need to study, practice in the field and maybe get some tips from an experienced tracker before you can tell the similar tracks of shrews, voles and other mice apart. Bigger than these and very common are the tracks of tree squirrels—the chickaree, the red squirrel and the less-common western gray squirrel. Squirrel tracks look like little rabbit tracks, with the long narrow prints of the hind feet in front of the small round prints of the front feet. The front feet tend to be even with each other in squirrel tracks and one behind the other in rabbit tracks. As you might guess, tree squirrel tracks usually start and end at the base of a tree.

The most common tracks you'll see are those of rodents, rabbits and deer. There are quite a few other possibilities if you do a lot of cross-country skiing and are very observant. Coyote and fox prints are a good possibility, but both look like dog prints and are hard to distinguish from each other. Sometimes you'll find scat on the trail, and that can be a helpful clue for telling these canines apart. Your friends may laugh as you kneel to examine poop in the snow, but scat can often tell you a lot. You no doubt have experience examining dog scat on your lawn and know that dog poop looks like reformed dog chow. Coyote or fox scat, on the other hand, looks different. It will have fur, bones, seeds, insect parts or any combination of these quite visible in it. Fox scat and tracks are "dainty" compared to the coyote's, but this distinction is often a fine one, and identification can be tough.

When trying to distinguish dog tracks from coyote or fox tracks, think of the differences in the behavior of these animals. Dog tracks will usually run all over the place, in circles and back and forth and all around people's tracks. The tracks of foxes and coyotes will not be connected with human tracks and will usually be in a fairly straight line, indicating purpose and awareness, and will often follow a natural feature such as a stream, the base of a cliff or a hedgerow.

The list of other mammal tracks that could be seen are those of the weasel, otter, beaver, porcupine, bear, bobcat and mountain lion. At lower elevations, raccoon, opossum and in some areas skunk are common, but these animals usually avoid human activity and are not seen in popular skiing areas.

Hot Spots

This book cannot begin to cover all the fabulous cross-country skiing opportunities in the Pacific Northwest; there are at least a dozen guide-books that do that. In addition to these, there are a variety of maps available. Unfortunately, cross-country ski trail maps and other printed information tend to be locally produced and not easy to obtain. Often, information for a particular area in a national forest is available only at the district ranger station. Call or write the headquarters of the national forests you are interested in and ask what is available, but also ask which district office you should contact directly. Without a doubt, the easiest way to get good maps and information about cross-country skiing is in the commercial guidebooks, but no one book can cover all areas.

Both Oregon and Washington have a state Sno Park program whereby the state plows and maintains many parking areas that provide access to winter recreation areas. To park in these areas you must display a current Sno Park permit. Permits are available by the day or the season, and the seasonal permit is by far the best deal. Each state honors the Sno Park permit from the other state (as well as from Idaho), but your permit must match the state of your license plate. Sno Park permits are widely available at almost any sporting goods store, any downhill or other developed ski area, and at many stores located near ski areas in Washington and Oregon. If you have any questions about the program or where to buy a permit, call the local state transportation department office.

Oregon

In Oregon, the national forests with the most cross-country ski areas are **Deschutes National Forest** and **Mount Hood National Forest**. Both have had several different maps available in recent years, some showing all the areas in the forest and others showing details of smaller areas. **Umpqua National Forest** and **Willamette National Forest** also have some maps available on specific areas.

A favorite area of Oregon skiers is **Crater Lake National Park** and nearby **Diamond** and **Lemolo Lakes**. The Umpqua National Forest Rim Drive, which goes around Crater Lake, is closed to vehicles and open to skiing in the winter and is popular for backcountry camping. Crater Lake is the most predictable place I know of to see Clark's nutcrackers in good numbers. Call or write Crater Lake National Park to ask for whatever printed information is available. **Diamond Lake Resort** (1-800-733-7593) is a center for the trails around Diamond Lake and nearby Lemolo Lake.

The **Willamette Pass–Odell Lake** area is partially in the Willamette National Forest and partially in the Deschutes National Forest. There are a variety of cross-country ski trails as well as a small downhill area, and **Odell Lake Lodge Resort** (541-433-2540) serves as a center for this area. Another well-known area shared by the two national forests is the **Santiam Pass Winter Recreation Area** off State Highway 20 near the Hoodoo downhill ski area. Some of the trails here go through the big airstrip burn of 1967, which has been a good spot for black-backed and three-toed woodpeckers, although sightings of these two sought-after birds are not predictable. Another major cross-country ski area where black-backed woodpeckers have been seen reliably is the **Swampy Lakes** area, about 12 miles west of Bend on Century Drive in the Deschutes National Forest. The gray jays here are the boldest I've ever seen—they have the shelters under close surveillance and show up quickly when the gorp appears.

Washington

There seems to be little question that Washington's **Methow Valley** has become the Northwest's cross-country skiing paradise. Amazingly, this fairly isolated valley has the second largest cross-country ski trail system in the United States! The 175 kilometers of groomed trails are maintained by the nonprofit Methow Valley Sport Trails Association, which is the source of information about skiing in the valley. A wide variety of lodging is available, from deluxe resort lodge to camping, and there is a central reservation phone number for the whole valley: (509) 996-2148.

The Methow Valley is home to Washington's largest mule deer herd, and the chances of seeing deer are excellent. Coyotes are heard regularly at night and are seen occasionally along the river bottoms. And there have actually been several sightings by skiers of mountain lions in the last few years. For information on the Methow Valley, write or call the Methow Valley Sport Trails Association at P.O. Box 147, Winthrop, WA 98862; (509) 996-3287.

Mount Rainier National Park is a popular area for cross-country skiing, and the Paradise area is heavily used. Better for wildlife is the less-used northwestern corner of the park, where people ski up the Carbon River or to Mowich Lake. Contact the park for printed information and to get current recommendations for specific areas. Elk are sometimes seen around the lower river bottoms.

Gifford Pinchot National Forest has a fairly large packet of information on winter recreation in the forest. One of the most popular areas with Portland residents is the **Upper Wind River Winter Sports Area.** The Wind River Ranger District offers a handout on wildlife viewing opportunities, as well as some good maps. This is one of those cases where you have to contact the district ranger station directly at (509) 427-3200. One disadvantage to the Wind River area is its low elevation (3,000 feet); the season isn't long, and conditions are good only during the coldest weather and when there has been snowfall at low elevations. It is important to check on conditions before going.

Washington has an extensive Sno Park system whereby the state uses parking-permit funds to groom cross-country ski tails in over forty areas throughout the state. What is great about these areas is that snowmobiles are not allowed at the sites that are groomed for cross-country skiing, although they are allowed at nongroomed Sno Parks. Write or call the state Office of Winter Recreation, Washington State Parks, P.O. Box 42662, Olympia, WA 98504 (360) 902-8552, and request the brochure "Groomed Cross-Country Ski Trails," which describes all the state's groomed areas. The one disadvantage to some of these areas is that they are close to highways and are heavily used, so there may be enough traffic and human activity to frighten wildlife into hiding.

British Columbia

It is difficult to get information about cross-country skiing in British Columbia from the United States. Two fine guidebooks—*Cross-Country Ski Routes: British Columbia,* by Richard and Rochelle Wright, and *Exploring the Coast Mountains on Skis,* by John Baldwin, are out of print. Maybe you can find them at a library. In general, there are not a lot of groomed Nordic ski trails in British Columbia, but backcountry skiing on hiking trails in provincial parks and on logging roads is almost unlimited to the experienced and adventuresome skier.

On the southwestern British Columbia mainland there are four main provincial parks that offer cross-country skiing with opportunities for viewing wildlife—Cypress, Mount Seymour, Garibaldi and Manning. Information about all these parks can be obtained from the appropriate district office of BC Parks (see appendix).

The most highly recommended place for cross-country skiing in our part of British Columbia is **Manning Provincial Park,** in the Cascade Mountains 130 miles east of Vancouver. Manning has a wide range of skiing possibilities, from many beginning and intermediate groomed trails to advanced backcountry overnight adventuring opportunities. There is also a downhill area, an ice-skating rink and a developed resort area with lodging, restaurant, store and equipment rentals. The developed ski areas and resort are managed by a private concessionaire, Manning Park Resort, (250) 840-8822. The area recommended for wildlife is **Strawberry Flats.**

Just north of Vancouver are **Mount Seymour** and **Cypress Provincial Parks.** Cypress has the most groomed ski trails of the two, and both have backcountry skiing for experienced skiers. Both also have downhill ski areas. Neither park is big by Canadian park standards, and the cross-country areas are not extensive, but both parks are popular because they are close to the Vancouver metropolitan area. Despite heavy use, Canadian naturalists still recommend them for winter wildlife viewing.

Farther north is **Garibaldi Provincial Park,** a big park with extensive backcountry skiing possibilities but no groomed trails. All the main trails in the park are available for skiing but are only suitable for more experienced skiers. The one exception is the **Diamond Head** area in the southwest corner of the park. A good day trip, suitable for intermediate-level skiers, is to **Red Heather Ridge,** where there is a small day shelter. This trail continues to an overnight shelter at **Elfin Lakes** that can be used as a base camp for exploring other areas in this part of the park, but this is definitely an overnight trip.

On Vancouver Island there are two major ski areas right on the border of the Forbidden Plateau section of **Strathcona Provincial Park: Mount Washington Ski Resort** and **Forbidden Plateau Ski Area.** Both are downhill skiing areas with access to backcountry skiing in Strathcona Park. The considerably larger Mount Washington Resort also has 35 kilometers of groomed Nordic trails, over half of which are actually in the Paradise Meadows part of the park. The Forbidden Plateau Ski Area is a small, low-key, family area. To get to both areas, head northwest on the Island Highway (Provincial Highway 19) out of Courtenay and follow the many signs to the area of your choice. For information about these areas, start by calling the Comox Valley Chamber of Commerce at (250) 334-3234, and ask them to send you the "Vancouver Island Ski Guide."

3

Swans

When I first moved to the Northwest and saw swans here I was astounded. I had never lived in a place where I could regularly see these magnificent birds. I haven't quite gotten used to them yet—they still seem exotic and special, much too extraordinary to be called a "common winter resident," which is what they are in much of our region. People don't realize how big swans are, but with an average weight just under 30 pounds and a record of 38 pounds for males, the trumpeter swan is the heaviest flying bird in the world. Only a few other birds have a wingspan greater then the 8-foot spread of the trumpeter. It truly deserves our respect and admiration.

Of the seven species of swan in the world, three live in North America, including the Pacific Northwest. The tundra swan (formerly called the whistling swan) and trumpeter swan are native to the continent. The mute swan from Europe has been introduced in many places and is now established in parts of the eastern United States and on southern Vancouver Island. The mute swan is considered a deleterious species in the U.S. and is actually being controlled in some eastern states. Because mute swans are not native or well established and occur in very limited areas, they are not covered in this book.

Tundra and trumpeter swans are very difficult to tell apart and are often seen together, so you'll need to do some careful reading of your field guides and get some practice before you can separate them consistently. Probably the best way to tell tundras and trumpeters apart is by their voices, but that takes plenty of practice in the field and the birds have to oblige by vocalizing. Birdsong tapes can help. The trumpeter got its name from its loud, low, buglelike call. Interestingly, both swans have extra long tracheas (windpipes) that have big loops, which gives them a more resonant call.

These two swan species are similar in many ways. They exhibit what we might consider model family values: They mate for life and appear to be very loyal. A mated pair selects the nest site and builds the nest, often using the same site from year to year. Although the female does all the incubating, the male remains close and guards his mate and the nest. Swans are very territorial—they will defend a large area from other swans and are very aggressive toward intruders, including people.

When the four or five young, called *cygnets,* hatch, both parents attend to them and are very protective. The family unit stays together for the rest of the breeding season and migrates together to wintering grounds. Young swans learn their migration routes on these first flights with their parents. Swans are very strong flyers—some migrate 8,000 miles a year, round-trip. It is suspected that some tundras actually fly as much as 1,000 miles at a time without stopping!

Over half of the world's trumpeter swans spend the winter in the Pacific Northwest.

The tundra swan is now the more numerous and widespread by far, outnumbering the trumpeter by about 40 to 1. In our region, though, trumpeters are much more common than tundras on Vancouver Island. As you would guess from the name, tundra swans live on the tundra. Actually, that is where they breed, on the Arctic tundra and in northern marshes from Alaska across North America to Baffin Island. During migration, they can show up in almost any bay, marsh or lake in our region. Significant numbers of wintering tundra swans are regularly found in the Puget Sound area, in the lower Columbia River and parts of the Willamette Valley and at many wildlife refuges east of the Cascades, such as Umatilla, Summer Lake and the Klamath Basin. Some are also found in coastal bays in Oregon.

The trumpeter swan has had a dramatic and all too familiar recent history. Before European settlement, trumpeter swans were widespread and abundant, nesting across half of Canada and Alaska and in at least a dozen of the contiguous United States. Like the American bison, they were hunted to the brink of extinction. In the U.S. in 1932 there were just under seventy left, in the Yellowstone area. Red Rock Lakes National Wildlife Refuge was established in Montana to protect this remnant population, which survived and grew until it reached the maximum number the area could support. Trumpeters were then taken from Red Rock Lakes and transplanted into other wildlife refuges in the west, including Malheur National Wildlife Refuge in Oregon and Turnbull National Wildlife Refuge in Washington. These transplants had spotty success, and the future for trumpeters would have been very bleak except that in the

1950s other populations of trumpeters were discovered in Alaska and northwestern Canada, where 75 percent of the world's trumpeters breed today. With protection and the adaptation to winter feeding on farmland, the population has risen to about 14,000, and trumpeters have been off the Endangered Species List since 1968.

Oregon plays an important role in the ongoing attempts to restore trumpeters to the lower 48. Although there have been trumpeters breeding at Malheur National Wildlife Refuge since the 1950s, it has been tough going, and the population there fluctuates drastically. The population centered around the Yellowstone area has also had problems. One reason these populations have not thrived is that the birds have become nonmigratory, and thus have suffered heavy winter mortality. They need to go to better wintering areas, and wildlife biologists believe the Summer Lake Wildlife Area, managed by the Oregon Department of Fish and Wildlife, is an excellent wintering site for birds from Malheur and the Yellowstone area.

In 1989, the Oregon Trumpeter Swan Program was started as part of an interstate cooperative program designed to expand the wintering and breeding range of the Rocky Mountain population of the trumpeter swan. Since then, swans have been brought to Summer Lake from Malheur National Wildlife Refuge and Red Rock Lakes in the fall to winter over. A few have returned in subsequent winters, and hopes are high that migrating populations will be established. Because of this and other research projects with swans, it is very helpful to report sightings of any swans that are marked with dyed wings or neck collars. Report the date, time and location of the sighting, as well as the swan's behavior and as much detail as possible about the markings and colors on the bird and its collar to: Marty St. Louis, Summer Lake Wildlife Area, 36781 Hwy. 31, Summer Lake, OR 97640. Your observations may be important data!

Oregon

Hot
Spots

Tundra swans are fairly common winter residents in much of Oregon, and many of the wildlife refuges in the state have wintering swans. The biggest population spends the winter in the lower Columbia River from Portland to the river's mouth, and the most reliable place to see some of these swans is just across the river in Washington.

Just east of Astoria, Oregon, is the **Twilight Eagle Sanctuary,** where an observation platform gives a good view of the Columbia estuary. Wintering swans are often seen here, but at a distance. To find the Twilight Eagle Sanctuary, go east from Astoria on Oregon Highway 30 for about 10 miles. Just after Milepost 88 turn left onto Old Highway 30. The street sign says Old Hwy. 30, but there is another sign on the right side of the road that says Burnside. Go about half a mile on this road and look for a wooden platform overlooking the estuary, on your left.

Tundras winter regularly at **Summer Lake** and in the **Klamath Basin.** Tundra swans can also be seen irregularly in marshes, flooded fields and lakes throughout much of the Willamette Valley, especially the northern end, and in bays along the Oregon coast, particularly near Florence.

Trumpeter swans occur in small numbers and are unpredictable in most of Oregon. If you see tundra swans, particularly during migration, remember that there could be a few trumpeters with them; it is always worth checking any group of swans carefully. The two reliable places to see trumpeters are **Malheur National Wildlife Refuge** (chapter 26) and **Summer Lake Wildlife Area.**

As described earlier, efforts are under way to establish Summer Lake Wildlife Area as a major wintering site for trumpeters, with the added hope that eventually they will start breeding there. The best times to visit Summer Lake are from the end of hunting season (usually around January 20) until March 15, and from August 15 until hunting season begins, in mid-October. During other times various roads and areas are closed because of hunting or nesting activity. It is important to call the refuge and get the dates for closures and hunting before you plan a trip. Winter is by far the best time to see swans of both species. You will also see large numbers and a good variety of other waterfowl and some wintering raptors during this time.

Summer Lake Wildlife Area and the tiny town of Summer Lake are about halfway between the towns of Lakeview and La Pine, on State Highway 31 in south-central Oregon. There is a store, gas station, small motel and cafe in Summer Lake. Across the street from the cafe and motel is the headquarters for the wildlife area. Here you will find maps, other information, a nice rest room and, if you're lucky, a staff member who can give you the latest tips on where to find swans and other wildlife.

From headquarters, take the tour route, which heads east for a couple of miles, turns north until it joins County Road A-17, and then continues west on A-17 until it joins Hwy. 31 near a roadside rest, north of headquarters and across from the gas station. Roads go south onto Windbreak Dike and Bullgate Dike from the first section of this tour route. If you drive the tour-route loop as described, counterclockwise, most birds will be seen on the outside of the loop, on your right. Cruise the road in standard bird-watching style, going slowly while looking very carefully in all directions and making your passengers nervous. Remember, your car is a good blind. Stay in it unless you must get out to scope birds that are at a distance.

Washington

Ridgefield National Wildlife Refuge (see chapter 58) is a very reliable place to see some of the swans that winter in the Columbia River. They are most often seen in **Rest Lake,** south of the observation blind in the River S Unit.

About three thousand tundra and a few trumpeter swans hang out in the myriad marshes, islands and sandbars in the estuary of the Columbia River between Longview, Washington, and Astoria, Oregon. Almost 40,000 acres of this area are included in the **Julia Butler Hanson** and **Lewis and Clark**

National Wildlife Refuges, but most of this acreage is actually out in the river and access is by boat only. Part of the Hanson refuge is on the mainland, however, and you can occasionally see swans when driving Steamboat Slough Road through the refuge. The Julia Butler Hanson refuge is discribed in chapter 67.

Both swans are found in **Willapa Bay,** which is north of the mouth of the Columbia and discussed in chapter 22. On the Columbia south of Willapa Bay, is the town of Ilwaco. Just north of Ilwaco on State Highway 103 is **Black Lake,** which often has trumpeter swans.

A mixed population of tundra and trumpeter swans spend the winter in western Skagit County, one of the Northwest's best winter birding areas. They can be found at the **Skagit Wildlife Area** (see chapter 56) or in the fields of the Skagit and Samish Flats (see chapter 1), especially during high tides. One spot in Skagit County that seems to be a favorite with trumpeters is around **Beaver Lake** and **Clear Lake,** just east of State Highway 9 south of Sedro Woolley.

Both swans are scattered throughout the Puget Sound area and can be found in river mouths and bays, or in fields feeding on grain. Tundras regularly winter in some of the wetlands in eastern Washington, such as the **Potholes Reservoir** area and **McNary National Wildlife Refuge,** but these areas can freeze up, and the swans will head south or to the Columbia River at places like **Umatilla National Wildlife Refuge.**

British Columbia

Half of the world's trumpeter swans winter along the southwestern coast of British Columbia, especially around Vancouver Island. Trumpeters can be seen in many of the island's estuaries and other appropriate wetlands, but two places really stand out as hotspots.

The largest single group of wintering trumpeter swans in the world, as many as two thousand, spends the winter in **Comox Harbor** and the farmlands of the **Comox Valley.** Since this population is of global significance, the Canadian Wildlife Service, Ducks Unlimited Canada, other conservation groups and local farmers have all teamed up to establish the Comox Valley Waterfowl Management Project (CVWMP). The story of swans in the Comox Valley and of the CVWMP is very interesting and deserves more space than we have here. Write the CVWMP at 1405 Argus Place, Comox, B.C. V9N 7Z7, and ask for any copies of their newsletters that are available and for their excellent booklet *Trumpeter Swans: A Story in Conservation on the Pacific Coast.* Also write the Comox Valley Chamber of Commerce, 2040 Cliffe Avenue, Courtenay, B.C. V9N 2L3, and ask for maps and other information about the area.

The swans can be seen in Comox Harbor or in farm fields. In the harbor, viewing is best during high tide, the higher the better. There are three particularly good spots for viewing the harbor. Two are along the southwest shore where the Island Highway (Hwy. 19) runs parallel to the shore, but this is sometimes too far to provide good views. In the small town of Royston, Marine Drive actually goes along the shore for about half a mile parallel to the Island Highway. Get onto Marine Drive at its intersection with the Island Highway or take any of the streets in central Royston north of the Island Highway and they will connect to Marine Drive. Cruise Marine Drive until you find a good place to park and get out to view the harbor. Just over a mile northwest of Royston on Hwy. 19, watch for the sign for the intersection with Fraser and Millard Streets. Turn onto Millard and take it until it intersects Sandpiper at the edge of the harbor. Park here—there are benches for birdwatchers.

The third spot is a viewing platform at the far northwestern end of the harbor, where the Courtenay River enters. In Courtenay, the Island Highway crosses the river and intersects Comox Road, which heads east to the town of Comox. Less than half a mile toward Comox from this main intersection the viewing platform is obvious on the shore.

The swans feed in many of the farm fields in the valley, but two seem to be big favorites. Farquharson Farm is right on the Island Highway just after it heads north from its intersection with Comox Road. You can park in the parking lot for the farm store and nursery and scope the fields. The other fields that are popular are along Knight Road, northeast of Comox. To get on the best section of Knight Road, take Comox Road into Comox. Just after the main part of town, turn left onto Pritchard Road and go just over 2 miles until it intersects Knight Road. Turn right and watch the fields to your right as you drive along Knight. An interesting way to return to Comox is to take Knight until it turns into Lazo Road, stopping at Point Holmes to look for waterbirds and seals. A quick side trip to Kye Bay, off of Knight Road, might also provide some good sightings. Take Lazo back into town, possibly stopping at Goose Spit (see chapter 22).

Martindale Flats is a favored area with local birders for swans, other waterfowl and raptors, and is only about 8 miles north of Victoria, east of the well-advertised Butchart Gardens. Martindale Road and Island View Road are less than a mile apart and both head due east from Provincial Highway 17 to the coast. Fields on both sides of both roads can be outstanding for birding, especially when flooded. Island View Road ends at **Island View Beach Park,** which provides excellent views of waterfowl and seabirds in Cordova Bay.

On the mainland, the farm fields around Delta and Ladner, south of Vancouver, are a regular winter hangout for both species of swan. They have developed quite a taste for pieces of potatoes left in the fields after harvesting. You can explore any of the roads in the area that go through farmland, but two spots are particularly worth checking. Drive the roads south of the Ladner Trunk Road north of Boundary Bay as described in chapter 1. The other area that is very reliable is Westham Island, sight of the **Reifel Migratory Bird Sanctuary** described in chapter 56.

4

Frozen Waterfalls

Life depends on water, so it's no surprise that water has always been a powerful symbol to humans. Moving water possesses a particularly strong fascination for people, and people love waterfalls. Here is moving water at its most dramatic—plunging into space or cascading over rocks, constantly changing its shape yet maintaining a character unique to that waterfall. And what could be more exhilarating than getting blasted by the spray of a big waterfall on a hot day!

The Pacific Northwest is a great place for waterfalls because we've got plenty of what it takes to make them—lots of water and lots of places for it to fall from. *A Waterfall Lover's Guide to the Pacific Northwest* (second edition), by Gregory Plumb, describes over five hundred waterfalls in the region.

Waterfalls vary in character depending on the amount of water they contain, but there is a more dramatic change that takes place during the coldest winter weather. Waterfalls can freeze into fantastic natural ice sculptures and sometimes will freeze completely. More commonly, especially with big falls, some water will keep flowing while an amazing assortment of different ice formations are created in the fall itself and on the surrounding cliffs. Spray from the falls forms beautiful delicate crystals on nearby rocks or plants. It is a unique and ephemeral winter display that doesn't happen every year. One thing you can count on when you go out in freezing weather to look at frozen waterfalls—no crowds! The most popular single tourist attraction in Oregon, Multnomah Falls, is almost deserted in the winter. The ideal time to go is on a sunny day with no wind and the temperature just below freezing after a stretch of really cold temperatures.

Any waterfall is worth checking out when it freezes, but there are two areas in Oregon that have more big accessible waterfalls in a small area than anywhere else in North America. They also happen to be exceptionally beautiful places with many other natural attractions besides the waterfalls—The Columbia River Gorge and Silver Falls State Park.

The Columbia River Gorge is one of the great scenic wonders of North America and is now, fortunately, protected to a degree by the 1986 legislation that established the Columbia River Gorge National Scenic Area. The Columbia River is the largest river, by volume, in North America that flows into the Pacific Ocean. The fact that this huge river has carved an essentially sea-level passage through one of North America's greatest mountain ranges, the Cascades, is totally astounding, and the geological history of The Gorge's formation is almost unbelievable. *The* Gorge, as it is commonly known, is appreciated for its geology, scenery, wildlife, wildflowers, economic importance, human history and recreational uses and is the subject of many fine books. For now the question is, Why so many waterfalls in The Gorge?

Waterfalls can present a fantasy of ice crystals in the winter months.

There are at least fifty accessible recognized waterfalls on the Oregon side of the 85-mile-long Columbia River Gorge. To understand why there are so many, we need to look at the geologic past and how The Gorge was formed. There was an ancient Columbia River flowing west to the ocean at least 40 million years ago, long before the Cascade Mountains were formed. About 15 million years ago, huge cracks opened in the earth's crust near the Oregon, Washington and Idaho border, and massive flows of lava poured out, eventually covering 60,000 square miles of eastern Washington and northeastern Oregon, and even reaching the coast. There were about three hundred different flows of varying sizes, and these flows are called the *Columbia River Basalts.* The flows poured out one on top of the other and piled up like a giant layer cake. This is important to our story, because Columbia River basalt is what makes up most of The Gorge and gives the cliffs their characteristic layered look. At Multnomah Falls you can clearly see six different layers and near Bridal Veil geologists have found sixteen exposed layers.

All these lava flows moved the ancient Columbia River around a bit, but the river kept on flowing west to the ocean. About 12 million years ago, the land was uplifted, and there were many faults and folds in the layers of basalt. Then, about 6 million years ago, there was a big increase in volcanic activity, and the Cascades began to form. Despite all this earth-moving and mountain-building activity, the Columbia kept on carving its valley through the layers of basalt as fast as the land rose around it. By the time of the Ice Age that started about 2 million years ago, the Columbia River had carved a deep V-shaped valley down through the rising layers of basalt.

Because the main channel of the river contained more rocks and gravel and a much larger volume of water, the main river channel carved down deeper than did the side streams flowing into the river. This meant that some of the side streams ended at the edge of the valley and then fell to the river below. These side canyons left high on the cliffs are called *hanging valleys,* and the streams pouring out of them became waterfalls. Over time, however, these side streams washed down plenty of debris, and large piles of rocks fanned out from each side stream into the main valley. Eventually the built-up debris and the downward cutting action of the side streams would eliminate many of the falls or make them much shorter. But then the most amazing event of all took place.

Toward the end of the Ice Age fifteen thousand years ago, a lobe of the Cordilleran ice sheet came down into the far northeastern corner of Washington and formed an ice dam blocking the Clark Fork River. A huge lake, now called Lake Missoula, formed and covered 3,000 square miles of Idaho and Montana and contained an estimated 500 cubic miles of water. Eventually the dam gave way and Lake Missoula emptied in the greatest flood the world has ever known. The water came pouring over 16,000 square miles of Washington and Oregon in a volume of water ten times the flow of all the present rivers in the world *combined.* The water was about 1,200 feet at its deepest, but by the time it reached The Gorge it was about 700 feet deep. Such a cataclysm is hard to imagine, but what is even more astounding is that geologists now think this happened at least forty times in just a few thousand years! These huge floods are called the Spokane Floods, the Missoula Floods or the Bretz Floods, after the geologists who first described them in the 1930s.

The Bretz Floods washed away everything that wasn't hard bedrock and left a large area of eastern Washington with a scoured terrain now known as the *Channeled Scablands.* As the water blasted through The Gorge, it carried away all the loose debris at the base of the cliffs and carved out the bottom of the valley, giving The Gorge its present broad U shape. The hanging valleys were left high on the smoothed-off cliff faces, and streams had to plunge to the valley floor. Our present waterfall paradise was completed. But how come there are so few waterfalls on the Washington side of The Gorge? There once were more, but the layers of rock in The Gorge were tilted slightly southward during all the uplifting. This resulted in many landslides on the Washington side that destroyed the cliff faces and their waterfalls.

Oregon

Hot Spots

Thanks to this unique set of circumstances we now have the ultimate waterfall-watching site for any time of year. In the 13 miles between **Corbett** and **Ainsworth State Park,** there are five major waterfalls between 150 and 620 feet high, all of which you can see after a very short walk from your car. Another six big falls, all over 100 feet, can be seen by driving 10 more miles. These require short hikes, the longest being 3 $^{1}/_{2}$ miles round-trip.

Interstate 84 goes through **The Columbia River Gorge** and in places is paralleled by the old **Columbia River Scenic Highway,** an engineering marvel of its time and a fascinating story in itself. At different exits you can cross over from I-84 to the Columbia River Scenic Highway, usually called the Scenic Highway or just "the old highway." (Be aware that not all exits are complete inter-changes, with access and exits in both directions.) The five biggest and easiest falls to see are all on the Scenic Highway between the Corbett Exit 22, and the Dodson/Ainsworth State Park Exit 35, both complete interchanges.

From Portland, take the Corbett Exit, drive up the cliff to the town of Corbett and turn left onto the Scenic Highway in Corbett. Head east, and in 2 miles you will come to the **Women's Forum State Park,** where you can get the classic scenic view up The Gorge. One mile farther east and you come to **Vista House Visitor Center** on Crown Point, complete with exhibits, rest rooms, gift shop and more scenic vistas. From Vista House, just head east on the Scenic Highway and watch for signs for the various waterfall areas. The "Big Five" going from west to east are Latourell Falls, Bridal Veil Falls, Wahkeena Falls, Multnomah Falls and Horsetail Falls. Multnomah Falls is the second highest year-round waterfall in the United States and the most famous in The Gorge by far. At its base is an extensive visitor area with restau-rant, gift shop, rest rooms and a forest service interpretive center. The next most spectacular falls within easy hiking distance are Upper Latourell Falls, Triple Falls, Ponytail Falls, Elowah Falls, Wahclella Falls, Metlako Falls and Punch Bowl Falls. All are located between Corbett and Cascade Locks.

Silver Falls State Park is Oregon's largest state park and is very popular. It is 25 miles east of Salem in the foothills of the Cascades. The same lava flows that created The Gorge also formed the bedrock of Silver Falls, again creating the right conditions for many waterfalls. The Trail of Ten Falls is just under 7 miles long and has views of ten waterfalls, half of them over 100 feet high. From Salem, take State Highway 22 east, then turn onto Hwy. 214 and take it to the park. The main visitor facilities are at the Nature Lodge, built by the Civilian Conservation Corps and located near South Falls, the highest in the park. Follow signs to the lodge or the day-use area. At the lodge you can get the park map that shows the trails and falls. A shorter route of $2\,{}^{1}/_{2}$ miles from the Winter Falls parking area will take you by five falls. Silver Falls State Park is also noted for its wildflowers and has a wildflower show every year on the Saturday and Sunday of the Mother's Day weekend from 11 A.M. to 5 P.M.

Washington

In Washington two areas with the highest concentrations of waterfalls are on the **Lewis River** and in **Mount Rainier National Park.** The section of the Lewis River with the most falls is between Mount Saint Helens and Mount Adams in the Gifford Pinchot National Forest. Access is from the Lewis River Road, which starts out as State Highway 503 at the Woodland Exit from I-5. Continue east on Lewis River Road, which will eventually become Forest Road 90. The falls start just east of Swift Reservoir. In Mount Rainier Na-tional Park there are about a dozen falls in the southern part of the park near Hwy. 706. Use Plumb's guide and forest service or park service maps to find these gems, but check on road and trail conditions first.

5

January Shorttakes

January Skies

The cold skies of winter are the clearest because there is less moisture, pollen and pollution in the air. This is also the time when the region of the sky most astronomers consider the richest is in full view. In winter you could see all the constellations if you stayed up all night, but the winter constellations are easily seen between about 7 and 9 P.M. The winter constellation most people know is Orion, which is distinct and easy to identify, and has the most bright stars. If you use Orion's belt as a pointer, toward the horizon you should see the star Sirius, the brightest star in the sky (after our sun) and part of the constellation Canis Major. Other classic winter constellations are Taurus, Gemini, Auriga and Perseus. In addition, you can see the circumpolar constellations that are visible almost all year—the Big and Little Dippers, Cassiopeia, Cepheus, Cygnus and Draco. The largest meteor shower of the year, the Quadrantids, occurs January 1 to 4 before dawn and appears to be coming from the constellation Boötes. There's a challenge for hardy folks who don't mind standing outside at the coldest time in the coldest month of the year!

Smelt

Late January and early February is the peak of the smelt run in the **Columbia River.** These little fish have many names—Columbia River smelt, candlefish, eulachon *(you-la-kon)* and the Canadian slang "hooligan." These prolific fish return by the millions to spawn in tributaries of the lower Columbia and provide an unequaled feast for dozens of predators who join in the mass multispecies feeding frenzy. Clouds of gulls swarm over spawning areas and are joined by other fish-eating birds such as cormorants, mergansers and a few loons and grebes. California sea lions and harbor seals swim up the river to join in the gluttony. Humans also pursue them, sometimes to eat but mainly for bait or animal food. Just where the smelt will spawn is unpredictable, except the **Cowlitz River** seems to have one of the biggest runs every year. Watch for the feeding action anywhere along the Cowlitz between its mouth and Castle Rock, Washington.

Starlings

Although they are scorned by most birders, European starlings form some of the largest flocks of birds you'll ever see when they gather to roost in winter. Drive over the **Broadway Bridge** in Portland around sunset during the winter and you will usually see tens of thousands, if not hundreds of thousands, of starlings settling on the bridge for the night.

6

A Closer Look:
Winter Survival

For animals living in temperate climates, winter usually provides the greatest challenge to survival. Problems caused by the colder temperatures are made worse by the concurrent decrease in the food supply. The populations of almost every Northwest animal are at their lowest after various types of winter mortality have taken their toll. How do the survivors make it?

Where an animal lives will determine the temperature extremes it will have to endure to survive. Animals living in the ocean have it the easiest, for the waters off our coast vary little, maintaining an easy temperature range for animals to tolerate, and the ocean never freezes. Most marine animals really don't need any special adaptations for winter weather. The same is also true for animals living in large bodies of fresh water that do not freeze. In contrast, animals living high in the mountains or in the eastern parts of Washington and Oregon may have to endure weeks of temperatures well below freezing. With many different kinds of animals living in a variety of habitats, it is not surprising that there are many different adaptations for winter survival.

It is important to appreciate how different types of animals are affected by cold temperatures. To do this we need to clarify the terms *warm-blooded* and *cold-blooded,* terms that are commonly used, poorly understood and mostly inaccurate. Animals that are commonly referred to as cold-blooded, such as reptiles, fish and insects, are animals that do not produce much heat inside their bodies and whose body temperatures are usually the same as the environment and change with it. They are able to regulate their body temperatures to some extent by moving to different parts of their environment or by behaviors such as basking in the sun. For the most part, though, they are thermal slaves of their surroundings. Biologists usually use the term *ectothermic,* which means "outside heat," for these animals.

The animals we call warm-blooded are quite different. Biologists call these animals *endothermic,* which means "inside heat." Endotherms produce a lot of heat inside their bodies with their high rates of metabolism and keep that heat in with insulation. They maintain a constant body temperature that is usually quite high in comparison to their environment. In a way, they have freed themselves from the thermal restraints of the environment—but at a cost. Warm-blooded animals need at least ten times the food and oxygen of cold-blooded animals to stay alive.

So why be an endotherm if it means that you constantly have to work harder to get more food and oxygen? The advantage is that activity level can be independent of the temperature of the environment. As the temperature drops and an ectotherm gets colder, all its bodily functions slow down until it can't even move. In contrast, when *its* environment gets colder (at night or during the winter), an endotherm can remain active and take advantage of whatever food is available, including tasty ectotherms too cold to move. Endothermy has allowed some animals to live in the coldest places on earth, the polar ice caps.

So who are these amazing endotherms? An outing in cold winter weather makes it obvious—usually the only active animals you will see are birds and mammals. Although there are a few scattered cases of other animals generating considerable heat inside their bodies at certain times, birds and mammals are the only animals that are all endothermic all the time. A good clue that they are the endotherms is their insulation—feathers on birds and fur or thick layers of fat on mammals. Ectotherms have no need for insulation and have none. You can't keep your pet turtle warm by wrapping it up in a blanket.

With this basic difference in metabolism, it follows that ectotherms and endotherms adapt to cold weather differently. Ectotherms don't have much choice in the matter. As their environment gets colder, so do they. Since all chemical reactions happen more slowly at lower temperatures, the metabolism and actions of ectotherms just keep slowing down until they can't move, and they become *torpid,* in a state of suspended animation. This would seem disastrous but actually works quite well because an animal in a state of torpor needs very little oxygen or food to stay alive. This explains how air-breathing animals like frogs and turtles can spend the whole winter in the bottom of a pond. They need so little oxygen in their torpid condition that then can get all they need from the surrounding water through their skin. The small amount of energy and nutrients they need comes from stored reserves such as fat.

So for ectotherms the basic winter survival strategy is to eat hearty while there's plenty of food and you can move around well to get it, store as much food as you can in your body and then be sure you are in a good safe place when it gets too cold to move.

It's basically a pork-up and chill-out life cycle. A good safe place would be a place where the temperature doesn't get too low for too long and where predators (endotherms, naturally) can't eat you up. Since the vast majority of animals on earth are ectotherms, this is the most common way animals survive the winter. They just get colder and colder and become less and less active until they are in a dormant state just above freezing. But there is a limit to how low their temperature can drop.

The bottom line for surviving cold is that an animal can't freeze solid. Animals are mostly water, and if all the water in an animal freezes solid, the formation of ice ruptures cells and kills the animal. This means that if an ectotherm gets much below 32 degrees Fahrenheit for too long, it will die. Or so scientists thought for years. It has only recently been discovered that the wood frog, a garter snake and some insects can actually freeze solid for short periods of time and then thaw out and still be alive! Exactly how these animals can do this is not known, but we do know that some animals produce natural antifreeze compounds that can stop ice from forming in the blood and tissues. Some animals (Arctic and Antarctic fish, for example) have even evolved to be active and live out their whole lives at near to slightly below freezing temperatures through physiological adaptations including these antifreeze compounds and special enzymes that are active at very low temperatures.

The simplest way for any animal, warm- or cold-blooded, to survive the cold is to avoid it entirely. If the animal is very mobile it can just leave and go some place warmer. It is no surprise that birds, with their amazing flying abilities, are famous for migration, and many species fly thousands of miles every year. Although birds are most commonly thought of, other kinds of animals also migrate. One of the best known in our region is the gray whale. There is even an insect, the monarch butterfly, that migrates up to 4,000 miles round-trip.

There are many animals that do not make long migrations but rather shorter seasonal movements to avoid the harshest weather or seek food. This is common among mountain dwellers. Deer, elk, bighorn sheep and mountain goats will all descend to wintering grounds from higher elevations. Some of our common winter feeder birds—juncos, pine siskins, evening grosbeaks and varied thrushes—are summer breeders in the mountains and regularly drop down to lower elevations as the snow piles up and the seeds get scarce. How many show up in lowland towns will vary with winter conditions in the mountains.

An animal doesn't have to travel a long distance to avoid the coldest temperatures. Just a foot below the earth's surface it may be many degrees warmer, not to mention drier and out of the wind. Many animals use burrows, cavities in logs and trees or cracks and caves in rocks for winter shelter. Snow is actually a good insulator and quite a few animals, like gophers, mice, pikas and soil invertebrates, remain active under a protective blanket of snow. A thick conifer covered with snow provides excellent shelter for birds who roost inside.

One question that should occur to the observant outdoor enthusiast in the winter is, Where are all the bugs? Insects are the most abundant life-form on the planet and though conspicuous most of the year, seem to disappear completely in winter. This effect will vary, of course, from place to place. In the milder western lowlands of our region the eager naturalist can still find plenty of arthropod action in winter, but in the mountains and on the east side, it's bugless.

The explanation is really quite simple. Most insects, and many other arthropods, don't even try to survive the winter as adults. The adults all die in the fall and the species overwinters in one of the other stages in the insect life cycle, most commonly as eggs but also as larvae or pupae, depending on the species. Insect eggs are extremely tough and can withstand much more severe conditions than can the adults, and the larvae and pupae of some species are stronger as well. Some insects do overwinter as adults, and some of these can keep ice from forming in their bodies at temperatures of 40 degrees below zero. And, as mentioned earlier, some insects can actually freeze solid and survive, although we don't know how widespread this ability is.

Endotherms, whether birds or mammals, have a completely different problem than the ectotherms. Their main problem becomes that of getting enough calories to keep the internal furnace burning. Of course, if they have the ability, they can migrate to warmer places. The main reason endotherms migrate is not so much that the weather is cold but that the food supply becomes inadequate.

For those that do not migrate, there are several possible adaptations. One of the first things we humans think of to get warm is increased insulation. Mammals are well known for their thick winter coats, and birds with their feathers fluffed to create a thick layer of insulating air are a common sight in winter. To increase heat production, endotherms can actually increase their metabolism. The most obvious sign of this is shivering—small, rapid, repetitive muscle contractions that generate heat.

A change in diet can also provide extra calories needed to stay warm. Fat has twice the calories per ounce than carbohydrates, and some animals seasonally seek foods that are high in calories, hence the popularity of suet bird feeders in winter. Stored food reserves often make the difference in winter survival, and many birds and mammals fatten themselves as much as possible in preparation. Then there are those animals that actually store food outside their bodies. Well-known examples are tree squirrels and jays, which bury nuts; honeybees, which store honey and the pika, which makes hay for its winter food supply.

Endotherms can conserve energy by seeking shelter and remaining inactive during the coldest times. Many mammals spend a lot of time in the winter sleeping; the most famous example of this are bears, which spend long periods of time in very deep sleep. The most extreme adaptation of endotherms to cold is to actually get out of the fast lane of endothermy and "go ecto," that is, hibernate. In hibernation it is as if the thermostat in the animal's brain has been set to a lower temperature. The animal's entire metabolism—heart rate, breathing, urine production, the works—slows to a level that just barely sustains life. The animal can't move, but it also doesn't need food to stay active and warm. If it can store enough fat and get in the right shelter, it can just wait out the winter and return to full activity when spring, warmer temperatures and food arrive. Some hibernating rodents will actually arouse occasionally during warmer times in winter and eat stored seeds in their burrows or even go out and forage.

True hibernation is not common. Among mammals, some bats and some rodents, particularly ground squirrels, are the most common and well-known hibernators. There is some debate among scientists as to what constitutes true hibernation. Hence, bears and some other mammals are called hibernators by some but not by others. The situation with birds is even more hazy and seems to be mainly a question of terminology. The only bird that is regularly called a true hibernator is the poorwill. Several species of hummingbirds are known to enter a torpid state on cold nights but will arouse quickly when necessary.

Regardless of how they do it, enough members of each animal population must survive the winter to reproduce. Changes in one species affect the other members of its community. Fluctuations in animal populations are part of the complex interactions among animals and between animals and their habitats.

February

Notes

7

Bald Eagles

Not everyone is thrilled by the sight of a sparrow in breeding plumage or an immature warbler, but most people seem to be impressed by the sight of an adult bald eagle. Winter eagle watching has become a popular activity in our region in recent years, and with good reason—the Northwest has the best areas for seeing bald eagles outside of Alaska.

It seems ironic that our national symbol has became an endangered species, but the decline of the bald eagle is a sadly appropriate symbol of our abuse of the land and its wildlife. Eagles have suffered from the triple threats of shooting, habitat destruction and pesticides. Fortunately, eagles have fared better in recent times as a result of much better enforcement of laws protecting them and improved regulation of some pesticides. Habitat destruction is now clearly the biggest threat to eagles, as it is with most wildlife, but there have been some significant gains in this area also.

Oregon and Washington have always been lucky in having more bald eagles than any of the other lower 48 states. In fact, the bald eagle is legally classified as threatened in these states, a more secure status than endangered. It is estimated that there are a little over three hundred nesting pairs of bald eagles in Oregon and Washington. In the winter, however, the total number of bald eagles in the two states may increase to almost two thousand. British Columbia is another matter entirely. With at least eight thousand bald eagles year-round, coastal British Columbia, along with southeastern Alaska, is the world's population center for these magnificent birds.

It is possible, then, to see bald eagles any time of year in the Northwest. In winter, however, observing these birds is much easier because there are many additional birds from farther north and because they gather in large numbers in traditional wintering grounds, where hundreds can sometimes be seen at one time. Bare deciduous trees also contribute to ease of observation. Eagles concentrate in certain areas for the winter because of food availability and good roosting sites. Their main food is either fish or waterfowl. They also are scavengers, and you can sometimes come upon them feasting on roadkill, especially freshly killed deer.

One very good reason for eagle watching in the winter is that the eagles are less affected by such human activities than they would be during the critical breeding season, when they are very sensitive to disturbance. It is still important, however, to disturb the birds as little as possible, regardless of time of year. When observing perched eagles in winter, do not do anything that will make them fly, causing them to expend critical energy reserves.

Back from the brink—bald eagles are one of the great success stories of the Endangered Species Act.

Novice eagle watchers are usually puzzled to see many bald eagles that aren't bald—they don't have a white head. Bald eagles do not get their beautiful all-white head and tail until they are four to five years old. Before this age, the young eagles are dark brown all over. As they get older, they start getting mottled with varying amounts of white before growing into their adult plumage of dark blackish brown with bright white tail and head. (By the way, no one ever thought that bald eagles were really "bald." At the time American colonists gave the name to these birds, the term *balled* or *balde* meant white or white-headed, not hairless.)

In many areas, western eagle watchers have the problem of trying to distinguish immature bald from immature golden eagles, which are very similar in appearance. The easiest way to tell them apart is by the distribution of white on the dark body. Immature golden eagles usually have patches of white that are neat and tidy and concentrated in two areas: the base of the wing primaries and the base of the tail. Immature bald eagles, by contrast, can have splotches of white anywhere on body or wings, they're a lot "messier" looking.

Oregon

Hot Spots

There is no question where the bald eagle hotspot is in the contiguous United States; it's the **Klamath Basin.** It's currently estimated that there may be as many as five hundred bald eagles in the basin at certain times. A new refuge was added to the complex of refuges in the basin in 1978 to protect an area of old growth forest that is a vitally important roost for the birds. The Klamath Basin has become very well known for its bald eagles partially because of the annual Klamath Basin Bald Eagle Conference started in 1979. The conference is held during the Presidents' Day holiday weekend every February. There are speakers, films, workshops, a photography contest and, of course, field trips to see eagles and other birds. At this time of year the basin is also one of the best spots in the Northwest for wintering waterfowl and raptors. The big highlight of the conference, or of any trip to the area, is the morning flyout from the major roost in the **Bear Valley National Wildlife Refuge.** To get information on the conference, write in early January to: Klamath Basin Bald Eagle Conference, c/o Oregon Department of Fish and Wildlife, 1400 Miller Island Road West, Klamath Falls, OR 97603. There are lots of motels in Klamath Falls, but make your reservations as soon as you can.

If you go to the conference you can go on the conference field trips, but in case you go on your own or do some extra birding, here is what I consider the basic tour of the Klamath Basin. This tour can be made in winter for raptors (including eagles) and waterfowl, made in March or early April for huge numbers of migrating waterfowl or made later in the spring (end of April to early June) for a good variety of waterfowl, raptors, shorebirds, herons and songbirds. The Klamath Basin is one of the Northwest's all-around great birding spots just about anytime. There are five national wildlife refuges in the basin plus the state's **Klamath Wildlife Area.**

Let's start with the bald eagle flyout. The one catch here is that you have to be at the site before sunrise. Find out when sunrise is by looking in the weather section of a local newspaper and plan on leaving downtown Klamath Falls about an hour or 45 minutes before that time. Head south on State Highway 97 from Klamath Falls (Main Street downtown turns into 97) for 13 miles. Just south of the little town of Worden you will pass Township Road on your left. Turn right onto the next road you come to on the right. The sign will indicate the way to Ashland and Keno. Cross the railroad tracks on this paved road, then immediately turn left onto a dirt road. In about 100 yards the road forks; go right. Drive west on this dirt road for about half a mile, then pull over as far as you can and park. Stand by your car and watch the hills to the northwest. As it gets light you should start to see bald eagles and rough-legged hawks fly right over your head and off to the sides. People have seen as many as one hundred eagles in a morning, but the number varies.

When you're ready to move on, turn your car around and go back to Hwy. 97. Turn left and head north, the way you came, but get ready to turn right onto Township Road, which comes up immediately. Township Road is great for a slow cruise through the farmland and along the northern border of the **Lower Klamath National Wildlife Refuge.** You'll see more eagles and rough-legged hawks, as well as red-tailed hawks, American kestrels and northern harriers. Township Road will intersect Lower Klamath Lake Road—the street sign says L. Lake Rd. Turn right and head toward the little town of Merrill. When you come to Merrill Pit Road, turn right and go south until it ends at State Line Road, or State Highway 161. Turn left onto State Line and go east about 4 miles and you will come to the intersection with Hill Road, where there is a small store. Turn right and go south about 4 miles to the visitor center and headquarters for the Klamath Basin refuges. This is a very nice

Klamath Basin

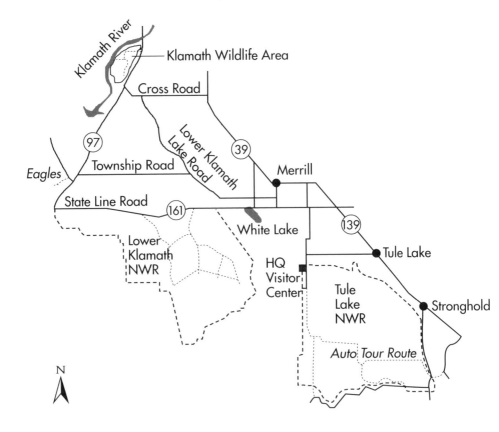

visitor center with displays, a slide show, maps, checklists, rest rooms and friendly people who can answer questions and probably give you some current information on birds.

There is a loop you can make from here that takes you through good wetlands and to a unique rock formation with petroglyphs. If you don't want to take this loop, return north to State Line Road. To make the loop, from the visitor center take the auto-tour route through **Tule Lake National Wildlife Refuge** to the Petroglyphs Section of **Lava Beds National Monument.** Follow the signs to the petroglyphs, and when you arrive you will see an amazing cliff pocketed with hundreds of holes of varying sizes. Scan these holes with your binoculars—barn owls and prairie falcons are often seen nesting and roosting in them. After checking out the cliff and the petroglyphs, continue on the road up and over the petroglyph hill, turn left when you come to an intersection, and drive to State Highway 139. Turn left and go north on

Hwy. 139 to the intersection with State Line Road (Hwy. 161), where you turn left and go west.

To view the main part of the Lower Klamath National Wildlife Refuge, go west on State Line Road about 7 $1/_2$ miles from the store at Hill Road. There is a signed entrance for the refuge on the south side of the road. Proceed into the refuge and follow the auto-tour route but head left when you come to the first fork. After that, if you come to an intersection, go right. It is very helpful to ask at headquarters about which roads are open and where the best viewing might be. Using the refuge map as a reference, I have found the best birding along the road that separates Unit 6 from Unit 7 and Unit 6 from Unit 11.

When you return to State Line Road, turn left and go west to Hwy. 97, where you turn right to go back to Klamath Falls. If you have time you might want to check out the **Klamath Wildlife Area** (Miller Island Unit) owned by the Oregon Department of Fish and Wildlife. It is best in March during spring waterfowl migration and is known for the large flocks of snow geese that pass through. To see Miller Island, turn left onto Miller Island Road, which is just south of where Hwy. 97 goes over the railroad tracks, about 5 miles south of Klamath Falls. There is just one road, with a few dead-end spurs, through the wildlife area.

Residents of the Portland area have a handy area nearby for viewing eagles, **Sauvie Island.** Sauvie Island is a large island where the Willamette and Columbia Rivers meet and is well known to Portlanders for bicycling, boating, going to the beach and buying fresh produce. It is also one of the best and most used birding spots in northwestern Oregon. To see bald eagles, leave Portland about 1 hour before sunrise and take U.S. Highway 30, or St. Helens Road, to the Sauvie Island bridge, just past the town of Linnton. Go over the bridge onto the island and as you do you will end up on Sauvie Island Road. Stay on Sauvie Island Road and keep going until you come to the sign for Columbia County. Park as far over on the side of the road as you can. Get out and watch the Tualatin Mountains to the west (which most people call hills), where the eagles have a roost. The eagles fly out onto Sauvie Island and the surrounding area to look for food starting about half an hour before sunrise. As many as forty have been seen in one morning, but a dozen is more likely. In January and February it is common to see individual bald eagles anytime during the day on Sauvie Island or across the river at **Ridgefield National Wildlife Refuge.**

Washington

Washington has a winter bald eagle spot as famous as the Klamath Basin and with just about as many eagles, about three hundred. Eagles come to the **Skagit River Bald Eagle Natural Area** to eat the spawning chum salmon beginning in November. Numbers build through January, and then the eagles slowly start departing until they have all dispersed by mid-March. A few nesting pairs do remain in the area all year. As in Klamath Falls, local eagle enthusiasts have started an annual Upper Skagit Bald Eagle Festival, which is at the end of January or early February. To get information about the festival, write Upper Skagit Bald Eagle Festival, P.O. Box 571, Concrete, WA 98237.

The center of the eagle gathering is along the Skagit River between the towns of Rockport and Marblemount on State Highway 20, the North Cascades Highway. Eagles may be viewed from two sites on Hwy. 20—Washington Eddy at Milepost 97, and Sutter Creek Rest Area at Milepost 100. There is concern that the dramatically increasing popularity of eagle watching on the Skagit will disturb the birds, so stay in the parking and viewing areas at these spots and do not try to get closer to the birds. People are allowed to boat down the Skagit through the area to see the eagles during the middle of the day, when they are not actively feeding. Commercial outfitters in the area offer eagle-viewing trips. All boaters are required to stay in their boats in the area and are asked to float quietly, with as little movement as possible.

Protection and management of the Skagit eagles is a cooperative project of The Nature Conservancy, the Washington Department of Fish and Wildlife, the U.S. Forest Service and the National Park Service, and is a good example of how different agencies and organizations often need to work cooperatively on natural resource issues, not always an easy task. For more information about the Skagit, write Mount Baker Ranger Station, U.S.F.S., 2105 Hwy. 20, Sedro Woolley, WA 98284.

The **San Juan Islands** have the highest density of nesting bald eagles in Washington, and these local birds are joined by others in the winter. The best way to view the eagles is by boat, and it is common to see bald eagles from the Washington state ferries that move through the islands. Another hotspot for Washington are the **Skagit** and **Samish Flats** described in chapter 1.

British Columbia

As you go farther north, especially along the coast, you run into more and more bald eagles. Hence, seeing bald eagles in British Columbia is almost considered ho-hum. As a matter of fact, in 1994 one area in B.C. broke the record for the largest number of eagles counted in one area in one day— 3,701. This beats the well-publicized Chilkat, Alaska, record of 3,495. This ultimate eagle hotspot is along the Squamish River near the towns of **Squamish** and **Brackendale,** just under an hour north of Vancouver. Eagles can easily be seen from Provincial Highway 99 and side roads that cross the tributaries of the Squamish. Brackendale has an annual Bald Eagle Festival, running through most of January. To get information, write the Squamish Estuary Conservation Society, P.O. Box 1274, Squamish, BC V0N 3G0.

In general, bald eagles are found regularly anywhere along the coasts of Vancouver Island and the mainland. Some areas on Vancouver Island that have concentrations are the **Cowichan River, Campbell River** and **Comox-Courtenay** (see chapter 3).

8

Wintering Waterfowl

If any wildlife is closely associated with winter in our region, it would be waterfowl. With its mild winters, thousands of miles of coastline, numerous bays and estuaries and freshwater wetlands, the Pacific Northwest is a waterbird winter wonderland. Not just ducks, but loons, grebes and gulls find our coast perfectly adequate for escaping the rigors of winter in their breeding grounds, thus escaping the longer and more dangerous flight to Latin America.

The bottom line in the winter survival of waterbirds is ice, or the lack of it. As long as there is enough open water for feeding, drinking and safety from predators, waterbirds can withstand very low temperatures. After all, they do possess the original down parkas. But when the water freezes solid, it's time to go. How far a particular bird migrates each year will vary somewhat with the weather. In our region, the area east of the Cascades may see a lot of variance from year to year, or even week to week, in the abundance and distribution of wintering waterbirds. The ocean, however, never freezes, and the western parts of our states (and province) are the winter home of millions of waterfowl and other waterbirds every year.

What's the difference between waterbird and waterfowl? "Waterbird" is a general term that varies in usage but usually refers to any bird that can swim— ducks, loons, cormorants, gulls and coots all qualify. "Waterfowl" means specifically the order or group of birds that consist of the ducks, geese and swans. Swans and geese have their own chapters, so here we'll concentrate on ducks.

Winter waterfowl first start arriving in September, and there is generally good winter birding from October all the way through spring migration. But one little problem gets in the way—hunting season. Waterfowl hunting usually starts in the second week of October and goes well into January. During this period there are breaks in the hunting, and it is possible to do some good waterfowl watching during the hunting seasons by knowing the right places and the right times. However, for many people it is a lot easier, and usually more pleasant, to just wait until all the hunting is over before doing serious waterfowl watching.

Ducks are some of the most familiar and well-known birds to North Americans. I bet that most kids can recognize and name a duck before any other type of bird. And no wonder; ducks are distinctive-looking animals and are very popular—everybody knows what a duck looks like. What most people don't realize, however, is how many different kinds of ducks there are. In the Northwest there are twenty-eight duck species that regularly occur, and that's not counting geese and swans!

Winter at Lost Lagoon in Stanley Park—thousands of ducks in downtown Vancouver, British Columbia.

With so many kinds, it's easy to get your ducks mixed up. Fortunately, ducks are easy to identify. If you get a good look at a male duck in breeding plumage, which occurs almost all year, you should be able to identify him with any good field guide. The females are much harder to identify because they are very plain and females of different species can look alike. Learn your males first, and then try your hand at the females. Be aware of what is known as the "eclipse plumage," the nonbreeding plumage ducks have for a few months right after the breeding season. During this period in summer and fall the birds go through a complete molt into a new breeding plumage. While "in eclipse" and molting, the males look like the females and everyone is pretty much a mess, making this the hardest time to identify ducks. This molting process is so variable that very few books illustrate it.

One way to sort out the ducks is to know the main groups or subfamilies to which they belong. *Puddle ducks* or *dabbling ducks* rarely dive or swim under water. They feed from the surface by sticking their heads under water and often "tip up," with their tails pointing toward the sky, to reach for plants or animal food. Our puddle ducks are the mallard, the northern pintail, the northern shoveler, the gadwall, the American wigeon, the Eurasian wigeon, the green-winged teal, the blue-winged teal and the cinnamon teal. All but the Eurasian wigeon and the blue-winged and cinnamon teal are very common winter birds. The Eurasian wigeon is here every winter but in very small numbers. The blue-winged and cinnamon teal are unusual in that they come here to breed and are the only ducks more common in the summer than the winter. The beautiful wood duck is in a group all its own, but its behavior is similar to the puddle ducks. Wood ducks are year-round residents but much more conspicuous in the winter.

The *diving ducks* or *bay ducks* dive under the surface and swim under water after food. Like puddle ducks, they eat both plants and animals, but diving ducks eat a higher proportion of animal foods. Many of these ducks have bold black-and-white patterns. They are usually seen in deeper water than the puddle ducks, and they have to run along the surface to take off—the puddle ducks seem to just jump into the air. Our diving ducks are the lesser scaup, the greater scaup, the ring-necked duck, the canvasback, the redhead, the bufflehead, the common goldeneye and Barrow's goldeneye. The redhead and the goldeneyes are the least common and most localized of this group.

Some of the diving ducks are often called *sea ducks* because they are usually seen in salt water, mostly in bays, but also out past the breakers in the ocean. Winter visitors on the coast, our sea ducks are the surf scoter, the white-winged scoter, the black scoter, the harlequin duck and the oldsquaw, the least common of the group.

Another small group of ducks are the three mergansers—common, red-breasted and hooded—all highly adapted for swimming after and grabbing fish under water. The merganser is easy to recognize by its unique bill, which is narrow, hooked and lined with teethlike serrations that give it the nickname "sawbill." In a group by itself is the little, plump ruddy duck, a common winter visitor west of the Cascades and a common breeder east of the mountains.

It is amazing that one can actually see almost all of these ducks in one day! Finding ducks in winter in the Northwest is about as easy as finding water. Almost any good wetland habitat with open water will have some waterfowl. The west side of the region has a lot more ducks more predictably than the east side. Since a majority of the national wildlife refuges were established primarily to protect habitat for waterfowl, almost any refuge is an excellent place to look for wintering waterfowl. Our many coastal bays and estuaries and the Salish Sea all provide a tremendous number of opportunities for viewing waterfowl.

Oregon

Hot Spots

Any estuary in Oregon has good waterfowl potential, but two favorites are **Tillamook Bay** and **Yaquina Bay**. U.S. Highway 101 borders the eastern edge of Tillamook Bay for several miles from the tiny town of Barview to Bay City. The well-known Harlequin Duck Rocks are described in chapter 64. Along Hwy. 101 there are several places where you can pull over to view the birds in Tillamook Bay, but use good judgment and watch carefully for traffic—101 is a very busy highway!

Yaquina Bay and the Newport area is one of Oregon's best birding sites as well as a center of many other recreational activities. It is the home of the excellent Oregon Coast Aquarium and the Hatfield Marine Science Center and the departure point for many whale watching (and a few pelagic birding) boat trips. There are three main areas for birding, all easy to find. The first, the south jetty, is described in chapter 9. The second area is the bay shore near the **Hatfield Marine Science Center**, which is also a great area for shorebirds. From the central part of Newport, go south on Hwy. 101 over the bay bridge. Turn right and follow the signs to the Marine Science Center and park in the main parking lot. From the parking lot you can see parts of the bay, but there is a trail that goes east from the parking lot that gives access and views to much more of the bay. High tide is the best time. This area has had many exciting sightings of shorebirds, gulls, jaegers and waterfowl over the years.

The third part of Yaquina Bay is the area known as **Sally's Bend.** On the north side of the bay get on the main road in the old waterfront part of town. (If you like saltwater taffy you can find more flavors here than you can imagine.) This road is Yaquina Bay Road, and it follows the north shore of the bay and heads east toward Toledo, which is what you want to do. About 10 miles out of town, you'll come to some huge storage tanks for natural gas. There is a dirt road that goes to a public dock for fishing and viewing near the gas tanks. This is the spot to scope the bay for birds. Waterfowl often hang out in the area just east of the viewpoint.

East of the Cascades there are three areas that are usually excellent for winter waterfowl, although they are subject to freezing, as all east-side locations are. **Summer Lake** is described in chapter 3. The **Klamath Basin** is described in chapter 7, but one spot in this area not mentioned earlier is **Lake Ewauna,** a small lake formed by the Link River just south of the old downtown part of Klamath Falls. To view the lake, go south on Main Street through downtown Klamath Falls. Just before you go over the Link River and under State Highway 97, turn left on a small road called Conger Avenue and take it to the parking area of the little park on the shore of the lake. Park and go to the main viewing area to scope the lake. There is usually a good variety of puddle and diving ducks, including goldeneyes, some gulls, Canada geese and often a bald eagle or two.

The third area is at the opposite end of the state. Near Hermiston are **Cold Springs** and **Umatilla National Wildlife Refuges.** Both usually have lots of waterfowl, and the birds travel between the two areas. Parts of Umatilla actually include the Columbia River, so when everywhere else freezes, birds can usually be found on the river. To get to Cold Springs National Wildlife Refuge from downtown Hermiston, take Main Street east until it angles off to the northeast and becomes State Highway 207. Go about 3 miles, and just past the fire station angle off to the northeast (a right turn) onto Punkin Center Road. Following signs to Cold Springs Reservoir, take Punkin Center Road about 2 miles until it turns to dirt. A little farther you'll come to a fork in the road. Go to the right, over the train tracks, and into the refuge. The road you are on goes over the dam and then follows the south shore of the reservoir. As you cross the dam you can see lots of birds from your car. As you take the road that runs south of the reservoir there are several places where you can park and walk to the lakeshore for viewing. The area is also good for raptors and wintering songbirds, which like the thick stands of cottonwood, willow and Russian olive.

Umatilla National Wildlife Refuge is spread out along the Columbia on the Washington and Oregon sides, and there are many different units to the refuge. The easiest viewing is usually in the McCormack Slough area, where there is a small information center. From Interstate 84 just east of Boardman, take the exit for U.S. Highway 730 to Walla Walla. After $3\,^1/_2$ miles, turn north, or left, onto Paterson Ferry Road (there is a sign for the refuge). In $1\,^1/_2$ miles you'll come to the information center, where you should be able to get a map. There are also outhouses here. Just south of the information center, back the way you came, is a dirt road that goes west on a ridge. It is usually closed at parking area A but it is well worth taking as far as you can to get a scenic overview of the area. You'll be able to spot geese and swans from here, but you're a bit too far for easy duck identification. Go north of the information center on Paterson Ferry Road and you'll cross McCormack Slough, getting good views from you car. There are two roads north of the slough that go west. The first goes along the slough and ends at a nature trail. The second goes through irrigated fields all the way to where the slough joins the river (bear left at any forks). Both roads are worth cruising.

Washington

The incredible array of little bays and coves in the vast shorelines of the mainland and all the islands in the Salish Sea present an overwhelming range of possibilities. Use any time you're near the shore as a opportunity to get to the waterfront and check the area for birds. Consider every ferry ride a wildlife-viewing trip. Some of the best spots are Ediz Hook, Port Susan Bay, Skagit Bay, Padilla Bay, and Birch Bay, all described elsewhere in this book.

Dungeness National Wildlife Refuge includes Dungeness Spit, claimed to be the largest natural sand spit in the country. The calm waters, beaches, and tide flats caused by this $5^1/_2$-mile-long spit next to the estuary of the Dungeness River provide lots of outstanding habitat for waterfowl, shorebirds, and many other birds. Hiking is permitted all the way to the tip, but a walk along any portion of the spit will provide some excellent wildlife views. The forested portion of the mainland, which the trail to the spit passes through, can be very lively with songbirds, including red crossbills and Hutton's vireos, birds often hard to locate.

Finding Dungeness National Wildlife Refuge is easy, for the way is well marked. From U.S. Highway 101, about 10 miles east of Port Angeles (4 miles west of Sequim), go north on Kitchen Dick Road. You'll make a short jog to the right on Lotzgesell Road, then turn left and drive through Dungeness Recreation Area, a large Clallam County Park, to get to the parking area for the refuge and the trailhead. Here you can find maps and bird checklists and pay the fee for visiting the refuge (on the honor system). The staff of Dungeness National Wildlife Refuge is currently concerned about the dramatically increasing use of the refuge, particularly for certain disruptive activities, and is considering some closures. Hike quietly and try not to disturb any wildlife.

In eastern Washington there is the problem of wetlands freezing completely during some winters, in which case the waterfowl will be on the Columbia River or farther south. **Wallula Habitat Management Unit** and **McNary National Wildlife Refuge** are two good areas near the Columbia that are usually open. The Wallula unit, managed by the Army Corps of Engineers, is along both sides of the Walla Walla River at its confluence with the Columbia. Best viewing is on the north side, in the area closed to all hunting and trapping. From U.S. Highway 12 just north of its junction with U.S. Highway 730, turn east onto North Shore Road. This is the first road north of the Walla Walla River and is also marked Madame Dorian Park. Take the left fork immediately after getting on North Shore Road and head east. In just under half a mile you'll come to an overlook where maps should be available and you can get your first good view of a lake that is usually loaded with birds. Continue along North Shore Road and you will have more good views of the lake for another half mile. After 2 miles you'll get good views of fields that are planted with food crops for waterfowl and are usually flooded in the winter and often as popular with waterfowl as is the lake.

McNary National Wildlife Refuge is just southeast of the confluence of the Snake and Columbia Rivers, near the town of Burbank. From Hwy. 12 turn east onto Maple Street, where there is a large sign for the refuge directing you to headquarters in 1/4 mile. From headquarters, where maps should be available, continue east on Maple a bit, then turn north onto South Lake Road. Soon after turning onto South Lake Road, you'll come to a small parking area on your right where you can park in order to check Burbank Slough, usually loaded with ducks. Regardless of how much you see here, be sure to check also the area where Humorist Road crosses the slough. In your car, head south on South Lake Road until you come to Humorist, turn left and head east until you cross the slough again. There are several parking areas near the crossing, but birds are often close to the road, so do as much viewing as you can from your car on Humorist (which has no traffic). After viewing the slough from your car, continue east a short distance to where the road ends at an overlook. Here you can get out to see much more of the slough and more distant birds without scaring everything away. Be on the lookout for white pelicans—McNary is one of the most predictable places to see these unique birds in Washington, although they may not be there during the coldest months.

British Columbia

The **Fraser River Delta** has the largest concentration of wintering waterfowl in Canada. The best areas are covered in other chapters as follows: Iona Island in chapter 45, Reifel Sanctuary in chapter 56, Boundary Bay in chapter 1 and Roberts Bank Coalport in chapter 62.

Stanley Park in downtown Vancouver is a huge park with a bird list of an astonishing 230 species. The best spots for waterfowl are **Lost Lagoon** and the seawall walk around the park, especially near Ferguson Point. There are regularly thousands of lesser and greater scaup and hundreds of common and Barrow's goldeneye as well as some of almost all the other divers. Over half the Barrow's goldeneyes in the world winter in this area, and an occasional tufted duck is found most winters. The southern part of the shore trail around Lost Lagoon, near the Nature House, has the best light and seems to be a particularly good spot.

Near Victoria are the **Victoria breakwater, Esquimalt** and **Witty's Lagoons** and **Martindale Flats.** The breakwater along the southeastern shoreline of Victoria between Clover and Cattle Points is good for many wintering water birds and is described in chapter 10. Martindale Flats is described in chapter 3.

To get to Esquimalt Lagoon, head east from Victoria on Trans-Canada Highway 1 about 5 miles to Provincial Highway 14 (Island Highway), and head south toward Sooke through Colwood. In $1\frac{1}{2}$ miles turn left onto Ocean Boulevard. Keep following signs for Ocean Boulevard and Esquimalt Lagoon, and in about 2 miles you'll end up on the sand spit that separates the lagoon from the Strait of Juan de Fuca. Ocean Boulevard goes the entire length of the spit. Pull over any place that looks interesting and scan both sides of the spit. There should be a good variety of loons, grebes and gulls in addition to waterfowl.

To continue to Witty's Lagoon, go to the south end of Ocean Boulevard and turn right onto Lagoon Road. In about half a mile turn left onto Mitchosin Road and head south. In a little over a mile you will come to the parking area and entrance to **Witty's Lagoon Regional Park.** If the little visitor's center is open you can get a map and a bird checklist. There are picnic tables and outhouses near the visitor's center. There are also lots of big beautiful madrone (arbutus) trees in the park. Walk the trail down toward the lagoon and go right and over the footbridge, taking the trail that goes near the south shore of the lagoon to the spit that separates Witty's Lagoon from Parry Bay. You will pass through several habitats and could see a good variety of land birds; the park's checklist is just over 120 species. As you near the spit you'll find several places where you can search both the lagoon and the waters of Parry Bay for waterbirds. To return to Victoria, take Mitchosin road north back toward Hwy. 14.

9

Winter on the Coast

After growing up going to beaches in San Diego, it was hard for me to call the Oregon coast a "beach," even in the summer. Now I'm less of a weather wimp, and I've found that an activity I once thought absurd, storm watching, is actually fun and very invigorating. To stand on a rocky headland in the middle of a big winter storm and watch the waves explode over huge rocks and smash up cliffs is an awesome experience that helps one understand just how coastal erosion happens.

Storm watching is enjoyable, however, only if you're dressed right and know you can escape to warmth and dryness when you've had enough. Rain pants were something I never even heard of in my Arizona and California days, but I now consider a pair a basic necessity for outdoor activities in the Northwest. Bundle up in layers, with a good waterproof outer layer, and find a headland or scenic overlook in the middle of a big storm. Plan on keeping your binoculars under your raingear except for occasional use if they're not waterproof. Those of us who wear eyeglasses have a real nuisance to contend with; I usually just take mine off most of the time I'm out in the storm, even if it means the world's a bit blurry.

There are other good reasons to go to the coast in winter even if you're not going to stand out in the rain. Although generally windy and rainy most of the winter, the weather can be very pleasant at times. Temperatures are mild because of the moderating influence of the ocean. In fact, it's not uncommon for the warmest spot in the Northwest in winter to be the southern Oregon coast, the "Brookings Banana Belt." And almost every year, usually in February, we will get a spell of clear, unseasonably warm weather. I've heard some longtime Portland residents call these periods the "February Fairs." If you can hit the beach during one of the February Fairs, you can have weather as good as, if not better than, many summer days. The trick is being able to take off at short notice—the Fairs are not predictable.

Even if you don't get to the coast during one of the spells of great weather, there are other advantages to going out in winter. The biggest advantage is the scarcity of other people. Places that are a madhouse in summer are nearly deserted in winter. If you like long walks on empty beaches, this is the time for you. Most motels have significantly lower rates in winter; be sure to ask when looking into accommodations. Serious beachcombers also like winter because winter storms wash up more goodies onto the shore and there are fewer people out looking for them. The same applies to rock fanciers who find storm-washed agates on beaches such as at Oceanside, Oregon.

As all birders know, winter is the best time to see many types of waterbirds that spend the nonbreeding season along the coast. Sometimes you can see these wintering seabirds from beaches and headlands, but they are often too far off-shore. The best way to see them is to go out into the water to get a closer look. This, of course, means having access to a boat, but there is another way to get offshore a bit without a boat, and that is by walking out on a jetty. Although walking on a jetty can be pretty hard and risky because most do not have any kind of road or trail and you must scramble over huge boulders, there are some jetties with roads that you can walk under most conditions and a few that are not bad if they are dry and the weather is nice. Walking out on a jetty is like walking out into the ocean. Even a modest jetty will take you outside of the waves, where many seabirds hang out. From jetties you even have the possibility of seeing some *pelagic* (living on the open sea) birds like jaegers and shearwaters. Most of the outrageous sightings of pelagic birds from land have been from jetties or prominent headlands during or just after storms. Jetties also attract "rockpipers," shorebirds such as wandering tattlers and turnstones, which like rocks. So pick a jetty and either try some storm watching mixed with searching for rare birds, or go during one of the February Fairs (they can also happen in January and March) and have a lovely day seeing wintering seabirds, sometimes even closer than you would from a boat.

Hot Spots

Any of the headlands mentioned for seeing gray whales (chapter 13) or nesting seabirds (chapter 31) are good possibilities for storm and wild-life watching, but you may be up too high for good views of most birds. These selected jetties give you unique views almost from eye level. Oregon has by far the most public access to the coast, for the entire shore-line (to high-tide line) is public property thanks to former Governor Oswald West. Oregon has over fifty state parks on the coast, and U.S. Highway 101 runs the entire length of the state either right along the coast or just a few miles inland.

Oregon

The **south jetty of the Columbia River** is very rough and difficult to walk on (or climb), but right at the base of the jetty there is a large lookout tower that gives you some great views. Although animals are usually pretty far away, they sometimes come in close. Seals and cetaceans are sometimes seen from the tower also. Directions to the jetty are in chapter 45.

The north jetty of Tillamook Bay, called **Barview Jetty,** still has an intact road on top of it from repair work done in 1991. The road is slowly washing away, but at this writing there is still enough there to make it a pretty easy walk just about to the end. The jetty is reached by driving west all the way through **Barview Jetty County Park** to a parking area at the base of the jetty. The road to the county park intersects Hwy. 101 in the tiny settlement of Barview, just over a mile north of the small town of Garibaldi. There are signs to the park.

The next best jetty south of Tillamook is the **south jetty of Yaquina Bay,** in the city of Newport. This is a jetty that you can drive on, but you'll have to decide when it's too rough and you should park and walk. Be sure to stop frequently and check out the whole channel from the bridge to as far out as you can see. An excellent variety of seabirds is seen here, and it is the most reliable spot in Oregon for the rare yellow-billed loon. Coming from the north on Hwy. 101, turn right just as you come off the Yaquina Bay Bridge onto the south side of the bay. There will be signs for the Oregon Coast Aquarium and the Hatfield Marine Science Center. As you come off Hwy. 101, you will swing around and head back north. After you pass the house with all the bizarre yard statuary and just *before* you go under the bridge, turn left onto 26th Street, which becomes the road going out onto the jetty.

The **south jetty of the Siuslaw River** is another great jetty with a partial road. Coming from the north on Hwy. 101, go through the town of Florence and cross the Siuslaw River on the bridge. About three-quarters of a mile south of the river, turn right onto South Jetty Road (it is well marked) and follow it as it goes west and then turns to head north. About $4^1/_4$ miles from Hwy. 101 is a parking area on the left (with outhouses) where you can park to scope the area to the east of road. Tundra swans winter here in large numbers, and the area is also good for other waterfowl and raptors in winter and migrating shorebirds in the fall. Continue north, and at $5^1/_2$ miles there is a parking area on your right that is good for looking over the estuary. From this parking area continue to drive north, then west onto the jetty road. Keep going until it gets too rough or too crowded or both. Park carefully—be sure you have room to maneuver when leaving and that other cars can get by. Don't get stuck in the sand! Once you have parked your car, you can continue out on the jetty as far as you like; the surface will continue to get worse as you go.

Washington

The **north jetty of the Columbia River** is a bit easier to get on than the south jetty, but this is still a jetty for dry weather. From Ilwaco, take Fort Canby Rd. to **Fort Canby State Park,** and as you see the big sign for the park you will also see a sign directing you to turn right for the north jetty. If you were to drive straight ahead at this point you would go to the **Lewis and Clark Interpretive Center,** which is worth a visit. But for now follow signs to the north jetty and drive to the end of the road. Walk on the sand along the base of the jetty on the north side as far as you can, and then climb up onto the jetty, aiming for the remains of an old wooden platform. This platform gives you a fairly level and secure spot to scope the south side of the jetty, which is where most birds usually are. There are outhouses at the parking area. This is a good stop to make when checking out other spots in the Willipa Bay area.

Ocean Shores Peninsula forms the northern side of the mouth of Grays Harbor, and on its seaward tip is **Point Brown,** which has a jetty. This jetty is fairly easy for walking out partway, but only when dry. To get to Ocean Shores,

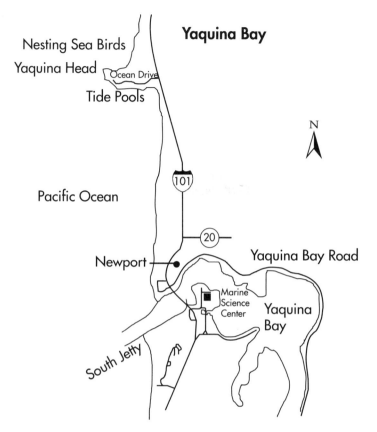

take Hwy. 101 and then State Highway 109 west from Aberdeen to its junction with State Highway 115. Turn left and head south on Hwy. 115 about 2 miles, then turn right onto Damon Road. Past the post office, turn left onto Point Brown Avenue and then turn right at the first street onto Ocean Shores Boulevard. At the corner of Point Brown Avenue and Ocean Shores Boulevard is the chamber of commerce, where you can get a good map of the peninsula and lots of other tourist information. After a quick turn to the left, Ocean Shores Boulevard goes down the entire west side of the peninsula. Take it south to the parking area (with restrooms) for Point Brown, at the end of the peninsula. Be sure to check the jetty rocks carefully for rock-loving shorebirds before climbing on top of the jetty to scan the south side. Walk out on the jetty as far as you feel comfortable, keeping in mind that during high tides or stormy conditions, waves can break over the top. In addition to the regular assortment of seabirds, harbor seals and California sea lions are common, and occasionally gray whales are seen during their migration north (chapter 13). Other parts of Ocean Shores are excellent for shorebirds (chapter 45).

Other good places for seeing wintering seabirds in Washington and British Columbia are described in chapter 62.

10

Great Gangs of Gulls

Ask any kid to name a bird that lives at the beach and the answer will likely be "sea gulls," for gulls are the most conspicuous wildlife along almost any stretch of coastline in North America. In our region, sea gull is one of the very first birds young children learn to identify, right along with duck and owl. It's kind of ironic, then, that there actually isn't any bird in the world that has the official common name of sea gull. This always comes as a big surprise any time I mention it in beginning bird-watching classes or programs. How can I say there is no such thing as a sea gull? What do I mean by "official common name?"

Bird-watchers are lucky, because ornithologists have made a great effort to establish a system whereby every bird in North America has one, and only one, official common name in English. This standardization may seem like no big deal, but it is not the case with other animals and plants, and there is often a lot of confusion over their common names. To be accurate and consistent with all other living things, scientists and amateur naturalists are forced to use the mumbo jumbo of scientific names, something that turns off a lot of people. But with birds it's different. The American Ornithologists Union (AOU) established the names; all books, birders and naturalists, professional or amateur, use them; and it's always clear what people are talking about. Sometimes the names are changed, such as "whistling swan" to "tundra swan," but overall, the system makes learning and using bird names really easy.

So, if they aren't sea gulls, what are they? Well, they are simply gulls. Lots of different kinds of gulls with different names like western gull or mew gull, but all gulls. Gulls are found all over the world in coastal areas, rivers, lakes and marshes. Sea gull is a somewhat misleading name, for few gulls spend much time in the open ocean and many live inland, in freshwater habitats. There are some gulls that never see an ocean in their lives. Even so, they are definitely waterbirds and are well adapted for swimming with webbed feet. Gulls do not swim under water as many waterbirds do, and only very rarely dive into the water, as do their close relatives, the terns. Gulls swim on the surface and either pick food off the surface or poke their heads underneath to grab it. They also spend lots of time walking on the shores of oceans, rivers and lakes eating whatever they can find that has been washed ashore.

Gulls are omnivorous and will eat almost anything, including carrion. Their importance as scavengers has long been recognized through legal protection. They are often called "the garbagemen of the beach." Like many other omnivores, gulls are quite intelligent and adaptable and are famous for some of their feeding behaviors. It has long been known that gulls will fly over rocks and drop mollusks onto the rocks to crack them open. Some gulls have even learned to leave hard-shelled animals scattered over parking lots, where cars will run over them and crack them open. If you have ever picnicked on the beach, you know that gulls will quickly determine who has food and will move in for handouts or the chance to snatch a morsel from an inattentive picnicker. Some people enjoy launching crackers or slices of bread like frisbees and observing the gulls' skill at snatching them out of the air.

Gulls are interesting creatures, and some have been very well studied. One of the great early classics in animal behavior is Niko Tinbergen's book, *The Herring Gull's World*. One famous behavior of gulls involves feeding young. Many gulls in breeding plumage develop a spot on their beaks. Many wondered about the function of these spots until Tinbergen demonstrated that they are targets for the gull chicks to peck. When the chicks see the spot, they peck at it, and when they peck, the adult bird regurgitates food for them. Gull chicks will readily peck at a stick with a similar spot painted on it, even when the stick doesn't look anything like a gull's head or beak. Gulls are among the most gregarious of birds and are always found in flocks, even when nesting. Sometimes they form huge flocks numbering in the thousands with several species mixed together. This can make for great birding, for you may see different species side by side, allowing for comparison of their field marks.

As birders know, gulls present some real identification problems. There are lots of different species, and most are very similar in appearance. To make matters worse, each has a breeding and a nonbreeding (or winter) plumage that differ. On top of that, you have the problem that gulls take two, three or even four years to attain their adult plumage. Immature gulls are a bird-identification nightmare; consequently, it would be impossible to cover gull identification adequately in this book. A good summary of our Northwest gulls can be found in Harry Nehls's *Familiar Birds of the Northwest*. The National Geographic field guide has the most illustrations of the different plumages of each species. But take my advice, and don't even think about trying to identify immature gulls until you've got a good handle on the adults. Gull identification usually centers on the color of the *mantle* (the top of wings and back), the contrast between the mantle and the wing tips, bill color and markings and leg color.

The Pacific Northwest, with all its coastline and freshwater habitats, is great gull country. Thirteen species of gulls, almost a third of the world's total species, are regularly seen in our region, although some are much more common than others. There are also a few rarities that only show up occasionally. Winter is the best time to see gulls, since many breed north of us or in the interior and spend the winter along our coast. During the winter there is a lot of gull movement, and many are seen along interior rivers and unfrozen lakes and in urban areas where there is food. The best gull action, however, is on the coast.

Two gulls breed along our coastline and are common there all year—the western gull and the glaucous-winged gull. Glaucous-winged gulls are more common as you go north. The opposite is true for western gulls; they are more common the farther south you go. The two actually interbreed regularly where they occur together, and there is some question whether they are really separate species. Ring-billed and California gulls are common breeders in the interior and spend a lot of time on the coast, so they are the other common year-round gulls in our region.

Six gulls breed north of us and spend the winter on our coast and somewhat inland—the Bonaparte's, mew, herring, Thayer's and glaucous gulls, and the black-legged kittiwake. Of these six, the glaucous gull (not to be confused with the glaucous-winged gull) is really a bird of the Far North and is the rarest of the gulls seen regularly. Small numbers of Sabine's gulls are seen regularly during migration but are usually well offshore, so they are very rarely seen except on pelagic birding boat trips. Franklin's and Heermann's gulls are summer visitors who stay into the fall but are not present in winter.

There are a few gulls that have been seen in the Northwest a number of times but are out of their normal range here, are unpredictable and are considered very choice finds by birders. These birds are usually seen, however, after the breeding season in late summer or fall. Many eastern gulls have been seen, and the most common of these rare gulls are the laughing, little and common black-headed gulls, and the red-legged kittiwake. The most likely way to see these birds is to follow up a report of a sighting from a rare bird alert.

It's so easy to find lots of gulls in the Pacific Northwest that it's hard to pick out any true hotspots. During the winter you can find gulls near almost any large body of water that isn't frozen. They are particularly numerous on the edges of estuaries and bays and in wet pastures and fields along the coast. They are common at garbage dumps and sewage treatment ponds—not the most scenic spots for birding but often productive. At city-park ponds where ducks are fed, they'll be there for a handout. They often congregate in large numbers around a good food supply, places like fish-cleaning tables on a wharf, for example. Unless regularly harassed, they show almost no fear of people and are usually easy to approach.

Oregon

Hot Spots

On **Sauvie Island** there is a small plant, the B.W. Feed Company, that makes cattle-food pellets out of old cookies. Gulls love this place, and it's usually crowded with them in winter. When the smelt start running in the Columbia River system, usually right at the end of February, they may all suddenly leave to go smelt fishing, so come in early February. The plant has just built a cover over an area where the gulls used to feed, and it's not clear yet what effect this will have on the birds. To find the plant, go northwest from Portland on U.S. Highway 30, the St. Helens Highway, to the Sauvie Island bridge just north of the little town of Linnton. Take the bridge to the island, and as you come off the bridge keep turning left until you make a complete circle and go back under the bridge. You are then on Gillihan Loop Road going southeast. In about half a mile you will see the plant by the side of the road where a dirt road takes off to the south. The plant and the area nearby will probably be swarming with gulls, crows, starlings and blackbirds—the land of opportunists! Park on the dirt road and get out to scan the gulls. Just about any of our gulls could be there, but the majority will be glaucous-winged gulls.

When they are flooded, the fields across the dirt road from the plant can be excellent for ducks, and if you're into searching for rare birds, occasionally a rusty blackbird has been found in with the others here.

Washington

Grays Harbor is one of the largest estuaries on the West Coast and is one of the state's most famous birding spots. At the southern end of the Ocean Shores Peninsula are several well-known birding areas—**Point Brown, Damon Point** and **Oyhut Wildlife Area**—that are good for gulls as well as shorebirds, waterfowl and seabirds. Chapter 45 describes this area.

The large spit that shelters Port Angeles harbor is called **Ediz Hook,** and it provides some interesting birding, including gulls. It is considered one of the best spots in the state to find large rare gulls such as the glaucous gull and is a good place to work on separating herring from Thayer's gulls. Ediz Hook is also good for common terns and parasitic jaegers during fall migration, and wintering waterfowl and seabirds, including oldsquaw and harlequin ducks and yellow-billed loons. All in all, it's a place you will want to check anytime you're near it, except maybe between spring and fall migration. In the town of Port Angeles, get on Front Street (one of the main east-west streets near the waterfront) and take it west until it turns into Marine Drive. Keep going on Marine Drive all the way to its end at the Coast Guard station. You will drive right through the middle of a huge paper mill, which will seem very strange, but just keep going and follow any signs you see to Coast Guard and Ediz Hook. The public road ends at the gate for the Coast Guard station, where there is parking. You cannot go into the Coast Guard area, but you can stop anywhere along the spit between the station and the paper mill. Most birds will be inside the harbor, but it's worth checking the other side a few times. The big rafts of logs often attract shorebirds and gulls as well as other birds.

British Columbia

The farm fields of the **Delta-Ladner area,** between Boundary Bay and Provincial Highway 99, are mentioned often in this book and are as great for gulls as they are for raptors and waterfowl. This area is described in chapter 1, and the time to go is during the highest tides.

Just a few miles to the northwest of Delta is another of British Columbia's hottest birding spots, **Iona Island,** which consists of a large sewage treatment plant and Iona Beach Regional Park. Directions to Iona are in chapter 45. Drive the road to its end at the parking area (with rest rooms). There are three main areas to bird from here. First is a pond, just east of the parking area, that was established for birds and is usually the best of all the ponds on the island

One of North America's most familiar birds, the American robin is common year-round in the Northwest.

for waterfowl, grebes, coots and gulls. Second, there is the beach with its dune grass and bushes that may have some interesting songbirds such as wintering sparrows (white-crowned, golden-crowned, white-throated, Harris's, juncos) or northern shrike. And last is the 2½-mile-long jetty, which contains the wastewater effluent pipe and heads southwest into the Strait of Georgia. You can walk or bicycle on the jetty, but if you're looking for gulls, you'll mainly see them around the ponds, mudflats and shores. However, a walk out on the jetty in winter is usually very productive for seabirds. In addition, the rocks of the jetty itself are good for rock-loving shorebirds such as tattlers, turnstones and surfbirds. Given all the possibilities, it's clear that a stroll on at least part of the jetty is in order during any visit to Iona. Iona is also known for a good variety of wintering raptors, so be sure to keep your eyes open for short-eared owls, merlin, peregrine falcons and maybe even a gyrfalcon!

A popular attraction on **Vancouver Island** is the drive along the southeastern coast of Victoria from Beacon Hill Park, near the Parliament Buildings, toward the University of Victoria. This is sometimes referred to as the Scenic Marine Drive. There are a few road-name changes, but basically you are on Dallas and Beach Drives. On this stretch there are two points of land that are city parks where you can stop and get out to search for birds—**Clover Point** and **Cattle Point**. Gulls hang out frequently at both places, in large part because people feed them there, and both spots are famous for having had rare-gull sightings. While at these areas looking for gulls, keep your eyes out for harlequin ducks (common) and ancient murrelets (regular but not common) in particular among the many waterbirds that are often present.

During the fall salmon run in **Goldstream Park** (chapter 47), large numbers of gulls show up to eat salmon eggs and spawned-out carcasses.

11

February Shorttakes

Sparrows

Seeds are a major food source during winter, so the seedeating sparrows are among our most common wintering songbirds. Song, fox, and white-crowned sparrows are present year-round and are abundant in winter, as are dark-eyed juncos. Lincoln's and savannah sparrows are mainly summer residents but are also present in small numbers during the winter, mainly in the warmer west. Winter brings thousands of golden-crowned sparrows to the Northwest from their northern breeding range (which borders the northern edge of our region). The real excitement comes from a small group of sparrow species that shows up almost every winter but that is unpredictable and includes small numbers. These species are often seen flocking with other sparrows, making it worthwhile to carefully check all sparrow flocks during the winter in the hopes of seeing these rare winter visitors. White-throated and Harris's sparrows are usually seen flocking with their relatives, the other "crowned" sparrows. Tree sparrows and snow buntings are usually seen on the east side only. Swamp sparrows and Lapland longspurs are most commonly encountered near the coast. Good places to look are in brambles near fields; often the best sites are fencerows along dirt roads in farmland.

Early Signs of Spring

Imbolc, the first day of spring in the ancient Celtic calendar, falls at the beginning of February, about the time of our Groundhog Day. To Northwest naturalists this makes more sense than does spring starting with the equinox, because we see many early signs of spring in February, at least we do west of the Cascades. The first trees start blooming—red alder, hazelnut, Indian plum; and by the end of the month the first migrating birds return—tree swallows and turkey vultures. By the end of the month you may also start to hear Pacific tree frogs calling and see skunk cabbage in bloom. So think Celtic and be on your toes for changes; by the equinox, spring will be well on its way.

12

A Closer Look:
East Side, West Side

Mention the Pacific Northwest to people in other parts of the country and you're likely to get a response like, Does it really rain all the time there? Certainly the most common image of our region is that of wet, green, lush forests. And that image is correct, for the Pacific Northwest has the greatest coniferous forests in the world (in terms of tree size and diversity) and the highest rainfall levels in the contiguous United States. People familiar with the region know, however, that such a portrayal is only half, or more accurately, one-third, the truth. Most of Oregon and Washington contain arid to semiarid lands, commonly called "high desert" by many residents. The Pacific Northwest has a wide range of climates and habitats that are intermingled somewhat, but in looking at the big picture it is easy to divide the region into two main parts—the wet part and the dry part.

The Cascade Range essentially makes a north-to-south-running barrier that divides the region into roughly one-third west and wet, and two-thirds east and dry. When a Northwest naturalist says "the east side" or "the west side," he or she means the appropriate side of the crest of the Cascade Range. Things get a little messy in British Columbia, because "the wall" is not as straight and gets closer to the coast, but British Columbia's Coast Mountains can be considered an extension of the Cascades.

The two sides of the Pacific Northwest have very different communities of plants and animals. Of all the many factors that determine what types of plants and animals will occur in a particular spot, climate is usually the most important. So what causes the Pacific Northwest to have the type of climate it does?

Latitude is usually ranked as one of, if not the most, important factors that determine the climate of any particular region on earth. Latitude certainly plays a big role, but other local factors can easily override latitude's influence. Hence, the Pacific Northwest has a significantly milder climate than Newfoundland, another coastal area at the same latitude. Three main factors determine the climate in the Pacific Northwest: the Pacific Ocean, the region's mountains, and the predominantly westerly winds. How do these three interact to give us our weather?

All bodies of water act as heat reservoirs, gaining and releasing heat slowly and thereby moderating temperature changes nearby. The bigger the body of water, the stronger the moderating effect. Since the biggest body of water on earth is the Pacific Ocean, it is no surprise that there is such a strong maritime moderating effect in our region. Surface temperatures in the Pacific off our coast are almost always about 50 degrees Fahrenheit and vary less than five degrees during a whole year. The farther you get from the ocean, the more temperatures will vary, but the maritime influence is so strong that it affects the climate as far as the eastern borders of Oregon and Washington.

Temperature differences between the east and west sides can be striking. Temperatures change much less on the west side, both daily and annually. For example, the two Washington cities of Aberdeen and Yakima are close to the same latitude but 160 miles apart. Aberdeen is on Gray's Harbor, just 15 miles inland from the coast, and Yakima is about 40 miles east of the Cascade crest. The average minimum temperature for January is a chilly 16 degrees in Yakima but a mild 34 degrees in Aberdeen. Come summertime, Yakima heats up with an average maximum for July of 88 degrees, while Aberdeen is again more temperate at 70 degrees. The range between average minimum and maximum temperatures is 72 degrees in Yakima but only half that, 36 degrees, in Aberdeen.

Oregon shows the same pattern. The average annual temperature range in Ontario, about as far east as you can get in Oregon, is over 80 degrees, while Brookings, on the southwest coast, is only 40 degrees, again about half the range. Daily temperature range shows the same pattern. The average daily temperature range in July is a phenomenal 80 degrees in Summer Lake but only about 45 degrees in Brookings. Brookings is so much warmer than the rest of Oregon during much of the winter that it is regularly called the "banana belt" by weather reporters.

The weather in our region can be seen as a battle between two great forces—the moist and mild maritime climate versus the dry and "temperature extreme" continental climate. The battle line is the Cascades, which keeps the two more or less separated and maintains the "typical" weather on each side. But exciting changes can occur when high- and low-pressure areas shift and either force contacts the other. Such a shift brings storms and can bring unseasonably extreme hot or cold temperatures to the west side or carry abnormal amounts of precipitation to the east side. The Columbia River Gorge is almost constantly very windy and is prone to storms because it is the big gap where the weather of the two sides is constantly mixing.

The mountains of the Northwest have a profound influence on precipitation. All mountains have some effect on their local weather, but when you have a major mountain range like the Cascades running the entire length of two states from north to south, the effect is dramatic indeed. It may seem obvious that such a massive mountain range would affect the weather, but the reason its effect is so strong is because of another factor not always recognized—the prevailing winds. There are semipermanent high- and low-pressure cells over the North Pacific Ocean that result in westerly winds blowing steadily from the ocean eastward over the land. These westerly winds are loaded with moisture from the ocean, and it is the interaction of these winds with the mountains that gives us our noted precipitation.

The warmer air is, the more water vapor it can hold. As warm winds blow over the ocean at about 50 degrees, the air becomes saturated with water. These moist winds come off the ocean and blow over the land. The colder air is, the less moisture it can hold, so if the temperature over the land is colder than the temperature over the ocean, a common situation for much of the year, condensation occurs, resulting in fog or precipitation. As the air moves farther east, hits the mountains and starts to rise, it gets even colder, about 4 degrees colder for every thousand feet in elevation. As the air gets colder, more water vapor condenses and falls as precipitation. Hence, the west, or windward, sides of the mountains get soaked. By the time the air has moved over mountains as high as the Cascades, it has lost most of its moisture. Then, when the air descends on the east side, the opposite process occurs. The falling air warms up and absorbs more moisture, actually drying out the land on the east side of the mountains. The resulting lower precipitation on the leeward side of the mountains is commonly called a *rain shadow.*

The Coast Ranges, the Olympic Mountains and the Vancouver Island Ranges all intercept a lot of moisture from the wet westerlies before they hit the Cascades. East of the Cascades, the interior mountains like the Blue Mountains and the Selkirks show the same rain shadow effect, although the difference is not as dramatic because the total amount of moisture is much lower. Because most of the mountains in the Northwest run north and south and the winds bring the moisture from the west, a map of the region color-coded for precipitation shows a series of north-and-south-running bands paralleling the mountains. It is clear from such a map that latitude has little to do with precipitation patterns here.

How dramatic this rain shadow effect is can be demonstrated with some precipitation records. Looking again at the two cities of Aberdeen and Yakima, we find that Aberdeen receives an average of 85 inches of precipitation a year while Yakima receives only 8, a difference of 77 inches!

Another striking example can be found on the two sides of the Olympic Mountains. The Hoh Rainforest, famous for its rain, averages 135 inches of rain a year, while the town of Sequim, just 40 miles to the northeast, receives only 15 inches. Of course, between the two are the 7,000-foot-high Olympics, which collect most of the moisture and have some of the highest snowfall levels in the lower 48. Another interesting statistic is the number of days in a year with at least half an inch of precipitation. Most of the Oregon coast has at least fifty such soggy days, while about half of eastern Oregon has less than five.

Many factors interact to determine which communities of plants and animals are found in a particular location. Topography, soil and interactions between living things all play a big part, but the single most important factor is climate. Understanding the basic climates of the Northwest makes the distributions of different plants and animals fall into logical patterns.

March

Notes

13

Gray Whale Migration

The change in common attitudes toward whales is one of the fastest and most dramatic such changes I have ever seen. In a little over a decade, from the 1960s to the 1970s, public opinion of whales went from exploitation or indifference to reverence. Creatures who once were seen as monsters by many and as floating bags of oil and fertilizer by a few are now widely respected and highly admired for their intelligence, beauty and exquisite adaptation to their marine environment. This change in human attitudes and behavior, brought about by a small but highly dedicated group of activists, is one of the most encouraging examples of what can be done to help our planet and its wildlife.

It is hard to imagine that whales *wouldn't* be highly significant to us in many ways; they are, after all, the largest animals that have ever lived on earth. Any animal that can reach 100 feet in length and weigh 220 *tons* is going to get some attention, even if it does live in a different world than ours.

It is clear that prehistoric peoples realized they could eat whales, and humans started actively hunting whales at least four thousand years ago. Hunting of whales increased slowly over the centuries, then increased tremendously in the last two hundred years. As with many other animals, whales were overhunted until many species were on the brink of extinction in this century. Fortunately, it appears that the Save the Whales campaigns of the last twenty-five years have actually stopped the killing in time for most species to survive, although some are clearly not yet secure.

As is commonly known today, whales are mammals, not fish, which they resemble superficially, and like all mammals they breathe air with lungs, are warm-blooded and nurse their young. Whales evolved from ancient ancestors that were land animals, and this evolution, with many adaptations, to a totally aquatic life has fascinated scientists for decades. The word "whale" is commonly used for the whole order or group of mammals named *cetaceans,* which includes whales, porpoises and dolphins. The cetaceans are divided into two big groups, baleen whales, and toothed whales, which includes all porpoises and dolphins.

The gray whale is a medium-large baleen whale about 35 to 50 feet long and weighing 20 to 40 tons. As you would guess, it is gray in color—but very blotchy with light- and dark-gray spots, patches of barnacles and white scars where barnacles have been. It does not have a dorsal fin but instead has a series of bumps on the rear of its back. Gray whales are unique in that they are the only living members of their family and fossils are unknown. They undertake the longest migration of any mammal, swimming 8,000 to 14,000 miles round-trip every year between their summer range in the North Pacific and their winter range in Baja California. They are the most coastal of all baleen whales, rarely venturing far out to sea.

Like all baleen whales, gray whales do not have teeth but sheets of baleen or "whalebone" that hang down from their upper jaw. Baleen is composed of the same material as human fingernails and looks and feels like plastic. The baleen sheets have fringed edges and make an effective filter or sieve, and these great animals feed by filtering vast quantities of small animals out of the water. It has seemed paradoxical to many people that the world's largest animals would feed on such small prey in contrast to the general tendency of large predators to eat large prey. But it is the incredible numbers of these small prey animals, such as crustaceans, and their reliable occurrence that has allowed the great whales to evolve to their huge size. Gray whales are again unique in that they are the only bottom-feeding whales, feeding primarily by sucking up and filtering soft bottom sediments.

Since gray whales regularly swim close to shore during their migrations, they were probably one of the first whales known to humans, and thus one of the first to be exploited. Aboriginal hunters in Asia and North America killed limited numbers for centuries, probably with little environmental impact, but the population was quickly decimated by modern whaling between 1845 and 1930. Fortunately, in the 1930s and 1940s various laws and regulations were passed by the United States, Mexico and the International Whaling Commission, resulting in complete gray whale protection by 1946. The result is one of the happiest stories of wildlife conservation. The recovery of the gray whale has been the fastest of any whale, and it is believed that the approximately twenty thousand now living comes close to the population of centuries ago. In 1994 the gray whale was removed from the Endangered Species List, the first marine animal ever "delisted."

The gray whale's amazing recovery, its habits and range, have made it one of the best known of all whales. Because gray whales migrate very close to the Pacific Coast every year, millions of people have seen them from shore and, increasingly, from boats and even small airplanes. Whale-watching boat tours have become a major business in many coastal towns, and whale watching has become so popular that there is concern over harassment by the boatloads of admirers. This is of particular concern in the shallow bays in Baja, where the calves are born during the winter and where whale-watching tours have increased dramatically. Government agencies and concerned organizations have produced various guidelines and laws governing whale-watching activities, and reputable tour companies will follow these procedures.

There are two periods during which gray whales pass our coast. The vast majority of gray whales spend the summer feeding in the Bering and Chukchi Seas. In October, the pregnant females are the first to leave for the southern wintering and calving lagoons, followed over the next two months by the males, juveniles and nonpregnant females. Peak numbers occur off our coast in December, with most animals making it to Baja by the end of January, although stragglers pass by for months. On their southward journey the whales tend to move faster and farther from shore than on their return in spring.

During December in the calving lagoons of Baja, females give birth to their single young, which grow quickly on their mother's rich milk, gaining as much as 60 pounds a day! By mid-February the first whales have already started back north, but the moms and their new calves won't leave until May or even June. Peak numbers of northbound whales occur from mid-March to mid-April. The whales, particularly the mothers and new calves, move slower and closer to shore during the spring migration, making this the best time for observation. Several hundred whales actually skip the long journey all the way back to the Arctic and hang out along our coastline all summer, joining the main population when it passes through the next winter. What with all the early starters, stragglers and dawdlers, it is now possible to see gray whales off our coast any time of year. The prime time, however, is during the peak of spring migration.

To see whales from land, one must get as far out into the ocean as possible, as on a point or headland. Being elevated is also a big advantage. You find whales by looking for their spouts ("thar she blows"), so the calmer the water, the better. This means early mornings are usually better than afternoons, when winds often pick up and make whitecaps. Watch the water about an inch below the horizon. (Overcast skies are best to reduce glare, which is not usually a problem in the Pacific Northwest.) Gray whales usually make three to five blows 30 to 50 seconds apart before they dive for 5 to 10 minutes. Since they usually travel in small groups, when you see one blow, you'll see others. Once you get used to the pattern of diving and blowing, it will be easier for you to find whales with binoculars and scopes for a closer look. If you are lucky you may see one breach, a spectacular jump almost out of the water.

Seeing whales by boat can be very exciting, and you will often see other marine mammals and seabirds also. This can be a great family outing, but take care to dress warmly, and take motion sickness medication, if necessary, well in advance of the trip. Ask at a chamber of commerce or visitor information center in coastal towns for information on tour operators. The Hatfield Marine Science Center in Newport has a listing of operators in Oregon. An excellent book is *Field Guide to the Gray Whale*, with information on charter trips throughout the Northwest.

Oregon

Hot Spots

Oregon is really great for gray-whale watching. The Oregon State Park Department and the Sea Grant Program at the **Hatfield Marine Science Center** in Newport, part of the Oregon State University Extension Service, have created an incredible program where almost four hundred trained volunteers staff twenty-eight whale-watching sites on the Oregon coast for two weeks each year. One week is the week of school vacation after Christmas, the second week is spring break, usually the third full week in March. There are volunteers at all twenty-eight sites from 10 A.M. to 1 P.M. every day during a Whale Watching Week, and they will help you spot whales and answer your questions. Signs are out on the highway at each site indicating Whale Watching Spoken Here. The winter week catches the whales headed south and the spring week is right at the peak of the migration north—the best time to see the most whales. Most tour-boat operators do not run tours during the winter migration but wait until March and April because of weather and sea conditions.

To get information on this program, and on the gray whale in general, write the Hatfield Marine Science Center (see the appendix). It will also provide a list of tour operators. Information about this program usually appears in major newspapers in the state the week before each Whale Watching Week. Listed next are eight of the best sites out of the twenty-eight, as selected by Bev Lund, OSU Whale Watching Volunteer Coordinator.

Ecola State Park, just north of Cannon Beach, is on Tillamook Head and has several easy trails leading to good observation sites. As U.S. Highway 101 traverses **Neahkahnie Mountain** in Oswald West State Park, there are some turnouts that provide breathtaking views of the coast all the way from Tillamook Head to Cape Lookout. The largest turnout, where there is a historical marker, is where the volunteers will be.

Cape Meares and **Cape Lookout** are on the **Three Capes Scenic Route** south of Tillamook. At Cape Meares you drive to a parking lot, then walk less than a quarter of a mile to the lighthouse on the tip of the cape for excellent views. Keep your eyes out for the unique population of gray jays that live on the cape and check out the Octopus Tree while you're there. At Cape Lookout you have to hike $2\frac{1}{2}$ miles out to the end of the cape to the observation area, but many consider this to be the best spot in the state because Cape Lookout sticks so far out into the ocean and the whales really hug the point.

Boiler Bay State Park, right on Hwy. 101 about halfway between Lincoln City and Newport, is one of the most convenient sites. **Yaquina Head,** just north of Newport, also has easy access and excellent viewing not only of whales but also of birds, seals and tide pools. (See chapters 31 and 38.)

Another very convenient spot is the turnout on Hwy. 101 between **Heceta Head** and **Sea Lion Caves.** And way down south near Brookings is **Cape Ferrelo,** one of the best spots from which to see gray whales during the summer.

Washington

Washington does not have the number of rocky headlands so characteristic of the Oregon coast and public access to the shore is much more limited. The best spots are in the coastal section of **Olympic National Park. Cape Alava** is the most westerly point of land in the lower 48 states and provides good chances of seeing not only gray whales but tide pools, seals and sea lions, many birds and even some of the few sea otters reintroduced along the Washington coast. Cape Alava is fairly isolated, and is a $3\frac{1}{3}$-mile hike from the Ozette Ranger Station in the far northwestern corner of the park.

A closer area is near the town of La Push. Just north of the town of Forks take the La Push road toward La Push, but follow the signs for Mora and eventually **Rialto Beach** in Olympic National Park. Whales will sometimes enter the estuary of the Quileute River and be quite close to shore. The easiest access to and viewing of gray whales in Washington is along the stretch of Hwy. 101 that hugs the coast from Ruby Beach to Queets. Any of the turnouts or parking areas on the cliffs will give you access to views of the water.

Without a doubt, the most popular way to see gray whales in Washington is by boat out of the busy seaport town of **Westport** at the mouth of **Grays Harbor.** Sometimes during spring high tides whales actually enter the harbor and come very close to the waterfront of the town. The municipal fishing pier, rock jetties, sea wall and inner harbor provide interesting sights and lots of opportunities to see a large variety of coastal birds, from loons to shorebirds. Call the chamber of commerce (1-800-345-6223) to get a list of charter-boat companies running whale-watching trips. Trips are 2 to 3 hours long and usually available March through May.

British Columbia

Although some gray whales occasionally wander into the Strait of Juan De Fuca, the vast majority migrate off the west coast of Vancouver Island, which has limited access. The best place for gray-whale watching is the **Long Beach Unit** of **Pacific Rim National Park** and the nearby towns of **Ucluelet** and **Tofino.** The two towns and the park have joined together to produce Whalefest, a two- to three-week festival celebrating the gray whale migration. There are lots of educational and entertaining events and activities, many geared toward families. To get information on the festival and other local attractions, write Whalefest, Box 428, Ucluelet, BC V0R 3A0.

To reach Pacific Rim National Park by car, drive west on Provincial Highway 4 from Port Alberni. When you reach the area, your first stop should be the Wickaninnish Center in the park to get maps and information. Coming from Port Alberni, you will come to a major junction where you can go left (south) to Ucluelet or right (north) to the park and Tofino. Just over 3 miles from the junction is the road to Wickaninnish. The center has some excellent displays, movies, outdoor observation areas, and park staff who can answer your questions. Wickaninnish Center is a great place to visit if it's raining, a likely possibility, for this area has the highest rainfall in British Columbia! The center is closed during winter and hours vary other times of year, so call the park office first.

The best spots in the park to see whales from are at **Wickaninnish Center, Wya Point** and **Box Island,** the eastern headland to **Schooner Cove.** The last two spots require hikes of about 2 miles round-trip. The best spot from land, however, is not in the park but at the Coast Guard station and lighthouse on **Amphitrite Point,** less than a mile south of Ucluelet. Drive through Ucluelet on the main road, and just south of town turn right onto Coast Guard Road. There is a small sign that reads Lighthouse. Go a short distance to the end of the road and park in the parking lot. Look in the carport for the sign to the viewpoint and follow it to a wonderful view off the point. Whales often pass close to the point, and bald eagles are commonly seen here.

There are several charter companies in Tofino and Ucluelet that run whale-watching boat trips. Ask for a list when you write about the whale festival, or call Super, Natural British Columbia and ask for the listing of companies in British Columbia that offer whale-watching excursions.

14

Early Bloomers

Winter is short in the Northwest at low elevations on the west side. From the time the last leaves fall until the first plants are blooming may be only a couple of months. The first flowers I notice every year are the long yellowish green catkins hanging down on the western hazelnut (wild filbert) in February or even late January. These are soon followed by the reddish catkins of the red alder. The extended catkins give the tops of the alders that fuzzy red look at the peak of their bloom, in late February or early March. These inconspicuous catkins are certainly not what most people think of when they think of wildflowers, so it is no surprise that this subtle sign of spring is missed by many.

The next tree (or, rather, big shrub) to show some action is the osoberry, or Indian plum, which is more noticeable. In February the flower clusters hang down from the branches, but it is the new leaves that come out at the same time that attract attention. These leaves are a bright green, almost chartreuse, and stand straight up on the branches. The trees look like some kind of strange candelabra with bright green flames. In the otherwise bare gray woods they really stand out. About this same time we get the first real splash of color from the large bright yellow spathes of skunk cabbage. Skunk cabbage likes it really wet, actually growing in standing water, so its distribution is spotty. It's particularly common in flooded pastures near the coast where it sometimes makes large displays.

After these earliest bloomers the wildflower season really gets under way with one of the showiest and most beloved Northwest flowers, the western trillium. These spectacular flowers have three large, bright-white petals that fade to pink or purple as they age, fooling many into thinking there are two different species in the same place (there actually are two other species of trillium in the Northwest, but they are not common and are quite distinctive). Once the trillium are out, the blooming season is really under way, and one can keep busy botanizing until the end of summer by going to different habitats and elevations. Some of our most common early wildflowers in west-side forests are wood violets, coltsfoot, wild ginger, bittercress, salmonberry, red-flowering currant and Oregon grape. These are closely followed by fairybells, bleeding heart, buttercups, false Solomon's seal and false lily of the valley, candy flower, large-leaved geum, star flower, vanilla leaf, mitrewort, youth-on-age, fringecup and foamflower.

As with animals, each species of plant has a preferred habitat. Some, like Douglas fir, are generalists and grow in a variety of conditions while others, like the cobra lily, are very restricted. And as with animals, the key to finding a particular plant, and often a helpful clue in its identification, is knowing the habitat where the plant lives. All good plant guides, therefore, will include some description of each plant's habitat. Some books are organized by habitat, such as *Plants and Animals of the Pacific Northwest,* by Eugene Kozloff, and *Wild Plants of the San Juan Islands,* by Scott Atkinson and Fred Sharpe. Kozloff's book covers the area west of the Cascades, and the Atkinson and Sharpe book is useful for the whole Olympic rain shadow area, including southern Vancouver Island, the Gulf Islands and Whidbey Island.

Scattered throughout the forests are areas with shallow and often rocky soil and lower rainfall, where conifers do not do well. This results in open meadows or woodlands with dominant trees of Oregon white (or Garry) oak and madrone, often mixed with Douglas fir. Many early wildflowers are found here because these areas get more sunlight and dry out faster, so plants have to get started early. Some conspicuous flowers of these habitats are blue-eyed grass and grass widows, yellow bells, fawn lilies, prairie stars, gold stars, drabas, spring gold, and the confusing desert parsleys, shooting stars, some buttercups and some saxifrages.

Just when a particular plant blooms can vary greatly from place to place and year to year. Such factors as elevation, slope, exposure and, of course, weather will all affect the particular microhabitat of each plant. In general, the blooming season is later east of the Cascades because of higher elevations and longer, colder winters. Blooming is also later, and the season shorter, the higher the elevation, so alpine areas aren't blooming until July or August (chapter 37). The big secret to being in the right place at the right time is to start going out early in the season and get out as much as possible as the season progresses. This chapter on wildflowers is in March so we can get going early! The areas mentioned will be blooming with different flowers throughout the spring, so plan on repeated visits.

Another way to know what is blooming where and when is to keep in touch with whatever networks of amateur botanists and naturalists there are in your area. These groups will usually be a native plant society or an Audubon chapter in the United States and a natural history society or the Federation of British Columbia Naturalists in Canada. Botanical gardens, natural history museums and occasionally garden clubs can also be good sources of information about wildflowers. Community colleges and parks departments may also have wildflower classes and trips.

Good books are the other important resource for flower identification. A favorite of many has been *A Field Guide to Pacific States Wildflowers,* by Theodore Niehaus and Charles Ripper. Even though this book works best in California and is better the farther south you go in our region, it can almost always get you to at least the right genus. A new (in 1994) excellent guide is *Plants of the Pacific Northwest Coast,* by Jim Pojar and Andy MacKinnon, which covers areas west of the Cascades from mid-Oregon to Alaska. It is a Canadian book and works better the farther north you are in our region.

Oregon

Hot Spots

The Klamath Mountains create a rain shadow effect in the valleys of the Rogue River and its tributaries, making the southwestern corner of Oregon just a bit sunnier and drier than the rest of western Oregon. Some animals that are much more common in California and are found here, but rarely in the rest of the state, include black phoebe, plain titmouse, blue-gray gnatcatcher, California towhee, California mountain and common kingsnakes, ringtail, valley pocket gopher and California kangaroo rat. The plants also show strong California affinities, with forests and woodlands of mixed black as well as Oregon white oak, madrone and Douglas fir intermingled with white fir, sugar pine, tan oak and incense cedar. Extensive stands of various species of ceanothus, manzanita and other chaparral species give a distinct California feel to the landscape. Southwestern Oregon is actually a great mixing area, with plants from the Cascades, the Sierra Nevada and the Northern California Coast Range all intermingled.

The **Table Rocks** are two conspicuous flat-topped mesas in the Rogue Valley that have a number of vernal pools and give a bright display of California and Northwest wildflowers in early spring. Both Upper and Lower Table Rock are a mixture of private and Bureau of Land Management (BLM) land, with the Nature Conservancy being a third owner of Lower Table Rock. Both Table Rocks are managed by a stewardship committee with representatives from all three groups. Everyone involved with the area is concerned about the impact of visitors, so be sure to stay on the trails or roads and avoid any disturbance to the vegetation and wildlife. As with all Nature Conservancy preserves, dogs are not allowed. The Medford office of the BLM conducts a series of guided hikes in the spring, and this is an excellent way to see the sites. Call (541) 770-2200 for information.

To reach either Table Rock, take the Central Point Exit 32/33 from I-5 north of Medford. Go east about one mile on Pine St. (which becomes Biddle Rd.), then turn left and go north on Table Rock Rd. After 5 miles you will come to the intersection with Modoc Rd. To get to Upper Table Rock, go right onto Modoc and in $1^1/_2$ miles, there is a parking area for the trail on your left. To get to Lower Table Rock from the intersection with Modoc, continue past Modoc on Table Rock Rd. for $2^1/_2$ miles, then turn left onto Wheeler and go $^3/_4$ mile to the parking area, also on your left. From both parking areas, it is about a $1^1/_2$-mile uphill hike to the tops of the mesas. The Upper Table Rock trail is a bit shorter and starts in better habitat.

This area can be hot and dry during sunny weather so take plenty of water and sun protection. You should also be aware of three pests—poison oak, ticks and rattlesnakes. Poison oak and rattlesnakes (which are rare) can be easily avoided but ticks are harder to detect. Spray your arms and legs well with insect repellent in tick country.

Another area in southwestern Oregon, near the Illinois River, is **Eight Dollar Mountain**. Twenty-four miles south of Grants Pass on Hwy. 199, turn right onto Eight Dollar Mountain Rd. and drive through the first mile of private property. After that, stop anywhere in the next few miles that looks interesting—many flowers can be found along the road. At $4^1/_2$ miles, there is a hairpin turn to the north. Park at this turn and a few hundred yards to the south you will find a huge bunch of cobra lilies (chapter 25).

Common flowers of the western forested lowlands can be seen in almost any good chunk of native forest, but four places in Portland and one in Eugene have a good variety of flowers, convenient access and visitor services and offer guided walks and other programs about wildflowers. The **Portland Audubon Society's wildlife sanctuary** presents an excellent sample of second growth forest and has several trails. The sanctuary is also the site of the society's book and nature store, meeting rooms and offices, and in Audubon House you can get trail maps and information from the friendly staff and volunteers. At various times there are wildflower walks in the sanctuary, wildflower classes and field trips and specimens of wildflowers blooming in the sanctuary on display.

Very close to Portland Audubon is **Hoyt Arboretum,** a city park. Much of the arboretum has plantings of trees and shrubs from all over the world, but there are plenty of native plants as well. Guided walks are usually held on weekend afternoons from April to October, and there are wildflower and other natural history classes offered. The visitor center for the arboretum is at 4000 S.W. Fairview. Adjacent to both Audubon House and the arboretum, and linking them via the Wildwood Trail, is **Forest Park**, at almost 5,000 acres the largest forested city park in the United States. There are 50 miles of trails in this undeveloped "wilderness park," and both the arboretum visitor center and Audubon House are good sources of information on Forest Park.

Tryon Creek State Park straddles the boundary between Portland and Lake Oswego and has basically the same habitat as the arboretum-Forest Park-Audubon ecosystem. Tryon Creek also has a visitor center and offers a variety of natural history programs. The trillium are so abundant at Tryon Creek that for seventeen years (as of 1996) the park has celebrated with the annual Trillium Festival, usually at the end of March. Not only are there guided hikes, activities and programs, but also a native-plant sale for those who want to try growing the locals at home.

Leach Botanical Garden is very different from the above destinations, and unique. While the Leaches were living in this lovely southeast Portland estate, Lilla Leach collected and transplanted plants from all over Oregon and developed a living collection of native plants that is now a city park. Though the plants are not in their natural plant communities, amateur botanists can become familiar with dozens of wildflowers all at once, with most of them identified. There are also tours and programs and a plant sale that features native plants for landscaping.

These Portland wildflower destinations are usually indicated on city maps, and all are listed in the appendix: call for current hours and programs.

The **Mount Pisgah Arboretum** is just east of Eugene and south of Springfield and occupies 118 acres within the **Howard Buford Recreation Area,** shown on more detailed maps. There are 5 miles of trails through a great variety of plants native to the Willamette Valley and some from outside the state. The arboretum has a full range of programs and activities, including a Spring Wildflower Festival and Plant Sale in May and a Fall Festival and Mushroom Show at the end of October. Both events have a lot going on besides the plant-oriented activities. In addition to being a great spot for botanizing, Mount Pisgah is considered an excellent birding spot for migrating songbirds.

From I-5, take Exit 189 for 30th Avenue. Go east on 30th just a few hundred yards, then turn left onto Franklin to go north. In another fraction of a mile turn right and head east on Seavey Loop Road. In a couple of miles you'll enter the Buford Recreation Area. Follow signs to the arboretum.

Washington

The most famous and popular wildflower area in the Northwest is the **Columbia River Gorge.** The Gorge has a wide range of habitats and is a mixing area for species from the west side, species from the east side, glacial relicts from colder times, southern species left from warmer periods and a number of endemics. At least eight hundred different species of flowering plants have been found in The Gorge. Such a botanical treasure deserves, and gets, its own book—*Wildflowers of the Columbia Gorge,* by Russ Jolley. Covering 744 species in detail, it's an extremely useful guide for finding the flowers of The Gorge. For positive identification between similar species, you will sometimes need another field guide.

The Washington side of The Gorge, with its south-facing slopes, is quite different from the cooler, wetter Oregon side. The Washington side greens up and blooms earlier than the Oregon side. The east end of The Gorge blooms earlier than the west end, so in March the best action is almost all in the pine-oak woodlands and the shrub-grasslands east of Hood River and mainly on the Washington side.

The Lewis and Clark Highway, Highway 14, winds it way along the Washington side of the Columbia River. Some of the best areas for early wildflowers in the region are off of the stretch of Hwy. 14 between Bingen and Horsethief Lake State Park, in the Columbia River Gorge National Scenic Area. You may find flowers anywhere along this section of the highway, but be very careful parking and getting out of your car. For about 6 miles, Hwy. 14 is paralleled by the old highway now called County Road 1230 but more commonly referred to as The Old Highway. Two outstanding floral areas are **Catherine Creek** and **Major Creek,** small creeks that are accessible from Rd. 1230.

Heading east on Hwy. 14 from Bingen, turn left onto Rd. 1230 just before you come to Milepost 71 at Rowland Lake. After $1^1/_2$ miles you'll see a small parking area in front of a green gate—the entrance to the Catherine Creek area. There is usually some information posted on a sign by the fence.

As you head north through the fence, head off to the right downhill toward the creek until you find yourself on an old dirt road. You can explore the different branches of this road as it heads up the drainage. Stay on this road (and its branches) to minimize impact on the area. Be aware that poison oak and ticks are common here.

Three quarters of a mile farther east on Rd. 1230 you'll come to Major Creek Road. Park on Rd. 1230 and walk up Major Creek Road. The road goes through a mix of forest service, tribal and private land, so it is best to stay on the road, which is public and has no traffic. Eighty different wildflower species have been reported from along this road during the spring! The Catherine and Major Creek areas are good viewing through May.

The **Dalles Mountain Road** leaves Hwy. 14 just west of Horsethief Lake State Park and winds up into the Columbia Hills. Along this road is excellent for early flowers such as grass widows, draba, poet's shooting star, a variety of lomatiums and the endemic Dallas Mountain buttercup. Horsethief Lake State Park has camping and other facilities and a good sample of wildflowers but does not open until April 1.

Washington's Olympic Mountains, with elevations around 7,000 feet, create a significant rain shadow to their northeast. This difference is impressive, with areas in the rain shadow getting under 20 inches of rain a year. This lower-than-average precipitation combined with the thin soils left by glaciation, has resulted in some plant communities much more like those of the Rogue Valley or eastern Washington than like the rest of the Salish Sea area. When you see Rocky Mountain juniper and prickly pear cactus growing here, you know something's different! Included in this rain shadow is the northeastern corner of the Olympic Peninsula, the San Juan Islands, Fidalgo, most of Whidbey and the Gulf Islands and the Saanich Peninsula (Victoria region). There are many open grasslands and rocky outcrops and woodlands of Garry oak, madrone and Douglas fir. The grasslands and rocky outcrops in particular start blooming early, and some years there is quite a display in March, although peak times are usually a bit later.

Any of the parks on the **San Juan Islands** are considered good for botanizing, but some areas worth mentioning are Mount Constitution in **Moran State Park** on Orcas, Iceberg Point on Lopez Island and Cattle Point on the southern tip of San Juan Island. Both **British** and **American Camp**, part of the National Historical Park, are good for flowers and excellent for spring songbirds. The most famous island for flowers is spectacular **Yellow Island,** a Nature Conservancy Preserve. Access is by boat only, and you should check with the conservancy before attempting to visit.

Washington Park in Anacortes and **Deception Pass State Park** both give you a taste of the San Juans without the boat trip. To get to Washington Park, head west on State Highway 20 through Anacortes, and before you get to the ferry terminal stay to the left and go onto Sunset Avenue, following signs to Washington Park. When you enter the park, you have a choice of going right to the beach or left onto Loop Road, which goes around Fidalgo Head. Going right to the nice pebble beach gives you some good views of Rosario Strait and waterbirds in season, but for flowers take the scenic Loop Road. There will be a number of places where you can pull out to explore the roadside and trails. On the south-facing slopes are the unique open woodlands of Douglas fir, madrone and Rocky Mountain juniper. Deception Pass State Park, Washington's most popular state park, straddles both sides of Deception Pass between Fidalgo and Whidbey Island. The trails on Goose Rock are considered the best for flowers.

British Columbia

The southeastern tip of Vancouver Island, the Saanich Peninsula, is very similar to The San Juan Islands. There are two things, however, that are very conspicuous by their absence from the oak woodland habitat—scrub jays and poison oak.

Some of the choice areas are **Mill Hill** and **Thetis Lake Regional Parks** and **Uplands Park** (Cattle Point) in Victoria. In Mill Hill, take the Summit Trail up to the top and loop back down on the Calypso Trail. In Thetis Lake also make a counterclockwise loop by starting at the sign showing wildflowers of the park and heading east on the Lewis Clark Trail, taking it to the Seymour Hill Trail, and then coming back near the lake. Wander the trails through the portion of Uplands Park across Beach Drive from the Cattle Point parking area in Victoria.

The most awesome floral display I've seen on the island is easy to miss. **Lone Tree Hill Regional Park** is just a few miles north of Thetis Lake and Mill Hill Parks. From Trans-Canada Highway 1, 2 miles west of Thetis Lake, head north on Millstream Road. After $3^1/_3$ miles head to the left to stay on Millstream Road and don't follow what seems to be the main road to the right, which is Millstream Lake Road. In just under a mile and a half you'll see a sign and small parking area on your right. There is just one trail, steep but only a mile, to the top. In addition to the floral display, the view from the top is spectacular and the madrones are exceptionally beautiful. Contact the Capital Regional District Parks Department (see appendix) for maps and other information.

15

Spring Waterfowl Migration

Say the word "migration," and the first images that pop into most heads are long V-shaped strings of geese flying over fields in autumn. Although a large majority of the birds in the Northwest are migratory species, waterfowl are so conspicuous, especially because of their huge flocks, that they have come to represent migration. All the waterfowl found in our region are migratory, although some wood ducks, mallards and Canada geese may move relatively little during a year. Most waterfowl migrate long distances, and round-trips of several thousand miles are common. Waterfowl fly at an average speed of about 50 miles per hour when migrating, and it is clear that some fly for as long as forty hours or 2,000 miles without stopping, some probably longer.

Birds that migrate to or through our region in the fall will be passing through again in the spring on their return to their breeding grounds. It seems that most people, however, are much more aware of the fall migration than they are of spring migration, with the exception of bird-watchers, of course. There are two reasons for this. First of all, fall migration is more spread out than is spring migration—there is a longer period during which birds are arriving and staying over as they pass through. In spring, birds seem a lot more anxious to get back to their breeding grounds. Unless something holds them up, like bad weather, most migrating birds really zip through in the spring, many at night, so it's easy to miss them. Second, when an animal that hasn't been around for months all of a sudden starts arriving in large noisy flocks, it is noticeable. If you catch it at the right time, however, spring migration is as impressive as the best fall migration, and the birds are in their peak breeding plumage.

Chapter 8 discussed our local ducks and waterfowl in general, and this chapter can be viewed as its second half. As mentioned in chapter 8, many waterfowl actually spend the winter in the Pacific Northwest. There are other birds, called *migrants* or *transients,* that pass through in fall and spring. During spring migration you can see them all—winter visitors, migrants and maybe the first cinnamon and blue-winged teal, which are summer breeders. The time of waterfowl migration varies with changing weather conditions and from one location to another, but the peak time for most species will be between mid-March and mid-April, although all of March and April are potentially good.

Hot Spots

Any place that is a major wintering area for waterfowl will be excellent for observing spring migration. The birds that have spent the winter will be there, and so will migrants passing through, because a good area to stay during the winter is also going to be a choice spot for stopping to

Like many ducks, the handsome, easy-to-identify, northern pintail winters on the west side but breeds east of the Cascades.

rest and feed. All of the hotspots for winter waterfowl in chapter 8 should be considered applicable to this chapter. Remember that most national wildlife refuges were established primarily for wintering and migrating waterfowl, so you can hardly go wrong at any refuge. There are twenty-five in Oregon and Washington that are excellent for waterfowl.

West of the Cascades there is so much good waterfowl habitat that the birds are spread out over large areas. On the drier east side, where wetlands are much more limited and scattered, you will get larger and more spectacular concentrations of waterfowl as they stop in these critical areas on their journeys north. This is a good example of what might be called the "oasis as magnet" phenomenon. The hotspots concentrate on these east-side locations.

Oregon

One of the West's largest inland marsh systems is in the Harney Basin, which includes Malheur National Wildlife Refuge, one of our most famous birding areas and subject of chapter 26. **Burns** is by far the largest town in the basin and is host to the annual **John Scharff Migratory Bird Festival and Art Show,** which will be held for the fifteenth year in 1996. Businesspeople, service clubs, agency personnel and lots of other folks from throughout the basin have joined together to develop what is one of the best examples of ecotourism that I know of in the West. The festival increases understanding and appreciation of local wildlife resources, provides some excellent wildlife viewing (especially for novices) without disturbing the animals and is a great addition to the local economy. The festival is usually held the first full weekend in April every year; for complete information and registration materials, write or call the Harney County Chamber of Commerce.

There is good birding in Malheur National Wildlife Refuge, but some of the best is actually just south of Burns in the pastures and fields that are normally flooded this time of year. Maps of the best areas around Burns are available at the festival and can probably be mailed to you in advance by the chamber of commerce. Write the refuge directly to get their maps and checklists. The best area is a rough rectangle bordered by U.S. Highway 20/395 on the west, Monroe Street/State Highway 78 on the north, State Highway 205 on the east, and Greenhouse Lane on the south. You can see almost everything from your car as you slowly drive along Egan, Hotchkiss, Hwy. 205 (watch traffic) and Greenhouse. Be sure to go all the way west on the unnamed continuation of Hotchkiss Lane to the sewage ponds, which are usually loaded and best seen from the roadside on their north side. Continue on this road as it turns south and goes between the sewage ponds and the lumber mill. The fields along this section of road are usually quite flooded and packed with birds. Sora and Virginia rails have been heard frequently (and seen rarely) at the bend in the road just before it turns, goes over the railroad tracks, and dead-ends at the mill. You can turn around at the road's end, but do not park on mill property (west of the tracks).

Be sure to ask at the Bird Central Booth at festival headquarters in the high school for the latest information on what has been seen and where. You especially want to see the huge flocks of snow, and some Ross's, geese. If they are roosting in a particular field, get there before sunset and you may be lucky and have five to ten *thousand* white geese swirling and honking all around you as they come to land and settle for the night. It's a transcendent experience. You will also see thousands of Canada and white-fronted geese, as well as a number of ducks. Some of the more conspicuous shorebirds will be American avocet, black-necked stilt, willet, long-billed curlew and snipe, which should all be feeding in the fields. And, of course, the sandhill cranes will be arriving to nest, and some will even be starting to do their spectacular courtship dance. To top it all off, one of the best ways to see sage grouse strutting is on an early-morning grouse tour. All in all, this is a fabulous time to visit a fabulous area. Be sure to make your motel reservations as soon as you can because the town will fill up for the festival.

Two other spectacular areas for spring waterfowl migration in eastern Oregon are **Summer Lake** (chapter 3) and the **Klamath Basin,** particularly **Lower Klamath** and **Tule Lake National Wildlife Refuges** (chapter 7).

Washington

There are two major areas in eastern Washington that are counterparts to the Harney and Klamath Basins in Oregon—**Turnbull National Wildlife Refuge** and the **Columbia National Wildlife Refuge/Potholes Reservoir** area. The two areas are about 100 miles apart and near I-90, making it possible to visit both in one big day of birding.

Turnbull National Wildlife Refuge is different from most wildlife refuges in a couple of ways. There is never any hunting at Turnbull, and there are almost 10 miles of hiking trails. The habitat is also different from most refuges in that it is mainly forested with scattered small lakes and marshes. There

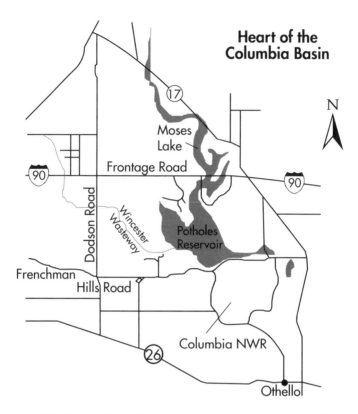

Heart of the Columbia Basin

is a beautiful mixture of ponderosa pines, aspen groves, rocky scablands, grasslands and the various wetland habitats. In addition to its animal life, Turnbull is noted for its spring wildflower display in early May. The refuge is easy to find, and visitor areas are well marked. The college town of Cheney is about a dozen miles southwest of Spokane. On Cheney's main street (State Highway 904), near the southern end of town, across from the IGA store, you will see a brown sign directing you to the refuge on Cheney Plaza Road. After about $4^1/_2$ miles, turn left onto Smith Road and drive into the visitor-use area, where you can get maps and checklists and pay the small daily-use fee. Drive the auto-tour route, and if you have time and good weather, hike some of the trails in the Middle Pine Lake area.

For a longer auto loop that goes around the refuge and through some good grasslands that are excellent for grassland sparrows, meadowlarks, eastern kingbirds and the like, go back to Cheney Plaza Road and head south (left turn). Stay on Cheney Plaza as it turns and heads east, then go left or west onto Pine Grove Road. Pine Grove ends at Wells Road, where you again turn left and go north until Wells turns into Cheney Spangle Road, which will take you back to Cheney. This trip would be best in May for the flowers.

The **Columbia Basin Habitat Management Area** has lots of excellent wildlife habitat, especially for waterfowl, but it's a confusing mosaic of federal, state and private lands. It's very helpful to get the map *Columbia Basin Recreation Areas* from the Ephrata offices of the Washington Department of Fish and Wildlife or the Bureau of Reclamation. The main area to bird is **Columbia National Wildlife Refuge,** which has the best access and for which a good map and checklist are available. A good loop through part of the refuge and state lands that goes by many small lakes is as follows. O'Sullivan Dam Road goes across O'Sullivan Dam, the longest earthen dam in the United States. At the very eastern end of the dam, turn south on a small dirt road named Rd. K.2 SE. This road (called Morgan Lake Road on the refuge map) is across O'Sullivan Dam Road from a big boat ramp and has a sign that says Soda Lake C.G. 1 mi. and Columbia N.W.R. Go south following signs to Othello, and in about 6 miles you'll hit pavement and then come to McMannamon Road. Go left on McMannamon, but in half a mile turn left again onto Seep Lakes Road (with a hard-to-see sign) and take it north. This is a rough road that takes you back to O'Sullivan Dam Road. Along this loop you go by many small lakes and wetlands and will see little dirt roads, some with signs, heading off to others. You can just follow your own instincts and explore what looks promising or call refuge headquarters and get the latest news on which spots are best at the time, which is always a useful thing to do.

To see some of the areas around **Potholes Reservoir,** head west on O'Sullivan Dam Road along the dam. If you see birds in the reservoir you can try scoping them from one of the boat ramps near either end of the dam. About $5^1/_2$ miles west of Potholes State Park, turn right onto Frenchman Hills Road and go west almost 5 miles to the intersection with Dodson Road, known locally as Birder's Corner or Audubon Corner. Along Frenchman Hills Road (and Dodson a bit) you will occasionally see little dirt roads heading off into the bush with signs that read Public Hunting, Public Fishing. All these roads go to the edges of the "wasteways," which are basically little rivers with marshy areas, and are public-access roads on state or federal land, so feel free to explore any that look interesting to you.

From Birder's Corner go north on Dodson Road, and in about 7 miles you'll pass through where the road crosses the **Winchester Wasteway.** You can see a lot by pulling over to the roadside or by parking in the area just north of the wasteway. There is also one of the little dirt roads on the south side of the wasteway going east to two parking areas.

To see another part of the Winchester Wasteway that is usually loaded with ducks, continue north on Dodson, cross I-90, and immediately turn left on the frontage road on the north side of I-90. Go west 2 miles to E N.W., turn right and go north 1 mile, then turn left to go west on 2 N.W. Notice that in this area east-west roads are numbered and north-south roads are lettered. A mile west on 2 N.W. you will come to the wasteway, which is a substantial lake at this point. You will see little dirt roads wandering south and north along the lakeshore that you can take to get different views of the lake. Either way, you will eventually get to another paved road, and you can find your way back to Dodson (or C Road), which has a complete interchange with I-90.

16

Nesting Great Blue Herons

Portland is "Heron Town." Although great blue herons are very common across North America, Portland is the only city that has adopted them as its official city bird. Artwork depicting this handsome bird graces publications and signs, not only from the city government but also from a variety of local businesses and organizations, including the Portland Audubon Society. The city's largest golf course has been renamed Heron Lakes in honor of the adjacent heron rookery, and we even have Blue Heron Ale, a popular local microbrew. And in late May or early June every year, Great Blue Heron Week honors our city's mascot. Why all the fuss about a "common" bird? It's because the great blue heron is big, beautiful and nests within the city limits, symbolizing the quality of life Portlanders value.

Although the great blue heron, or GBH, as birders call it, is one of the most familiar birds in the country, many people mistakenly call it a crane. Great blue herons are conspicuous, reaching a height of 4 feet and a wing span just over 6 feet. They often feed in open areas, making them easier to observe than many other animals.

Many people regularly see GBHs feeding but never nesting, for the birds tend to find isolated undisturbed areas for their nesting colonies or *rookeries*, as they're called. Sometimes, however, a heron rookery will be accessible for easy viewing, giving an unusual opportunity to witness some very interesting behavior. The large size of the herons and the presence of many nests together makes for entertaining bird-watching, often suitable for children and others who like their nature observation on the lively side.

Wherever possible, GBHs nest in trees, and an established rookery may be used for decades. Nest use varies from year to year: a bird doesn't necessarily use the same nest each year, not every nest in the rookery will be used, and every year some pairs will build new nests. In the rookeries, other birds such as cormorants and other herons may nest alongside the great blues and the accumulated droppings may actually kill the trees. Preferred sites for rookeries are on islands or frequently flooded land because this reduces the risk from ground predators like raccoons. The young have an interesting defense against predators—they will lean over the edge of their nest and regurgitate onto the unwelcome and unfortunate intruder, humans included.

The herons start returning to the nests and pairing up as early as February, but March is when they start becoming really active with nest building, territorial displays, courtship displays and mating. The action in the rookery continues to build as the first young hatch in April and stays busy through June. Unfortu-

The large nests of great blue herons are easy to spot in bare deiciduous trees.

nately, here in the Pacific Northwest great blue herons almost always nest in cottonwoods, and it becomes very difficult to see what's going on once the trees leaf out. Viewing in late February and early March is usually the best compromise between visibility and activity. Starting in February, watch the cottonwoods in your area carefully, and get out to do your rookery viewing just as soon as the trees show the first signs of new growth. This will vary from year to year with the weather.

Great blue herons have been well studied, and they have many interesting displays that one can easily see. Great books for understanding bird behavior are the three volumes of *A Guide to Bird Behavior* in the Stokes Nature Guides series. The third volume includes the GBH, and I highly recommend it if you want more details on heron behavior.

Some of the interesting behaviors seen at the nest are the "head-down," the "stretch" and "swaying." In the head-down, a heron stands in the nest, stretches its neck and head out very straight and at an angle downward, on the outside of the nest and snaps its bill. Often it raises the feathers on its head and neck at the same time. This is a territorial display that signals others to stay away. What's really fun is when both members of a pair display at the same time, crossing necks and clacking away with their beaks.

You might call swaying kissing heron-style. A pair will lock bill tips and move their heads back and forth together. In the stretch, a bird points its beak and head straight up in the air, then lowers its head toward its back while making a sound described as crooning or howling. This is sometimes done after the male brings the female a gift of a nice stick to add to the nest, which is a common practice. The male usually brings sticks to the female, who actually does the work of building a new nest or remodeling an established one. Both birds take turns incubating the three to five eggs, which hatch in about a month, and caring for the young. Three months after hatching, the young will be fully grown and independent.

It's easy to see great blue herons feeding in almost any kind of wetland throughout the year. Herons are wading birds and will stand in shallow water and spear or grab just about any animal they can get, although fish make up about two-thirds of their diet. Sometimes you will see them feeding in fields, and people often wonder what they're getting on dry land. Their main upland prey is mice, although they will eat just about any animal they can get such as big insects, frogs or snakes.

Great blue herons are common throughout our region year-round, although there will be some seasonal movement on the east side when water freezes. You can find them almost anywhere near water, from mudflats in saltwater bays to freshwater marshes in the desert. Although GBHs are considered shy and sensitive to disturbance, some have shown themselves to be quite adaptable and can be found in disturbed areas and places with significant human activity. By far the most common location for rookeries in our region is in cottonwoods in riparian woodlands. Be on the lookout for rookeries during the winter when the trees are bare, then come back and check for activity in late February or early March. Remember to observe from a distance, and be careful not to disturb the birds. A scope is necessary because you should not get close enough to see the birds well without one.

Oregon

Hot Spots

Since Portland is Heron Town, it's appropriate to mention the two rookeries in the city. The most famous is the rookery on **Ross Island**, a large island in the Willamette River just south of downtown. There are about fifty nests on Ross Island, and the herons feed up and down the Willamette and at wetlands such as **Oaks Bottom Wildlife Refuge.** The best view of these nests is actually by boat, and the Portland Audubon Society occasionally offers boat trips on the Willamette for viewing the rookery and other wildlife along the river. The best view of the Ross Island rookery from land is in the Johns Landing area; the rookery is across the river from the Willamette River Greenway just north of the Heron Pointe condos. Even though this rookery is well known and noteworthy because of its location in the city, it is hard to see much because viewing from land is at a distance.

A much smaller rookery, with about half as many nests, is the one that led to the naming of the **Heron Lakes Golf Course** in north Portland. It is possible to get much closer to this rookery and get outstanding views of the birds. This rookery was barely saved from destruction by a road realignment thanks to the action of concerned citizens. Since human disturbance is a major concern here, call the Portland Audubon Society and go on one of the many organized field trips to view the rookery.

Another rookery is on **Goat Island,** south of Portland near Oregon City, at the confluence of the Willamette and Clackamas Rivers. The rookery can be seen from **Clackamette Park,** which can be reached by following signs from State Highway 99E (McLoughlin Boulevard) just north of I-205 and south of the Clackamas River. Park at the far northwestern corner of the park and take the rough trail through the blackberries to the last point of land separating the rivers, and look northwest to the trees on the island. Clackamette Park can also be an interesting place for gulls in the winter as well as some waterfowl, but don't get confused by all the strange "mongrel ducks."

For information about Great Blue Heron Week activities, call the Portland Audubon Society (503) 292-6855, city of Portland's Bureau of Parks and Recreation (503) 823-2223 or the Wetlands Conservancy (503) 691-1394 in early May.

Washington

Just across the mighty Columbia River from Portland in the **Shillapoo Wildlife Area** is the best rookery I know of for heron watching. The rookery has about two hundred active nests and can be clearly seen from a reasonable distance without disturbing the birds. The Washington Department of Fish and Wildlife is monitoring the rookery closely and knows that it has been declining in recent years but doesn't yet know why. It is not thought that disturbance by people is a factor, but given the situation, it is important that observers do not try to get any closer than the road. From I-5 in Vancouver take the Fourth Plain Boulevard Exit and head west on Fourth Plain Boulevard, which becomes River Road, and is also State Highway 501. After about $4^3/_4$ miles you will come to the entrance to Vancouver Lake Park. Instead of going into the park, turn left onto Lower River Road (there probably won't be a sign) and go another 2 miles. The rookery will be on your right, and on your left there is a small dirt road marked Frenchman's Bar Temporary Access. Go down this road to the parking area (with outhouse), park there, and walk back to Lower River Road (300 yards) to scope the rookery from the roadside. You may want to walk farther north on the road to get different angles. This area is also excellent for waterfowl, and possibly cranes, this time of year.

Terry Wahl and Dennis Paulson's *A Guide to Bird Finding in Washington* describes a small but easily observable rookery in **Auburn** that is a great example of how community action can save a natural resource. There is a sign at the site that describes how the marsh was saved from destruction when the state highway department wanted to wipe it out for a road realignment. Take Exit 143 from I-5 in Federal Way and go east on 320th, which will turn into Peasley Canyon Road. In just under $3^1/_2$ miles Peasley Canyon will end at West Valley Highway, where you turn right and go immediately into a little parking area. There are signs that direct you to the viewing area. From the main informational sign, look south into the tops of the alders to see the nests. This is a good example of a small group of herons that have become acclimated to a surprising level of human activity all about them.

In the Columbia Basin near **Moses Lake** is a large and active rookery in the middle of one of the best areas in eastern Washington for migrating waterfowl. It is in the far northwestern corner of **Potholes Reservoir** a few miles south of I-90. Six miles west of the city of Moses Lake, take the Hiawatha Exit 169, and go south to the frontage road that parallels I-90 on its south side. Go east (back toward Moses Lake) about 2½ miles, and just before you get to a big power line, turn right (south) onto a dirt road. The only sign here says Public Fishing, Public Hunting, but just east of the power line is a sign that labels this road D 5 NE. You'll pass a sign that reads Potholes Wildlife Area, and you'll come to a couple of forks in the road—always go to the right. Pretty soon you will start to see a line of trees to the northwest and eventually some nests in them. You'll drive on a dike through some good wetland habitat, and the road will end at a locked gate and parking area about 5 miles from the frontage road. Park here and continue walking on the road and you will circle around on the west side of the rookery. You'll have to judge how close you can or want to get, but be sure you are not disturbing the birds.

Another eastern Washington rookery is located in the area near **Touchet** that was described for wintering raptors (chapter 1). About 6 miles east of Touchet, McDonald Road goes south and intersects Detour Road in about a mile. Go east on Detour (toward Walla Walla) and watch the cottonwoods growing along the Walla Walla River. You should see the nests almost immediately. Park in a good place along Detour Road and get out to scope the rookery. Unfortunately, the rookery is at quite a distance and you can't get closer, but this is a nice stop to add to any birding trip in the Walla Walla area.

British Columbia

This is the easiest one yet! In some tall conifers next to the **Vancouver Aquarium** in Stanley Park is a small rookery with about fifteen active nests that is clearly visible from the deck north of the killer whales. The aquarium has turned this naturally occurring rookery into an exhibit by placing interpretive signs on the deck and by usually having a spotting scope set up. The rookery has been here at least sixty years. The Vancouver Aquarium is one of North America's best and has many exhibits on Northwest aquatic life. It is open every day from 10:00 A.M. to 5:30 P.M. with extended hours in the summer.

17

March Shorttakes

Herring

The herring family contains some of the world's most important fishes used for human food and includes sardines, alewives, menhaden and shad. Herring are extremely important in many food chains. The Pacific herring spawns in shallow coastal waters, and the greatest concentration of spawning herring in our region is along the eastern coast of **Vancouver Island,** between Ladysmith and Comox. This gathering of hundreds of thousands of tasty fish and their eggs attracts an awesome assemblage of mammalian and avian predators. During the peak of the spawn, in one-half-mile stretch of coastline wildlife biologist Neal Dawe estimated that he saw over 50,000 gulls, 10,000 scoters, 5,000 brant, 3,200 oldsquaw, 3,000 red-breasted mergansers, 1,000 harlequin ducks, about another 10,000 diving ducks and 10,000 dabbling ducks, dozens of bald eagles and scores of northern and California sea lions and harbor seals. What a feast! One of the best places to witness this feeding frenzy is from **Hornby** and **Denman Islands,** accessible by ferry from Buckley Bay, about 12 miles south of Comox and Courtenay. Both islands have a couple of provincial parks and many bed-and-breakfasts, making them very attractive for a spring wildlife-watching getaway. Commercial wildlife-watching boat trips are offered in Nanaimo Harbor, and south of Nanaimo, around **Yellow Point,** are some coastal resorts with great viewing.

Worm Piles

Ever notice those funny little piles of dead leaves on bare soil at the edge of a lawn or under a tree? Carefully lift up the whole pile and you'll see a hole in the ground about as big around as a pencil. This is the burrow of a night crawler, and it made the little pile by reaching its head end out of the hole, grabbing the leaves with its mouth, and pulling them back toward (and sometimes into) its hole. Night crawlers do this when it's raining or very damp, and if you're sneaky enough you can catch them in the act. The amount of earthworm activity varies with temperature and moisture, so you will see more piles at certain times of the year. In areas where the soil freezes, earthworms hibernate together in little dens below the frost line. When the soil finally thaws completely there is a sudden reappearance of earthworm activity. Some Native Americans called the full moon of March the "Worm Moon." Is there a worm moon where you live?

18

A Closer Look: Owling

Owls have always fascinated people and have been powerful symbols for many different things throughout history. Because they are nocturnal, it's not surprising that they have been associated with dark, mysterious and spooky things. But they have also been symbols of wisdom. This is a bizarre image because, compared to other birds, owls are not very intelligent. How did they come to be a symbol for intelligence? Well, owls are unique among birds in that their eyes are close together on the face, just like human eyes. Owls are the only birds with faces that are remotely humanlike; maybe that's why we think they're smart. Another factor may be the fact that owls are nocturnal and secretive, thereby making them mysterious, and mysterious things are often thought to have special powers.

Although they might not be the Einsteins of the bird world or magical spirits, owls do have some amazing adaptations for their way of life. The positioning of their eyes gives owls excellent binocular vision—the ability to judge depth and distance. This is important for a predator that has to drop from the sky and hit its prey dead-on. Although owls are not unique in having binocular vision, they have the best by far among birds.

The owl's huge eyes are extremely sensitive to light, allowing it to hunt by moonlight and starlight. But even an owl can't see well when it's really dark. That's when its equally acute hearing comes in. Owls have among the most sensitive ears in the animal world, and their stereoscopic hearing can pinpoint the source of a sound better than any other animal. The two ear openings in an owl's skull are even shaped differently and located so as to exaggerate the stereo effect. To help collect sound waves and direct them into the ear openings, owls have a circular pattern of feathers around their eyes called *facial disks*. These feathers are a distinctive part of an owl's appearance.

An owl's superior hearing wouldn't help much if the birds made a lot of noise themselves, so they have specially built feathers that result in silent flight. It is a startling experience to see a big owl fly right over your head yet not hear a sound. This silent flight also means that their prey can't hear them coming. Owls, then, are the stealth birds of prey. Instead of using high speed and diving on their prey as hawks do, owls sneak up on their prey, silently flying low and slow over the ground and suddenly dropping out of the night sky.

Sightings of owls are among the most sought-after by birders and are very exciting to more casual nature observers as well. I've known birders who rate the success of an outing by the number of owls they see! Make no mistake about it, finding owls is tough. They are nocturnal and do their best to hide during the day. Owls are notoriously elusive, and this behavior, coupled with their silent flight, camouflage and keen senses makes owling one of the most challenging tests of observational skill and patience. Fortunately, some naturalists have become quite expert and share their experience through field trips and classes and in books. A great book that really tells the secrets of finding North America's owls is *How to Spot an Owl*, by Patricia and Clay Sutton. Watch for special owling programs offered by local Audubon Society chapters or other natural history clubs. Here are some basics to get you started.

The Pacific Northwest has the greatest diversity of owls in the United States. This reflects the diversity and extent of forest and woodland habitats, the preferred habitats of most owls. We have ten owls that can be found year-round in the proper areas—great horned owl, western screech-owl, common barn owl, short-eared owl, northern pygmy-owl, northern saw-whet owl, spotted owl, great gray owl, long-eared owl and barred owl.

The flammulated owl is highly migratory and is here only for the summer breeding season, when it is actually quite common, although almost never seen, in pine forests. The declining burrowing owl is also migratory and is here mainly in the summer, with a few wintering west of the Cascades. Two more owls are northern species that are sometimes pushed far south of their normal range by severe winter weather and population crashes in their prey population—the snowy owl and the very rare northern hawk owl. There is evidence that the boreal owl is a year-round resident and breeder in a few limited areas, but little is know about its status.

The easiest way to find owls is not to look for them but to listen. Most owling, including an official census, is done by sound. During the breeding season most owls become quite vocal, calling off and on all night but especially just after dusk and just before dawn. March is an excellent month for owling because all our resident owls will be into their breeding season by then and should be calling. Calling will continue into June. To find owls by sound, go to an area of good habitat and listen carefully. You have to be as quiet as possible, which means going by yourself or with one other person. Wear clothes that don't make noise when you walk or make other movements such as putting your hands in your pockets. Still clear nights are best, and the more moonlight the better. Temperature seems to have little effect on the owls but can affect the owlers—dress warm.

To pick areas of good habitat, read about the preferences of the owls in your area and ask local birders for tips on good owling spots. In general, the best habitat for most owls is at the edges of forests and woodlands that are adjacent to open fields or meadows where they can hunt. The less human disturbance the better, although some owls are fairly adaptable to the presence of people, the barn owl being a prime example. Go just before sunset and plan to be out a couple of hours, or start two hours before sunrise. It is wonderful if you can go with a knowledgeable owler who can identify the different calls for you to learn. The next best thing is to listen to tapes of owl calls before you go out.

At your selected area pick a route and walk it slowly, stopping frequently to listen and look carefully. Check all possible perches on the tops of trees or poles.

When you hear an owl you can try to move closer and locate it. You have to move as silently as possible. If you actually see an owl, slowly sink to the ground or move behind a bush or tree to hide yourself as much as possible. Watch the owl carefully and you can tell by its behavior whether it knows you're there and is alarmed or if it is relaxed. Remain still and hidden until it is relaxed, and you may be able to see some common behaviors, such as hunting. Seeing an owl, of course, depends on having enough light. Carry a good strong flashlight for safety and in case you actually get close enough to an owl in the dark to toss a beam on it. Many owls do not seem to be bothered by flashlights. Most of the time, however, you'll have to be satisfied just to hear the owls.

It is also possible to owl by car. Slowly drive roads through good habitat. Stop frequently and listen for several minutes while looking carefully at all good perching sites. Needless to say, the quieter your car, the better. The Suttons suggest bicycling as an excellent way to cover a lot of territory quietly.

A well-established but controversial technique for finding and seeing owls is to copy their calls with your voice or to play recordings of their calls. Several owls are very responsive to this technique and will start answering back when you make the calls. Some may even fly over to check you out, allowing for some incredible sightings. The most responsive to such calls are the great horned, screech, pygmy, saw-whet and barred owls. Unfortunately, as is often the case, some birders have overused tapes and disturbed the birds' normal breeding behavior. It is now generally recommended that people do not play tapes or make calls of owls during their breeding season. Fortunately, this is when the owls are calling the most anyway and usually don't need much coaxing. Outside of the breeding season, from July through January, tapes can be used sparingly to try to get owls calling or to lure them in for a closer look. I have always felt that trying to copy owl calls with my voice instead of using tapes is less intrusive and more fair, as well as more fun and a lot more convenient. And trying to imitate owl calls is the best way to learn them.

If you decide to dabble in playing tapes, check on local restrictions. It is illegal to play tapes in national parks, in some national wildlife refuges and in some special areas of national forests. It is also illegal to play tapes of spotted owls because they are an endangered species. Play tapes at moderate volume. You should play calls for three to five minutes, then stop and listen for at least five minutes. Don't play a tape any more than two or three times in one place. Once you get a good response, stop playing the tape.

You can also look for owls during the day. Short-eared owls, pygmy owls and burrowing owls are often active during the day, especially in the early morning and late afternoon. You may also be able to find owls perched and snoozing by noticing clues such as "whitewash" (droppings) or pellets on the ground. But to really get into the owl's world, it's more fun to go out at night. Of course, when you're out looking for owls during the magic hours just after dawn and before dusk, your chances are good for seeing other wildlife.

April

Notes

19

A Million Sandpipers

Shorebirds are a good example of the tremendous advantages flight provides birds. Because of their fabulous flying abilities, shorebirds are able to take advantage of two different and greatly separated habitats that are rich in food resources. The typical shorebird spends the majority of the year along seacoasts in the mid to low latitudes, then migrates long distances to breed in very high latitude tundra, marsh or prairie. The big question is, of course, Why? If the west coast of Mexico is a great habitat for ten months of the year, why risk all the dangers of flying 3,000 miles to the Alaskan tundra for only a month or two to nest? The two-part answer reveals the two most important factors affecting the survival of almost every animal—food and predators.

The northern nesting grounds are frozen and covered with snow most of the year. This makes these areas very inhospitable, and few animals live there on a year-round basis. But as bleak as these regions are most of the year, when the brief Arctic summer comes, there's an explosion of life. Hundreds of Arctic plants and invertebrates (mainly insects) come out of dormancy and go about the business of growth and reproduction with amazing speed and intensity. Suddenly there is lots of food and not much around to eat it. If an animal can get there, it will have plenty of food for the energy-intensive process of reproducing, and there will also be a big food supply for its babies when they arrive. What's more, there is plenty of room to nest if nesting on the ground isn't a problem. All one has to do is get there, and for birds that's actually possible.

In addition to lots of food and few competitors, there is also a lack of predators. Few predators can survive on the slim pickings during the winter in the Arctic, so there just aren't many around. The logical question is, Why don't a bunch of predators bop on up to the Arctic and eat all those birds that flew up there? Well, some predators do, but the only ones that can really make such a journey are other birds. The predatory skuas, jaegers, gulls, hawks and owls all take their toll, but it's nothing like the predation nesting birds would experience in regions with warmer climates and a host of predators on the ground, in the trees and in the water. This is especially important because shorebirds are ground nesters.

So there are great benefits to nesting in the Arctic (and near-Arctic) that birds can take advantage of because they can fly. Shorebirds are fast, strong flyers, and most of them fly thousands of miles a year. This is particularly amazing when you think of some of the small sandpipers that weigh only a couple of ounces and nevertheless zip on down to Argentina from Alaska—and back. When not on their nesting grounds, shorebirds feed in other habitats that are also incredibly rich with life. The intertidal areas of seashores and estuaries are home to a huge variety of invertebrates. The mudflats in estuaries, in particular, are some of the most productive habitats in the world in terms of total biomass. It is no surprise then that mudflats, much more so than sandy beaches or rocky shores, are the feeding grounds with the biggest variety and largest numbers of shorebirds.

As a group, shorebirds are easy to recognize. Shorebirds comprise about two hundred species of birds in twelve families that are found worldwide. In general, shorebirds have long legs and long narrow bills, and most spend their time wading in water or walking near the edge of water in fresh- and saltwater habitats. In Europe this group is called "waders," and in the United States it is sometimes called "the small waders" as distinguished from the herons or "long-legged waders." Most shorebirds look very much alike, and it is usually easy for beginners to classify an unknown bird as a member of this group.

There are some interesting variations on the basic sandpiper theme. All shorebirds have basically the same diet, which is any animal they can catch. Each species, however, has adapted to eating a particular type of prey, and the most obvious evidence of this specialization is seen in the variety of bill sizes and shapes we see on different shorebirds. There are those, like the plovers, that run and pick small creatures off the surface of the sand. Many sandpipers probe the mud for prey at different depths, depending on the length of the bill. Oystercatchers have chisel-like beaks for whacking and prying limpets and mussels off rocks, and avocets use their unique bills for filtering crustaceans out of the water. And those long, curved curlew bills fit perfectly into the burrows of marine worms and crabs. Because of a variety of bills and feeding styles, many different shorebird species can all feed in the same general area without being in direct competition.

Most of the thirty-five or so species of shorebirds seen regularly in the Pacific Northwest are primarily migrants; we see them as they pass through in spring and fall. Almost all of these migrants can also be seen from time to time during the winter, but there are a dozen common species that regularly winter in significant numbers: black-bellied and semipalmated plover, killdeer, black oystercatcher, black turnstone, surfbird, sanderling, western and least sandpiper, dunlin, long-billed dowitcher and common snipe. Roughly the same number of species are the only regular breeders in our region: snowy plover, killdeer, black oystercatcher, black-necked stilt, American avocet, willet, spotted sandpiper, long-billed curlew, common snipe and Wilson's phalarope. For complete details on every aspect of all our shorebirds, I highly recommend Dennis Paulson's *Shorebirds of the Pacific Northwest*.

There are some big differences between the spring and fall migrations of shorebirds. In spring the birds are adults in breeding plumage, making identification a lot easier than at any other time. But the period of migration is very short and the birds move through quickly, so it's easy to miss the main movement if you're not in the right place at the right time. When you do hit it right, however, the numbers can be astronomical since shorebirds travel in much larger groups in spring. In general, the peak of spring migration for all shorebirds is between mid-April and mid-May. Although numbers of individual species are high in spring, the overall variety of different species is lower than in the fall. Red knots and ruddy turnstones are the only shorebirds that are more common during the spring migration than in the fall.

Oregon

Although we think of shorebirds migrating up and down the coast, most of our regular migrants can be found on both sides of the Cascades. On the drier east side, shorebirds will be more concentrated around the few choice wetlands. It is no surprise that two areas mentioned often in this book are the best for shorebirding in Eastern Oregon—**Malheur National Wildlife Refuge** and **Summer Lake Wildlife Area.**

Seven shorebird species breed in eastern Oregon and are therefore more common there than on the coast. They are easier to see in the spring because they aren't just passing through—once they've arrived, they're here for a while. These species are the black-necked stilt, American avocet, willet, long-billed curlew, Wilson's phalarope, and two very localized species, the snowy plover and upland sandpiper.

Washington

The most famous shorebird spot in the West is **Bowerman Basin** in Grays Harbor. Over one million shorebirds stop here on their way north, making this the largest concentration of shorebirds on the West Coast south of Alaska. The majority are western sandpipers; the other most common species are dunlin, short-billed and long-billed dowitcher and semipalmated plover. An additional dozen shorebird species occur regularly. This is a particularly good spot to see red knots. In 1988 this critical area was saved from potential development by the establishment of **Grays Harbor National Wildlife Refuge,** and more land is being acquired to add to the refuge. Bowerman Basin has been featured in magazine articles and on TV programs and has become so popular that a shuttle bus runs between Hoquiam High School and the viewing area during the peak period.

The popularity of Bowerman Basin presents a classic example of the paradox in publicizing a good wildlife viewing site or other natural area. By making Bowerman better known, conservationists were able to get enough support to have it protected. But now many people are worried that the area is being "loved to death." The U.S. Fish and Wildlife Service now has the challenging responsibility of managing the refuge for the birds while at the same time trying to provide visitors with a unique wildlife-viewing opportunity. This is becoming a more common problem throughout the country as both the human population and the popularity of such activities continues to grow. It is the responsibility of all of us to do what we can to minimize our impact and support good management by the agencies we have chosen to protect these resources.

The peak time at Bowerman is sometime between April 15 and May 8 and will vary from year to year. Timing your visit with the tides is critical, for

Although they are adorable, give baby harbor seals a wide berth. A human's presence could keep mom from her pup.

the birds concentrate in Bowerman Basin for a period of about an hour or two on both sides of the high tide. To find out when the best viewing times will be, write to Grays Harbor National Wildlife Refuge in care of the Nisqually National Wildlife Refuge (see the appendix) and ask for a brochure with the current year's schedule of viewing times. This is usually available by March. During the busiest weekends, usually the last two in April, all visitors to Bowerman are asked to park at Hoquiam High School and ride the shuttle bus to the viewing area. The shuttle bus runs continuously during the best viewing times; the schedule is in the brochure. To avoid some of the crowds, try to pick a weekday when you can arrive early in the morning, and consider coming just after the peak period; there will still be thousands of birds.

Hoquiam High School is just west of the town of Hoquiam on State Highway 109. (Do not go to the old Hoquiam High School building in the middle of town.) If you are coming when the shuttle bus is not running, turn left onto Paulson Road off of Hwy. 109 just west of the high school and follow the signs to the airport. Turn right when you come to the T intersection and drive toward Lana's Hangar Cafe (great for lunch) and the FAA building. Park only in designated parking areas (not at Lana's) and follow signs to the viewing area.

You will walk in mud and water several inches deep, so rubber boots or other waterproof shoes are necessary. Also, be well prepared for cold wind. The trail will lead you out onto a higher spot of dry sandy ground where there are lots of driftwood logs convenient for sitting. There will be a twine barrier set up to keep people from getting too close to the shorebird area. Needless to say, you should stay behind the barrier and feel free to remind anyone else who doesn't. Even with the string barrier you will be within 50 feet of some birds. While watching the shorebirds, keep on the lookout for raptors—peregrine falcons regularly hunt here during migration.

20

Botanizing to the Max

April and May are the peak of the blooming season almost everywhere in our region below about 3,000 feet, so this is the best time for getting out and botanizing. Botanizing? Is that a word? You bet it is! It's in the dictionary but is rarely used, unlike the similar term "birding," which is quite common. Sure, birders are the largest identifiable group of nature hobbyists, but my impression is that wildflower watchers are the next most numerous. But what do you call people who go out looking for wildflowers? Are they botanists? Botanizers? Wildflower watchers? Flower people? I think this is one reason that "looking for wildflowers" is not recognized as the popular activity it is. Without a good name, this group just doesn't have much of an identity.

Botanizing has actually been getting more attention lately. Celebrating Wildflowers is a new cooperative program of the U. S. Forest Service, National Park Service, Fish and Wildlife Service and Bureau of Land Management. Personnel at various offices of these agencies are developing guided hikes, brochures, displays and other activities highlighting native plants in the lands they manage. Agency people are volunteering their time for much of the work and are getting help from native plant societies and other organizations in some communities. There is even a National Wildflower Hotline with recorded information about wildflower viewing throughout the country: 1 (800) 354-4595.

Because Celebrating Wildflowers is a relatively new program and depends a lot on volunteer time, programs vary a lot from place to place and from year to year. Almost every national park will have some regular programs relating to plants, but those in national forests are not as predictable. In 1994 and 1995 the Colville, Mount Baker–Snoqualmie and Okanogan National Forests in Washington and the Deschutes, Fremont, Ochoco and Willamette National Forests in Oregon had Celebrating Wildflowers activities, mainly guided hikes. Probably the best way to find out about these programs is to contact your local parks department, ranger district or other agency offices directly in early spring. Participating national forests will usually have a brochure about their hikes or activities. Mount Baker–Snoqualmie National Forest seems to have the most extensive program and has even printed a booklet describing twenty self-guided wildflower hikes in the forest.

Another sign of the interest in botanizing is the growing number of wildflower shows or festivals being held in the Northwest. At a wildflower show there are samples of the local blooming plants displayed and identified. This is really an easy way to get to know your flowers! Wildflower festivals may or may not have actual samples of plants on display but commonly have guided walks, slide shows and other activities. Sometimes there are other cultural or social events taking place with a wildflower show or festival. These events are usually in small towns and have plenty of local character.

Wildflower Shows and Festivals

Trillium Festival. Tryon Creek State Park, 11321 SW Terwilliger Boulevard, Portland, OR 97219; (505) 653-3166. There are hikes, programs, kids' activities, a native plant sale and music. Saturday and Sunday; 9:30 A.M. to 3:30 P.M.; usually the last weekend in March or first in April.

Mosier Wildflower Show. Mosier School, Mosier, OR. Take the Mosier Exit 69, off I-84 about 5 miles east of Hood River and drive into town to the only building that looks like a school. A large collection of blooming flowers from the Columbia River Gorge are displayed. One can do some serious botany here, maybe even try to tell the lomatiums apart! This show is held the same day as the Mosier Volunteer Fire Department's annual Fireman's Smorgie fund-raising feast. For the date, call the Mosier Volunteer Fire Department at (503) 478-3391 in March. Sunday; 10 A.M. to 4 P.M.; usually held in the last two weeks of April.

Glide Wildflower Festival. Glide Community Center, Glide, OR. Glide is about 20 miles northeast of Roseburg on State Highway 138 (North Umpqua Hwy.). Blooming flowers of Douglas County are displayed. Food is available. Saturday and Sunday; 9 A.M. to 5 P.M.; held in late April. Call the Glide Community Club at (503) 496-3736.

Shady Cove Wildflower Show. Shady Cove School, Cleveland Street, Shady Cove, OR. This little town is about 20 miles north of Medford on State Highway 62, on the way to Crater Lake. There is a lot going on besides the flower show, including an art show, plant sale and spaghetti feed. Saturday and Sunday; 10 A.M. to 5 P.M.; usually the first weekend in May. Call Shady Cove City Hall at (503) 878-2225.

Mother's Day Wildflower Show. Silver Falls State Park, OR. Oregon's largest state park is about 25 miles east of Salem on State Highway 214. There are identified wildflowers on display, guided hikes, slide shows, a plant sale and a barbecue dinner. Saturday and Sunday; 10 A.M. to 5 P.M.; held the weekend of Mother's Day.

Mount Pisgah Spring Wildflower Festival and Plant Sale. Mount Pisgah Arboretum, 6 miles southeast of Eugene, OR (see chapter 14); (503) 747-3817. This is a big festival with displays, hikes, plant sale, nature store, food and music. Sunday; 10 A.M. to 4 P.M.; the Sunday after Mother's Day. There is also a big mushroom festival at the end of October.

Darrington Wildflower Festival. Darrington School, Darrington, WA. Washington's only wildflower festival does not have picked flowers on display but has guided walks, slide shows, displays, kids' activities and other events, including a square dance Saturday night. Saturday and Sunday; 10 A.M. to 5 P.M.; usually in mid-June. Call the Darrington Ranger District during the week, at (360) 436-1155.

Oregon

Hot Spots

As mentioned in chapter 4, the **Columbia River Gorge** is considered one of the premier wildflower spots of the West, and the places described in that chapter will continue to be interesting into June. But as spring progresses the action shifts from the drier Washington side to the shady, moister Oregon side and moves up in elevation. You really can't go wrong hiking on any of The Gorge trails in spring. The heart of the west Gorge is the section of the old Historic Columbia River Highway (also called the Scenic Highway and Crown Point Highway) between Corbett (Exit 22) and Dodson/Ainsworth State Park (Exit 35). This section is almost all public land, there are waterfalls and lots of trails and various plants blooming from March through July. Other areas just to the east are the trail to Elowah and Upper McCord Creek Falls from Yeon State Park and Lower Tanner Creek Road (County Road 777), which starts at Exit 40.

About 35 miles farther east in the oak woodland belt of The Gorge is one of the most popular botanizing spots in The Gorge, the **Rowena Plateau.** The plateau is a mixture of state park land and the Tom McCall Preserve of the Nature Conservancy. From I-84 take the Rowena Exit 76, then head west on the Mosier–The Dalles Highway (Hwy. 30), following signs to Rowena Crest Viewpoint. In about $3\frac{1}{2}$ miles you'll come to the parking area for the viewpoint, and the view is indeed awesome. The preserve is across the highway, and there is a large sign that has a map of the area and other information. Please, stay on the trails and don't bring dogs.

On the Washington side there are two popular hikes known for wildflowers and for providing a good workout (most trails in The Gorge do go up). **Dog Mountain** is 12 miles east and **Hamilton Mountain** is 7 miles west of the Bridge of the Gods at Cascade Locks. On either trail you will go through several different habitats with a variety of flowers and birds, and both provide some great scenic views of The Gorge. If it's very windy, consider making it a short hike and coming back another time because the wind gets worse the higher you go.

There are still new plants blooming as the season progresses into June and July, so don't hesitate to return to favorite spots at a later time. In the summer there are more plants blooming at higher elevations; start exploring places like **Larch Mountain, Wahtum Lake** and **Rainy Lake.** Be sure to get the 1995 forest service map *Columbia River Gorge N. S. A.* For finding the flowers of The Gorge, nothing can compare to Russ Jolley's *Wildflowers of the Columbia River Gorge.*

Washington

Since **Olympic National Park** is the largest national park in the Northwest, you might expect lots of good wildflower habitat, and you wouldn't be disappointed. The park ranges from sea level to almost 8,000 feet, and there are flowers blooming somewhere for half the year! Park Ranger Rod Norvell suggests five easy-to-moderate hikes in the northern part of the park that give an excellent representation of typical west-side forest flowers.

Right at the main visitor center in Port Angeles is the very easy **Aldwell Nature Trail.** Five miles up the road to Hurricane Ridge (excellent for alpine flowers) is the **Heart of the Forest Trail.** Just to the east on the north shore of Lake Crescent, the **Spruce Railroad Trail** goes through some open rocky areas for a little variety. Calypso orchids and chocolate lilies are favorites on this trail. On the south shore of Lake Crescent is the heavily used **Marymere**

Falls Trail, which passes through some excellent old growth forest. In the Sol Duc Valley a 6-mile loop can be made by using the **Sol Duc Falls** and **Lovers Lane Trails.** Of course, maps and information about these hikes and areas are available at park visitor centers.

The **Mount Baker–Snoqualmie National Forest** is particularly active in the wildflower area. The forest has native plant checklists (and hiking guides) for some of its more popular trails. The favorite of several botanists is the **Asahel Curtis Nature Trail,** #1023, which passes through some old growth, is easy going for all ages and has interpretive signs. The trail begins in the Asahel Curtis Picnic Area, just off I-90 about 3 miles west of Snoqualmie Pass. Coming from the west (Seattle) on I-90, take the Asahel Curtis/Denny Creek Exit 47, and turn left to cross over the freeway. When you come to the T, turn right and go straight into the picnic area. A couple of miles east, just past Denny Creek Campground, is the Franklin Falls Trail, another easy trail through similar habitat. For detailed directions, plant checklists and suggestions for other wildflower hikes, call or write the North Bend Ranger District (see the appendix).

A very different type of habitat can be found just south of Olympia in the prairies of **Mima Mounds Natural Area Preserve.** About 10 miles south of Olympia take Exit 95 from I-5 and go west on State Highway 121. In 3 miles drive straight through Littlerock, leaving Hwy. 121, which turns left, and in about another three-quarters of a mile the road will end at Waddell Creek Road. There is a small sign for the preserve here. Turn right and go north about half a mile and turn left at the signs. Mima Mounds Preserve is full of unusual mounds of soil. There are interpretive signs explaining the mounds and theories as to how they formed. The preserve has lots of flowers all spring, but there are two peak times, one in mid-April and another in mid-June.

East of the Cascades is really a different world with different flora, but most of the wildflowers are close relatives of flowers common on the west side. Although they will be different species, those familiar with west-side plants will recognize the many buckwheats, daisies, larkspurs, paintbrushes, lupines, penstemons and desert parsleys. Other common east-side flowers are locoweeds, balsam roots, sandworts, phlox, evening primroses and mariposa lilies. *Sagebrush Country: A Wildflower Sanctuary,* by Ronald Taylor, is a handy photo guide for all of eastern Washington and Oregon. Often the wildflower displays on the arid east side are more spectacular than on the wetter west side because blooming times are compressed into a shorter period and the flowers stand out in bold contrast to the normally more barren landscape. Much of eastern Washington is BLM land, and the agency's Wenatchee office is producing a "watchable wildflowers" guide (to be available in 1997) that will cover about ten sites in the southeastern quarter of the state.

Two large national wildlife refuges in eastern Washington are great for wildflowers, and springtime visits are very productive for both plant and animal observing. **Turnbull** and **Columbia National Wildlife Refuges** are both described in chapter 15. It is worth a call to either refuge for information about blooming activity because east-side weather, and blooming times, can vary from year to year.

If you're heading east on I-90 from the west side to either of these refuges, there is a scenic alternative for a section of I-5 that is known for wildflowers. The Vantage Highway goes from Ellensburg to Vantage on the Columbia River, just north of I-5, and on most maps is keyed as a scenic route. The area along the highway itself can be good for flowers, but the interpretive trail for **Ginkgo Petrified Forest State Park,** 2 miles west of Vantage, gives you a chance to get out and hike around. Immediately north of the highway and the town of Vantage, on the Columbia, is the interpretive center for the park—a good source for tips on the best wildflower areas and times. Unfortunately, center hours fluctuate with the budget, so call for information: (509) 856-2700.

Two other eastern Washington state parks noted for their wildflowers are **Steamboat Rock State Park** and **Fields Spring State Park.** Steamboat Rock is at the north end of Banks Lake, and the best area is the top of the rock itself, which can be reached by a steep 1-mile-long trail that starts at the entrance to the northern campground. Across State Highway 155 from the main park is Northrup Canyon, which is excellent for flowers and songbirds. Fields Spring State Park is down in the far southeastern corner of the state and is worth a visit if you are in the Hells Canyon area or the Blue Mountains. Trails through the open forest to Puffer Butte have lots of flowers, and the view from the top is great.

British Columbia

Just north of the U.S. border east of White Rock is **Campbell Valley Regional Park.** This large regional park is a bit out of the way, so it is not as heavily used as most others. There is a good variety of habitats, with meadows, marshes, forests and woodlands, resulting in a variety of flowers. The two main access points are the North and South Valley entrances. The South Valley entrance is the most developed, with many facilities, while the North Valley entrance just has parking, picnic tables and pit toilets. The Little River Loop Trail, from the north entrance, is a good introduction to the habitats of the park and is an easy $1^1/_2$ miles long.

From Provincial Highway 99 take Exit 2, the White Rock and 8th Avenue East Exit, and go $4^3/_4$ miles east on 8th Avenue to the south entrance. To get to the north entrance, take 200th Street north from 8th Avenue to 16th Avenue and go east about half a mile to the parking area. There are lots of signs; maps are usually available at the south entrance or from the Vancouver Regional Parks office. This park is also very good for migrating and breeding songbirds in the spring.

Three good spots on Vancouver Island for April and May flowers are **Honeymoon Bay Ecological Reserve, Francis/King Regional Park** and **Goldstream Provincial Park.** Honeymoon Bay is a small preserve established primarily to protect the pink fawn-lily, uncommon on the island and very rare elsewhere in British Columbia. In addition to the fawn-lily, for which it is famous, Honeymoon Bay has an excellent sample of the common west-side forest flowers—trillium, wood violet, bleeding heart, vanilla leaf, wild ginger, candy flower, false lily of the valley, fringecup, fairy lantern, foamflower, both species of false Solomon's seal and starflower, among others. As of 1995 there were no signs of any kind for the preserve, making it a bit tricky to find. Because there is concern about the negative impact of too many visitors, this probably won't change.

Honeymoon Bay Ecological Reserve is near the south shore of Cowichan Lake about 24 miles west of Duncan. As you head west on South Shore Road from the town of Cowichan Lake you will go through the small village of Honeymoon Bay. Mark the store as zero and continue another mile to where South Shore Road turns left; stay on it instead of going straight to Gordon Bay Provincial Park. Go another $3/5$ mile and turn left into the unmarked and inconspicuous little parking area that looks like a dirt driveway. You will know you've come to the right place when you see the sign with the paintings of common flowers. While botanizing you'll have a chance to try to identify the Hammond's flycatcher, which is very common and nests here.

Goldstream Provincial Park, just 11 miles northwest of Victoria, has several different habitats, resulting in a good variety of flowers. The main parking area is just off Trans-Canada Highway 1 in the northern part of the park. From here trails lead through wet forest habitat to the Freeman King Visitor Center, which has displays and a bookstore as well as helpful naturalists. Hours vary seasonally, so it would be worth a call in advance to the BC Parks district office at (604) 391-2300. Even if the center is closed, the trails to the center and into the marsh are worth taking for the flowers and birds of those habitats. The uncommon and exotic-sounding black lily can be found in the marsh area.

To get an excellent look at the drier madrone-Douglas fir-oak forest habitat, drive to the park campground off of Sooke Lake Road in the southern end of the park. Across from campsite 40 is a small parking area at the trailhead for the Arbutus Ridge Trail. A great loop can be made by taking this trail to the Arbutus Loop Trail and then back to your car. A park trail map will help. This trail is "Saprophyte Lane," with lots of coralroot (including the albino form) and the bizarre candystick. While looking for spring flowers in Goldstream you'll be hearing lots of bird songs with winter wren, Pacific slope flycatcher and Townsend's and orange-crowned warblers particularly abundant.

Francis/King is a Capital Regional District Park west of Vancouver. It has moist forest habitat and flowers similar to those mentioned for Honeymoon Bay. An outstanding feature of the park is the Elsie King Trail, a universally accessible boardwalk trail that is the longest and nicest I have seen for those with limited mobility. To get to Francis/King Regional Park from Victoria, head west on Hwy. 1 to the Helmcken Road Exit (the exit for Victoria General Hospital). Turn right and go north on Helmcken less than half a mile to West Burnside and turn left. In less than a mile turn right off West Burnside onto Prospect Lake Road (there is a small sign for the park here). Soon you'll see signs for the park showing you where to turn off Prospect onto Munn Road and into the parking area.

21

Sage Grouse Strut Their Stuff

We could hear the weird popping-gurgling sound coming out of the dark around us. We were three graduate students in a tiny wildlife blind stuck in the middle of a high sagebrush plain in northern Colorado. It was March and we were at about 6,000 feet. I had just become an active birder and had started the serious pursuit of what would become my career as a naturalist, and this trip to see sage grouse was one of my earliest and most memorable wildlife adventures.

As the first rays of dawn brought some faint light to the scene, we started seeing flashes of white accompanying the noise. With more light we could see that these were the bright white breast feathers of the birds and that there were bizarre yellow air sacks in the feathers. The yellow sacks were being inflated and deflated by the birds, thus making the unique sounds and highlighting the white feathers. While they made the pop-and-flash display, the birds held their wings down stiffly at an odd angle and their tail feathers straight up, keeping them erect and fanned out evenly. To top it all off, they had bright yellow eyebrows that they seemed to arch and lower.

Well, this was worth it—I had never seen anything like it before. Since then I have taken people to see sage grouse displaying on other leks and many have considered it one of the most fascinating wildlife experiences they have had. Unfortunately, it is a sight that is getting harder and harder to see.

The sage grouse is truly an animal of the American West. As John Terres says in his *Encyclopedia of North American Birds,* the sage grouse is "as western as a Stetson hat and sagebrush." The sage grouse is an excellent example of an animal that is highly specialized for a very specific habitat. Sagebrush is almost 100 percent of the grouse's diet in winter and 75 percent from late spring to early fall. During the warm growing season the birds will add to their diet whatever shoots, buds, blossoms and succulent new leaves become available. They also eat insects, a food source critical to the chicks. All other members of the sage grouse's group, the order of chickenlike or *gallinaceous* birds, are known for their large, very muscular gizzards adapted to grinding seeds. But the sage grouse has a soft, thin-walled gizzard that is just right for a diet of soft sage leaves. In addition to food, sagebrush provides cover for nesting, shelter from the weather and protection from predators.

Sage grouse are big birds, the males tipping the scales at over 6 pounds. Like many gallinaceous birds, sage grouse were an important and favored food of western settlers. They are still legally hunted today in many states. Although overhunting was clearly responsible for the decreasing number of sage grouse in the past, habitat destruction is now their biggest threat, as is the case with most wildlife.

The range of sage grouse and their numbers have decreased dramatically this century because of the systematic destruction of sagebrush. Although it is the dominant plant of one of the main natural habitats in the West, sagebrush has been treated as if it were a weed that had to be eliminated. Why? One reason is that the cows and sheep many of us like to eat don't like to eat sagebrush. So the sagebrush is removed through the use of fire, chains and bulldozers, or herbicides, encouraging grasses to grow or followed by seeding of the area, usually with non-native grasses. This manipulation is termed "range improvement" or "rehabilitation," but in reality it is the destruction of a natural habitat and its native wildlife. Ironically, it is overgrazing by domestic sheep and cattle in the first place that is one of the main causes for the increased proportion of sagebrush over grasses in many areas.

Much easier to see is the complete and total conversion of large areas of sagebrush to irrigated agricultural fields and urbanization. Because of habitat loss, sage grouse have been extirpated from British Columbia and are just barely hanging on in Washington. Southeastern Oregon is the place to see this resident of the Great Basin sagebrush steppe. There is still a limited hunting season on sage grouse in Oregon even though they are listed as "sensitive" in some parts of their range and are a candidate for listing under the Federal Endangered Species Act.

It is possible to come upon sage grouse any time of the year in the right habitat, but they are very unpredictable and hard to find when not on their display grounds or leks. One way to increase your chances is to be near a body of water where they come to drink early in the morning or late in the afternoon. If you're lucky enough to be near their route from the water to the sagebrush you might catch them going from one to the other.

To see sage grouse displaying, you must know where there is a lek. Unfortunately, publicizing sage grouse leks is a good example of a dilemma faced by wildlife managers and authors of books like this one. On the one hand, you want people to see wildlife and to have outstanding and unique experiences, but on the other hand, you know that too many people can have a negative impact on the wildlife being observed. Some areas simply can't be visited by the public. Other sites can be visited by people who practice proper wildlife-watching etiquette. With sage grouse this is especially important. All those who visit a lek must follow the single most important rule for lek watching: Do not get out of your car!

Oregon

Hot Spots

There is one well-known sage grouse lek in southeastern Oregon that wildlife biologists with the Bureau of Land Management (BLM) feel can withstand its current visitation. This is the lek on **Foster Flats Road** near Malheur National Wildlife Refuge. Staying at the Malheur Field Station gives you the shortest drive to the lek in the early morning hours. Plan on getting to the lek while it's still dark, at least half an hour before sunrise. Foster Flats Road heads west from State Highway 205 about 20 miles south of the turnoff to refuge headquarters. After you turn onto Foster Flats Road, drive $8^{1}/_{3}$ miles, then pull over as far as you can on the side of the road and park. Many people feel it is better to slowly drive past the $8^{1}/_{3}$-mile point a bit and then turn around and drive back to park. This way, when you leave you can just go forward out of the area and not disturb the birds as much as you would making the turn and driving back through the lek once the sun is up. Foster Flats Road is sometimes very muddy and can be impassable, so it is a good idea to call refuge headquarters or the Hines Office of the BLM to get road conditions and any other information pertinent to visiting the grouse lek.

Once you have parked at the lek site you'll just have to sit in the dark until it starts to get light and you can see the birds. Leave your engine and lights off and be as quiet as possible. It will probably be very cold, so dress warmly for sitting in a parked car. Watch with the windows rolled up to prevent any incidental noises from inside your car from reaching the birds. At some point you will want to roll down a window to better hear and appreciate the sounds the birds are making. Photographers will also want to lower a window to take pictures. Get set up in advance, and be sure everyone is as quiet as possible while the window is open. Most important of all—never open a door or get out of your car. If someone gets out of a car (usually an overzealous photographer) the birds immediately fly away, and that's it for the day. Such thoughtless behavior will make instant enemies of all other grouse watchers present and could eventually result in the area being closed.

When you have seen your fill, start your car and creep out of the area as quietly as possible. If you cannot get to the Foster Flats Road before first light, do not drive into the area during the day.

The grouse may start displaying as early as late February, and a few may persist until early May, but March and April are the best times. Another way to see this lek is to go on one of the organized grouse field trips offered as part of the annual waterfowl festival in Burns the first weekend in April (see chapter 15).

Washington

The **Yakima Training Center** of the U.S. Army is now the only place in Washington where people can regularly see sage grouse at leks. Access is limited, and the only way one can visit these leks is as part of an organized sage grouse trip with the Seattle Audubon Society or possibly with other local chapters. Call Seattle Audubon in January or February to find out when trips are and how to register: (206) 523-4483.

22

Brant Migration

During September and October virtually the entire Pacific population of brant, about 140,000 birds, gathers at the tip of the Alaska Peninsula to get ready for their mass migration south. Then, almost overnight they're gone, on a 3,000-mile, 60-hour nonstop flight to Mexico. An impressive flight for a little goose barely bigger than a mallard.

In the past, many brant spent the winter along the coasts of Washington, Oregon and California. But starting in the late 1950s, more and more started skipping these states entirely and went straight to Mexico. This was particularly true of California, which went from being a major wintering area to having almost no wintering brant today. The Salish Sea in Washington is now the only area in our region with a significant number of brant in winter. What happened? The consensus is that the birds couldn't take the disturbance created by the water-skiers, boaters, anglers and others using the bays they favor.

Fortunately, there was and still is plenty of good wintering habitat in Baja and along the west coast of mainland Mexico, so the brant adapted by changing their wintering grounds and appear to be doing just fine today. And fortunately for us, we get to see them on their trip back north in the spring, when they hug our coast and travel at a much more leisurely pace. As they travel north, they stop for days at a time in different spots, eating almost constantly to put on weight so as to arrive at their breeding grounds in peak condition. While feeding in big flocks, they keep up a honking-croaking sound that has led some to call brant "the talking goose."

The brant is a small dark sea goose, one of the smallest geese in the world and one of the few that spend their entire life in or right near salt water. They breed in the tidal wetlands of the Arctic, farther north than any other goose. In the Arctic they eat a small variety of plants and invertebrates, but in the bays and estuaries of their wintering grounds, western brant feed almost exclusively on eelgrass. Eelgrass is very unusual in being one of the very few flowering plants in the world that grows in salt water. When eelgrass becomes established in the right environment, it can quickly spread to form huge beds, or meadows, that are an ecosystem unto themselves.

The brant's dependency on eelgrass proved disastrous during the early 1930s when disease killed most of the eelgrass along the Atlantic Coast. The Atlantic brant population (considered a separate species for many years) crashed and extinction was feared, but the birds proved adaptable and switched to other aquatic plants. Eelgrass along the Pacific Coast has not suffered similar epidemics, and in the West the association between eelgrass and brant is still very strong—no eelgrass, no brant. The spots along our coast where the brant stop on their

The east coast of Vancouver Island plays host to thousands of brant during their spring migration.

northward migration all have rich eelgrass beds, although you will also see brant eating sea lettuce, a favored algae.

Brant follow the typical breeding behaviors of other swans and geese: they mate for life, the female does all the incubating while the male stands guard, they are very defensive of their nest site and both parents rear the young. Brant have a pronounced tendency to return to the same nest area each year. The Arctic summer is short, and young brant must therefore grow quickly. Young brant can walk and swim within a day of hatching, dive in two days and fly in six weeks. The family group stays together until just before the migration south.

From November through April it is possible to find brant in any bay or estuary along the coast, but large numbers are regularly seen in a fairly limited number of hotspots. The only place where significant numbers actually spend the whole winter is the Salish Sea. Otherwise, one must wait until large numbers pass through during the spring migration, which peaks in April. For some residents in these areas, the real harbinger of spring is the "little talking sea goose."

Oregon

Hot Spots

In our region, Oregon has the fewest brant. The estuaries with consistently good numbers of brant during migration are **Tillamook, Netarts, Yaquina** and **Coos Bays.** Of these, Yaquina is probably the best and is described in chapter 8. Tillamook is also mentioned in that chapter as well as in chapter 45. In Coos Bay the best spot for finding brant is from the boat basin in the town of Charleston, reached by Newmark Road and the Cape Arago Highway from U.S. Highway 101. The whole eastern shore of Netarts Bay is hugged by a road that is named Cape Lookout Road, Whiskey Creek Road or Netarts Bay Drive in different sections. There are areas for parking on the side of the road to check the bay.

Washington

Washington now has the largest population of wintering brant north of Mexico in the numerous bays, coves, harbors and inlets of the Salish Sea. This population of about fifteen thousand is joined by thousands more during the April migration. As you would expect, the places that are good for seeing brant in winter are also good during migration. Any of the Salish Sea spots mentioned in chapter 8 are good bets, but the best spot is probably **Padilla Bay.**

Most of Padilla Bay is included in the 11,000-acre **Padilla Bay National Estuarine Research Reserve,** one of the twenty-one reserves in the little-known National Estuarine Research Reserve System managed by state agencies in conjunction with the National Oceanic and Atmospheric Administration. Padilla Bay is one of only four reserves on the West Coast and was selected because it has the largest known eelgrass meadow in the Pacific Northwest (7,000 acres). Brant are regularly seen in Padilla Bay during the winter, and during April tens of thousands are sometimes seen.

Access to Padilla Bay is along Bayview-Edison Road, which goes up the eastern shore of the bay. Bayview-Edison Road intersects State Highway 20 at a major intersection with a signal roughly halfway between Anacortes and Exit 230 on I-5. From Hwy. 20, go north on Bayview-Edison Road $3^1/_2$ miles and you'll come to **Bayview State Park** where you can park right on the shore and look over the bay. About another mile north is the very nice **Breazeale Interpretive Center,** which has exhibits, including aquaria of bay life, and is your resource for information about the bay. The center is open all year Wednesday through Sunday, from 10 A.M. to 5 P.M. Another good place to watch the bay for brant and other birds is from the **Shore Trail,** parking for which is just over a mile south of the interpretive center (ask for a map). If you're in the area any time between October and April, be on the lookout for other waterfowl as well as for raptors in the nearby Skagit and Samish Flats.

Another major stop for migrating brant is Willapa Bay, the largest estuary in Washington. **Willapa National Wildlife Refuge** consists of five different units that include several thousands of acres of tidelands with eelgrass, as well as some upland habitats. Willapa Bay is an excellent spot for observing wintering and migrating waterfowl and migrating shorebirds as well as the brant. Unfortunately, viewing of the bay is somewhat limited or involves long hikes. Hwy. 101 hugs the southeastern shore of the bay from near the refuge headquarters south to the Lewis Unit. Along this stretch are some places to pull over on the side of the road in order to search the southern part of the bay. Refuge headquarters, on Hwy. 101 about 4 miles west of its junction with State Highway 4, is the place to stop for maps, checklists and current information.

The best all-around birding spot in the Willapa area is the **Leadbetter Point Unit** of the refuge at the tip of the **Long Beach Peninsula.** Just take State Highway 103 north up the Long Beach Peninsula from its junction with Hwy. 101 and follow signs for Leadbetter Point State Park. Hwy. 103

ends at Leadbetter Point State Park, where there is a parking area with a big interpretive sign. There is a very short tail that goes due east to the shoreline—be sure to take it and check out the shoreline and bay from this point. Then drive the short distance to the final end of the road and the parking area for the trail heading northeast into the refuge. Rubber boots are a good idea here because the ground gets muddy and you may have to walk in some shallow water to go as far as you want. As you look out over the bay and shoreline along this trail you should see plenty of brant and other waterfowl, gulls, herons, some loons and grebes and flocks of shorebirds. You will see a big sign at the trailhead showing you which part of the point is closed from April through August to protect nesting snowy plovers.

As with most tidal areas in the Northwest, the birding is best at high tide or as high tide is receding. Find the times for tides in local newspapers, at sporting goods stores or at visitor information centers. In the Willapa area, tides are usually given for the Columbia River at Ilwaco. The tides are 2 hours later at Nahcotta, inside the bay, so use this as your adjustment for Leadbetter Point or the southern end of the bay.

Willapa Bay is home to one of the biggest oyster fisheries on the West Coast. In Nahcotta there is a small museum worth a stop, the Willapa Bay Interpretive Center, that tells the story of the Willapa Bay oyster industry and has some natural history information. Turn onto 273rd Street from Hwy. 103 in Nahcotta (there is a big sign for Jolly Roger Seafoods). The Long Beach Peninsula is a major tourist area, and the visitor center at the intersection of Hwys. 101 and 103 can give you lots of information on the area.

British Columbia

Twenty thousand or so brant migrate up the Strait of Georgia and stop along the east coast of Vancouver Island. The two beach resort communities of **Parksville** and **Qualicum Beach** have held the Brant Festival every April since 1991 to celebrate the arrival of the geese and to focus attention on the importance of coastal wetlands. There is an assortment of activities, including birding competitions, exhibits and workshops on wildlife art and photography, field trips for wildlife viewing and various feasts. If you are interested in the Brant Festival, write Brant Festival, Box 327, Parksville, British Columbia V9P 2G5.

There are four main areas on the east coast of Vancouver Island that provide excellent views of brant and the many other waterbirds present in April, including hundreds of western grebes and surf scoters and many harlequin ducks and oldsquaw, to name a few. In Parksville, **Rathtrevor Beach Provincial Park** is the easiest site to find—there are signs that lead you right to the best viewing spot (near parking lot 1). It is important to go at high tide or just as high tide is receding. Sometimes brant are just offshore from Rathtrevor but are hard to see from the park.

There is another nearby site that may give a better view. There is a small residential neighborhood adjacent to the park on the west. As you leave

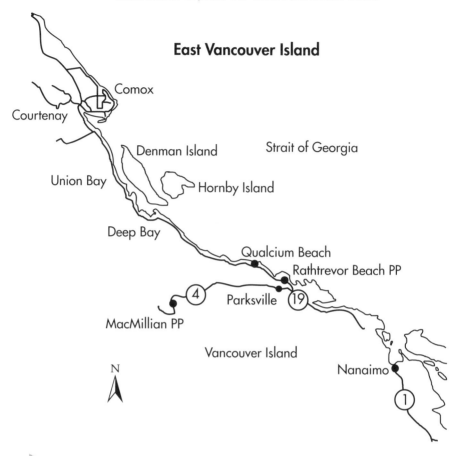

East Vancouver Island

Comox

Courtenay

Denman Island

Strait of Georgia

Union Bay

Hornby Island

Deep Bay

Qualcium Beach

Rathtrevor Beach PP

④

Parksville

⑲

MacMillian PP

Vancouver Island

Nanaimo

N

①

Rathtrevor, go northwest a short distance on the Island Highway (Provincial Highway 19) and turn right onto Plummer Road. Stay on Plummer until it turns into Shorewood Drive, and take Shorewood until it intersects Mariner Way. At this T intersection, left will put you on Mariner, right is the continuation of Shorewood. There are three little unpaved sections of road that lead in less than one block from Mariner and Shorewood to the shore. All are posted with a No Camping or Overnight Parking sign. These are public roads, and you can park here and walk to the shore for good views of the Strait of Georgia near Rathtrevor and toward the mouth of the Englishman River.

The second main area for brant viewing is **Qualicum Beach.** The Island Highway hugs the shoreline for about a mile in Qualicum Beach, and there are several areas where you can pull over, including a roadside rest with a Brant-Viewing Area sign.

The third area is the stretch of coast between Qualicum Beach and Courtenay. One excellent spot here is **Deep Bay,** just off the Island Highway a bit over 2 miles north of Bowser. Heading north, turn right onto Gainsburg Road following the sign to Deep Bay. Stay on Gainsburg, going left at the

Mama mallard and her young are a common spring sight in wetlands throughout the Northwest.

train tracks, then turn right onto Burne Road and then left onto Deep Bay Drive. Where Deep Bay Drive curves left there is a place to park where you can see the Chrome Island Lighthouse. Get out here and check the shore and water carefully. Then drive all the way to the end of Deep Bay Drive, park, and walk out to the end of the point on a short trail to search the shoreline and channel. Be sure to check the charming little harbor itself on your way back out to the highway. You should see ducks galore, brant, scads of western grebes, some loons, gulls, herons, cormorants and shorebirds.

Continuing north on the Island Highway, there is a stretch between Fanny Bay and Union Bay where the highway runs right along the shore. There is an official roadside rest that provides a great view across Baynes Sound toward Denman Island. This can be a productive stop.

The fourth excellent area for brant is **Comox Harbor,** noted for its large population of wintering trumpeter swans but great for waterfowl in general. All the spots covered in chapter 3 on swans are also possible brant spots, but there is one more not mentioned there that can be excellent. **Goose Spit Regional Park** is on the neck of Goose Spit, which sticks out into Comox Harbor from the north shore. To get onto the spit, go through the center of Comox on Comox Road and turn left onto Pritchard, following the sign for Goose Spit. Continue on Pritchard to the first stop sign and turn right onto Balmoral. Go a few blocks and Balmoral ends at a stop sign on Lazo Road but continues on the other side with a new name, Hawkins. Go straight onto Hawkins and stay on it until you drive out onto the spit. Park along the road and get out to scan the area. You may want to move your car to another spot once you see where the birds are. You can't go to the end of the spit, which is a military installation. I once saw eighty brant here feeding right along the eastern shoreline on big clumps of sea lettuce.

23

April Shorttakes

Animal Babies

Harbor seals are the most abundant and familiar of the *pinnipeds* (seals and sea lions) seen in the Northwest. They are year-round residents and are commonly seen resting on beaches, mudflats and low rocks. In the spring the females seek shallow protected waters to have their pups, and the mother will sometimes leave her baby parked on a beach while she hunts for food. This usually starts happening in April and continues into May. People will occasionally see these baby seals lying all by themselves on the beach and sometimes they assume that the babies are abandoned and need help. They pick up the baby seal and then try to find a place to take it where it will be cared for. They may try the police, the Humane Society, an Audubon Society or a zoo. Some of these kidnapped babies end up at a proper wildlife rehabilitation center and eventually are released, but they would all be much better off if they were left alone.

The same thing happens with fawns and some other mammals, but the biggest number of animal kidnappings are the thousands of baby birds picked up by people during the nesting season, which starts in earnest this month. In almost every case of an "abandoned baby," the parents or mother is nearby and will return to take care of the youngster once people are gone. This tendency of many people to want to do something for these young animals is a wonderful indication of care and concern, but the general rule is, *leave them alone.*

Nighttime Mammal Movement

The spring breeding season is also a time when many mammals start roaming more than usual in search of mates. Since most mammals are nocturnal, this means a big increase in mammal traffic across roads at night. We are all too familiar with the tragic end of some of these creatures when we see their carcasses on the road. The most common victim on the west side seems to be North America's only marsupial, the Virginia opossum. It may be that the frequent encounters between people and the unattractive remains of deceased opossums on roads contributes to the generally negative attitude most people seem to have toward these benign and helpless creatures. As sad as these deaths are, they sometimes provide opportunities for examining animals you might not otherwise see. I've seen mountain beaver and long-tailed weasels on the road at the Portland Audubon Wildlife Sanctuary that I didn't know lived there.

24

A Closer Look: Territories and Leks

Bushtits may be buddy-buddy all year, but when it comes time to breed, even these highly social birds are driven by their raging hormones to seek their own space. Territoriality is a very common and widespread phenomenon among animals and is one of the main causes of the patterns of animal distribution in an area. Because birds are so conspicuous, noisy and easy to study, their territorial behavior is the best known. Some animals, like mountain lions and eagles, maintain territories all year, but the majority of animals maintain territories for a limited period and a specific purpose.

The word "territory" has a very definite meaning in animal behavior and biology and should not be confused with "home range" or "range." An animal's home range is the area within which it is usually found and that it rarely, if ever, leaves. Thus, an animal's home range would have to provide all the necessities for life. The term "range" is used for the total geographic area in which that animal occurs and is often used for the area in which a whole species occurs. It is common to see terms like "winter range" or "breeding range" used to describe different parts of an animal's total range. In contrast, an animal's territory is specifically the area that it will actively defend against other animals, usually of its own species, and is usually much smaller than the animal's total range, although it may sometimes be close in size to the home range.

Some territories have a single purpose, such as a feeding territory. A good example would be the feeding territory of a rufous hummingbird, which would be an area of blooming flowers that one rufous hummingbird would aggressively defend against all other rufous hummers. Sometimes individuals will keep out members of other species as well as their own. Clearly, this type of territory would change greatly over time with changes in the blooming flowers. Sometimes a group of animals will defend an area against other groups of the same species. This is common among chickadees and some rats and mice.

The most common type of territory is the all-purpose breeding territory established by a breeding pair of animals for the purpose of raising their young. This defended territory provides food, shelter and space for displays and other activities. The classic example of this is the nesting territory used by a pair of breeding songbirds. In these cases, the work of establishing and defending the territory is mainly carried out by the male, although this does vary among birds and other animals. When birds sing in the spring they are saying, "Keep out—this is my space, reserved for my family alone." If a male bird does not yet have a mate, his singing also functions to advertise for one.

Why do animals set up territories? The overall function of territories is to somewhat evenly divide up or partition the limited resources in an area so that each animal, or group of animals, gets enough. This is demonstrated most obviously with food. By establishing an exclusive foraging area for himself and his family, a male robin greatly increases the chances that his offspring will survive. Besides providing a stable food source, the territorial system reduces predation because nests are dispersed and harder to find.

This all sounds great, but doesn't establishing and maintaining a territory require a tremendous amount of time and energy? Actually, the return on the investment is a big *savings* in time and energy. If an animal had to constantly fight with outsiders over food, nesting sites, space and mates, it would use up a lot more energy and actually be at risk of injury. Once territories are established, boundaries are amazingly well respected and require relatively little energy to maintain. And actual fights are almost completely eliminated.

There are many interesting variations in animal territories that are adaptations to the particular challenges faced by each species. One of the most interesting is the lek system. A lek is a special area where the males of a particular bird species traditionally gather every year during the breeding season to strut their stuff for the females, who come to the lek and select a mate for breeding. Ten different bird families around the world contain species that show lek behavior, but one of the most famous, and the classic example for North America, is the sage grouse featured in chapter 21.

In the lek, also called an "arena" or "strutting ground," each male has a very small individual territory around him that he defends against all other males. Sometimes fights over territories can get bloody. The cocks put on elaborate displays for the sole purpose of attracting the hens. Unlike most birds, sage grouse form no pair bond for breeding and raising young. The hens saunter on over to the lek and cruise through the males, who are each displaying away in the hope that one of the seemingly indifferent females will pick him for mating. The female picks the cock of her choice and enters his territory, where the two copulate. Then the female leaves and goes off to do all the nesting, incubating and raising of the young by herself. The cock then continues his display in the hope of attracting another hen.

The territories in the center of the lek are the most valued because the males that occupy these territories will mate with a large majority of the females. The most dominant male sage grouse, or "master cock," in the center of the lek may mate with 80 to 90 percent of all the hens that visit that lek. Some master cocks have been recorded mating with twenty hens in a morning. Once the territories are well established, the males will spend several hours every day—morning and evening, for as long as two months—giving their best displays in the hope of attracting females. Males have less time to eat and rest then, and some biologists believe that these spring mating rituals are a major factor in the mortality of male sage grouse.

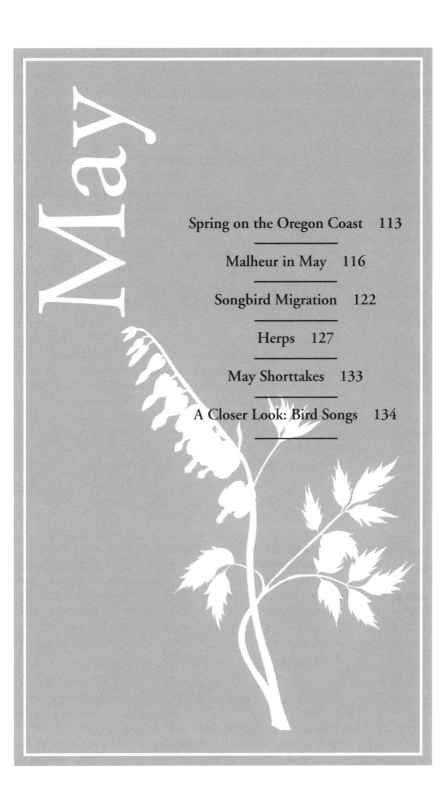

May

Notes

25

Spring on the Oregon Coast

This month we have two chapters that describe a particular place rather than an animal or group of animals. Malheur in May (chapter 26) covers one of the West's greatest birding areas, which is also endowed with many other interesting species of wildlife as well as beautiful scenery. In this chapter we explore a section of the central Oregon coast that is one of the most outstanding chunks of coastline in the United States in terms of both scenery and wildlife. In the 100 miles between Yachats and Bandon there are twenty state parks and waysides; two wilderness areas and the Cape Perpetua Scenic Area, the nation's first national estuarine reserve; Sea Lion Caves; the Oregon Dunes National Recreation Area and a dozen big county and city parks.

During spring, the major natural attractions of this stretch of coast are: gray whale migration; shorebird, waterfowl and songbird migration; the state's best tide pools; the arrival and beginning of nesting by breeding seabirds; ancient forests; breeding newts; wildflowers and two plant specialities. In addition to the natural wonders, there are many tourist attractions and accommodations in the towns, three of which are considered among the most charming on the Northwest coast—Yachats, Florence and Bandon. Public access is almost unlimited, and about 50 miles of beach are included in the Oregon Coast Trail.

May is a wonderful time to go just about anywhere, but here there is one extra reason—the "rhodies." The Pacific rhododendron *(Rhododendron macrophyllum)* ranges from northern California to just inside southern British Columbia and is common in many areas west of the Sierra Cascades crest. But this showy rhody really flourishes and reaches peak densities in the understory of the transition coniferous forests that dominate the sand-dune area of the coast from Coos Bay to a bit north of Florence. U.S. Highway 101 goes right through the heart of the rhododendrons. **Heceta Beach Road,** just north of Florence, usually has a spectacular display. South of Florence, trails in **Honeyman State Park** and in the **Siltcoos** and **Tahkenitch Lake** areas of **Oregon Dunes National Recreation Area** provide opportunities for hiking among the rhodies. For over seventy-five years Florence has celebrated this spectacle with the annual Rhododendron Festival the third weekend in May, complete with floral parade, carnival, arts and crafts booths, sock hop, Rhody Run and other events. This is a homespun event and not swarmed with big crowds, but if you go, make your lodging arrangements well in advance.

Florence is also a great place for seeing one of the most unique and bizarre plants in the West—*Darlingtonia,* commonly called the cobra lily or California pitcher plant (never the latter in Oregon, however). Just by looking at this strange plant you will know right away that there is something weird about it, and you're right—it eats insects. *Darlingtonia* is so unusual that it is in a genus all its own. It is the only member of its family in the West and grows only in very limited parts of northern California and southern Oregon.

Like other pitcher plants, the cobra lily catches insects passively by forming a trap with its leaves. The highly modified leaves form a hollow tube up to 2 feet long with an enlarged bulbous "hood" at the end. On the underside of the hood is a small opening into the hollow leaf, and projecting downward from this opening is a forked, petal-like appendage that looks like a giant snake's tongue. The leaves usually grow straight up from the base of the plant, although some may lie along the ground. All the leaves twist as they grow so they end up facing to the outside of the plant, presumably because this is better for catching insects. The leaves range in color from green to yellow to red, changing from the base to the top and with age. These features make the plant look very much like some kind of stylized cobra rising up and flaring its hood—hence the name cobra lily. When the tall leaves with their hoods and tongues sway in a breeze, they look all the more snakelike and menacing.

Why would any insect be foolhardy enough to enter the rather small hole on the underside of the hood? The cobra lily uses that age-old lure, nectar. Nectar glands on the tongue and lip of the opening attract insects, who venture farther inside the hood seeking more goodies. Once inside, they may start to slip on the waxy surface and then try to crawl or fly back out the opening. Distributed about the hood, however, are spots where the leaf tissue has lost almost all of its usual contents (such as chlorophyll) and has formed translucent spots. These thin "windows" look like openings, and the confused insects keep trying to fly out these spots until they fall exhausted into the bottom of the leaf. Those that try to crawl out have a little surprise also. The inside top of the leaf is covered with a slick waxy secretion that makes secure footing practically impossible. As the hapless insect slides farther down the leaf it then encounters a myriad of tiny but sharp downward-pointing hairs. These hairs make progress down the tube of the leaf easy but escape upward impossible. Bit by bit the victim sinks lower and lower into the tube of doom until it finally falls into the water contained in the bottom of the leaf.

Once in the water, the insect drowns. Unlike some carnivorous plants, such as sundews and Venus's-flytraps, the cobra lily does not produce enzymes to digest its prey. Instead, the bugs just rot, and as bacteria go about their usual business of breaking down the bodies into simpler compounds, the useful nutrients are absorbed by the plant. Like almost all carnivorous plants, *Darlingtonia* grows in boggy soil, which is very low in nitrogen, so the plant has adapted to the situation by getting its nitrogen the way many animals do, from the protein in animal flesh. From an evolutionary standpoint, carnivorous plants are doubly fascinating, because several different types in unrelated families have developed different methods for eating bugs, all to solve the same basic problem of low nitrogen in the soil.

It's easy to see a healthy stand of cobra lilies in the **Darlingtonia Botanical Garden,** a state wayside, just 5 miles north of Florence off Hwy. 101. Heading north from Florence, watch for the signs and turn right onto Mercer Lake Road. The trail to the plants is very short and level, and there are rest rooms at the parking lot.

Another unique natural attraction near Florence is America's largest sea cave, home to the only permanent colony of Steller, or northern, sea lions on the mainland of North America. Steller sea lions are the largest members of the eared seal family, and big males can weigh a ton. Ten miles north of Florence is **Sea Lion Caves,** a private wildlife sanctuary that has operated continuously since 1932. The 208-foot elevator descent into the grotto provides a truly unique experience and a great opportunity to see these marine mammals up close.

Fall and winter are when the largest number of sea lions are inside the cave. By May the sea lions have started to spend most of their nonswimming time at the rookery on the rocky ledges just outside the cave entrance. There is an observation deck near the top of the cliffs where you can view the rookery (take your binoculars), so you can always see sea lions regardless of the time of year. Other marine mammals sometimes seen are harbor seals, California sea lions, gray whales and, rarely, orca. In spring and summer there are a number of seabirds that nest in and about the cave. Gulls, cormorants and pigeon guillemots are the most common, but other seabirds are also seen. The outside viewing decks are excellent for seeing migrating gray whales earlier in the spring and afford a great view of the Heceta Head Lighthouse, considered one of the most scenic on the West Coast.

Here is just a quick summary, from north to south, of the main natural (and a few human-made) attractions in this amazing hundred miles of coast.

Yachats. Tide pools.

Cape Perpetua Scenic Area in Siuslaw National Forest. Tide pools, ancient forest, giant Sitka spruce, gray whales, great scenic overlook, visitor center.

Neptune State Park. Tide pools, harbor seals at Strawberry Hill.

Devil's Elbow State Park and **Heceta Head.** Tide pools, seabirds, gray whales, lighthouse.

Sea Lion Caves. Sea lions, whales, seabirds.

Darlingtonia Botanical Garden. Cobra lilies.

Florence. Siuslaw estuary and south jetty for seabirds, waterfowl, shorebirds.

Honeyman State Park. Rough-skinned newts breed in Cleawox Lake.

Oregon Dunes National Recreation Area. Florence to Coos Bay: spectacular rhododendron display. Siltcoos Lagoon: freshwater wetlands, beaver, waterfowl, herons, osprey. Lots of good hiking trails, hiking guide available from Siuslaw National Forest. Large sand dunes.

Coos Bay. Shorebirds at Pony Slough in North Bend.

Cape Arago. Chain of three great state parks: Sunset Bay, Shore Acres, Cape Arago. Tide pools; seals and sea lions, including possibly elephant seals; seabirds.

South Slough National Estuarine Reserve. 4,400 acres of outstanding wetland and upland habitats; best seen by canoe.

Bandon. Nesting seabirds (including puffins) on offshore rocks, Bandon Marsh National Wildlife Refuge.

26

Malheur in May

The most famous birding spot in the Northwest is **Malheur National Wildlife Refuge** in southeastern Oregon. Roger Tory Peterson named it one of the "Dozen Birding Hotspots" in the nation. The 185,000-acre refuge is the second largest in the Northwest and contains one of the West's largest freshwater marsh systems. What makes Malheur dramatic is that this huge wetlands system is surrounded by the arid and rugged country of the northern Great Basin. This oasis-in-the-desert setting has two major effects. One is diversity: Within a relatively small area you can find wildlife from several different habitats. The second is that Malheur "sucks in" traveling birds that are seeking the water and vegetation so scarce in the surrounding hundreds of square miles. Malheur regularly produces many of the most unusual bird sightings in the region, and many Oregon birders consider no year complete without at least one trip to this legendary hotspot.

A trip to Malheur can be very productive almost any time of year. Late May, however, is the birder's favorite time. May has the greatest diversity of species, and most of the unusual bird sightings occur in that month. In spring there is the great advantage of seeing birds in their finest breeding plumage and hearing them sing, both extremely helpful for identification. In a two- or three-day visit an experienced birder can expect to see at least 110 species in 35 different families!

The northern part of the refuge is located about 25 miles south of the town of Burns, Oregon. The long T-shaped refuge then stretches for another 30 miles south, more or less along State Highway 205, to the tiny town of Frenchglen. Since most visitors get to the refuge via Burns and proceed from north to south, I'll do the same. Take State Highway 78 east from Burns almost 2 miles to the intersection with Hwy. 205. Turn right and head south on Hwy. 205. En route to the refuge you will drive through hay fields that when flooded provide some excellent birding. These fields south of Burns are an excellent birding area on their own, especially during waterfowl migration (see chapter 15).

About 10 miles south of Hwy. 78 you will drive over an interesting geological formation called **Wright's Point,** a tongue of basalt that is actually a cast of an ancient river canyon. Just before coming to the top as you go up the northern side of Wright's Point, you will see a small rough turnout on your right. This turnout is in a jumble of collapsed rimrock and chokecherries that for many years has been a good location for finding both rock and canyon wrens, ash-throated flycatchers and, sometimes, sage thrashers. From this spot you also have a great view north to Burns and the Strawberry Mountains.

Ten miles south of Wright's Point you will find yourself driving on a causeway. You are going through **The Narrows,** the point where the road separates Malheur Lake on the east from Mud and Harney Lakes on the west. The amount of water in these lakes has varied phenomenally over the last decade—you may find yourself driving in the middle of a lake or over dry and cracked mud. As you would guess, what birds there are will depend on the amount of water present, but The Narrows almost always produces some interesting waterbirds and shorebirds.

Just south of The Narrows, turn left at the clearly marked Princeton-Narrows Road going east to the **refuge headquarters.** The headquarters make a logical starting place for exploring the refuge. Here you can pick up maps and checklists, visit the excellent museum with mounted specimens of birds of the area, use the nicest public restroom in the whole area and bird one of Oregon's most famous hotspots.

A variety of native and exotic trees have been planted around the headquarters over the years, and these have created a wonderful migrant trap. This artificial oasis in the Great Basin desert pulls in birds like a magnet. Some of the rarities seen over the years are the yellow-billed cuckoo, gray catbird, veery, black-and-white warbler, northern parula, Cape May warbler, scarlet tanager, indigo bunting and rose-breasted grosbeak. You can always count on finding a few great horned owls hanging out in the larger cottonwoods, usually young ones in the cute "ball o' fluff" stage. It will be easy to find out what has been seen and what's around while you're there—just ask the other birders! In the unlikely event there aren't other birders around, you can check the bird-sighting records in the office and museum where birders record their noteworthy finds. The best time to bird headquarters is early in the morning, but there is always something going on. The refuge office is open 7:00 A.M. to 3:30 P.M. Monday through Friday, but the museum, which usually has everything you'll want, is open every day sunrise to sunset.

After spending time at headquarters, drive south through the refuge down the dirt **Central Patrol Road,** called the CPR by locals and regular Malheur birders. There are two parts to the CPR. The upper or northern part goes from near headquarters to the Buena Vista area. At Buena Vista the CPR ends and you have to go west to get back on Hwy. 205 and continue south. About $8^1/_2$ miles south of Buena Vista, off the Krumbo Reservoir Road, the CPR starts again and heads south to P Ranch. This second section is the lower or southern CPR. Although there is much to see along the whole CPR, you may want to drive just one section if your time is limited and you have recent bird news indicating one section is more lively than the other.

For a basic tour, leave headquarters and drive southwest through the Wright's Pond area until you come to the CPR. The road coming in from your right is the road from **Malheur Field Station.** This area, at the head of the CPR near Wright's Pond, is one of the most reliable places in the state to see short-eared owls. Look for their unusual butterflylike flight in the morning and late afternoon. Proceed

Malheur National Wildlife Refuge

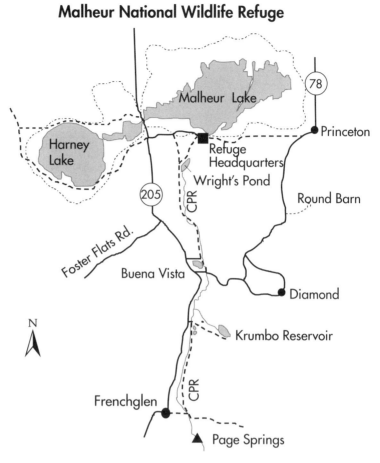

south on the CPR, keeping a sharp lookout in all directions. As usual, it's best to stay in your car and use it as a blind, but some spots will be so tempting that you'll want to get out to scan the marsh and enjoy the scenery. The list of possible birds is enormous, just about any freshwater bird found in the Northwest could show up. As the surrounding land gets drier you can pick up your pace a bit until you get to Buena Vista.

In about 12 miles you'll come to a sign that reads Buena Vista, State Hwy. 205. Turn right and head west on the road that is the northern border of the **Buena Vista Ponds.** This area is usually an excellent place for soras and Virginia rails. These birds are notoriously difficult to see but can often be heard calling. There has been much debate about the ethics of using recorded bird songs to attract birds. You will have to use your judgment and develop your own guidelines for the use of tapes. If you decide to play rail calls at Buena Vista, you will almost surely get some response. If you do get a good response, do not play the recording any more. The soras here in particular are usually pretty noisy without encouragement.

Other birds to look for in the fields north of the road are sandhill cranes, common snipes and a variety of blackbirds. The Buena Vista Ponds south of the road are a good place to see the resident trumpeter swan, lots of other waterfowl, grebes, black terns and common freshwater marsh birds like the marsh wren and common yellowthroat. Seeing a marsh wren can be almost as difficult as seeing a rail. Pick a place where you can hear several of them making their incessant fussy songs and just watch and wait. Sooner or later one will pop into view on the top of a reed, vibrate like mad while giving a song, then hop back into the marsh. You've got to be quick to get your binoculars on this one!

Just before the Buena Vista road intersects Hwy. 205 there is a short road that goes south to the scenic overlook. This is well worth the few minutes it takes to get to the top of the rimrock for a fantastic view across the marsh to the Diamond Craters area. If it is warm and sunny, the rocks around the scenic overlook are usually alive with side-blotched lizards, one of the most common reptiles in the area.

After exploring Buena Vista, get on Hwy. 205 and head south toward Frenchglen. For most of this drive you will have wetlands on your left (east) and rimrock and sagebrush on your right (west). The rimrock is excellent for raptors. There is a section of the road between Mileposts 42 and 46 where rimrock rises around you on both sides of the road. I call this Eagle Alley because it is the most reliable place I know to see golden eagles. I've also seen red-tailed hawks, prairie falcons, northern harriers, turkey vultures, American kestrels and, once, a short-eared owl. On the rimrock just after Milepost 44 red-tailed hawks and great horned owls have nested, and you can sometimes find their nests and young. When you're not watching raptors, keep your eyes on the marshes and ponds as you drive along and you may see trumpeter swans. There will be myriad waterfowl, herons, gulls and terns, white-faced ibis, and probably shorebirds.

Eight and a half miles south of Buena Vista, a dirt road heads due east to **Krumbo Reservoir.** The deep water of Krumbo sometimes attracts diving birds like loons, grebes and diving ducks that you may not see elsewhere on the refuge. If you decide not to go all the way to Krumbo Reservoir, be sure to go the short distance to a pond by the road that is great for ducks. "Krumbo Pond," as it is informally called, is $1\frac{1}{3}$ miles east of Hwy. 205, and there is a rough pullout where you can park. Scan this pond carefully; on some trips I've seen the trip's greatest number of duck species in one place at this spot! From Krumbo Pond go about 4 more miles to Krumbo Reservoir for a quick look, or turn around and head back toward Hwy. 205.

As you drive west toward Hwy. 205, watch for the beginning of the southern CPR. It is the dirt road heading south just east of the Blitzen River, which you crossed coming from Hwy. 205. From here the CPR heads south toward the P Ranch, Frenchglen and Page Springs. Depending on your time and the latest bird-sighting news, you may not want to drive the entire length of the southern CPR. You will get to Frenchglen and Page Springs much faster by going back out to Hwy. 205 and driving south that way. However, there is one close stop that is worthwhile even if you don't take the CPR all the way.

Just off the CPR a mile south of the Krumbo road is **Benson Pond.** On the northern edge of Benson Pond is a road that goes east to a big grove of cottonwood and willow trees. Drive into this grove until the road ends (in less than half a mile). You'll see a small abandoned stone building. Often this grove of trees at Benson is like birding around headquarters, with lots of migrants swarming through the treetops. This is a surefire place to find great horned owls and a very likely place to find porcupines in the cottonwoods. Benson is best in the early morning but always seems to end up in the middle of a day's itinerary. Regardless of time of day, Benson is a lovely spot and always has some interesting wildlife sightings. From Benson go back out to the CPR and turn left (south), or go right to backtrack to Krumbo Road and Hwy. 205 and then head south.

The tiny town of **Frenchglen** is historic, quaint and your only chance for gasoline and munchies for many miles. It is also a migrant trap because of the many planted trees, and sometimes Frenchglen will produce bird sightings as exciting as those at headquarters. Good places to check are the cottonwoods nearest the hotel (good for sapsuckers and orioles) and the willows around the little stream and outhouse. This is another good place to introduce yourself to other birders and get the latest birding gossip.

One of my favorite places at Malheur is actually just outside the refuge on BLM land. **Page Springs Campground** is a beautiful little campground with tables, water and outhouses located in a little valley where the Blitzen River comes rolling off the base of Steens Mountain. This is certainly one of the nicest places to have a picnic lunch if the weather is good. There are open meadows, streamside thickets and juniper woodlands. Because it is at the base of Steens Mountain and has junipers, this campground gets birds you don't always find on the refuge, such as the Townsend's solitaire, house wren, ash-throated flycatcher, mountain bluebird and Cassin's finch (rare). The open grassy fields sometimes have lesser goldfinches and lark sparrows.

From the campground, a trail follows the river up the canyon. In sunny weather this is a beautiful hike and leads to excellent spots from which to see yellow-breasted chat and lazuli bunting, or on which to lie in the grass and soak up some sun. Along the swiftly flowing river itself you will usually see spotted sandpipers, sometimes common mergansers and belted kingfishers, and, occasionally, osprey. This is also a great place to find snakes. Garter snakes are by far the most common, but gopher snakes and racers are also regularly seen. So is the western rattlesnake, although this unfortunate snake has been so relentlessly persecuted by humans that its numbers are quite low. Its presence does, however, mean that hikers should exercise the normal cautions of traveling in rattlesnake country.

The preceding is what I would consider the essential Malheur tour. There are many other areas in and about the refuge that are just as productive for wildlife and very scenic. One area that is worth fitting into any trip is the **Diamond area.** The paved Diamond Lane goes east from Hwy. 205 just south of Buena Vista. At $6^4/_5$ miles is Diamond Junction. If you go straight ahead (this section is not paved) you will arrive at the Diamond Hotel and store (gas, food and lodging) after driving through usually lush fields commonly loaded with white-faced ibis. If you turn left at Diamond Junction and head north, you will drive through some other fields that often provide exceptional birding. There are usually plenty of ibis as well as some sandhill cranes and herons, including an occasional American bittern or cattle egret. These fields are one of the best sites in Oregon for seeing the bobolink, a very rare bird for the West. They are usually west of the road about half a mile north of Diamond Junction (before you get to the farmhouse).

After you drive through the fields north of Diamond Junction, you will start rising onto higher, drier land. At $3^1/_5$ miles north of Diamond Junction, near a small red cinder cone, an inconspicuous dirt road heads west into the **Diamond Craters Outstanding Natural Area,** managed by the BLM. Turn onto this road, stay to the left, and drive to the first crater. Sit on the crater's edge, and after soaking in the magnificent views, search the crater walls opposite you for baby great horned owls. They are usually there but hard to see. This crater is a good place to find rock wrens, canyon wrens, and Say's phoebes. If it is warm enough, side-blotched and western fence lizards are usually active on the rocks. The rest of the Diamond Craters Outstanding Natural Area has much to offer in terms of geology, birds and reptiles. The BLM office in Burns has a self-guided tour brochure available for the area.

From Diamond Craters you can make a long loop trip back to refuge headquarters by returning to the paved road and going north to the historic and unique **Round Barn,** then continuing north to the Princeton-Narrows Road (all paved) and then taking the Princeton-Narrows Road west to headquarters (this section is dirt). Some of the dry grasslands near Round Barn are excellent for loggerhead shrike, horned lark, and vesper and lark sparrow. As you near Princeton, you start entering a rich area for raptors. The first few miles of the road from Princeton to headquarters, through irrigated fields often swarming with ground squirrels, can be truly awesome. It is possible to see golden eagles; turkey vultures; red-tailed, ferruginous and Swainson's hawks; northern harriers; prairie falcons and American kestrels in one drive down this road. About 6 miles from Princeton start watching carefully for burrowing owls; there have been a few recent sightings in this area, especially near some dirt piles by the road. In addition to the birds, this loop often provides some good views of pronghorn (see chapter 61).

One possible big day's trip would be to stay at the Malheur Field Station, start early at headquarters, go down the upper CPR to Buena Vista, take Diamond Lane to Diamond Junction and go north, stopping at the first Diamond Crater. Continue north to Round Barn, then to Princeton, then return to headquarters from Princeton. Another day could be spent exploring the southern half of the refuge and Page Springs.

27

Songbird Migration

The return of migrating songbirds to their breeding grounds in the north has captured the attention and romantic spirit of people since ancient times. And no wonder, for after the quiet, drab winter all of a sudden there is color and singing everywhere. When songbirds, or *passerines,* come north to breed, they are in their full breeding plumage and singing their hearts out. At no other time could birds be more conspicuous.

Spring, in many ways, is the zenith of the natural year and the time when naturalists are dying to be outside every possible moment. For birders it is the time when they do wild things like Birdathons and Big Days, trying to find as many species as possible in a single day. Not only are there new arrivals from the tropics, but the year-round residents have also been swept away by hormones and are acting like different birds than they did just months ago.

Spring songbird migration starts with the return of tree swallows in February and proceeds species by species from then until late May, or even early June for the last arrivals. Although all of April and May are dynamite, the real peak is probably about mid-April to mid-May. Things are delayed at higher elevations, so spring follows the melting snow as it retreats up the mountains.

Songbirds tend to concentrate in certain areas and such places are often called *migrant traps.* Migrant traps are islands of choice habitat in the midst of mediocre habitat. There are three basic types of migrant trap:

1. Oases. Areas with water, and therefore lots of vegetation, in an otherwise arid and sparsely vegetated region. Urban wetlands function in much the same way, only in this case the "wasteland" is the urban area, not a desert.

2. Forested hills in urban areas. These are usually city parks with mixed woodlands or forests and with openings and edges. Lots of birds seem to congregate at the tops of hills, so if the habitat is good and there is good access, you've got a birding hotspot.

3. Headlands. Isolated clumps of trees or big shrubs on a point of land sticking out into the ocean.

Always be on the alert for places that meet these conditions and you may discover your own migrant trap. What really excites birders is when a migrant trap is so good that it attracts the few migrating birds in the area that are really lost and totally out of their normal range. These lost birds are called *vagrants,* and nothing gets a serious birder drooling like a good vagrant trap.

In spring, birds are active and singing very early, so birding is better the earlier you can get going. In some cases, access to an area like a city park may be closed until 6 or 7 A.M. The eager and early birder should verify opening times before trying to get into a park at, or before, dawn.

Oregon

The most famous migrant traps in the Northwest are two oases in southeastern Oregon that are 75 miles apart. **The headquarters of Malheur National Wildlife Refuge** was covered in chapter 26. A very similar situation is found at the tiny settlement of **Fields,** 75 miles south of Malheur headquarters and included by most birders in any spring trip to Malheur. From Frenchglen (another birding oasis), head south on State Highway 205 and stay on the main road (Catlow Valley Road) following signs to Fields or Denio, Nevada. When you get to Fields you should probably think about getting one of the famous milkshakes at the cafe before doing any birding. It's also useful to know that there is a small store and gas station in Fields. You might even hear some bird news in the cafe.

Bird around the Fields Cafe and then cross the street to the big clump of trees just to the east known as the **Fields Oasis.** Explore every nook and cranny of this little microhabitat. Many of the rarest sightings in Oregon and the whole Northwest have occurred in this small clump of trees and bushes. It is most famous for spring vagrants—mainly eastern songbirds that are *really* lost, like the least flycatcher; blue jay; gray catbird; black-and-white, magnolia, Tennessee and Cape May warblers; wood and gray-cheeked thrushes; summer tanager and rose-breasted grosbeak. Great horned owls nest here every spring, and it is almost unheard of to visit the Fields Oasis in May and not see baby owls in the trees. From Fields you should consider heading north through the Alvord Basin to State Highway 78 or east through Hart Mountain for some beautiful Great Basin open vistas.

Portland and Eugene both have some well-known spots for spring migrants. The **Pittock Mansion,** an interesting historical attraction, is on top of one of Portland's West Hills and is surrounded by a small park. From Powell's Books in downtown Portland, head west on Burnside Street. Watch closely on the right for green signs to the mansion, and in about 2 miles turn right and keep following signs up Pittock Avenue. Park in the parking lot (a left turn as you come to the mansion), and start by checking all the trees surrounding the parking lot. Walk all the way around the mansion looking down on the hillsides as well as in the trees.

Sometimes the first part of the **Wildwood Trail** heading north is very productive. Pick up the trail in the northwest corner of the parking lot. If you want more exercise, you could hike from here down to the Audubon Society sanctuary. On the return you could cover some new ground by coming up the **Upper Macleay Trail,** which splits off from Wildwood for a while. A word of warning: many maps show the main part of the Portland Audubon Wildlife Sanctuary as the "Pittock Bird Sanctuary," and people are always getting this mixed up with the Pittock Mansion. The two are more or less connected by the Wildwood Trail and you could probably see one from the other if there weren't any trees, but they are not part of the same concern and there is no easy, direct way to drive from one to the other.

Another favorite migration stop in Portland, this time east of the Willamette River, is **Mount Tabor Park.** Coming from the river, take Belmont Street east until it ends at 69th Avenue. Turn right and go south into the park. Go left when you get to the fork and drive around the east side of the mountain almost a quarter of a mile, then make a hairpin turn to your right and head toward the top. In a fifth of a mile you'll come to a small parking area with roads on either side blocked by locked gates. Park here and walk up the road to the top (to the east, or your left as you sit in your parked car), looking and listening everywhere. You can explore any other part of the park that looks inviting. You may be surprised at the number of crowing pheasants you'll hear. The entire park is closed to all vehicles on Wednesdays, so plan on more walking if you go then.

In Eugene a very similar situation exists in **Skinner Butte Park,** on the Willamette just north of downtown. Take High St. north and curve to the left as the road enters the park and becomes Skinner Butte Loop. Before reaching the playground, turn left onto a small, paved road and drive to the parking lot on top. Another excellent spot for songbirds is **Mount Pisgah Arboretum,** just southeast of Eugene and described in chapter 20. Just west of Eugene is one of the best all-around birding spots in the area, **Fern Ridge Reservoir.** The three parks at the north end of the reservoir (Richardson, Kirk and Orchard Point) are good for migrants and can be reached from Clear Lake Road from northwest Eugene. Fern Ridge is also great for fall shorebirds and wintering waterfowl and raptors.

In the southwestern corner of the state there are birds that are much more common farther south in California. These birds, the "California specialties," are the California towhee, blue-gray gnatcatcher, plain titmouse, ash-throated flycatcher and black phoebe. Every Oregon birder has to make at least one trip to the area to add these birds to his or her state list. Joe Evanich's excellent *The Birder's Guide to Oregon* covers all the best spots except for one. **Salt Creek Road** is about 20 miles northeast of Medford. Going north on Hwy. 62, turn right and head east on Lake of the Woods Highway (Hwy. 140). In $12^1/_3$ miles, turn left onto Salt Creek Rd. The road goes through private property for the first 3 miles, where you could stop and bird from the road, but then it enters BLM land with public access. In the next few miles you go through a great sample of different habitats.

On the southern Oregon coast, **Cape Blanco State Park** provides an example of a headland vagrant trap. The park is 4 miles north of Port Orford and 5 miles west of State Highway 101. The area around the lighthouse at the tip of the cape has produced a few sightings of eastern warblers but is not in the same league with the Malheur area.

Washington

Washington birders say there just aren't any migrant hotspots like those in southeastern Oregon, but there are places that have a good variety of the regular transients and resident species. The **Blue Mountains** in the southeastern corner of the state, east of the charming city of Walla Walla, has lots of wildlife and scenery and is lightly visited except during elk-hunting season. It is known as "woodpecker heaven," because all species resident in the state can be found there. There are also mountain quail, green-tailed towhees, broad-tailed hummingbirds and turkeys. Local birders favor **Coppei Creek** in the western foothills of the Blues.

Coming from Walla Walla, head northeast on U.S. Highway 12 and pass through Dixie at 8 miles. Two more miles from Dixie, turn right just before the large grain elevator covered with graffiti, and cross the old railroad bed. The road then forks; go to the left and you will be on Walker Road. In about a mile Walker Road intersects South Fork Coppei Creek Road. Park on the side of the road near this intersection and do a "birders walk" north on South Fork Coppei Creek Road until you come to North Fork Coppei Creek Road, then return to your car. A birder's walk is when you're listening like an owl and watching everywhere like a hawk for bird life as you creep along, taking 1 or 2 hours just to cover a mile.

When you get back in your car, drive south about $5^1/_2$ miles on South Fork Coppei Creek Road until it ends. Park here and explore the immediate area for birds found at slightly higher elevations. To get higher into the mountains, drive north, back the way you came, until you come again to North Fork Coppei Creek Road. Turn right and head up this road, stopping in any areas that look like good habitat.

Across the state on the southern coast are three points of land that represent headlands. **Leadbetter Point,** in Willapa Bay, is described in chapter 22, and **Ocean Shores,** in Grays Harbor, is described in chapter 45. The farthest north you can go on the Washington coast is that little bit of land that should belong to Canada, **Point Roberts,** described in chapter 62.

The **San Juan Islands** are very beautiful and therefore very popular. Summer on the islands can be extremely crowded and hectic, so it is advantageous to visit off-season when, among many other benefits, some great bargains in lodging can be found. Wildlife watching and nature appreciation on the islands are actually best outside of the summer months, with the exception of orca watching. **San Juan Island National Historical Park** has two units, **American Camp** and **British Camp,** and a visitor center in downtown **Friday Harbor.** Both camps are great for birding; British Camp is one of the easiest places in the state to see wild turkeys, and American Camp is about the only place in the United States in which to see the Eurasian skylark! San Juan Transit (1-800-887-8387) provides public transportation to both spots if you don't bring a car to the island, a big advantage any time the ferries are crowded. For details on birding the San Juans, see Mark Lewis and Fred Sharpe's *Birding in the San Juan Islands.*

Large parks in urban areas often act like an island, attracting many more birds than would normally be found in an area of the same size. One such urban oasis is **Discovery Park** in Seattle, a big favorite of Emerald City birders. An oft-quoted factoid is that half of the bird species found in the state have been seen at least once in the park. The visitor center is at the east entrance to the park at West Government Way and 36th Avenue. It is open from 8:30 to 5:00 daily and has maps and a bird checklist. The best area for migrating songbirds is near the north parking lot, reached by a short road from the east entrance and visitor center.

Park in the north lot and walk the road (usually closed to cars) to the Daybreak Star Indian Cultural Center. From here walk back toward the parking lot on the trails that go around the ponds (the north pond is largest) and eventually hook up with the **Wolf Tree Nature Trail,** a half-mile self-guided interpretive trail. Other trails in other parts of the park reach the shoreline, which is good for seabirds, waterfowl and gulls during fall migration and into the winter.

In northern Washington a lot of spring migrants actually stop to nest, and **Okanogan County** may have the highest number of nesting species of any county in the state. Good habitat is widespread. **Loup Loup Campground,** off State Highway 20 about halfway between Twisp and Okanogan, is known for a good assortment of nesting birds, including several owls.

British Columbia

There are classic hilltop migrant traps in Victoria and Vancouver. **Queen Elizabeth Park** is south of downtown Vancouver, between Main and Cambie. The weather greatly affects the birding here. When there are thick low clouds and it is cool the park can have many migrants, but it can be very quiet during warm, still, sunny weather. From Granville Street (Provincial Highway 99), go east on 33rd Avenue, which heads right into the park. The eastern side of the park has more varied habitat. The Bloedel Conservatory is a giant greenhouse with a tropical rain forest inside, complete with many tropical birds. **Stanley Park,** one of the largest urban parks in North America, is also an excellent spot for birds. In winter, waterfowl and seabirds are abundant, but during spring migration the trees around **Lost Lagoon** are often lively with migrating songbirds.

In Victoria there are two big hills near each other that are similar yet different enough that checking both is worthwhile. **Mount Tolmie** is near the University of Victoria. Go east on Cedar Hill Cross Road from its intersection with Shelbourne Street. Be aware that there is a Cedar Hill Road and a Cedar Hill Cross Road. In about five irregular blocks turn right onto Mayfair Drive, where there is a big sign for Mount Tolmie Park. You will be driving up the northeast slope of the hill to the top. You will want to go to the top to see what birds are there and maybe check the view, but the best habitat is the oak woodland you must drive through on the northeast side. Park in any of the parking areas and hike any trails that look inviting.

Mount Douglas Park, about $2\frac{1}{2}$ miles north of Mount Tolmie, is higher, much larger, and more forested. Drive north on Shelbourne and turn left into the park on Churchill Drive, then drive up to the top and park. There are two small peaks on either side of the parking area with slightly different views from each, so you might want to visit both. Look, and listen of course, down the sides from each peak. You can take somewhat roundabout routes back from the tops of the peaks to the parking area. After checking the area around the top, walk back down the road. A different group of birds can be found by parking in one of the lower parking areas near the entrance and hiking through the lush forest below. Both parks are very good places to see wildflowers in May.

28

Herps

Herps is a slang term commonly used by biologists for reptiles and amphibians. It is derived from *herpetology,* the study of reptiles and amphibians, which is in turn derived from *herpeton,* Greek for "creeping thing." That there is one term for the study of two distinctly different groups of vertebrates is a historical accident that adds to the high level of confusion about these two groups of animals. Amphibians really have as much in common with fish as they do with reptiles, and reptiles have more in common with birds than they do with amphibians. Regardless, the words herpetology and herp are here to stay. The word *herptile* has even slipped into print but is scorned by most biologists.

Herps have certainly been among the least-favored animals in human history. Even today in highly educated societies they remain mysterious, and the amount of confusion, misinformation and mythology circulating about them is astounding. Some are more acceptable than others. Frogs and turtles are generally considered cute and harmless, and lizards, as long as they're small, seem to be more or less tolerated. Salamanders, though, are borderline—maybe a bit cute but often considered repulsive. Several crocodiles (and alligators) are clearly dangerous to humans, so their unpopularity is fairly understandable. Nothing, however, approaches the worldwide fear and loathing of snakes.

There is a logical basis for some fear of snakes, for there are, after all, a small but significant minority of them that are venomous, and in some parts of the world hundreds of people die from snake bites each year. In North America, however, we have very few venomous snakes, and most of them are of moderate size and do not have highly toxic venom. Most modern Canadians and Americans hardly see snakes of any kind and very rarely encounter any venomous snakes. Yet fear and hatred of snakes is still very high. In every survey of people's attitudes towards animals I have ever seen, snakes are by far the most universally disliked and usually the most feared animals. Snake phobia is so strong and persistent that some biologists have argued that it is an innate part of our primate heritage.

Fortunately, we have little to worry about in our region. In the entire northwestern quadrant of North America there is only one venomous reptile, the Western rattlesnake. Western rattlesnakes are of modest size, rarely over 3 feet long, and are not very aggressive. On average, only a dozen people are hospitalized for rattlesnake bites every year in the Northwest, and only one person dies from a bite here every *ten years.* All one has to do is exercise reasonable caution when in rattlesnake habitat during the half of the year when they are active, April through October. Watch where you're stepping, don't try to handle any snake that you can't identify and don't put your hands under logs or in cracks in rocks. The Western rattlesnake tends to like rocky areas and open sunny habitats with scattered brush or trees. It is widespread east of the Cascades but on the west side is usually only found in the Willamette Valley and the valleys of southwestern Oregon.

Although it is one of the most interesting herps in the Northwest, the rattlesnake is only one of about sixty-five different species found in our region. Despite the number of different kinds, most of our herps are not common and are rarely seen. The best time to see them is in the spring as they emerge from hibernation or start breeding. At this time reptiles are active on sunny days, some amphibians are in their breeding ponds and frogs are calling at night.

Amphibians prefer cool, moist habitats, especially forests, so it's no surprise that the Northwest has a good complement of frogs and salamanders, mainly on the wetter west side. Reptiles, on the other hand, tend toward warmer, drier habitats, resulting in a small number of species in our region. The Northwest has eight native salamander species and is one of the world's centers of salamander diversity. Our reptiles, on the other hand, are basically all common western species that reach the northern limit of their range here.

Amphibians are the class of vertebrates with the biggest identity problem as a group. Everybody recognizes a frog as a frog (toad is close enough), but far fewer know what a salamander is or that the two are related and in a group called amphibians. One big reason for the confusion is the existence of the adjective *amphibious,* which can refer to anything that can live in water and on land. Hence, many animals that are not amphibians—alligators, turtles, beaver—are sometimes called amphibians because they are *amphibious.* Another problem is that salamanders look a lot like lizards, so they are frequently mistaken for reptiles.

Go into almost any freshwater wetland on a warm spring night and what do you hear? Chances are good you'll hear the familiar *rib-bit* or *kreck-ek* calls of Pacific tree frogs. The Pacific tree frog, also called the Pacific chorus frog, is our most conspicuous frog, amphibian and herp. These small frogs, just under 2 inches long, are widespread throughout our region from sea level almost to timberline. You've heard them call all your life because they are just about the only frog sound you hear in movies or on TV. This is because they live near Hollywood and are easy to record in big choruses. Though they're usually green, these little creatures can be gray or brown, so look for the dark mask extending from their nostrils to their shoulders and their little toe pads to confirm identity.

The other frog commonly seen by many people is the bullfrog, conspicuous by its large size. Unfortunately, when you see bullfrogs you usually won't see any other frogs because the bullfrogs eat them. The introduction of bullfrogs, native to the east, into parts of the West has been disastrous. Bullfrogs eat any creature they can swallow with their huge mouths, including fish, snakes, small turtles, birds (especially baby ducks) and other frogs. They have clearly played the major part in the disappearance of the spotted frog from western Oregon and Washington and are suspected of being a major factor in the dramatic decline of the western pond turtle and all of our native frogs. Bullfrogs were purposefully introduced as a new game species by state wildlife agencies and are still classified as a game animal regulated by state hunting and fishing regulations. If you or anyone you know ever ends up with a bullfrog or bullfrog tadpoles, *don't release them into the wild!*

The only other amphibian that is common and conspicuous in our area is the rough-skinned newt, described in chapter 32. The Pacific Northwest has twenty other species of salamanders, but they are so secretive and many have such limited ranges that most people never see them. If you spend time looking for them, or you move old rotten logs around in your garden a lot, you may find the long-toed salamander, the western red-backed salamander or the ensatina. If you spend a lot of time hiking in the woods on rainy days (or better yet, on warm rainy nights) you may be lucky enough to find a Pacific giant salamander, largest land salamander in the world and one of our claims to amphibian fame. The others are hard to find without damaging their habitat.

A very peculiar and unique Northwest amphibian is the tailed frog, the only frog in the world with a "tail." It's not actually a tail but a copulatory organ, making this unusual herp the only frog in the world with internal fertilization. Internal fertilization is an adaptation to mating in the fast-flowing streams that are the frog's habitat. Sperm would be washed away with the typical external fertilization characteristic of other frogs.

Since the Northwest is pretty reptile-poor, few are a conspicuous part of our wildlife. The most commonly encountered reptiles are the garter snakes. The four species (and numerous named subspecies) of garter snakes in the Northwest are difficult to tell apart because there is so much variation in coloring within each species. Almost all garter snakes, however, will have a light stripe down the spine, which is a dead giveaway that this is a garter snake of some kind. These snakes have many local names—water snake, red racer, and ribbon snake— in addition to the variations of garter such as garden, gardener and gartener. Having lots of names like this is usually a sign that an animal is very common. Like all snakes, garter snakes are predators and eat insects, worms, fish, frogs and (gardeners take note) slugs. Almost all snakes are beneficial from our standpoint because they often eat animals we consider pests. Garter snakes are completely harmless and are frequently caught by interested humans, but they will often try to bite, which is an ineffectual defense, and almost always let go with their extra stinky feces in a usually successful attempt to be set free.

The other two snakes you are most likely to encounter are the gopher snake and the racer (sometimes called the yellow-bellied racer). Both are widespread and common east of the Cascades and are found locally west of the Cascades in Oregon but are rare on the west side in Washington and British Columbia. They prefer open sunny habitats and are fairly tolerant of human presence if they are not harassed. They are often found around farms, pastures and sources of water that attract their prey.

The beautiful collared lizard is one of the Alvord Desert's lizard specialties.

Although widely recognized as beneficial rodent eaters by farmers and ranchers, gopher snakes are sometimes killed because they make a great rattlesnake impersonation. This may have been an effective defense for several million years but has certainly served them poorly since the arrival of humans, who seem to have a powerful urge to kill anything resembling a rattlesnake. The gopher (or bull) snake is the biggest snake in western North America and can be over 6 feet long in the Northwest. Although they may appear intimidating because of their size, gopher snakes are actually fairly mellow snakes and can often be handled. This is in sharp contrast to racers. Racers, as the name suggests, move fast and are generally high-strung and aggressive. If you try to catch one, assume you'll be bitten several times by a strenuously thrashing snake.

As someone who grew up chasing lizards in the Sonoran Desert, I consider the Northwest's lack of lizards one of the region's major drawbacks. In most of our area lizards are few and far between. Lizards like open sunny areas, so few are found in the typical forested habitats west of the Cascades. The most common, and often the only, lizard on the west side is the alligator lizard. This aggressive lizard is very distinctive and easy to recognize, although its two species are hard to tell apart. The northern alligator lizard is usually the only lizard found in dense forests.

In most parts of Oregon one can find western fence lizards and western skinks in the right habitat. These lizards range north into scattered parts of eastern Washington, and the skink even reaches British Columbia. The short-horned, sagebrush and side-blotched lizards all range through eastern Oregon and into the Columbia Plateau of Washington. The short-horned lizard is another of the few that reaches southern British Columbia.

Part of southeastern Oregon is the northern limit of the Great Basin, and there are four lizards common in the Great Basin that range into this part of the state and are not found anywhere else in the Northwest. These "Great Basin lizards" are the desert collared, longnose leopard and desert horned lizards and the western whiptail.

It's hard to write about turtles and not use the word "venerable." They live longer than any known vertebrate and are the oldest living type of terrestrial vertebrate in the world—having existed virtually unchanged for 250 million years. There are just two native turtles in the Pacific Northwest, although various others show up from time to time that were brought here as pets and set free in one way or another. Our native turtles, the western pond and the painted turtles, have both shown drastic population declines and are classified as protected and sensitive or endangered species in Oregon and Washington. As with most vanishing wildlife, the greatest threat to these turtles is habitat change by humans, although predation of the young by bullfrogs is a significant problem. It is to be hoped that the current conservation effort being spent on these reptiles will result in some stable populations.

Although generally ignored by most folks, many reptiles and amphibian populations have been severely affected by collecting—for the pet trade, for biological supply companies and for gung-ho herp collectors. For many species in the Southwest, illegal collecting for a thriving black market has become the greatest threat to their survival. Wildlife laws have been changing recently to provide more protection for reptiles and amphibians in much of the West. It is illegal to sell or trade any native reptiles or amphibians in Oregon, Washington and British Columbia without special permits. Laws vary from state to state and will change over time, but it is generally illegal to catch or keep most herps in our region without a permit from the state or provincial wildlife agency.

It is too bad that it has become necessary to enact such strict protection of reptiles and amphibians. One great thing about herps, unlike other vertebrates, is that most of them can be safely caught and examined closely, and then released without harm. Many can also be kept humanely in captivity for a period of observation and study and then returned to their original home. An important experience for many of today's adult naturalists was catching frogs, lizards or snakes as kids. It is now important to check local regulations before considering catching or keeping any native reptile or amphibian.

Hot Spots

Except for rough-skinned newts, there are no specific hotspots for amphibians. Those that are easy to find are widespread throughout the proper habitat and those that are difficult to find are too sensitive to disturbance to be listed here. Pacific tree frogs can be found, and heard, in just about any still fresh water from March to June. They are even common in flooded roadside ditches in rural areas. Bullfrogs are, unfortunately, also widespread and can be found in many ponds and small lakes. Salamanders can sometimes be found by hiking through our dense moist forests on warm, rainy spring nights with a flashlight or headlamp.

Reptiles are also hard to pin down to specific sites, except for the two Oregon areas listed below. Look for garter snakes in grass along the edges of thick bushes or forests on sunny spring mornings. They are also very common around fresh water. Other reptiles are pretty much a "see them when you see them" deal, but always be on the alert for snakes in sunny areas near water and lizards in rock piles when you are east of the Cascades this month.

Oregon

Southern Oregon has by far the best assortment of reptiles in the region. The two **Table Rocks** (chapter 14) near Medford, famous for their spring wildflowers, are also known for their nice complement of reptiles, reflecting the California affinities of these two "mesas." In the other corner of the state is **Malheur National Wildlife Refuge,** which has its own chapter this month, and the nearby Alvord Desert. Be on the lookout for garter snakes, gopher snakes and racers in any grassy areas near water, such as the trail up the Blitzen River from **Page Springs Campground.**

Lizards can be found in many rocky areas on the refuge (**Diamond Craters, Buena Vista Overlook**), but the lizard capital of the Northwest is the **Alvord Desert,** on the east side of Steens Mountain. This is where the Great Basin lizard specialties—horned, desert collared, leopard and whiptail—can be found along with the more widespread western fence, sagebrush and side-blotched lizards. The dirt road that runs up the east side of Steens Mountain, from Fields to State Highway 78, could well be called Lizard Lane but is instead unimaginatively named Fields-Denio Road. Several small dirt roads head east from this road, and driving and walking any of these could be productive, but the best-known is the road to **Micky Spring.**

About 2 miles north of the Alvord Ranch, the Fields-Denio Road makes a right-angle turn to the east, goes 1 mile, then makes another right-angle turn to the north. Right at this turn north, near a small tree an unsigned dirt road heads east. Take this road and drive slowly, getting out to hike around anyplace you spot some lizard action or that looks interesting. In about 6 miles you will come to Micky Spring, where there is a sign and small parking area. The spring is too hot for bathing, but there is a mini-geyser that erupts occasionally. This is a BLM Wilderness Study Area, so no off-road driving is allowed. Keep out of any posted areas near the springs. Collecting or otherwise harassing wildlife is prohibited in a wilderness study area. You can continue to explore on roads to the northeast and southeast from the spring. It is a good idea to call the Burns BLM office to check on road conditions and get any other pertinent information before heading out in this fairly remote area.

29

May Shorttakes

Upland Sandpipers

There are plenty of reasons to visit the beautiful high mountain meadows of **Logan Valley,** about 30 miles southeast of John Day. For active bird-listers, though, it is the best place in the Northwest, and probably west of the Rockies, to see the very local and uncommon upland sandpiper. At dawn from mid-May through June, the males of this small breeding population can be seen and heard as they stake out their territories in the lush meadows west of **Big Creek Forest Camp.** Conveniently for visiting birders, they often perch on fence posts and low snags where they can easily be seen. The Logan Valley and Big Creek, are about 20 miles east of Seneca on Forest Road 16.

30

A Closer Look: Bird Songs

Bird songs are the most complex, musical, and downright pleasant natural sounds that humans have ever heard. I would bet that a case could be made for birdsong being the original inspiration for human music. The two have a lot in common structurally, and some of the intervals and harmonies we find so innately pleasing in our music are present in birdsong. The sound of the clarinet, for example, has a harmonic structure very similar to the songs of thrushes.

Bird songs have been the most conspicuous and constant component of the ambient sounds of life on the planet since they evolved at least 100 million years ago. It's only in recent times that large numbers of people have become isolated from this experience. But it doesn't have to be that way. Even someone living in our urban centers will be exposed to at least fifty or so different bird sounds during a year if he or she spends any significant time outdoors. An experienced birder on a prime day in spring might be able to identify close to one hundred birds by sound in one day. Tuning in to bird sounds is a great way to tune in to nature and seasonal changes.

Why do birds sing? Almost everybody knows that it's the way they talk to one another, although some people will answer, Because they're happy. They may be happy, but we know that bird vocalizations serve as communication with other birds. Birds say different things at different times and to different audiences.

It is helpful to distinguish what are normally called "songs" from what are called "calls," even though the distinction is not absolute. In general, the word *song* is used for the complex, melodic, species-specific vocalizations made by birds during the breeding season. Songs are characterized by patterns of notes grouped into phrases that are repeated. Songs are made, for the most part, by male birds to identify themselves, defend a territory and attract a mate.

All other vocalizations made by birds are usually called *calls,* a catchall term. Different calls can be made by either sex, at any age, during any time of day or year, and can have a great variety of meanings. The calls baby birds make to be fed are very specific and appear for a very short time. For baby birds born in big colonies, their little peeps are identification badges, allowing their parents to pick them out of the hundreds of others the same age. Some birds make alarm calls that warn others of danger, some give calls that alert others to food, others make calls that gather the flock together.

In almost all cases, birds vocalize to communicate with their own species and for the most part completely ignore the sounds made by other kinds of birds. There are noteworthy exceptions, however, where another species has learned the significance of its neighbor's calls. The classic example in the West is the Steller's jay, the "sentinel of the forest." These common jays are well known for the raucous alarm calls they often make when there is an intruder in "their" forest. Other animals, mammals as well as birds, have learned to respond to these calls. The jays also seem to use this call to intimidate smaller birds and scare them away from bird feeders.

Bird vocalization is a fascinating subject and has been studied a great deal. Modern technology has allowed scientists to analyze birdsong in ways that were impossible only a short time ago. The details of the physiology and anatomy of sound production are fascinating. Birds have a unique anatomical structure called the *syrinx,* which produces all the sounds we call songs or calls. One of the earliest discoveries in bird vocalization no doubt happened centuries ago, when our ancestors noticed that chickens and ducks occasionally continued to cluck and quack even after their heads were chopped off. Though this was not a very precise procedure, it was clear enough to demonstrate that the source of bird sounds was somewhere in the body, not the head (or neck).

It wasn't too hard for early scientists, and cooks, to discover the location of the bird syrinx or "song box," as it is sometimes called to distinguish it from the mammalian "voice box." The syrinx is located right where the trachea joins the two bronchi, near the lungs. The location of the syrinx is an example of how much of the weight of birds is concentrated toward the center of the body for better aerodynamic balance. Membranes in the syrinx vibrate with passing air and can be controlled with sets of muscles, giving different pitches and timbre. Amazingly, the two halves of the syrinx can operate independently, allowing some birds to make two different sounds at the same time!

Generally, the more pairs of muscles a species has in its syrinx, the more complex is its song. Pigeons have only one pair of muscles and make very simple "coo" calls. Songbirds, which comprise well over half the birds in the world, have five to nine pairs of muscles, and some of the super songsters have the highest number. Vultures, storks and a few other birds have no syrinx muscles (or may even lack a syrinx) and can only make hisses, grunts or booming sounds. Some birds, like swans and cranes, have greatly elongated and folded trachea in their breasts that act as resonators, increasing the volume of their calls.

Do birds learn their songs or are they born knowing them? The answer seems to be that they do both. Like almost all behaviors, vocalizations are the result of inherited characteristics or innate factors interacting with the animal's environment. Bird songs appear to fit along a continuum from innate to learned. Some birds seem to have their songs "hardwired" in them from birth and will sing the correct song upon maturity if raised in total isolation from any bird songs. Other birds have to hear their song and practice it. Others are in between. Some birds are very flexible in their songs and mimic other birds as well as other sounds occasionally. The most famous mimics are parrots, starlings (including the my-nah) and mockingbirds. It is thought that mimics do not copy other birds in order to somehow fool them, but rather are just borrowing new material to add to their elaborate and changing repertoire.

Since one of the main purposes of songs, and of many calls, is the identification of the singer, bird vocalizations are an invaluable aid to bird-watchers. The vast majority of birds make distinctive sounds that can be used by humans to identify the bird. Most birders find that as they get more experienced, they use sound more and more for identification. Some birds are actually much easier to hear than to see, and there are other birds that are much easier to identify by sound than by sight (*Empidonax* flycatchers, for example). Bird sounds, then, should be given equal status to field marks as a tool for identification but are, unfortunately, often neglected in bird-watching classes and on field trips.

Unfortunately, most people seem to have a much harder time learning bird sounds than they have learning what birds look like. Maybe this is because we are visual animals and learn by seeing. It is also the result of technology. It is easy to have a good illustration or photograph of a bird in a field guide to study and review, but it is much harder to try to represent sounds and to store and use recordings. The age of the CD-ROM could have a great impact on the learning and studying of bird songs, but there still isn't anything that identifies sounds with the ease and convenience of a handy field guide for visual identification.

What is the best way to learn bird vocalization? I have found that nothing comes close to the experience of seeing and hearing the real bird singing in its natural habitat. When you hear live birds singing, you don't hear them in isolation, as through a set of headphones in a dark room. You hear the bird while you see its habitat, feel the weather, smell the air and hear other sounds. The bird's sounds fit into a big picture, and the other parts of that picture go along with the sound to tell you who that bird is. When I hear a new bird sound I try to find the bird and watch it sing. I try to establish a link between the sound and the visual image in my brain. I'll close my eyes and listen and try to imagine the bird I just saw, then open my eyes to confirm and reinforce my associated image. I'll do this over and over again, though it may take years until that sound is as familiar to me as the caw of a crow.

One handicap to learning bird songs is that most birds sing only during the breeding season. With migrants you may only get to hear the bird singing for maybe a month while it's passing through in the spring. This gives you plenty of time to forget what you just learned, and I find that every spring I have to relearn some songs I knew the previous spring. But those are fewer and fewer every year. Like learning anything, it just takes time and practice. Be patient, and get out in the field and listen as much as you can, and keep listening everywhere you go outside. You'll find that you're hardly ever without some bird sounds around you.

June

Notes

31

Nesting Seabirds

"Hey, do you guys know about the penguins at Cannon Beach? I was at the coast this weekend and there were dead penguins all over the beach!" These are common phone calls to the Portland Audubon Society every summer. People from the Portland area have seen, for the first time, a common bird of the Oregon coast—the common murre (pronounced *mur* as in murmur). They have seen an animal and have no idea what it is, so they give it the name of the only thing they know of that looks like the strange new beast. Birders and knowledgeable nature folk may laugh at an idea as wacky as penguins in Oregon, but these untrained observers have actually done a great job of matching an unknown object with the next closest thing.

The *alcids* or *auks* are a family of birds that are unknown to the vast majority of Americans. Alcids are considered pelagic, which means they spend their lives on the open sea, and are rarely seen except by avid birders and those spending lots of time at sea. Alcids are an example of just how much a bird can adapt to swimming and still be able to fly. In their extreme adaptation for swimming and living in the oceans, the alcids have only one rival group among birds, the penguins. What is fascinating is that these two quite unrelated families, penguins and alcids, are very similar in many ways and have divided up the earth, as it were, into exclusive fishing grounds. The well-known penguins inhabit the Southern Hemisphere and the alcids inhabit the Northern.

Both families of birds have many similarities: webbed feet; thick layers of fat; large preening glands; extrastrong rib cages to withstand pressure when diving; large salt glands; short, narrow, flipperlike wings; countershading and legs far back on the body. As with owls and hawks, penguins and auks are an excellent example of *convergent evolution:* Both groups have the same set of adaptations because they do the same thing. What they do best, among all birds, is dive deep and swim fast by "flying" through the water. The vast majority of swimming birds swim with their webbed or lobed feet—rarely if ever using their wings for propulsion. Auks and penguins, however, swim under the water by flapping their wings and using their webbed feet only as rudders or for paddling about when on the surface. This method of swimming allows these birds to dive deep in pursuit of prey. The common murre can dive over 500 feet, and the emperor penguin can almost reach 800! Among "foot swimmers," only loons can compete in this league.

How come all alcids fly and all penguins don't? It's an evolutionary trade-off—loss of flight for deeper diving. The bigger and heavier a bird the deeper it can dive, but the harder it is to fly with the small flipperlike wings required for deep diving. The common murre and the little blue penguin are the largest alcid and the smallest penguin and are just about the same size. The little blue penguin, however, is a bit larger than the murre and can't fly, while the slightly smaller murre can (just barely). The murre is apparently the maximum size possible for a bird that swims and dives and is also able to fly. The little blue penguin is just over the limit in weight and can't fly. These two birds can be seen as being in a transition zone of evolution toward the ultimate diving bird.

What advantage could explain selecting diving ability over the power of flight? Auks and penguins live in a band around the earth of about 20°–50° latitude away from the North and South Poles, respectively. That part of the Southern Hemisphere is 90 percent ocean, and the same chunk of the Northern Hemisphere is about 80 percent land. Since they live in such a watery world, being great swimmers has been very advantageous for penguins. However, it appears that flight is necessary when faced with a variety of land predators, as the auks are! Flight probably would have helped the one auk that could not fly, the now extinct great auk, when it was faced with that clever and most ruthless of predators, the human.

All alcids live in salt water, coming to land only to breed. They can be sighted from shore, but the most predictable ways to really get good looks at them are either by boat or by watching them at nesting sights that are close to land. In our region, three alcids nest on islands and offshore rocks and on a few cliff faces where they can easily be seen—the common murre, the pigeon guillemot and the tufted puffin.

Rhinoceros and Cassin's auklets also nest here but are primarily nocturnal and much harder to see at their nesting sites. The endangered marbled murrelet is another local breeder, but it nests high in ancient forests and is so hard to see nesting that it was the last bird in North America to have its nesting site discovered—in 1974. These last three alcids may be hard to see nesting, but they are regularly seen at sea most of the year. Rhinoceros auklets are actually common during summer in open water near some of their nesting sites.

Nesting in the same areas with these alcids are other seabirds that contribute to making the nesting colonies very lively, interesting places. Birds number in the tens of thousands at some sites! The word "seabird" doesn't have an official definition; it is generally used for any swimming bird that spends much of its life in salt water. Always included as seabirds are the families of pelagic birds, the tubenoses and the alcids. Usually included as seabirds are several groups that are primarily coastal—cormorants, pelicans, gulls and terns, and several groups that winter in salt water—loons, grebes and some waterfowl (swans, geese and ducks). Chapter 62 covers wintering seabirds in depth.

The seabirds that nest with the alcids along our coasts are the double-crested, Brandt's, and pelagic cormorants; western and glaucous-winged gulls; Leach's and fork-tailed storm-petrels. The cormorants and gulls are easy to see, for they are among the most common and conspicuous residents of the coast. The storm-petrels, on the other hand, are only present in small numbers in scattered locations and are nocturnal, making them among the hardest birds to find.

Some islands may have as many as half a dozen different seabird species nesting together. How can they all compete for the same limited nesting area? As is usually the case when there is competition for limited resources, the different species have all specialized a bit for slightly different nesting sites. The gulls like flat ground, guillemots prefer rock crevices, pelagic cormorants seem to hang on impossible cliff ledges and puffins dig burrows in soil. The brochure "Oregon Coastal National Wildlife Refuges," from the U.S. Fish and Wildlife Service, has a nice explanation of the birds' different nesting needs. In that regard, here is an important tip for finding puffins. Look for islands that have grass growing on them and look in the grass for the puffins. Since puffins dig fairly deep burrows (down to 6 feet), they need lots of soil, and if there is enough soil for puffin burrows, there is usually grass growing on it. As is usually the case on the West Coast, morning is best for viewing anything offshore, because the sun will be at your back.

In general, the breeding season for all these birds is from April through August, with June and early July being the peak of activity at the nesting colonies. Seabird colonies are very sensitive to disturbance and are all strictly protected by federal and state laws. In Oregon and Washington, 2,270 islands, offshore rocks and reefs are protected as national wildlife refuges, and human entry is prohibited.

Oregon

Hot Spots

Haystack Rock is discussed in chapter 38 on tide pools. It is an important nesting site for western gulls, pelagic cormorants, pigeon guillemots and tufted puffins, which usually steal the show. The puffins nest in the grassy area on the north side of the rock. If you are there during one of the days when the Haystack Rock Awareness Program is in action, someone with the program may know where to find the puffins—be sure to ask. You might find one right away, or you might have to wait until one pops out of a burrow or comes flying in. To spot a flying puffin, look for what appears to be a black football with a red tip flying through the air with small rapidly beating wings.

Cape Meares is about 10 miles west of Tillamook. In downtown Tillamook take Third Street west from U.S. Highway 101. Keep following signs for Cape Meares State Park, Three Capes Scenic Loop, or the Octopus Tree. Third Street will turn into the Netarts Highway and you will turn right onto Bayocean Road after crossing the Tillamook River. Stay on Bayocean Road as it winds along the southwest shore of Tillamook Bay, following the signs and turning left to head uphill toward Cape Meares. Note that just before this turn is Bayocean Peninsula, an excellent shorebird spot. You will get some great views of Tillamook Bay and the coast north to Neahkahnie Mountain, on your right, just before you get to the park. Cape Meares State Park is surrounded by Cape Meares National Wildlife Refuge, but you can't tell which is which. Drive into the park, and the road will end at a circular parking area. There is a picnic table, drinking fountain, rest rooms and some new interpretive displays on wildlife.

A trail goes to the Octopus Tree, an amazing old Sitka spruce worth a look. Most of the surrounding forest is old growth Sitka spruce and western hemlock. Opposite the trail to the Octopus Tree is a paved trail that heads due west to the end of the cape and the lighthouse. This trail goes through a younger Sitka spruce forest with dense salal thickets. All of the forested areas can be quite lively with common perching birds such as chickadees, nuthatches, creepers, juncos, white-crowned and song sparrows, winter wrens, warblers and varied thrushes. Occasionally you can see gray jays. Most people are flabbergasted to see gray jays, or camp robbers, anywhere else except in high alpine areas, but there is a small population in this part of the Coast Range, and Cape Meares is the best place to see them.

On the north side of the trail to the lighthouse are two lookout points with a fence at the edge of the steep cliffs. Go to both of these points for good views (with a scope) of two offshore rocks that will be densely covered with birds, mainly murres. Scan all the nearer cliff areas that have grass, and the water below you, for puffins. They nest in the cliffs under the lookout points. If you are lucky enough to find one perched on the cliffs, it will probably be the closest view you'll ever have of these delightful birds. If you can't find puffins on the cliffs or in the water, check out the other areas on the cape, then come back, or just hang out at the cliffs and wait. Often people first see the puffins when the birds come flying back to the cliffs. Keep your eyes open for the flying black football. You should also see most of the other summer seabirds, and chances are quite good that you will see the peregrine falcons that have been nesting here for several years. The short hike to the tip of the cape gives you some great views up and down the coast, and the historic lighthouse is usually open for visitors. You can have some good views of birds from the tip, but they are usually far away. The cape is also a great place to see migrating gray whales, and once I saw a huge sunfish floating just offshore!

Just south of Cape Meares is **Three Arch Rocks National Wildlife Refuge,** the first wildlife refuge in the western U.S. and home to the largest murre colony south of Alaska. You can see the rocks from Cape Meares, but you are too far away to see wildlife. To get a closer look, leave the cape and head south for about 2 miles on the Three Capes Scenic Loop to the tiny town of Oceanside (watch for a right turn into town). Drive through town and park at **Oceanside Beach State Wayside.** You can scope the rocks and water from the parking area or walk down onto the beach and get a bit closer. In addition to a couple hundred thousand birds, you will usually see some northern or Steller's sea lions on the lower rocks. Rosanna's Restaurant in Oceanside is the best within many miles.

Yaquina Head Outstanding Natural Area, just north of Newport, is described in chapter 38. Yaquina Head truly is outstanding; not only is it a fantastic seabird spot, but it is also excellent for seeing gray whales and tide pools. Enough superlatives? To see the seabirds, head toward the lighthouse and it will be obvious where the action is.

Near **Bandon** there is a chain of over a dozen offshore rocks, some with interesting shapes, names and stories. The most striking by far is Face Rock, which looks so much like the face of a giant looking up out of the sea that it can give you the willies. Legend has it that it is Ewauna, daughter of Chief Siskiyou, who was turned to stone by Seatka, evil spirit of the sea. Start at the **Face Rock Wayside** and work your way north on Beach Loop Drive, stopping wherever possible on the cliff top to scan the bigger rocks, like Elephant and Table Rocks. To get to Beach Loop Drive, turn right onto 11th Street half a mile south on Hwy. 101 from the big Old Town Bandon sign. There are no street signs at Hwy. 101 and 11th, but there are signs reading To Scenic Beach Loop Drive, State Park and Golf Course. Go west on 11th until it crosses Scenic Beach Loop Drive and ends at the tip of Coquille Point. This parking area, called Masonic Viewpoint (there is no sign) is one of your best views of the rocks. Face Rock is half a mile south of this point on Scenic Beach Loop Drive, and about a quarter of a mile north is a pullout near the Table Rock Motel, where you can get a good view of Table Rock. All of our summer seabirds can be expected here.

Washington and British Columbia

Unfortunately for wildlife watchers, there are no seabird colonies in Washington or British Columbia where people can get as close as to those in Oregon. The exception is for those who own boats, a significant number of people in the Puget Sound–Vancouver Island area. Private boaters have many opportunities to see breeding seabirds but must take care to stay at least 200 yards away from any rocks or islands with colonies or any evidence of bird activity. Just about every rock and island in Oregon or Washington waters is national wildlife refuge land and protected by federal law.

If you don't own a boat, you can go with the **Port Townsend Marine Science Center** (see appendix) on one of their cruises to view wildlife around Protection Island. An easy way to see some seabirds is from the numerous ferries. The **Keystone Ferry,** from Port Townsend to Whidbey Island, the **San Juan Islands Ferry,** through the San Juan Islands, and the **Tsawwassen–Swartz Bay Ferry** are considered the best for birds during the summer, although all are better in the winter. Be aware that traffic on the ferries can be heavy during the summer with people waiting many hours to get their cars on. Foot passengers, on the other hand, can always walk right on, and the fare is much less than for a car. Just over half of all the seabirds that nest in the Washington part of the Salish Sea, including thirty-five thousand rhinoceros auklets, nest on nearby **Protection Island,** making a Keystone Ferry ride the best bet for seabirds in June.

32

Newts

The rough-skinned newt should certainly be considered for the post of mascot of the moist forests west of the Cascades. It is common and widespread from the Coast Range near San Francisco through the entire west side of our region all the way into southeastern Alaska. It is by far the most conspicuous salamander in the Pacific Northwest and in many areas is the most common of all amphibians and reptiles. Rough-skinned newts are much more familiar to us than are other amphibians, because they are the only ones that are regularly active above ground, in the open, during the day. They are also commonly found in huge populations, as high as five thousand in one lake, making them pretty hard to miss.

Although they're common, newts suffer from the high level of confusion about herps in general. May people think they are lizards, and I've often heard people discussing whether they are newts or salamanders. A newt is a kind of salamander the same way a mallard is a kind of a duck. The easiest way to tell salamanders from lizards is to look at their skin. Like all reptiles, lizards are covered with scales, while salamanders have the smooth wet skin of amphibians. Rough-skinned newts, however, do look a lot more like lizards than any other salamander because on land they actually have fairly dry granular skin, which can appear scaly.

It is assumed that the reason newts can crawl around in the open during the day and are so abundant is because of their highly poisonous skin. Many amphibians have poison glands in their skin, but newts have the most potent toxin of any amphibian in North America. Any animal that eats a newt, including a human, will die, with the possible exception of some garter snakes. Many people are shocked to hear this because they have caught and handled newts many times with no ill effects. Teachers who have had newts as classroom pets are especially distraught to discover the potential danger from newts, widely believed to be totally harmless.

The danger of newt poisoning is actually very slim because the poison cannot penetrate skin and has to be eaten to have any effect. However, some people (including myself) have been mildly poisoned by handling newts and then eating without washing their hands, thereby transferring some poison onto their food. Newts *can* be handled safely—just make sure that hands are washed well afterwards and fingers are kept out of mouths, noses and eyes. Given the number of kids handling newts in the Northwest, it's astounding that there aren't more cases of poisonings and that newt toxicity isn't well known.

Like some other poisonous animals, our newts have a "warning color" that stands out and lets predators know that they are nasty to eat. The rough-skinned newt's entire underside is a bright orange, and when one is disturbed, it will

Newts are one of our most common amphibians. Although docile and many youngsters do handle them, you should be cautious of their poisonous skin.

often make an unusual defensive posture, arching its head and tail up and toward each other to show more orange color.

Newts are very amphibious amphibians and have distinct terrestrial and aquatic periods each year. As adults they spend most of the year on land in the leaf litter, rotten logs and soil of moist forests. When the breeding season starts, they migrate to traditional breeding sites in ponds, small lakes and slow-moving eddies and edges of streams. Newt migrations can be large, and there are areas near San Francisco with Newt Xing signs and temporary road closures meant to alleviate the slaughter of hundreds of amorous newts by cars. The males arrive at the breeding sites first and have undergone a remarkable transformation into an aquatic stage, which is characterized by smooth slimy skin, a vertically flattened tail for swimming and a swollen area around the cloaca. The cloaca is the common opening of the urinary, digestive and reproductive systems that is found in all vertebrates except mammals.

When the females arrive at the breeding ponds, they are often overwhelmed by a number of waiting males resulting in the "ball of newts" sometimes seen in early spring. Eventually, one male and one female pair up and go through a courtship routine that includes the male rubbing the female's snout with his chin, which has a gland that produces secretions to induce appropriate mating behaviors by the female. Fertilization takes place in a rather unique way that is very different from the "squirting gametes" style of external fertilization characteristic of frogs. After holding and rubbing the female, the male releases her and does a special walk in front of her on the bottom of the pond. She follows him closely. The male deposits a "gumdrop" of sperm, called a *spermatophore,* on the bottom of the pond, and the female moves over it and picks it up with her cloaca. She stores the sperm inside her reproductive tract and uses it to fertilize the eggs internally before she lays them.

Newts start their migration to the breeding ponds sometime between February and July, depending on the elevation and climate. This is a wide range for breeding dates, but these adaptable salamanders do range from sea level to just about timberline, over more than 20° of latitude, so there is a lot of variation between populations. During the winter and early spring you may come upon newts if you are hiking in forests during or just after it rains, certainly an easy thing to do in the Pacific Northwest. At lower elevations there is a lot of newt activity in ponds by April, with May and June being very lively. In the mountains, newts are common in shallow lakes in June and July, assuming, of course, that snow and ice have melted. Toward the end of the summer the adults and the recently metamorphosed young migrate onto land. In mountain lakes the young have such a short growing season that they may not change into adults until the next summer.

Oregon

Hot Spots

The rough-skinned newt is an animal so widespread that it's hard to name specific places as hotspots. Any shallow, quiet, permanent body of fresh water in or near forests and woodlands (and sometimes in grasslands) west of the Cascade crest is a good possibility for newts. The pond in the **Portland Audubon Wildlife Sanctuary** is a sure bet and a great place to visit in general. Maps to the sanctuary trails are available in Audubon House—a multipurpose visitor center, meeting hall and natural history bookstore. Audubon House is open every day from 10 A.M. to 6 P.M., 5 P.M. on Sundays. In northwest Portland, head west on Lovejoy and follow it as it curves to the right after crossing NW 25th (there is a sign here to Bird Sanctuary and Macleay Park). You are now on Cornell Road, which you continue on more or less west as it weaves up into the West Hills. Turn right at the stop sign, go through two tunnels and the Audubon sanctuary is on your right. Some maps still have the antiquated name Pittock Bird Sanctuary for the Portland Audubon sanctuary's location. The location is correct, but don't get the Pittock Sanctuary mixed up with the Pittock Mansion, a historical home and city park that is great for songbirds during spring migration.

Many lakes in the **Mount Hood National Forest,** near Portland, have good populations of rough-skinned newts. **Mirror, Lost, Trillium** and both **Twin Lakes** are some of the most well known. On the way up Mount Hood, the BLM's Wildwood Recreation Site has some good examples of newts using slow-moving side channels and meanders (of the Salmon River) for breeding, and this can be seen from the new Wetlands Trail (chapter 46).

Washington

West of Olympia is the **Capitol Forest Recreational Area,** managed by the Department of Natural Resources. Within this area is the **McLane Creek Nature Trail,** one of the department's few interpretive trails. The old beaver ponds on the creek, seen from the nature trail, are loaded with newts, as well as Pacific tree frogs and many other wetland species. Head west 4 miles on State Highway 101 from I-5 in Olympia and take the Mud Bay Exit. Take McKenzie Road south a couple of miles to Delphi Road, and then continue south just over 3 miles and turn right. While in the area, be sure to stop at **Mima Mounds Preserve,** another Department of Natural Resources natural area just 6 miles south of McLane, and a good spot for wildflowers and butterflies.

33

Mountain Birds

Because spring comes later in higher elevations, peak times for most natural events are different in the mountains than in the lowlands. Spring songbird migration and the onset of the nesting season are delayed a bit, making June an excellent month for birding in the mountains. Some of the birds seen in the mountains during the breeding season are year-round residents there, others are long-distance migrants and others are commonly seen in other parts of our area at different times of year.

Many birds that breed in the mountains move down the slopes into the foot-hills or valleys for winter. How low they go will depend on the weather and food supply; some years they may be very common in a particular area, but during another year with a milder winter, they may be scarce. Such "altitudinal migration" is common in the Northwest and is typical for juncos, varied thrush, evening grosbeak, pine siskin, mountain bluebird, Townsend's solitaire, mountain chicka-dee and Cassin's finch, among others. As the snow melts and more food be-comes available, these birds move back up into the mountains, and then they are in their breeding plumage and singing.

Some of our other mountain birds are actually neotropical migrants and come long distances to breed in our mountains. Good examples of these are the flammulated owl; calliope hummingbird; Hammond's, dusky and olive-sided flycatchers; most ruby-crowned kinglets; Townsend's warbler and hermit thrush (some winter here); green-tailed towhee; hermit warbler and western tanager. Then there are the *real* mountain birds, the ones who tough it out and spend the whole year, including the winter, high in the mountains. However, even these hardy birds will sometimes travel to avoid the most severe weather. Characteris-tic examples are blue and spruce grouse, several woodpeckers, pine grosbeak, rosy finches, raven and those two bold marauders of the high country, the gray jay and its cousin the Clark's nutcracker. Both these jays are often called camp robbers, although this name is most common for the gray jay. The gray jay, nutcracker and raven are the most noticeable mountain birds because they act like most members of the jay family—smart, noisy and bold. The gray jay and nutcracker are common companions of lunching cross-country skiers, and ravens do a lot of scavenging after humans also, but usually after the people are out of sight.

The Pacific Northwest is known for its coniferous forests, and where there are lots of trees you can expect those very important forest residents, the woodpeck-ers. About 60 percent of all North American woodpecker species live in the Northwest, so they are a common group of mountain birds. Three of our woodpeckers have a fairly limited range in the western U.S. and are not common, making them much sought-after by birders. White-headed woodpeckers can actually be easy to see in some locations. Look for them in ponderosa pine forests on the east slope of the Cascades. The two woodpeckers with three toes, the black-backed and the three-toed woodpeckers, live almost exclusively in lodgepole pine forests, where they are rarely common. Look for the trees with bare patches, where they have pecked off the bark.

Why are woodpeckers important? Everyone knows woodpeckers carve holes in trees for their nests, but what many people don't realize is that the excavating woodpeckers will usually use the hole only once, and then it's up for grabs by other forest creatures. Woodpeckers will sometimes even drill a hole that they never use, so there are even more holes to go around. These abandoned woodpecker holes are used by many other animals for nesting and sometimes for shelter. One study in eastern Oregon found sixty species of birds and mammals that used old woodpecker cavities. This makes woodpeckers very important members of any forest community.

Much of the forested mountain habitat in the Northwest is very similar from one place to another, so any of your summer travels in our mountains are potentially good birding trips. Just be on the lookout for good habitat and, of course, listen carefully. Check likely places early and late in the day. As usual, many of the most productive areas are along the edges where one habitat meets another. In the mountains this usually means openings in the forest cover around mountain meadows and areas near water.

Oregon

Hot Spots

The most reliable and easiest place in the world to see Clack's nutcrackers must be in the parking lot of the visitor center at **Rim Village** in **Crater Lake National Park**. The birds are always here because people continue to feed them despite pleas by the park staff. Please help out by resisting the urge to toss a few potato chips. Gray jays will sometimes hang around the lot also. Some people will find that seeing these beggars in the parking lot is not a satisfying wildlife experience and will instead seek them out in their natural habitat. Two of the highest trails in the park that are good not only for mountain birds but for wildflowers and marmots are the Mount Scott Trail and the Garfield Peak Trail.

About 50 miles north of Crater Lake is an area with over a dozen lakes within 40 miles, all accessible by road. These lakes are along the **Cascades Lakes Highway**, officially Forest Road 46, starting as Century Drive in Bend and eventually joining State Highway 58 near Odell Lake. The whole area is considered good mountain birding, but two places that stand out are **Crane Prairie Reservoir** and **Davis Lake**. Crane Prairie Reservoir is famous for its large number of nesting osprey. Davis Lake simply has a great variety of all the Cascade Mountains birds, plus some interesting waterbirds from the east side such as eared and western grebes and Forster's and black terns. Osprey are also common at Davis Lake, as they are at almost all high Cascade lakes. The north and south ends of the lake are considered the best birding. The Deschutes National Forest map is very helpful for exploring this area, which makes an excellent three- to five-day camping trip.

Near the touristy town of Sisters are two forest service campgrounds with good ponderosa pine forest that are known for all three nuthatches and for white-headed, hairy and downy woodpeckers, flicker and red-naped sapsucker. Many other mountain birds are usually seen, and a few vagrants have turned up at Cold Springs. **Cold Springs Campground** is about 5 miles west of Sisters on State Highway 242. The actual springs are to the west of the parking area and are a must, but be sure to check all habitats. **Indian Ford Campground,** also about 5 miles west of Sisters but on Hwy. 20, has birds very similar to Cold Springs. You'll always see at least one species at one campground that you don't at the other. They are connected by a good dirt road, Forest Road 1021, that travels from Hwy. 20 to Hwy. 242, east of both campgrounds. If I'm in a hurry and can only stop at one place, I always make it Cold Springs.

Washington

Mount Rainier National Park is one of the best places in the Northwest for seeing wildlife and flowers in summer. Two popular visitor areas give easy access to trails near timberline, where the high-mountain birds can be relatively easy to see because trees are few and short. Both **Paradise** and **Sunrise** have lots of visitor services and are centers for activity in the park, so both are quite crowded in the summer. Of the two, Sunrise has significantly less visitors, so it is a better destination for nature watchers. Special birds sought in the park are white-tailed ptarmigan and rosy finch, all sometimes seen on the Burrough's Mountain Trail out of Sunrise. This is also a good area for marmots, pikas, mountain goats and wildflowers.

Between Yakima and Ellensburg and to the west of them in the eastern foothills of the Cascades is **Wenas Creek.** This has been a popular east-side birding spot for many years, and the Washington Audubon Society chapters have a big campout here each summer. It can be reached from Ellensburg via Umtanum Road or from Naches via Wenas-Naches Road and Longmire Road. The route from Ellensburg is easier to describe and more scenic. Take Damman Road west from Ellensburg and it will turn south and become Umtanum Road. Stay on Umtanum as it climbs and goes over Ellensburg Pass. In about 20 miles you'll get to pavement. Go just under a quarter of a mile, then turn right and go almost 2 miles. Take the left-hand fork onto Dry Creek Road, which goes to Wenas Campground. There is a variety of vegetation from aspen and cottonwood along Wenas Creek to the ponderosa pine and sagebrush on the slopes, resulting in a great variety of birds.

The true birding potential of **North Cascades National Park** is not really known because it is a large wilderness park and simply hasn't been covered well. One speciality of the park in the adjacent **Ross Lake National Recreation Area** can be seen from the outdoor observation deck at the new North Cascades Visitor Center at Newhalem. From this deck you can look up at the cliffs towering above you to the north, on the other side of the highway. This is considered the most reliable spot in Washington to spot black swifts, a very difficult bird to find in the Northwest. Hundreds are sometimes seen circling overhead before dusk in June.

Farther east on State Highway 20 is an area with several trails leading into high country that has mountain birds, pikas and marmots. At **Rainy Pass** there is a major parking and picnic area with two trailheads. On the trail going south, it's easy to take as long, or short, a hike as you'd like. The 1-mile, paved and level trail to **Rainy Lake** is very easy and universally accessible. Farther and harder are **Lake Ann, Heather Pass** and then **Maple Pass.** A loop can be made back down to the Rainy Lake Trail for a total of almost 8 miles, an ambitious day hike. To Lake Ann and back is about 5 miles. On the other side of Hwy. 20, the **Pacific Crest Trail** heads north for 4 miles to **Cutthroat Pass** at 6,820 feet. Mountain goats are sometimes seen along this trail. The Cutthroat Pass and Cutthroat Lake area can also be reached from another trailhead at the end of a spur road that leaves Hwy. 20 farther east, near Milepost 167.

The highest road in Washington, and probably the most dramatic, goes to **Hart's Pass** and **Slate Peak,** to the north of Rainy Pass and on the edge of the Pasaytan Wilderness Area. This area is probably the only place in Washington where you could possibly see such northern treats as the three-toed woodpecker, boreal chickadee, Bohemian waxwing, white-winged crossbill and just maybe even white-tailed ptarmigan all in one day. It is also considered a good spot for migrating raptors.

British Columbia

Manning Provincial Park is another place like Mount Rainier that has it all for summer in the mountains and shows up repeatedly in this book. The subalpine area near Blackwall Peak is great for easy access to extensive subalpine meadows. For real alpine habitat and the best chance of seeing white-tailed ptarmigan and rosy finches, you'll have to backpack up to Mount Frosty, the highest point in the park and a 14-mile round-trip. Strawberry Flats and Beaver Pond both have an excellent variety of mid-elevation mountain birds. The park is a good place to see such mountain birds as pine grosbeaks, three-toed woodpeckers and boreal chickadees.

One feature that makes Vancouver one of the most attractive places in the world to live is the large provincial parks just north of the city. **Cypress Provincial Park** and **Mount Seymour Provincial Park** both have large areas of mountain hemlock forest and many desirable mountain birds like the pine grosbeak, three-toed woodpecker, red and white-winged crossbills, black swift and the regular guys like gray jay and blue grouse. The best areas in Mount Seymour are Goldie Lake Loop, with lots of wetland habitat, and Mystery Lake Trail, which also goes around Mystery Peak. Both leave from the same main parking lot at the end of the road. In Cypress the Yew Lake Trail and the Black Mount Loop Trail are favorites.

34

Butterflies

Butterflies have always been popular and a major subject of interest to naturalists. As with birds, there has been increasing interest in butterflies during the last few decades. Birds and butterflies are both popular for some of the same reasons. Both groups of animals are colorful, active, diurnal, harmless and have many common species that are easy to see. Unfortunately, one reason for the interest is increased concern over the fact that many butterfly species are showing dramatic population declines as their habitats are altered. There are about twenty species of butterflies in the United States now on the Endangered Species List, and there are many others to be concerned about. The Xerces Society was started in 1972 by butterfly expert Robert Pyle to promote the conservation of invertebrates and their habitats. It is named after the Xerces blue, the first butterfly in North America known to become extinct because of human activity.

As everyone knows, butterflies do not start life as a butterfly. All members of the insect order Lepidoptera (butterflies and moths) start as eggs and undergo a radical metamorphosis from larva to pupa to adult. The larva of all butterflies and moths is called a caterpillar, and all a caterpillar does is eat, poop and grow. Unfortunately, some caterpillars, as well as some other insect larvae, are called worms, which is confusing and about as accurate as calling a worm a snake. Worms are worms and are always worms—they don't change into something else. All caterpillars, like all larvae, eventually turn into adult animals that usually look very different from the larvae.

Once a larva has eaten enough it turns into a pupa, a resting stage when nothing seems to be happening but when the animal is actually undergoing a radical transformation into the adult form. The pupa of all butterflies and moths is called a *chrysalis,* but many moths spin a *cocoon* that surrounds the chrysalis for extra protection. The pupal stage can last days or months, depending on the species and its life cycle. Eventually the adult butterfly or moth emerges from the bare chrysalis or cocoon and pumps up its folded wings until they are fully spread, dry and ready for flight. Then off it flies to mate.

Adult butterflies have a different purpose then do the larvae. The adult stage is the reproductive stage, and mating and egg laying are the main activities. Some do not even have functional mouth parts and therefore don't eat. The bold, colorful patterns on the wings that we find so beautiful serve several functions. First and foremost they proclaim the identity of the butterfly and are important in courtship and territorial displays. The colors may also identify the animal as poisonous, as in the case of the monarch, or attempt to frighten predators with patterns that resemble eyes. And for many butterflies, wing coloration is camouflage to fool predators into thinking there isn't a butterfly there at all.

The conspicuous anise swallowtail is one of the Northwest's most widespread butterflies.

Adults have a long thin tube for sipping nectar instead of the munching jaws of the larvae, and this means you will find butterflies where there are flowers. Butterflies like sunshine and rarely fly in the rain, so you do not have to brave the bad weather to see them the way you sometimes must to see birds or mammals. From April through October, almost any place that has flowers will have some butterflies on a warm and sunny day.

Most butterflies die within a few weeks of emerging, but there are some notable exceptions. Many members of the brush-footed butterfly family (also called nymphs) can hibernate and overwinter as adults, living from early fall until early the next spring. The best known of these is the mourning cloak, which can be seen flying about on warm days in the middle of winter. Other members of this family that live through the winter include Milbert's tortoiseshell, and the saytr anglewing. Some species in this family will migrate to survive the winter, but the champion insect migrator is the famous monarch, which is known to migrate up to 1,000 miles.

The Pacific Northwest does not have a lot of butterflies. As with most insects, the species diversity increases the closer you get to the Tropics, and the cool, wet Northwest just isn't butterfly paradise. There are about two hundred species of butterflies in our region. Following are the most common and conspicuous.

In the lower elevations west of the Cascades there are forests and woodlands and lots of land that has been converted to agricultural uses and urban and suburban development. This is, of course, where the vast majority of the Northwest's people live, so the butterflies here are some of the best known as well as some of the most widely distributed. Swallowtails are the biggest butterflies in North America and because they are also very brightly colored it is no surprise that they are the most familiar. There are actually several kinds of swallowtails, and the two most common are the western tiger swallowtail and the pale swallowtail.

The other butterfly everyone has heard of is the monarch, famous for its long migrations. Monarchs are not common in the Northwest, but many people think they have seen them, mistakenly identifying any of the other butterflies with orange-and-black wings, such as the fritillaries, as monarchs.

The family of sulphurs and whites is widespread. Among the first butterflies to emerge in spring are the cabbage white and the distinctive Sara's orange tip. The cabbage white, introduced from Europe, is one of the few butterflies whose larvae are a major agricultural pest. Cabbage whites are adaptable and abundant in most of North America, sort of the starling of butterflies. A widespread and common relative of the cabbage white that is also an agricultural pest is the alfalfa butterfly or orange sulphur, the easiest sulphur to identify.

Many members of the brush-footed butterfly family mentioned above are common in western valleys. These include the mourning cloak, the painted lady, the mylitta crescent and Lorquin's admiral. The mourning cloak is one of our most distinctive butterflies and is easy to identify on the wing. Because it is a hibernator who sometimes comes out on warm winter or early-spring days, the mourning cloak is often the only butterfly around. The cosmopolitan painted lady is famous for being one of the most widespread insects in the world, being found almost everywhere.

Another big and particularly confusing family contains the blues, coppers and hairstreaks. There is at least one species of each type of these little butterflies just about anywhere, but they can be hard to see and are often difficult to tell apart. Blues are the most noticeable, with the echo blue or spring azure being a fairly common early-spring butterfly. Skippers are another large and confusing group that look a lot like moths. The peppy little woodland skipper is common in grassy areas, but telling the species apart is tough.

Because butterflies favor open sunny areas, they are not common in the thick coniferous forests west of the Cascades except around openings and edges. As you start climbing in elevation in the Coast Range or on the western slope of the Cascades, you start to see some mountain butterflies that are found at mid-elevations. The anise swallowtail becomes a common swallowtail here, and their close relatives, the parnassians, can be very common. Parnassians are noted for the unusual "chastity belt" that forms on the female after mating, presumably to keep out additional sperm from other males. Fritillaries are common in moist meadows and riparian areas. The great spangled fritillary is the most well known of this group.

Once you get above about 5,000 feet in elevation and start getting into the sub-alpine and alpine meadows, you will see a whole new set of high-mountain butterflies. The anise swallowtail and clodius parnassian will continue to be common, as will several fritillaries. Both California and Milbert's tortoiseshells are great wanderers that can show up almost anywhere but are seen most frequently in mountains, with the California generally at lower altitudes. The California tortoiseshell is famous for occasional population explosions that result in mass movements of millions of butterflies. Driving through one of these swarms can be hazardous as windshields become coated and roads turn slick with the smashed bodies. These two tortoiseshells are hard to tell apart and can be confused with their relative, the painted lady.

The arctics and alpines are characteristic of the high mountains, but these are small, drab butterflies that escape the notice of most people. The common alpine and the great or Nevada arctic are the most widespread species. In the Olympics, the North Cascades and farther north into British Columbia, Vidler's alpine and the chryxus arctic become common.

You would, of course, expect to find different butterflies on the arid east side, and indeed you do. Many familiar friends from the west side are here also, such as the western tiger and anise swallowtails, the mourning cloak, and the cabbage white. Out east, the Oregon swallowtail joins the anise, and several more whites, especially Becker's white, are common. The small tullia ringlet is widespread on the east side as are the wood nymphs. There are several checkerspots that are hard to tell apart and that are similar to fritillaries but lack the silver spots on the underside of the hind wings that are usually noticeable on fritillaries.

Blues are common in arid habitats and are represented by several similar species, and the common, acmon, lupine and silvery blues are all encountered regularly. There are also many species of the related coppers and hairstreaks, making this group very confusing and not an easy one for the casual butterfly watcher. Unfortunately, the exquisite, minutely detailed markings on these little beasts can only be appreciated by viewing a collected specimen.

There are enough names to get anyone confused. A good start for learning to identify these beautiful animals is that old standby Golden Guide, *Butterflies and Moths.* As is typical of field guides that cover the whole country, it has a strong eastern bias, but you can get a good idea of what the main butterfly groups look like from this inexpensive classic, which is one of the few books to focus on moths as well. The next step would be *The Audubon Society Field Guide to North American Butterflies,* by Robert Pyle, the best comprehensive butterfly field guide available. The disadvantage to this book is that it contains so many butterflies that it can be overwhelming. The butterfly section in Dan Mathews's *Cascade-Olympic Natural History* is an excellent summation of the mountain species, half of which are widespread in our region. Fortunately, Robert Pyle is working on a new regional guide, which should be available soon.

The moths get stuck playing second fiddle to the butterflies and are usually left out of butterfly books altogether! This seems illogical, given that there are usually *ten times* as many species of moths as butterflies in any particular area. Moths are very important because in their larval stage many are serious agricultural pests. However, it is easy to understand why moths are not as well known and popular as butterflies. Most moths are small, very plain and drab and nocturnal. Some moths, however, are very noticeable and merit mention.

The giant silk moths are the most spectacular moths but unfortunately are represented by only a few species in the West. Occasionally, people find the huge Polyphemus moth west of the Cascades, and if you are so lucky you'll never forget it. On the east side, the ceanothus silk moth is equally spectacular and is more common. The Pandora moth is smaller and plainer than most of its relatives but makes up for its looks by its numbers. These moths have a two-year life cycle and often show extreme population fluctuations. In July of each odd year since 1989 there has been a large outbreak of Pandora moths near Bend. This population may eventually crash, but was still huge in the summer of 1995.

Sphinx moths are large, very active moths often called hawk moths or hummingbird moths. They are noticeable because they often feed during twilight, hovering over flowers and making a humming noise with their wings that one can hear as they swoop past.

Hot Spots

There are not specific hotspots for butterflies as much as there are general guidelines for finding good habitat. The most important key to finding butterflies is simple—go where there are lots of flowers. All the areas described in chapters 14, 20 and 37 for wildflowers should also be considered for butterflies. East of the Cascades is significantly better than the west side for butterflies, for the best habitats are open and sunny. Particularly good habitats on the east side are in canyons and along riparian zones, places where there is moisture and a variety of plants. Open woodlands are much better than dense forests, which sometimes seem to be devoid of butterflies. As summer progresses, the action moves up into the mountain meadows, just as it does with wildflowers.

Oregon

All of the eastern Oregon mountain ranges (Ochoco, Strawberry, Blue and Wallowa) are equally productive where dry open forests meet moist meadows. **Big Summit Prairie**, about 40 miles east of Prineville, has been considered a good spot for years. In the southeastern corner of the state, near Malheur National Wildlife Refuge, is **Steens Mountain** (see chapter 55); the area around **Fish Lake** and higher in the alpine zone is best for butterflies.

In south-central Oregon, between the town of Lakeview and Hart Mountain National Antelope Refuge, are several areas that have been favored by collectors. **Warner Canyon** and **Camas Creek**, along State Highway 140, are good, as are the shores of nearby **Crump Lake**. North of Hwy. 140 is **Bull Prairie** and the area around **Light** and **Drake Peaks**, reached by Forest Roads 3615 and 019. Heading west from Lakeview to Klamath Falls, Hwy. 140 goes over **Bly Mountain Pass** about halfway between the little towns of Dairy and Beatty. There are a number of little roads heading in all directions around the pass that are worth exploring if flowers are blooming.

Open meadows and riparian zones in the Sisters area are representative of the ponderosa pine forest of the east slope of the Cascades. The shores of the **Metolius River** from Camp Sherman downstream are worth checking for mountain birds and butterflies, as is **Three Creeks Meadow,** about 5 miles south of Sisters via FR 16.

Washington

Hurricane Ridge in **Olympic National Park** and the **Sunrise** and **Paradise** areas in **Mount Rainier National Park** (see chapter 37) provide easy access for high-mountain butterflies. The highest road in Washington is the **Hart's Pass Road** described in chapter 51. The road up is a little scary, but the views are unbelievable. This is an excellent starting point for trails into the **Pasaytan Wilderness Area** and provides instant access to high-mountain meadows for viewing wildflowers and their attendant butterflies, as well as marmots and pikas in the rocky areas.

The riparian areas in the canyons near Leavenworth and Yakima are some of the favorites of Washington butterfly watchers. Icicle Creek is a main tributary of the Wenatchee River and joins it in the unique Bavarian-theme town of Leavenworth. Upstream on the Wenatchee is **Tumwater Canyon,** known as a great place to see spawning salmon in the fall (chapter 57) and a good spot for a mix of butterflies because of the mix of plants. **Icicle Canyon,** upstream from the Leavenworth National Fish Hatchery, is the same habitat but with less traffic and lots of little campgrounds. Be sure to stop at the fish hatchery in the summer, when there should be lots of fish to view.

The **Oak Creek Wildlife Area,** northwest of Yakima, is described in chapter 69. The road up Oak Creek Canyon itself starts just south of the elk feeding station on U.S. Highway 12. Just under 5 miles farther southwest on Hwy. 12 is the start of the Bear Canyon Road, which eventually connects with the Oak Creek Road. Both are good dirt roads that wind through some great oak woodland habitat with riparian vegetation along the creeks. This is an all-around great place for wildflowers and wildlife. It's one of the best places in the state in which to see the declining western gray squirrel. Spring and early summer are best because things get pretty hot and dry up soon in most years. Be sure to come back in winter to see elk and bighorn. Other good canyons nearby are the **Yakima River Canyon** and the upper parts of two tributaries of the Yakima River, **Wenas** and **Umtanum Creeks.**

35

June Shorttakes

More Wildflowers

June is bustin' out all over! Wildflowers that began in March and April continue to bloom in massive numbers through May. In June, the peak of flowering activity moves up in elevation. Three modest peaks in Oregon are famous for their June blooms. **Iron Mountain** is about 34 miles west of Sweet Home and just north of U.S. Highway 20. There is a well-marked parking area for the trailhead off of Hwy. 20. **Saddle Mountain State Park** is 12 miles east of Seaside as the raven flies, and they do, because they nest on the mountain. Reach the trailhead on a park road from U.S. Highway 26. **Humbug Mountain** is in **Humbug Mountain State Park**, about 5 miles south of Port Orford.

Stoneflies

An awesome display of insect abundance is the stonefly hatch on the **Deschutes River.** Stoneflies, locally called salmonflies, spend most of their lives as aquatic nymphs in streams. At breeding time, the nymphs climb out onto plants or rocks, their backs split open and out come the winged adults. The adults' only purpose is to mate and lay eggs; they usually die within a week. While they are present there is a feeding frenzy of insect-eating animals, from trout to magpies. Two stoneflies, one the biggest in America, emerge along the Deschutes River from about May 25 to June 20. The peak is usually between June 10 and 15. The best place to see this natural wonder is from the trails along the east bank of the Deschutes between the Hwy. 26 bridge at Warm Springs and the BLM campground and boat ramp 7 miles downstream, at Trout Creek Campground. Access to the trail is by rough dirt or gravel road at each end. From Warm Springs, take the small dirt road that starts just east of the bridge northeast about $1^1/_2$ miles to Mecca Flat, where you can park and pick up the trail.

American Shad

American shad were introduced to our area from the East Coast in the 1870s. Their numbers started to increase with the building of the dams. The slow water of the reservoirs that have contributed to the demise of Columbia River salmon have benefitted the shad. Once the Dalles Dam submerged Celilo Falls in 1957, the upper river became shad country, and the population exploded. Shad, like salmon, are anadromous, and during the peak of their run upstream in late June, sixty thousand may go through the Bonneville fish ladders each day. This "chrome tide" of the largest members of the herring family can easily be witnessed at the **Bonneville Dam** fish-viewing rooms on both sides of the Columbia.

36

A Closer Look: Songbird Nesting

The major activity of spring is reproduction, and we have already discussed some of the behaviors associated with breeding birds—singing and establishing territories. All this is leading up to the main event, the laying of eggs and the raising of young. Because all birds lay eggs, they are all faced with the same major problem: finding a safe place to incubate them. For most birds the solution is to build a special structure specifically for holding and protecting the eggs and, in most cases, the baby birds. This is, of course, a nest.

There is a lot of confusion about nests. Strictly speaking, a nest is a structure built by an animal for the sole purpose of raising its young. Nests are not used for anything else except breeding and are, therefore, not used at all for most of the year. Unfortunately, people commonly use the words nest and nesting in different ways, and most think of a nest as the equivalent to a home.

Birds aren't the only animals that make nests. Nests are made by members of all vertebrate groups, and many invertebrates as well. Squirrels make nests, but the big balls of leaves we usually see that we call their nests are actually shelters. Of all the nest builders in the world, birds are considered the champs. They build the biggest and most complex nests in the widest variety of locations and with the greatest diversity of styles.

Some birds do not build nests at all but just lay their eggs on the ground. This is true of many seabirds, shorebirds and some goatsuckers and vultures. Almost all other birds, make nests of some kind, even though these may be relatively simple. The master nest builders are the song or perching birds, the passerines.

Nests perform several functions. The main purpose of a nest is to hold the eggs and young and protect them from predators and bad weather, but to some extent it also needs to protect the parent bird from the same dangers. The nest can also be important for incubation because it acts as insulation, helping keep the eggs at the proper temperature. With their powers of flight, birds can put their nests in an amazing variety of places, and their main technique for keeping them away from predators is to build them where predators can't go. This isn't always possible, so birds also use camouflage. In other parts of the world birds use some neat tricks to protect their nests. Some build their nests near a larger predatory bird that isn't able to catch them but that can catch *other* predators. Some birds build their nests near, or even in, wasp nests.

The variety of materials used is pretty dazzling, especially when one considers that many birds have started to incorporate human-made items. I remember an oriole nest at Malheur that lasted several years and attracted a lot of attention with the orange, blue and green plastic strings incorporated into the design.

Probably one of the most unusual nests in our region is that of the Vaux's swift. This fragile shelf is made of nothing but little sticks and dried saliva, which glues the sticks together and attaches it to the inside of a hollow tree or chimney. The biggest nests in our area are bald eagle nests which can weigh 1 *ton.*

Each bird builds a very specific type of nest in a particular type of site, and nest-building behavior is innate. Birds will adapt, however, and can use innovative materials or locations when the need arises. There is almost always competition for choice nest sites among species, and laying claim to a good site is one of the main functions of bird songs and other territorial behavior. Nest sites may be selected by the female alone, as would obviously be the case with polygynous birds like grouse. In many species the male and female select the nest site together, and this process is an important part of their courtship. In many migratory songbirds the male arrives first and establishes his territory around a choice nesting site or sites. In some cases, such as that of the house wren, the males even start building the nest before the females arrive. What optimists!

If the female is going to do all the nesting herself, as do grouse and most ducks, she builds the nest by herself and does all the incubation. She's a single parent from the moment she mates. For most songbirds the typical pattern is the selection of the nest site and then the building of the nest by both male and female. After the nest is finished, the female will start laying eggs, usually one a day, until the clutch is complete. The number of eggs in a clutch is genetically determined, although there are cases in which birds will lay more eggs if food is abundant. The female usually does the incubating, with the male often feeding her in the nest so she can keep the eggs at a constant temperature. There is a lot of variation in this pattern, however, with many songbird parents working in shifts. Incubation for most songbirds is just under two weeks; larger birds have longer incubation periods.

Once the eggs hatch, the parent birds really have their work cut out for them, because the babies will grow to adult size in about two weeks. That means lots of food given virtually constantly during daylight hours. While the young are in the nest they are called *nestlings,* and when they leave the nest they are called *fledglings.* The parents will continue to feed and take care of the young after they leave the nest anywhere from a week or two to a whole year for some larger birds. Once the young have left the nest, the nest itself is history. Most birds will never use a nest more than once, and as soon as the young fledge they will have nothing to do with it. There are exceptions, such as large birds of prey, which use and modify the same nest for years, or some cavity-nesting birds, which may use a particular cavity more than once. So a bird's nest is not like a home; the birds don't want to be near it any more than is necessary because being there puts them at a greater risk of predation.

The nestling and fledgling phase is a period about which there is a great deal of confusion. Every spring, thousands of fledglings are found on the ground by people who "rescue" them. There are a few wildlife rehabilitation centers in the Northwest, the largest being the Wildlife Care Center at the Portland Audubon

Wildlife Sanctuary, where people can take these fledglings, but the birds didn't need to be rescued in the first place. It is very common for young birds to leave their nests just before they are able to fly, and many of them end up on the ground for a few days. Their parents will find them and feed them wherever they are if they are left alone. A common misconception is that once a baby bird is out of its nest, its parents won't (or can't) take care of it, and it is therefore doomed. When people pick up these fledglings they are not rescuing them, they are kidnapping them!

Of course, people who see a helpless fledgling on the ground want to help it, and most people correctly realize that the bird faces a high risk of being killed by cats or dogs, which are abundant wherever there are people. This period is actually when birds do suffer the greatest mortality, and many fledglings die every spring. If you find a fledgling and feel you must take action, try to get the bird off the ground as near as possible to where it fell. Sometimes you can find the nest and get to it, in which case you can put the bird back in, if you are sure it's the right nest. Since this is usually impossible, what some people do is mount a small box or empty margarine tub in a tree and put the bird in that. Sometimes you can find a crotch in the branches in which you can set the bird. The parents will find it and feed it. Do not put the bird where it will be in the sun. The idea is to leave the fledgling where it is, but away from Fido and Puffy.

Now you're thinking, If I touch the baby bird with my hands, its parents will smell my scent and won't take care of it. This has got to be one of the most widespread, persistent myths in America. Some people even believe that the parents will kill the fledgling if it has been touched. As far as we can tell, most birds have almost no sense of smell, so they can't tell if you've touched their baby or not. It is true that birds will sometimes abandon their nest or young if there is too much disturbance. But this will happen because of what the birds *see* and *hear,* not what they smell. So your touching the baby bird once for a short time will not have any influence over the parents' care of their young.

Another tricky situation between nesting birds and people is when birds build a nest where people don't want one. Barn swallows commonly build their mud nests on buildings, and Vaux's swifts seem to be increasingly building their nests in chimneys. The important thing to remember is that the situation is temporary. The birds are only going to be using that nest for about a month, and once they are gone, you will not be harming them by removing the nest. If you can wait it out, it will be over soon.

The preventative approach is best. As soon as you see birds starting to nest in an inappropriate place, start shooing them away, without hurting them, before they finish the nest and lay eggs. They will try to find another location. Once the eggs are in the nest, though, you either have to wait it out or have the deaths of baby birds on your conscience. Maybe by putting up some nesting boxes or similar structures you can attract the birds to areas more acceptable to you. Remind yourself that every swallow that nests in your yard will eat thousands of mosquitoes while it is there.

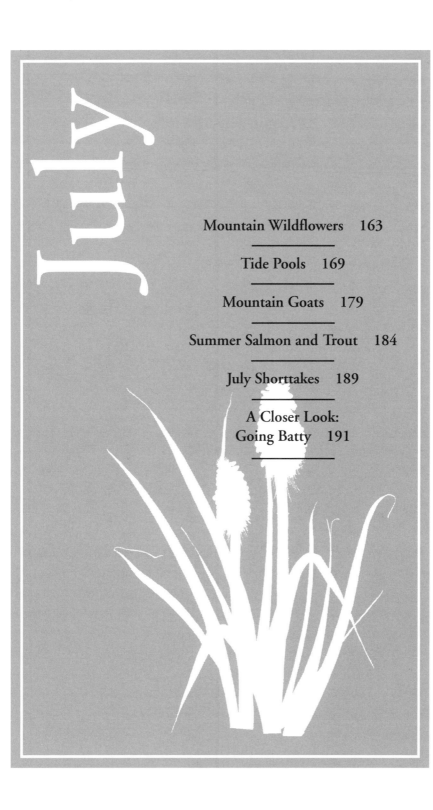

July

Notes

37

Mountain Wildflowers

Northwesterners have been heading up into the mountains in the summer for thousands of years. Native Americans moved up the slopes following game or other food resources, such as the many delicious berries with which the Northwest is blessed. Modern Americans head for the hills in droves for recreation—backpacking, fishing, climbing, camping, hiking, boating or just loafing around the lodge or cabin. We go, of course, because we can. Areas that present life-threatening tests of winter survival skills become sublime alpine paradises offering escape not only from the heat down below but from everyday life. Many backpackers live for the summer, when mountain wilderness becomes accessible and just plain pleasant.

There are many wonders and activities to be enjoyed high in our dramatic mountains during the three-month window of the warmest and driest weather, July through September. In a region of scenic superlatives, the display of mountain wildflowers has got to be near the top of the list. I use the term mountain wildflowers as a general term for flowers that grow from about 5,000 feet on up, in the regions formally called *montane, subalpine* and *alpine.* These words are used to describe the different habitats found around timberline, the region in which we go from the continuous thick closed forest (montane) to the completely treeless alpine tundra of higher elevations. None of these terms can be precise, because they all deal with a transition zone where there are no clean borders. What they all attempt to define is the result of the continuously more difficult conditions for life that occur as one goes up in elevation—the slope is steeper, the soil is thinner, the weather is more extreme.

The area that is most appealing for flowers are the meadows interspersed with small clumps of trees in the subalpine zone and the alpine meadows just above timberline. It is in these open sunny habitats where we see the explosion of flowers typical of plants that live where the growing season is very short. Just when any particular area reaches peak bloom will vary, of course, but count on the first plants blooming as the snow retreats. Some plants will even send blossoms right through the last thin layer of snow! For most of our region this means the best time for mountain flowers is generally from mid-July to mid-August. If you are planning a botanizing trip to a specific area, it is particularly worthwhile to get accurate and timely information about current conditions from someone familiar with the spot.

It's impossible to mention here all the common flowers one might expect to see. There are a number of books about mountain flowers of particular areas, but one of the best for the most common flowers in our region is the flower section in Dan Mathews's *Cascade-Olympic Natural History.*

Among the most common white flowers are the spectacular avalanche lily, beargrass, Sitka valerian, partridge foot, yarrow, pearly everlasting, western pasqueflower (conspicuous seed heads are also called tow-headed baby), white heather and American bistort.

There are lots of yellow members of the sunflower family that are hard to tell apart, but the most common are arnicas, groundsels, goldenrods and mountain-dandelions. Other common yellow flowers are sulphur flowers and other buckwheats, desert parsleys (another identification challenge), stonecrops, monkeyflowers and buttercups.

The red-to-pink flowers really stand out, and the various types of paintbrushes probably are most conspicuous. Others include fireweed, spreading phlox (which actually varies in color to blue and white also), Lewis's or pink monkeyflower and various louseworts and penstemons, a confusing group. Lupines probably dominate the blue-to-purple group. Others in this color range include monkshood, larkspur, Jacob's ladder, asters and fleabanes, gentians, bluebells and more penstemons. There is one very conspicuous and distinctive plant with green flowers—the corn lily or false-hellebore.

Oregon

Hot Spots

Oregon's only national park, **Crater Lake National Park,** has some of the great interpretive programs we've come to expect from our national parks. The **Castle Crest Wildflower Trail** is a short, easy hike that lives up to its name—many of the plants are labeled and there are brochures on wildflowers available at the trailhead (and at the visitor centers). Other trails in the park that are favorites with amateur botanists are **Annie Spring Canyon Trail** at Mazama Campground, and **Garfield Peak** on the south rim. There are ranger talks about plants and guided hikes among the many programs offered in summer. One of the greatest things about national parks, of course, is that you can go to a visitor center and ask about what you are particularly interested in and get up-to-date information (and maps and checklists) from the helpful staff, who are usually delighted to talk to someone about something other than where the bathrooms are. Many national park rangers are knowledgeable naturalists.

At the other end of the state is Oregon's highest mountain, **Mount Hood,** which is within Mount Hood National Forest. Circling the entire peak at about timberline is the appropriately named **Timberline Trail,** about 75 percent of which is in the Mount Hood Wilderness Area. Although the whole Timberline Trail is good for flowers because it winds in and out of subalpine meadows and forests all around the mountain, there are two really choice areas. **Cloud Cap Campground** is on the northeast side of the mountain and on the Timberline Trail (#600). This provides very easy access to the timberline region. Drive to the campground and head west on the Timberline Trail toward **Elk Cove.** It's about 5 miles to Elk Cove, which is great in itself, but it really doesn't matter how far you go because you start seeing plenty of wildflowers almost immediately. It's

Beargrass in bloom on Mount Hood—a summer floral spectacle.

nice to go as far as you can, though, because you will see a bigger variety of flowers, and the scenery gets more dramatic.

To get to Cloud Cap from the town of Hood River, head south on State Highway 35 (13 miles south of Hood River is the Hood River Ranger District office, an excellent source of maps and information). After $21^1/_2$ miles, turn right onto Forest Road 3510 and follow the signs to Copper Spur. Head north, then west for $2^1/_2$ miles, until you come to the Inn at Copper Spur, and then turn left onto Forest Road 3512, and continue to follow signs to Copper Spur and Cloud Cap. At the next two forks keep to the right and follow the signs to Cloud Cap. The dirt road gets pretty narrow and rough for the last mile or so, but a passenger car can make it just fine if you take it easy. The parking area and sign for Trail #600 are easy to find.

Almost directly opposite Cloud Cap on the other side of the peak is **Paradise Park**, which is most easily reached by hiking 5 miles west on the Timberline Trail from Timberline Lodge. This is a popular backpacking destination and gets a lot more traffic than the northern side of the wilderness area.

Washington

On the southeastern slope of **Mount Adams**, in Tract D of the Yakima Indian Reservation, is **Bird Creek Meadows**. This is where I saw the most awesome display of mountain flowers in my life. Trails into the area originate at **Bird Lake**, which has a large camping area managed by the Yakimas. For years there has been a $5 per vehicle day-use fee and a $10 per day fee for camping at Bird Lake, so be sure you have some cash.

Bird Creek Meadows

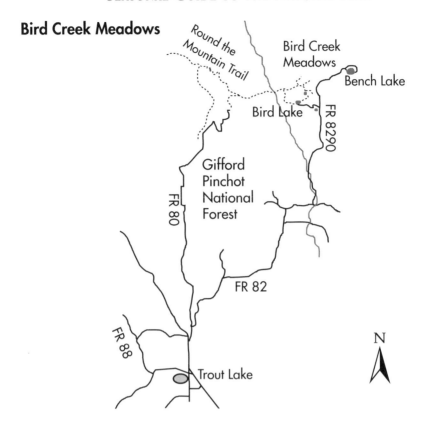

Getting to Bird Lake and knowing where to go when you get there are a bit tricky, so get the best map available. The forest service's *Mount Adams Wilderness* map was best for the trails in 1995. To get to Bird Lake from the town of Trout Lake, head north on the main road out of town, which is called the Mount Adams Road or Mount Adams Recreation Area Road, but which does not always have signs. In about a mile the road will curve to the right, where it intersects Forest Road 23 to Randle. Stay on the main road as it curves to the right. Stay to the right on the main road again in about half a mile, at the intersection with Forest Road 80. In a couple of miles you will enter Gifford Pinchot National Forest, and the road you are on becomes Forest Road 82 and turns to gravel. Stay on FR 82 and follow signs to Bird Creek Meadows. Just as the road enters Tract D it becomes Forest Road 8290. In about $3^1/_2$ miles after entering Yakima land you will come to Mirror Lake; turn left and head west just over half a mile to Bird Lake. These roads have changed in the last few years, so contact the Mount Adams Ranger District office in Trout Lake for current information.

From the southwest end of Bird Lake is the trailhead for the **Crooked Creek Falls Trail,** which goes north to meet the **Round the Mountain Trail.** From this junction there are wonderful wildflower meadows to the east and west on the Round the Mountain Trail for a couple of miles. Bird Creek Meadows proper is to the east. If you go west, you will go into the Mount Adams Wilderness Area (in the Gifford Pinchot National Forest), where backpack camping is permitted (the Yakimas do not want people camping on reservation land outside of their developed campgrounds). A slightly shorter hike can be made by going to the northwest corner of Bird Lake and taking the trail to **Bluff Lake** and then heading northwest into the heart of the meadows. A great loop can be made by combining these two. Bird Creek Meadows does not open until July 1 and is usually at its best at the very end of July or the beginning of August.

Washington's two well-known national parks, **Olympic** and **Mount Rainier,** are both famous for mountain wildflowers. Mount Rainier National Park has two areas that are very accessible—too accessible for the welfare of the plants. **Paradise** and **Sunrise** are both major visitor sites with visitor centers and services, and both have suffered from being loved to death. Fortunately, visitor awareness of the problem is increasing significantly, and some volunteer groups have been heavily involved in revegetating some damaged areas. It is very important in high-use areas like these to stay on established trails and follow all regulations. Between the two areas, Paradise gets significantly heavier use. Mount Rainier gets lots of weekend use from the Puget Sound metropolitan area, making midweek trips desirable. Both areas are easy to find with a park map, and there are rangers to ask for suggestions of the best current flower spots.

Hurricane Ridge on the northern end of Olympic National Park, offers some great wildflowers, as well as opportunities to observe Olympic marmot and deer. Hurricane Ridge is a major tourist attraction 17 miles south of Port Angeles. On the way, you will pass the park's main visitor center and two spots described for spring wildflowers in chapter 20. On a clear day, views from the road and the top of the ridge are spectacular. There are daily interpretive programs in summer, some highlighting wildflowers, as well as some exhibits and services. *Guide to Hurricane Ridge,* by Charles Stewart, for sale in the gift shop, is a nice little guide to the area and features the most common plants and animals.

British Columbia

There is widespread agreement that on the mainland of southwestern British Columbia the best alpine flower spot is **Manning Provincial Park,** 135 miles east of Vancouver. Provincial Highway 3 runs through the park, and the two other roads in the park head in different directions from the visitor center and lodge area. Both go to fabulous wildflower areas. A paved road heads from Hwy. 3 to **Cascade Lookout,** and a gravel road continues to **Blackwall Peak.** From here, trails wander through a subalpine meadow area of almost 50 square miles! There is the self-guided **Paintbrush Nature Trail,** as well as guided walks based at the Naturalist's Hut. These are the most accessible and some of the most extensive subalpine meadows in all British Columbia.

Just across Hwy. 3 from the road to Blackwall Peak is the road to **Strawberry Flats.** The road ends at the Strawberry Flats parking area, and from here a trail winds through the flats and up to the **Three Falls Trail.** Strawberry Flats is lower and more lush than Blackwall Meadows and is famous for its diversity. About 150 different species of wildflowers have been found in the 12-acre area. Peak blooming time for both areas is mid-July into August, and Strawberry Flats is a bit earlier than Blackwall. But don't worry, at any time during this period there will be more than enough to keep you busy if you start trying to identify all you see!

Garibaldi Provincial Park is much closer to Vancouver and also has outstanding mountain meadows, but they require considerably more effort to see. The area is ideal, however, for backpacking and botanizing. The **Black Tusk** is a 7,600-foot rock "fang" sticking up over Garibaldi Lake. Around its southern base are extensive meadows that are well known for their dazzling display of mountain wildflowers toward the end of July. The trail to Black Tusk starts at the Rubble Creek parking area. The short road to the parking area joins Provincial Highway 99, 22 miles north of Squamish near the dam for Daisy Lake. About $3^1/_2$ miles up the trail is a junction. The right fork goes to the camping area on the shore of **Garibaldi Lake** in just under 2 miles. From here a trail heads north into the meadows. The left fork leads to Taylor Meadows (in another mile), and provides more direct access to the meadows. At both camping areas there are a few shelters. This area can be seen in a long day hike (10 miles round-trip), but wouldn't you really rather wake up in the meadows and have a whole day to explore? By the way, the Black Tusk is a popular climb with incredible views, but it is for experienced climbers only.

Strathcona Provincial Park is British Columbia's oldest provincial park, and the biggest one on Vancouver Island by a long shot. Most of the park is total wilderness without trails, an unusual situation for many Americans to experience. Strathcona has two main trails noted for flowers, **Marble Meadows** and, appropriately, **Flower Ridge.** Unfortunately, the trailhead for the Marble Meadows Trail is in the Phillips Creek marine campground, on the other side of Butte Lake from the road. If you don't have a boat, you're out of luck unless you can get a ride from another vacationer who does.

The Flower Ridge Trail is accessible from Butte Lake Road near its southern end. The trail climbs steeply for $3^1/_2$ miles into the alpine zone. It then continues for another $3^1/_2$ miles. Two short and easy nature trails with flowers typical of lower-elevation forests are **Lupin Falls** and **Wild Ginger,** both right off the main park road.

38

Tide Pools

Few people have had direct experience with life in the vast oceans, but one place where we can come into contact with the marine world is where the oceans meet the land—the seashore. When the tide goes out, this area between land and ocean reveals a wondrous sample of marine life that is easily accessible to land dwellers.

This is the *intertidal* zone, the land between the tides. Although it is in many ways one of the harshest environments on earth, the intertidal zone is packed with an astounding variety of plant and animal life that has adapted to the daily changes in temperature, moisture, oxygen, food availability and predation. It is dominated by invertebrates and algae, life-forms unfamiliar to most humans. But many cultures throughout the world and throughout history have relied on this ecosystem for food and special materials. Peering into a tide pool is like looking through a window into another world, and exploring the intertidal zone can be a fun and very rewarding outing for people of all ages.

Tides are caused by the pull of the moon's and the sun's gravitational fields on the earth and its oceans. Because the earth rotates while the moon orbits, a point on earth will experience two high tides and two low tides every 24 hours and 50 minutes. This difference of 50 minutes is the reason why the tides do not occur at the same time every day.

An important characteristic of tidal cycles that causes some confusion is the difference between *spring tides* and *neap tides*. When the earth, moon and sun are arranged in a straight line with one another (at the new and full moons), the difference between high and low tides is at its greatest—high tides are at their highest and low tides are at their lowest. These extreme tides, both high and low, are called spring tides (from the verb for jumping) and occur every month, not just in the spring. When the moon is at right angles to a line between the sun and the earth, there is less difference between low and high tides and these more equal tides are called the neap tides. It is during the spring tides that you want to go looking for life in the intertidal zone.

Tides vary greatly from place to place depending on many factors. On our Pacific Coast we usually have very clearly defined sets of tides—two unequal high tides and two unequal low tides every day (approximately), and two sets each of spring tides and neap tides each month. During part of every set of spring tides, one of the two low tides each day will be a "minus" tide, below the average low-tide level. It is these minus tides that provide the golden opportunities for finding the greatest variety of intertidal life because the greatest area is then exposed. During the wintery half of the year most minus tides are at night.

It is from April through September that most minus tides occur during daylight hours and most of the lowest tides of the year occur.

In order to plan when to go tidepooling, get a tide table for the area in which you're interested. Tide tables are available from many different sources. It is quite common for sporting goods stores, charter-boat companies, motels and chambers of commerce in coastal towns to have tide tables for their area printed for free distribution. Get one for the current year and look for the days with minus tides occurring at convenient times. Some tide tables highlight the minus tides, making it very easy to find the best days and times for exploring the intertidal zone.

Canadian tide tables use a different datum, or zero point, that is $2^1/_2$ feet lower than that used in the United States. This means that if you are using a Canadian tide table, any tides below $+2^1/_2$ feet will be the same as minus tides in the United States and will be great for tidepooling.

Rocky shores provide the best opportunities for viewing intertidal life. Exploring these areas is often called tidepooling, even though most of the area is not actually made up of tide pools but consists of ledges, boulders, vertical rock faces and crevices. One of the first things many people notice when viewing a rocky intertidal area during a minus tide is the bands or layers of different living things at different heights. Each zone has characteristic animals and plants, and once you know which zone you are in, you will know what organisms to expect. We'll keep the terminology simple with "high-tide zone," "midtide zone," and "low-tide zone."

The distribution of organisms within the intertidal zone is the result of complex interactions between many things. An organism's tolerance of changes in temperature, moisture and oxygen availability, as well as of other physical factors like wave action and substrate, are some of the more obvious influences. Often more subtle and harder to study are the interactions between organisms, such as predator-prey relationships and competition between similar species for the same resources.

Let's take a quick look at some of the most obvious animals found in the three zones. These animals are common and conspicuous in most rocky intertidal areas that get some direct wave action. This is just a general guide, of course, and there will be variation from place to place. Protected waters, such as in the Salish Sea, will vary considerably, and some organisms will not be present. There are many good books to aide you in your intertidal journey of discovery (several are listed in the bibliography). One of the best beginning guides, and a good bargain, is the booklet *Plants and Animals of Oregon's Rocky Intertidal Habitat,* available from the main headquarters of the Oregon Department of Fish and Wildlife for $4 (postpaid). It includes a listing of all the better tidepooling areas in the state.

The highest parts of the intertidal zone receive water only occasionally, and there are few marine animals that can survive there. The most conspicuous are the small acorn barnacles that often cover large areas by the thousands in tightly packed mats. When out of the water they appear quite dead, but if you get a chance to see them covered by water in a pool, you may observe them extend their feathery feet out of their shells and sweep them through the water to gather food. Although they have shells and look like mollusks, they are actually crustaceans, like their relatives the shrimp. A barnacle starts life as a free-swimming "shrimpy" larva but then finds a suitable place and attaches itself there by its head, using the original "super glue." The barnacle then starts growing the plates of shell that will protect it for the rest of its life.

Of course, predators are never far away. Among the acorn barnacles you will usually find their main predator—dogwinkles or rock whelks of several species. Rock whelks (genus *Nucella*) have an elongated shell of about an inch long, usually with distinct striping. These snails drill a hole in a barnacle's shell, squirt digestive juices inside, and then suck out the contents. These snails are known for their characteristic eggs, called "sea oats," and for a high incidence of cannibalism.

Also found in this highest zone are different kinds of limpets, another mollusk with a very different lifestyle. Limpets have one shell that looks like a little volcano and are very slow-moving vegetarians, much more like the snails we find in our gardens than the ferocious rock whelks.

The small shore crabs become quite abundant below the barnacles and range from the high- into the midtide zone. During low tides in the daytime, shore crabs remain hidden in nooks and crannies in rocks or among mussels and may be hard to see at first. Sometimes you'll see them scurry for cover as you approach a tide pool. At night they are out and active on exposed rocks and in the water, nibbling on seaweed and playing an important role as scavengers. Another small crab, the porcelain crab, can normally be found by looking carefully under rocks. This distinctive crab is recognized by its uniquely flattened body and large claws.

The black turban snail is the most common and conspicuous snail in the high-tide zone in areas with significant wave action. The shell is quite spherical and dark black when wet, dingy gray when dry. We would expect turban snails to be as slow as limpets because they are also vegetarians that scrape algae off rocks. But these snails often wander into lower zones where sea stars try to eat them, and apparently they can move very fast, for a snail, in escaping from this predator.

The midtide zone is marked by a very distinctive animal community that often makes the most clearly defined band in the intertidal area. This community is dominated and defined by the California mussel and the goose (or gooseneck) barnacle, but both must have wave action and are not found in more protected waters. In good habitat, the California mussel forms huge clusters, called mussel beds, covering large areas of rock. The goose barnacle is usually scattered irregularly through the mussel beds in smaller clumps. Both animals are sedentary filter feeders but use quite different feeding techniques.

Like all other bivalve mollusks, mussels draw water into their bodies through a siphon. The water passes over the gills, which remove oxygen from the water but which also are covered with a layer of sticky mucus. Particles of food in the water become stuck in the mucous layer, which slowly moves across the gills and into the mussel's mouth. The used water is sent out the exit siphon. Instead of bringing the water into their bodies as mussels do, barnacles stick their highly modified legs, called *cirri,* out of their shells and wave them through the water, catching the same types of small food particles, which are then scraped off the feathery cirri into the mouth. Barnacles have no gills, so it is assumed that oxygen is absorbed by the cirri. Both animals have the same adaptation for being left high and dry by the low tide—close up the shell and wait it out.

Mussel beds are a major food resource for anything that can get inside the shells. Humans have been a major consumer of mussels for millennia, and the California mussel is prized for its taste. The mussels' worst nightmares, however, are the sea stars or "starfish" (they are no more a fish than we are). Sea stars are uniquely adapted to eating bivalves because of their amazing hydraulic system of tube feet and their bizarre technique of extruding their stomach out of their bodies and into the pulled-open shells of their prey, where most digestion takes place. The most conspicuous sea star by far is the ochre or common sea star. Don't be fooled by all the different colors of this fairly large (up to 1 foot in diameter) sea star. It comes in orange, purple and brownish tones but all are of the same species, with different color variations. These stars range into different tidal zones but are usually concentrated at the lower edges of the mussel beds. Indeed, they cause the edges like the browse lines made by cows on trees.

The midtide zone is loaded with a variety of mollusks. There are many different kinds of snails, limpets and chitons. Check snail shells carefully; some will contain hermit crabs instead of the original owners. Chitons are fairly flat and oval-shaped and have eight interlocking plates in their shells instead of the much more common one or two. You usually have to look closely to find chitons because of their protective coloration and hiding habits. The easiest to spot is the large black chiton (also called leather chiton or black katy). This bold chiton is out in the open more than others and is easy to identify because its *girdle* (the soft stuff) covers all of its plates except for a row of roughly diamond-shaped patches in the middle of its back.

The next distinct band of animals, and the border with the low-tide zone, consists of two sea anemones, relatives of jellyfish and coral. The aggregating anemone is about an inch in diameter and lives in huge groups, which are all clones, sometimes completely covering a rock. When they close up during low tide, sand and shell fragments are usually stuck to them, making them easy to overlook. Once you recognize them, though, you'll be astounded at their numbers. When open, they have pink in their tentacles.

Found lower in the low-tide zone than the aggregating anemone is the handsome green anemone, one of the world's largest anemones. Big specimens can reach a foot across, but half that is the norm. These are often seen completely opened up in tide pools and can be fed small crabs, snails or mussels. Their tentacles push the food into the digestive cavity, and they digest all the good stuff and spit out the shells. If you gently rub your fingers on the tentacles you will feel a strange stickiness caused by stinging cells firing into your skin, which is fortunately tough enough to prevent them from penetrating. The green color comes from algae living inside the anemone's body, a relationship of apparently mutual benefit.

Found with or below the green anemones in some areas are two sea urchins, the purple and the red. The red sea urchin is really an animal from below the tidal zone and is not common. The purple urchin, in contrast, can be very abundant and can completely line the sides of some tide pools. These mellow algae grazers will actually carve out little depressions in the rocks, in which many generations may live. Sometimes a small urchin will enter one of these pits and then grow too large to get out the opening, trapping itself forever. But that's no problem, for as long as it gets enough food it's as happy as, well, as happy as a sea urchin in a sea urchin pit!

There are many animals in the low-tide zone, but they require some searching to find. The most famous are the gumboot chiton and the nudibranchs. At a length of a foot, the gumboot or giant Pacific chiton is the largest chiton in the world. This behemoth's plates are completely covered by its bumpy, dark orange girdle. Nudibranchs, or sea slugs, are the jewels of the tide pool—delicate, often brightly colored and hard to find. The most commonly seen is also the most common in appearance, the sea lemon. This bright yellow fellow, a couple of inches long, looks just like a piece of its namesake.

Intertidal Etiquette

Hot Spots

Naturalists, resource managers and marine biologists throughout our region are extremely concerned about human impact on intertidal areas. Intertidal habitats may well be the most sensitive areas listed in this book. Please observe proper intertidal etiquette when you visit these areas:

1. Do not collect any living organisms. Look at them where they are and don't remove anything.

2. Do your best not to step on any plants or animals. Step on bare rock or sand.

3. Do not remove animals attached to the rocks. A few animals, such as hermit crabs, can be picked up gently from the bottom of pools, but if you have to use any force, don't do it; you can damage the animal.

4. Don't move animals from one place to another. If you do pick up something, put it back exactly where you got it, and without delay.

5. If you look carefully under seaweed or rocks, return them gently to their original positions.

6. As always, remove any litter when possible.

Note that many biologists and managers feel that people visiting intertidal areas should not touch anything, including disturbing rocks in any way. Some areas, such as marine gardens and national parks, are legally protected from all disturbance.

Tidepools near Cape Perpetua.

In addition, be very careful about your own, and your companions', safety. Wear shoes with soles that grip. Avoid stepping on seaweed—it's as slippery as mucus. Keep a careful watch on the waves and incoming water. Be sure you always have a good escape route when the tide starts to come in or if a "sneaker wave" tries to catch you.

Oregon

Because of the geology of the Oregon coast and the terrific public access to many intertidal areas, Oregon provides the best opportunities in our region for tide pooling. A good resource for information on Oregon tide pools is the **Hatfield Marine Science Center,** which has a printed list of favorite areas.

Cannon Beach is one of the most heavily visited tourist towns in the Pacific Northwest, and right in the middle of the beach, at the edge of the ocean, is **Haystack Rock.** This giant monolith of basalt, and the surrounding reefs and smaller rocks, has provided some of the best tidepooling in the Northwest for many years. But decades of ever-increasing impact by thousands of tourists, many collecting animals willy-nilly, threatened to destroy this wonderful area despite its legally protected status. Haystack Rock is also a very important nesting sight for many seabirds, and this use was also threatened by people climbing the rock during the nesting season. Wildlife managers debated about what sould be done, but then a wonderful thing happened.

A group of concerned residents from the surrounding area started the **Haystack Rock Awareness Program.** The purpose of the program is to protect Haystack Rock through a public education program, and it is one of the best examples of such a program I have ever seen. Paid seasonal staff and many volunteers provide a range of programs about the rock; the most exciting and effective take place right at the rock itself during the lowest tides of the summer. There are demonstration aquaria with sample animals and plants, telescopes for watching the birds, interpretive signs and lots of friendly guides showing people around the rock.

These activities allow everyone to see all the neat stuff living around the rock without hurting anything and to actually learn what the organisms are and what they do. People experiencing the program have a greater understanding of the importance of the Haystack Rock environment and have learned to treat it properly. Word has spread, and the negative environmental impact has been reduced. Plan a trip to Cannon Beach during a minus tide and visit Haystack Rock when the program is going on. To find out more about the Haystack Rock Awareness Program and to get their printed materials and schedule for the summer, write Haystack Rock Awareness Program, P.O. Box 368, Cannon Beach, OR 97110.

Heading south on the coast, the next great intertidal areas are just north of Newport. The **Marine Gardens at Otter Rock** are 6 miles north of Newport. From U.S. Highway 101, take the road to Otter Rock and Devil's Punch Bowl State Park. Follow the marine gardens parking signs, park, and take the trail that goes down to the beach. During minus tides a huge expanse of sandstone is exposed that is richly covered with algae. There are some animals in the crevices and holes in the sandstone, but the best area is north of where the trail joins the beach. Go to the rocky areas at the base of the cliffs directly west and northwest of the big point of land on which The Inn at Otter Crest stands.

The tide-pool area at **Yaquina Head** suffers from heavy visitation but is still an excellent outing. Two and a half miles north of Newport, on Hwy. 101, turn west onto the well-marked road to Yaquina Head and drive to the parking area at the end of the road. The BLM has been developing the Yaquina Head Outstanding Natural Area as a major interpretive site, and you'll find rest rooms, interpretive signs and, during most minus tides, rangers to answer questions. A very exciting project that was finished in 1994 is the **Quarry Cove Tide Pools,** the world's first "man-made natural tidepool area." An old quarry was converted into a rocky intertidal habitat that now functions as a natural system—it is flushed by the ocean and is being colonized naturally by plants and animals. The area features a system of universally accessible trails that are all exposed during any zero, or lower, tide. The "completely nature-made" tidepool area is at the bottom of a long staircase just to the west of the main parking area. Yaquina Head is also an excellent place to see nesting seabirds (chapter 31) and gray whales (chapter 13). Call the BLM at Yaquina Head for more information, (541) 265-2863.

From Yachats south for about 5 miles there is an almost continuous wide rocky ledge in the intertidal zone that provides many excellent opportunities for tidepooling. On both sides of the mouth of the Yachats River is a state park with access to good areas. **Yachats State Park** is on the north and is reached by following the sign in central Yachats and going west on 2nd until it ends in the park parking lot. From the parking lot go down the stairs to the intertidal area and work your way north to the best spots. South of the river is **Yachats Ocean Wayside State Park,** reached by turning right on Yachats Ocean Road just after crossing the bridge. Drive about half a mile until you see informal parking areas overlooking a rocky area.

Just 2 miles south of Yachats is the **Cape Perpetua Visitor Center,** managed by the U.S. Forest Service and a good source of information on the area. A trail leads from the visitor center to the tide pool area. For closer access, you can park in a parking area across Hwy. 101 from the visitor center road and take the trail that goes south to join the trail from the visitor center. Head toward the ocean and go straight at the next junction.

A couple of miles south of Cape Perpetua are the **Strawberry Hill** and **Bob Creek** areas in **Neptune State Park.** Although it's an excellent intertidal area, Strawberry Hill is best known as a great place to see harbor seals, especially babies in the summer. Please be careful not to disturb the seals while you're exploring. Another mile south of Strawberry Hill is Bob Creek, another good access point to the rock ledge extending south from Cape Perpetua. There is a very large rocky area south of the parking lot.

Washington

Not as many choice intertidal areas are accessible in Washington because of private land ownership and limited roads to the rocky seacoast. The three areas described below are a sample of the different types of exposure found in Washington. **Olympic National Park** represents maximum exposure to the open Pacific; **Salt Creek** represents the partially protected waters of the Strait of Juan de Fuca and **Rosario Beach** represents the more protected waters of the San Juans and other islands in the northern Salish Sea.

Sixty miles of beautiful wilderness coastline is included in Olympic National Park. In the **Kalaloch** area, Beach 4 is the favorite tidepooling spot and the site of guided ranger walks in July and August. Check on times for walks and tides at the Kalaloch Information Center, (360) 962-2283. To go on your own, park in the Beach 4 parking area, take the trail to the beach, and head north for the rocks. Farther north in the park is **Rialto Beach,** near the Mora campground and ranger station and reachable by La Push Road from Forks. The road to Mora ends at Rialto Beach, and it is a mile-and-a-half hike from the parking area to the tide pools near **Hole-in-the-Wall.** Plan on leaving the Rialto Beach parking area an hour to an hour and a half before low tide. The rangers schedule tide-pool walks during July and August; check at the Mora Ranger Station for a schedule.

On the north shore of the Olympic Peninsula is **Salt Creek County Park,** a great spot for camping and wildlife viewing. Most of the surrounding intertidal area is a marine sanctuary. From Port Angeles head west on U.S. Highway 101 to the junction with U.S. Highway 112. Go west 7 miles on Hwy. 112 to the well-marked turnoff to Salt Creek–Tongue Point (Camp Hayden Road). After entering the park, go straight, past the road to the bunkers, then head west (left) on any of the next roads and go as far as you can into the camping area toward the northwest corner of the park. There is a small parking area with an informational sign near stairs heading down to the intertidal area. There are two more nearby stairways to other rocky areas. In addition to intertidal creatures, you should have excellent views of seabirds, although these are most numerous in the fall and winter.

Deception Pass State Park is Washington's most popular state park, and within the park is **Rosario Beach,** probably the state's most visited intertidal area. Rosario is a classic example of a great place being loved too much, but increasing awareness of the sensitive nature of intertidal habitats and their inhabitants is helping. Like Yaquina Head in Oregon, Rosario is still an excellent tide-pooling spot despite heavy visitation and is located in a scenic area. From State Highway 20 south of Anacortes, take the Hwy. 20 spur south to Whidbey Island. Follow the signs to Rosario Beach, which is about 5 miles from Hwy. 20 and before the bridge to Whidbey Island.

British Columbia

Most of the British Columbia coast in our region is protected and not as rich as the west coast of Vancouver Island, which has direct exposure to the Pacific. Access by road is very limited on the wild west coast of Vancouver Island, so choice spots are limited. The two best places are **Botanical Beach Provincial Park** and the **Long Beach Unit of Pacific Rim National Park.**

Botanical Beach Provincial Park may well be British Columbia's most famous intertidal area. Botanical Beach is near Port Renfrew at the end of Provincial Highway 14, about 65 miles west of Victoria. Fortunately, the road, parking area and trails have recently been improved. As you near the end of the highway in Port Renfrew, just before coming to the dock and the Port Renfrew Hotel turn left (the only turn possible) onto the dirt Cerantes Road. There is a sign for Botanical Beach and a street sign for Cerantes Road. In about 2 miles you'll come to the new parking area. From here one trail (eastern) goes to Botanical Beach, and another (western) goes to Botany Bay. There are outhouses at the end of each trail near the beach.

Take the trail to **Botanical Beach,** the best tide-pool area by far, and when you get to the shore, walk out onto the exposed rock and work your way to the right to the best areas. There are some amazing pools and other interesting formations carved in the easily eroded sandstone. This area is particularly rich in mollusks, with many limpets and chitons. Instead of returning the way you came, you can take the new trail from Botanical Beach over to Botany Bay and then take the trail back up to the parking area from there. This route gives you a triangular loop, goes through some nice forest habitat and adds about half an hour to your trip. The whole area is very scenic, and if you want to explore further, the new **Marine Trail** goes from Botanical Beach east all the way to China Beach Provincial Park.

Pacific Rim National Park, the only national park in southwestern British Columbia, consists of three separate units. The **Long Beach Unit** has the easiest access and visitor facilities; the other two units are wilderness. The Long Beach Unit offers fantastic scenery, wonderful hikes in ancient forests, bogs and beaches and great viewing opportunities for birds, marine mammals and intertidal life. The nearby towns of Tofino and Ucluelet offer a wide range of visitor services and provide an interesting contrast to each other.

A visit to **Wickaninnish Center** is a must. It is a beautiful visitor center with great displays, rest rooms, the South Beach Trail, and a surprisingly elegant little restaurant with great food, a fabulous view and reasonable prices. It is a great place to hang out if it's raining, which is a very common occurrence. The best tide-pool areas are on the **South Beach Trail** and at **Box Island.** The South Beach Trail starts at Wickaninnish Center and within a quarter-mile goes past good rocky habitat. Pick one of the little side trails that leads to a promising area and start exploring.

Box Island is the biggest of several offshore rocks in **Schooner Cove.** You can walk out to these rocks at low tide from the beach at Schooner Walk-in Campground. The parking area for Schooner is about 9 miles north of Wickaninnish. From the parking area, the Schooner Campground trail descends through beautiful, lush ancient forest habitat to the walk-in campground and beach, a great place to camp.

Whenever you are on the west coast of Vancouver Island, be on the lookout for whales in season (see chapter 13).

39

Mountain Goats

Ghostly white, shy enough to be mysterious and living on the most rugged peaks, mountain goats are the spirits of the high mountains in the Pacific Northwest. These animals are superbly adapted for their extreme environment, easily scampering across rocky cliffs using the smallest ledges for footholds. Their legs are short for their size, giving them a low center of gravity. Their feet have tough inner pads that are rubbery and rough for traction, and hard outer hooves for gripping ice and rock. As you can guess, their sense of balance is excellent. To survive the subfreezing temperatures and severe winds of winter in the high mountains, they have an impressive coat of shaggy white fur. The outer coat consists of hollow guard hairs up to 8 inches long that are loaded with lanolin to repel water. Underneath is a 3-inch layer of wooly underfur. Mountain goats are born to climb, and kids start instinctively hours after birth.

Mountain goats are not closely related to our domesticated farm goats, although they are both in the large bovid family. The mountain goat's closest relatives are the chamois, serow and takin, which live similar lives in the high mountains of Europe and Asia. Actually, mountain goats are also from Asia, although they have been here for about 500,000 years. Mountain goats crossed into North America over the Bering Strait land bridge during the Pleistocene Ice Age in the great ungulate invasion that also included bighorn sheep, musk ox, elk, bison and caribou. As with many other subarctic organisms, they were once much more widely distributed throughout the West when the climate was colder. With the post–Ice Age change to a warmer climate they have retreated to the mountains of Alaska and Canada, still ranging into the lower 48 in the Washington Cascades and the northern Rockies of Idaho and Montana. In the last eighty years there have been intentional introductions into some other western states.

There seems to be a lot of confusion as to whether mountain goats are native wildlife in the Pacific Northwest, especially in Washington. I have heard many strange tales of mountain goat origins from "informed locals" in eastern Washington. Mountain goats are definitely native wildlife in Washington, although their numbers and distribution have varied greatly during the last two hundred years. Washington currently has six thousand to eight thousand mountain goats in about one hundred scattered populations. Some of these populations are the results of reintroductions of goats into areas in which they originally occurred but had since disappeared.

Mountain goats were introduced into the Olympic Mountains in the 1920s, and have been the center of much controversy. Despite some recent claims otherwise, the scientific evidence is clear that mountain goats were never native to the Olympics and that they are having a negative impact on the alpine vegetation. Many goats have been removed from Olympic National Park by live trapping and released in other parts of the state. I suspect the controversy about introduced mountain goats in the Olympics and the fact that many goats now living in other parts of Washington are the results of reintroductions is the source of much of the confusion among the general public about their actual origins and status.

There's no question that British Columbia has always been the world's headquarters for mountain goats, with an estimated fifty thousand to sixty thousand in the province today. In Oregon there is still debate about the original status of mountain goats in that state, although Patrick Matthews and Victor Coggins of the Oregon Department of Fish and Wildlife have recently presented evidence for the existence of mountain goats in Oregon—in Hell's Canyon and the Wallowa Mountains—prior to European contact. Since 1950 there have been introductions of mountain goats into the Wallowa and Elkhorn Mountains. These introductions have had limited success and at this time there are no more than one to two hundred mountain goats in Oregon.

Because mountain goats live in remote, rugged, mountainous terrain and are very wary of humans, they are not easy to see. They are rarely found below 5,000 feet elevation, even in Alaska. There are a few spots in Washington where your chances of seeing mountain goats are good, but your view will almost always be from a distance. Binoculars or a scope are a must. Fortunately, their white fur makes mountain goats easy to spot unless they're on snow. To find them in summer, look for rocky cliffs near timberline and then search grassy areas between the base of the cliffs and the edge of the forest. They are most frequently seen in this band of scattered trees and openings. They will sometimes be on the cliffs themselves, and at higher elevations may be out in the open on alpine tundra. Be patient; you may have to wait hours before they wander into view from out of the trees or from rocks. They are most active early and late in the day and on overcast days. If they are in grassy areas or on the typically dark rock of the Cascades, they will stand out clearly with good light. As biologist Ron Warfield at Rainier National Park put it, "If you see a patch of snow get up and move, you've got yourself a goat."

At reasonable range, with binos or a scope, mountain goats are unmistakable. About the size of a small deer but much more compact and stocky, they are completely white except for the black nose, eyes, hooves and small curved horns. They have big humped shoulders and goatees that get longer with age. Males and females are very similar looking, though males are slightly larger and have bigger shoulders. The best way to tell them apart is by behavior. Nannies and their young live in small groups while adult males are usually solitary. The sure way to tell them apart is to watch them urinate—nannies squat and billies stretch.

Speaking of urinating, Dan Mathews makes an unusual suggestion in his excellent book, *Cascade-Olympic Natural History.* Mountain goats crave salt and will search for salty soil to eat—even traveling long distances to frequent salt licks. When hikers urinate on alpine turf, the goats will sometimes eat the anointed soil to get the salt, destroying the fragile vegetation in the process. Dan recommends that all hikers urinate on rock or gravel when in mountain goat habitat.

Mountain goats are not finicky and eat a wide range of plants. The availability of winter food is their main problem, but their extraordinary climbing ability allows them to feed on steep slopes and cliffs where snow doesn't accumulate. As spring approaches they are often found feeding on south-facing slopes, which are the first to green up with new plant growth. Their climbing ability also makes mountain goats fairly safe from predators. The main causes of death for them are extreme winter weather, a scarcity of food and accidental falls. All these factors affect young goats more severely.

Washington

Hot Spots

The best spots in our region for seeing mountain goats are all in the southern Cascades near Mount Rainier. In **Mount Rainier National Park** itself, the **Sunrise** area in the northeast corner of the park has several spots the goats frequent. Sunrise also provides spectacular views, alpine wildflowers, marmots and pikas and is a must-see in the Northwest. There is also a ranger station, visitor center, and other services, including an overpriced snack bar. The road up to Sunrise makes a sharp turn at Sunrise Point, where there is a parking area and some interpretive signs. Park here and go to the wall with the north view and find the sign reading The Cascade Range. Using this sign as your guide, locate Dege Peak and The Palisades. Carefully search the area between these points for goats, keeping in mind the preferred habitat described earlier. If the goats are not in that area, search all other suitable areas in view. Occasionally goats get quite close to the road here. For another vantage point, continue to Sunrise and go to the southern edge of the main parking lot. Scan the top of **Goat Island Mountain**, about 2 miles south on the other side of the White River Canyon. This is a distant view, and a scope is needed to see the dots in the distance.

Several good areas for goats can be seen by hiking west from Sunrise on the **Sourdough Ridge Trail** until it joins the **Wonderland Trail.** One and a half miles from Sunrise and just west of Frozen Lake there is a major four-way trail junction. Here you have views of Mount Fremont, Burroughs Mountain and part of the Berkeley Park area, and from the junction trails head to these three areas, where goats are regularly seen. Ask the rangers at Sunrise where the latest sightings have been, and don't be shy about asking hikers coming from any direction if they have seen goats (or marmots and pikas). You may locate goats from the junction and be able to hike closer to them on one of the trails, or you may have to hike on a trail awhile before getting any sightings. Or you may hike all over the place all day and never see one! Such are the risks of wildlife viewing, but hey, you're in one of the most beautiful places in the world, so why worry?

East of Mount Rainier National Park and right on the eastern edge of the **William O. Douglas Wilderness Area** is what could well be the most reliable place to see mountain goats in the Northwest and one of the places where people can get the closest to them. **Timberwolf Mountain** is as high as Sunrise (just over 6,400 feet), and a forest service road goes right to the top. The breathtaking panorama rivals any in the state, with great views of the Goat Rocks and Mounts Rainier and Adams (30 and 40 miles distant, respectively) towering above the surrounding Cascades.

For a trip to Timberwolf Mountain, a Wenatchee National Forest map is very handy, but not essential. Forest Road 1500, also called the Bethel Ridge Road in places, travels about 30 miles from State Highway 410 at Nile Road south to U.S. Highway 12 near Rimrock Lake. The road is paved for about the first 10 miles heading south from Hwy. 410, and the rest is good dirt road (but with plenty of washboard), except for the last spur to Timberwolf, which is one lane, steeper and rougher, but still passable in a regular passenger car if the road is dry. If you have any doubts about the road, be sure to check with the Naches District Ranger Station at (509) 653-2205.

You can start at either end of FR 1500—the distance from Hwy. 410 is almost twice as long, but easily twice as pretty, as the route from Hwy. 12. Let's take the pretty route here. Twelve miles northwest of Naches, turn onto Nile Road from Hwy. 410 (the Chinook Pass Highway). In just about a mile and a half, turn left onto FR 1500 and follow the signs to Hwy. 12. You'll come to several intersections, all of which are well marked with signs to Hwy. 12 or with the brown binocular sign. Except for one. Just about 10 miles from your start at Hwy. 410 is an unmarked fork in the road—go right. At 10.8 miles is a nice scenic-vista turnout with a great "name that peak" sign to help you get oriented and a good view of Timberwolf Mountain from below.

From the turnout, FR 1500 goes up and over the ridge that includes Timberwolf. A small spur road, #190, goes from FR 1500 to the top of the mountain. What is pretty bizarre is that, after all the brown binocular and other signs leading you up to Timberwolf Mountain, the most important road, #190, is by far the most poorly marked! At $18^1/_3$ miles you will see a road going to the right. The only sign is a small yellow diamond, stuck up in a tree on your left, indicating an intersection. After you turn onto this road you may see the small brown stake hidden in the vegetation with 190 on it, but you will definitely see the Narrow Rough Road sign. Two and a quarter miles up this road and you're on top. On the way you'll pass some pretty mountain meadows.

Once you're on top, enjoy the view and start looking around the mountain right below you. Move around the top to get different angles of view. Search areas of good habitat on nearby peaks and slopes. Be sure to ask anyone else up there if they have seen any goats (or other wildlife). The majority of people you'll find on a place like Timberwolf are interested in wildlife and can sometimes be a good source of information. On the other hand, you may hear some pretty colorful tales of dubious authenticity. Sometimes if a small group of people gathered in a spot like this are compatible and sociable, you find yourself at a pleasant wildlife-viewing party. If you don't find goats right away, make yourself comfortable, get out some snacks, enjoy the view, and hang out for several hours. You may also spot elk, mule deer, ravens, red-tailed hawks, mountain bluebirds, gray jays, Townsend's solitaires and other mountain birds.

It's easy to follow FR 1500 in the other direction to Hwy. 12 if you don't want to backtrack. To get to Timberwolf Mountain from Hwy. 12, turn onto Bethel Ridge Road just west of Hause Creek Campground. When you're coming from the east on Hwy. 12 the road sign is a bit hard to see (until someone prunes the tree), so watch for Hause Creek and get ready to turn right after you pass the campground. When you're coming from the west, from Rimrock Lake, there is a warning sign for Bethel Ridge Road, and the green road sign is much more visible. After you turn onto Bethel Ridge Road you'll see a 1500 sign. Stay on FR 1500, following the signs for Hwy. 410. Main intersections are marked, but there are a few unsigned roads that head right at various points at around 5 and 6 miles. Continue straight ahead on FR 1500, which is clearly the main road. After going $10^1/_5$ miles from Hwy. 12 you will come to the poorly marked spur road #190 described above, only from this side you'll have an extra little orange diamond sign with an arrow.

Our last spot is near the **Goat Rocks Wilderness Area** just south of Mount Rainier National Park. The Goat Rocks got their name for good reason. Mountain goats are regularly seen by backpackers in the wilderness area, especially near—where else—**Goat Lake.** For those who want to see some goats without backpacking, head for **Stonewall Ridge,** a major geological feature along Johnson Creek south of Packwood. It is important to try this spot in the morning, when the light is best. Take Forest Road 21 (Johnson Creek Road) south from Hwy. 12 just $2^7/_{10}$ miles west of Packwood. Using this as your zero point, go 9 miles and turn left onto Forest Road 2140, which is considerably rougher. Forest Road 2140 is narrow and there is little room to pull over, but there are a few wide spots in the road at just over half a mile and again at 1 mile up the road from Forest Road 21. These points will give you great views of Stonewall Ridge rising up before you on the other side of Johnson Creek. Search the band of good habitat along the base of the cliffs. If you don't find any goats you can wait for a while or go to the next viewpoint and come back later if you still haven't found them. You need to go to both of the viewpoints described here because they give different angles of view and the goats can be visible from one but not the other.

The second viewpoint for Stonewall Ridge is a bit tricky to describe. Get back on Forest Road 21 and go another 7/10 mile south. Just after you pass a small sign for Wright Lake on your left, there is a small overgrown road that goes to the right as the road you're on goes uphill and makes a turn to the left. This road is actually marked #107 with a small brown stake hidden in the bushes, but it is not on the Gifford Pinchot National Forest map. Where this road takes off there is plenty of room to pull over and park. Walk back down FR 21 until you can get a good view of Stonewall through the trees. Again search carefully, especially at the edge of the trees below the cliffs. If you don't find goats at either place, I'd suggest that you go back and wait up on FR 2140, which is off the main road and more scenic.

40

Summer Salmon and Trout

If one animal were chosen to symbolize the Pacific Northwest, it would surely have to be the salmon. Some have defined the Northwest as "where a salmon can swim to," and others have called salmon "the silver thread that weaves through the entire tapestry of the Northwest ecosystem" or the "soul of the Northwest." To the first Americans living in the Northwest, salmon were the abundant and dependable food source that permitted the development of the wealthiest native cultures north of Mexico. And today, in a region packed with anglers, where fishing is sometimes treated as a spiritual quest, salmon are revered as the ultimate fish.

Who are the Pacific salmon? A newcomer to the region will hear more names for salmon than for different types of rain. There are seven species of salmon that belong to the genus *Oncorhynchus* and live in the northern Pacific, spawning in the rivers and streams of western North America from Alaska to California. This is a confusing group that has been split up into species a number of different ways in the past and will probably be split up again as we learn more about their complex genetics. Any difficulty keeping them straight is compounded by the multiple names applied to most species.

Chinook salmon are the biggest and least abundant of our salmon. Big chinooks can grow to 4 feet long and weigh 100 pounds, so they deserve their other common names "king" and "tyee," which means "big chief." Chinook are found in large streams and rivers, and many spawn far inland. The Columbia River Basin was the world's greatest producer of chinook, and it was these fish that gave the Columbia its reputation as the great salmon river and that started the canning boom along the river. Because chinook travel far up the biggest rivers in the region, they have been heavily affected by dams.

The other salmon that travels far inland is the sockeye, or "blueback," "red" or "Alaska" salmon. These are the most colorful salmon, turning bright red with a green head before spawning, and are often depicted in artwork. Sockeye differ from the others in that they spawn in lakes, where the young fish mature before leaving for the sea. Some sockeye have become landlocked and are then called kokanee.

Coho and chum salmon are similar in size and appearance, but the chum is much more widespread and abundant than the coho. Both commonly use coastal streams for spawning. Coho are also called "silver salmon," and chum are called "dog salmon." Both can reach a length of 3 feet and a weight of around 30 pounds, but most are around 10 pounds. The most abundant and the smallest of the fish usually called salmon is the pink salmon, also called "humpback" or "humpy." Pink salmon are known for their rigid two-year life cycle, and in our region spawn in odd years. They rarely spawn far from the sea and are the salmon least dependent on fresh water. Pinks are only found in large numbers north of the Columbia.

Two fish that are usually called trout are now considered part of the salmon group. A strain of rainbow trout that go to sea and return to spawn in fresh water, just like other salmon, are called steelhead. Some steelhead actually survive their first spawning and can spawn again after returning to the sea. Steelhead are about the size of chum and coho and are highly prized game fish. There is also a strain of cutthroat trout that spend some time at sea and can also survive their first spawning. These "trout" are often called coastal cutthroat or sea-run cutthroat and are the smallest of the Pacific salmon. Since both these sea-going trout spend so much time in fresh water, both steelhead and coastal cutthroat are very sensitive to habitat disturbance, especially to loss of riparian vegetation and silting, and therefore have been heavily affected by logging.

Everyone living in the Northwest knows the amazing life cycle of the salmon. Many actually know the term *anadromous,* which describes those fish, like salmon and shad, that are born in fresh water, migrate to the sea, where they live for an extended period, and then return up rivers and streams to spawn. Salmon are famous for their ability to return to spawn in the exact location where they were born after years roaming the Pacific. How they are able to do this is still not entirely understood, although it is currently believed that they use the earth's magnetic field to some extent for navigation and that they "smell" their way back to their home stream. In the Northwest, the annual cycles of the salmon have been one of the most important rhythms in nature since the last Ice Age. Many animals in addition to humans have depended on them, and their death after spawning returns needed nutrients to the land. The current environmental crisis involving our Northwest salmon is discussed in chapter 57.

There are three main ways by which to see returning salmon and resident trout (other than catching them or skin diving). The most aesthetically pleasing is to frequent those rare settings where you can actually see the fish in their natural habitat. When looking for fish in the wild it is very helpful to use "fish glasses"—inexpensive polarizing glasses that greatly improve your ability to see through the water. These are available at any store with fishing gear.

The easiest way to see fish is at fish hatcheries, where you can often watch artificial spawning and other hatchery operations in season. Some hatcheries have fish ladders or holding ponds where you can see fish in a somewhat natural-looking setting, but some people find hatcheries too artificial. However, hatcheries can provide some excellent opportunities to see fish up close and often have educational exhibits and materials that are very useful.

The third way to see returning salmon is by using the fish-viewing facilities at the fish ladders of major dams. This is a mixed experience, because even though you may get some great views of fish swimming under the water, you are seeing them at the very dams that have been the main cause of their decline.

Oregon

Hot Spots

The **North Umpqua River** is world famous for its summer steelhead fishing (artificial flies only) and for its scenery. Thirty-four miles of the river are designated as a Wild and Scenic River, and the road that follows the river, State Highway 138, is designated the North Umpqua Scenic Byway. The BLM's **Deadline Falls Watchable Wildlife Site** is near the downstream end of the Wild and Scenic section, where Rock Creek joins the North Umpqua 23 miles east of Roseburg. Coming up Hwy. 138 from Roseburg, turn right about a mile after Idleyld Park and cross over the North Umpqua River on the Swiftwater Bridge. Turn left into the **Swiftwater Recreation Site** immediately after crossing the Swiftwater Bridge. The trailhead for the North Umpqua Trail starts here, and the first quarter-mile section of trail provides very easy access to the Deadline Falls viewing site (and goes through beautiful old growth forest). During the summer you can see chinook and steelhead jumping the falls very early or late in the day. The very best times to come are during May for the spring chinook and right after a freshet in December or January for the winter steelhead.

Down the Umpqua River near Roseburg is the **Winchester Fish Viewing Area,** which has got to be the "fishing viewing area with the closest freeway access." Take Exit 129, North Roseburg, off I-5 and turn left at the first stop. You're now headed east. At Hwy. 99 turn right to go south just a bit, then turn left into the fish viewing area parking lot. The fish are using a ladder to pass an old dam on the Umpqua. Fish can be seen almost any time of year, and you could see steelhead or chinook and possibly coho.

The **Metolius River Fish Overlook** is in **Camp Sherman,** about 15 miles northeast of Sisters, and provides an opportunity to see big resident rainbow trout. From U.S. Highway 20 head north on Forest Road 14, following the signs to Camp Sherman/Metolius River. In $2^{1}/_{2}$ miles bear left at the fork, then in about another $2^{1}/_{2}$ miles turn right for Camp Sherman (you want to be on Forest Road 1419). Immediately after you cross the bridge, park on the right for the viewing platform. There are huge "tame" rainbow trout here all year (these are not sea-run trout), usually just upstream from the platform. Sometimes you can also see kokanee salmon moving upstream in September and October.

It is sadly ironic to see salmon at dams, but the big dams on the Columbia River between Oregon and Washington all have fish ladders and fish viewing facilities that are well marked and easy to find. **Bonneville and McNary Dams** have the best viewing on both the Oregon and Washington sides. Different runs of different species pass through at different times—the best time is in the middle of the summer, when there are runs of summer chinook, summer steelhead and sockeye. Since each dam will stop a percentage of the fish, Bonneville has more than does upstream McNary. At Bonneville there is also a large fish hatchery with outdoor display ponds where huge specimens of several species can be seen any time of year. The fish hatchery is reached from the Oregon side by the Bonneville Exit from I-84.

Washington

The Little White Salmon National Fish Hatchery is well developed for visitors; everything for the public is universally accessible. For those interested in hatchery operations, there are large viewing windows where one can watch the artificial spawning when it's taking place. Call ahead for schedule: (509) 538-2755. There are also underwater windows in the adult holding tanks, unusual at a hatchery, affording good views of huge mature adults. Fish can also be seen jumping up the ladder and in the river. This is the oldest federal fish hatchery on the Columbia and celebrated its centennial in 1996.

Twelve and a half miles west of Stevenson on State Highway 14, turn left just before the bridge over the Little White Salmon River. Go north about a mile along the river and drive through the lower part of the hatchery to the upper area. Visiting hours are 7:30 A.M. to 4 P.M. daily. There is a run of spring chinook from May through August, and spawning (artificial) takes place from mid-July into August. There is also a good fall run of coho and fall chinook from October to mid-November.

Leavenworth National Fish Hatchery opened in 1940 as the world's largest salmon hatchery. It was meant to try to ameliorate the loss of salmon caused by Grand Coulee Dam, which completely blocks fish from going any farther upstream. The hatchery now produces about 2,500,000 spring chinook and 100,000 steelhead each year and is designed for visitors, with displays and an interpretive trail that describes the history and operations of the hatchery. The peak of the returning chinook is in July, when adults can be seen in the holding tanks as well as in Icicle Creek from the interpretive trail bridge. Head west from Leavenworth on U.S. Highway 2, and just outside of town turn south on Icicle Road. In about a mile and a half watch for the hatchery sign and turn left. To see wild salmon spawning in the Wenatchee River, come in October for the Salmon Festival (chapter 57).

Migrating salmon can be seen in Seattle at the **Lake Washington Ship Canal Fish Ladder** (or Chittenden Locks) in the Ballard neighborhood. Chinook, coho, sockeye, steelhead and coastal cutthroat all pass through the ladder at various times of year, but the most action is from early July through September. The viewing area is a huge room with lots of interpretive displays and information and is open every day from 7 A.M. to 9 P.M. The fish ladder can be reached from the north side of the canal, which has the main visitor facilities and botanical gardens, or from the south side for a more direct route. To get to the north side, take NW Market Street west from the Woodland Park area, and after 28th Avenue head to the left onto 54th Street, then turn left into the visitor parking area. NW Market Street can be reached from the North 45th Street Exit from I-5 near the University of Washington. From the south the fish ladder is accessible from Commodore Park, which is on Commodore Way north of Discovery Park.

Two of the dams on the Columbia River between Richland and Chelan have good fish viewing facilities, but fish numbers are lower than at Bonneville or McNary. Hours for the visitor areas are roughly 8:30 A.M. to 5:00 P.M. daily, but you should call and check on hours and the amount of fish action before going. The visitor center at **Wanapum Dam**, (509) 663-8121, is the most developed, with a nice museum on local Native Americans in addition to the fish viewing room. Access is from the east side of the Columbia from State Highway 243 just south of I-90. **Rocky Reach Dam**, (509) 663-7522, is about 5 miles north of Wenatchee on U.S. Highway 97 (west side of the Columbia) and is well developed for tourists with a snack bar, gift shop and nice picnic area in addition to the fish viewing.

British Columbia

Stamp Falls Provincial Park on Vancouver Island offers a chance to see wild fish jumping falls in a dramatic setting. A run of sockeye move up the Stamp River from mid-July through August, followed by coho in August and September and chinook in September and October. Drive west on Provincial Highway 4 through Port Alberni (this is a good stop on the way to Pacific Rim National Park), and on the west side of town turn north on Beaver Creek Road. After 7 miles watch for the big park sign and turn to the left. Drive through the park to the locked gate, then continue on foot down the road, which becomes the trail. Be sure to go to the end of the trail, where there is an overlook of a big pool where the fish pile up waiting to go up the falls or to the ladder that was built to make the trip easier. There are good interpretive signs along the trail and a nice camping area in the park.

The **Capilano Fish Hatchery** provides a chance to see salmon right in Vancouver. The hatchery is in **Capilano River Regional Park**, off Capilano Road in North Vancouver. This is a major tourist attraction, so try to come early or late in the day, hours are 8 A.M. to 9 P.M. in summer and until dusk after Labor Day. This is an artificial hatchery setting, but it has some great exhibits and fish are usually on view from July through October.

The booklet *Where and When to See Salmon* from the Department of Fisheries and Oceans office in Vancouver lists more than 50 sites in British Columbia.

41

July Shorttakes

Osprey

Osprey are common summer residents along rivers and at many lakes in the Northwest. The males and females arrive separately in March, unite with their former mates and immediately begin establishing their territory and rebuilding their nests from previous years. The breeding season lasts until the end of August, and there is plenty of activity to see all summer. Most osprey have headed south by the end of September. **Crane Prairie Reservoir,** about 35 miles southeast of Bend, Oregon, is a major osprey nesting area because of the large number of snags there. There are also a few nesting bald eagles. This mountain reservoir is on the Cascades Lakes Highway (Forest Road 46) and can most quickly be reached from Bend by driving 15 miles south on U.S. Highway 97, then 21 miles west on Forest Road 40, the road to Sunriver. Turn left from FR 40 on to FR 46 to go down the west side of the reservoir to Quinn River Campground. Half a mile south of the campground is a wide spot in the road where you park for the **Osprey Point Observation Trail** (there is a small sign). Walk to the shore of the lake for great views of osprey and bald eagles as well as a number of waterfowl. Rock Creek, Crane Prairie and Cow Meadow Campgrounds also have good wildlife-viewing opportunities.

Chicory and Queen Anne's Lace

Along many roads that haven't been sprayed, and in other disturbed areas on the west side, you will see lots of blue chicory and white Queen Anne's lace, two of our most abundant and hardy wildflowers. Both were introduced from Europe and are commonly called weeds, but weediness is in the eye of the beholder, and most folks find them a beautiful addition to the midsummer landscape, especially so because they grow in disturbed places that need some natural color. Queen Anne's lace is also known as wild carrot and is presumed to be the wild source of the domesticated carrot. Chicory was brought here to be grown commercially as a coffee substitute (the roots are roasted), and it "escaped" into the wild. The leaves have been considered a choice salad green since the time of the ancient Greeks and are still popular in parts of Europe.

Crane Flies

Leave your windows or doors open and the lights on sometime this month and you can be sure of getting some crane flies as houseguests. These impressive insects are often called "mosquito hawks" but, unfortunately, they do not eat mosquitoes. Many people seeing them for the first time are horrified, because they look like enormous mosquitoes, and the thought of being bitten by one of these big bruisers is creepy. But these gentle giants from the largest family of flies in the world are as harmless as can be; many of them don't even eat as adults. The larvae are tough-skinned maggots called "leather jackets," which live in lawns, decaying vegetation, moist soil or even water. Those adults that do eat sip nectar or nibble on rotten plants primarily, although a few apparently do eat tiny insects. Be careful as you escort them back outside—their legs are notorious for falling off easily.

42

A Closer Look: Going Batty

Figure this one out: The more ancient forests we cut down, the more we'll be bitten by mosquitoes. What? How does that one work? The answer is a classic example of how everything in an ecosystem is interconnected. As you have probably guessed from the chapter title, the important link in this relationship is bats. Bats eat mosquitoes. Not just a few mosquitoes, but as many as one thousand to two thousand *per bat, every night,* for some species! In the Pacific Northwest most bats roost in big old trees and snags when they are not hibernating, which is, of course, when mosquitoes are present. Big old trees and snags are the classic components of ancient forests, and bat populations are dropping as this type of habitat disappears. Fewer roosting sites—fewer bats; fewer bats—more mosquitoes.

Bats are also suffering from other human activities and pesticides. The greatest threat to bat survival today seems to be human disturbance to bats roosting in caves during hibernation and during the period when the females are raising young. Few animals could be less deserving of the hard time we've given them than bats. Any animal that eats insects, our main competitors on this planet for food, usually has a good reputation. But in some parts of the world, mainly America and temperate Europe, bats are among the most feared, misunderstood and ruthlessly persecuted animals.

Fortunately, public knowledge and opinion about bats is changing for the better, thanks to the efforts of groups like Bat Conservation International, some Audubon Society chapters, the National Wildlife Federation and the nongame programs of wildlife agencies. More and more people are becoming aware of how harmless and beneficial bats are, and they are also becoming more concerned about declining bat populations. One response made by bat fanciers has been to provide roosting habitat by putting up bat houses. A small industry has blossomed in the making and selling of bat houses and bat-house kits.

Bats deserve our respect and appreciation. After all, they are a fairly close relative of ours and the only mammal capable of true flight. Bats are often mistaken for rodents and described as "flying mice," but they are very different from rodents, and the current scientific thinking is that they could be closely related to primates. One thing is clear, and that is that bats have been very successful in an evolutionary sense. Bats are an ancient type of mammal, and one-quarter of all mammal species in the world are bats. They totally dominate the nighttime sky and are without a doubt the main predator of nocturnal flying insects.

Actually, it can be downright scary to imagine what would happen if there were no bats. Studies have carefully estimated that one huge colony of bats in

Braken Cave, Texas, eats 250,000 pounds of insects every night! That's 45,625 tons of bugs a year! And in just one part of Texas. (I know, I know. It just doesn't seem possible that there are that many bugs, even in Texas, but the figures are entirely reasonable.) Can you imagine what it would be like if there were no bats eating all these bugs? Among the many insects bats eat are some of the worst agricultural pests, such as corn borer and cutworm moths, potato beetles and grasshoppers. In the Tropics, bats are also extremely important as pollinators and seed-dispersal agents.

Despite some improvement in bat public relations, though, many of the Euro-American myths about bats are still prevalent. Four of the most common are that they are aggressive and vicious, that they get tangled in people's hair, that they are blind and that most of them have rabies. All of these are far from the truth.

People who have worked with bats extensively know that they are not vicious or even ill-tempered. On the contrary, bats are very gentle and nonaggressive animals. And why would a bat want to get into someone's hair? Isn't it a bit absurd to think that an animal that can precisely determine the location and movement of a mosquito flying at night cannot avoid running into a human head? No one really knows the origin of this "bats-in-hair" fear, but it is possible, of course, that it has happened a few times over the centuries. But bats do not *try* to get into people's hair. And blind as a bat? Not quite—bats have eyes, and most of them can probably see about as well as we can, except for color.

Like most mammals, bats can get rabies, but they are not infected at a rate any higher than some other mammals, and most of the rabid bat stories in the news media are distorted or just plain not true. Everyone, children especially, should know not to touch wild animals except in safe circumstances, such as when catching a garter snake or picking up an earthworm. One should always be especially cautious when an animal is acting odd, which for almost any wild animal will mean that it allows a human to touch it. It is true that a few people have gotten rabies from bites by rabid bats (that they picked up), but the number is less than one person every two or three years in all of North America. There is a much greater chance of getting rabies from a domestic dog or cat.

There has been a great increase in knowledge about bats in the last couple of decades, and there are many good books available if you decide to go batty. One of the best introductions to bats and their relationship to people is *America's Neighborhood Bats,* by bat expert Dr. Merlin Tuttle. Certainly one of the most fascinating adaptations of bats is their amazing ability to "see" the world through echolocation. Another unusual characteristic of bats is their longevity. Usually, smaller animals live shorter lives, but bats can live from twenty-five to thirty years.

So who's who in our regional bat fauna? Here are some brief sketches of the most common and conspicuous bats in the Pacific Northwest.

Little brown bat. These bats are just what the name says—they are small (with a 9-inch wingspan) and brown. Little browns are the most common bat in the Northwest and are usually seen near water. They use a wide variety of places for summer roosts, including buildings in which they can form large colonies—putting them into conflict with humans. Little brown bats are often seen roosting and flying with big brown bats, which are, you guessed it, bigger. Both are sometimes seen feeding around streetlights.

Big brown bat. Another of our most common and widely distributed bats, the hardy big brown bat is the only bat that overwinters in Canada. This is another great bat name—individuals are big (13 to 14 inches) and brown, with short black ears. They are most common near forests and water but are frequently seen in cities and towns. Big browns readily use buildings (sometimes all year) where, like their small cousin, they can form large colonies—putting them also into occasional conflict with people.

Pallid bat. One of our bigger bats (14 to 16 inches), the pallid bat has pale brown to tan fur and huge ears. It occurs locally on the east side in rocky areas and canyons. Pallid bats are unusual in that they commonly feed on the ground, and their diet includes scorpions (now there's a helpful friend). These bats rely heavily on caves, so it is no surprise that they are on the Oregon Sensitive Species List.

Western pipistrelle. This is the smallest bat in the United States, and it seems to be teamed up with the pallid bat as another pale bat of east-side river canyons. Although generally buff, the contrasting black feet, face and ears make it easy to identify in the unlikely case you ever got close to one. These bats are easy to see flying over rivers in desert canyons before sunset because they emerge earlier in the evening than most bats.

Hoary bat. The biggest bat in North America (up to 17 inches) is also the most widely distributed. The brown fur is tipped with white (hence the "hoary") and there is an orange-to-yellow throat collar. Hoary bats are solitary, living in forests and woodlands, including wooded areas of towns, and roosting in trees. They are unusual in almost always giving birth to twins. The huge drop in their population recently is most likely due to the loss of ancient forests.

Because bats are so sensitive to disturbance, biologists, resource managers and responsible spelunkers who know of bat roosts do not reveal their location to the general public. For this reason, there are no recommendations here for specific places to go looking for bats at their roosts. Instead, try to find the places where they feed and you can then watch without disturbing them. This is actually fairly easy.

The basic strategy for finding bats, as with all wildlife, is to think like a bat. This boils down to knowing the animal's needs, picking the right habitat and the right time. The right time of year for bats is during the summer, when there are lots of flying insects, and the right time of day is dusk. Find a good spot just before sunset, settle in comfortably and wait. Many bats come out to start feeding during twilight, and you can watch them as long as the light lasts. Under these conditions you are basically watching silhouettes and won't be able to see any markings or colors, making identification pretty tough. I've never had the opportunity to go out batting with a real expert, but I'm sure there are those who can identify some species by their size, shape and behavior.

To find the right habitat for bats, look for places where there are lots of flying insects. Generally, quiet bodies of water are excellent locations. On the west side, small quiet ponds with trees nearby are best, although quiet stretches of rivers may be just as active in some areas. Small lakes and ponds are also good places to try in the mountains, and sometimes very wet meadows will also have good bat concentrations. On the drier east side, water plays an even bigger role in concentrating feeding bats, and most rocky canyons with water flowing in them will have bats, mainly pallid bats and the western pipistrelle. People river-rafting in the summer, especially in the warmer, drier areas, will regularly see bats around sunset. Don't forget to slather yourself with insect repellent before going bat-watching, unless you happen to be in a very arid area with no mosquitoes.

People should not look for bats in caves, because human disturbance of bats roosting and hibernating in caves is thought to be the biggest cause of the decline in bat populations. Any time you do happen upon roosting bats, do your best to leave the area immediately without disturbing the bats in any way. If you have problems with bats roosting in a building, seek advice from your state wildlife department or read *America's Neighborhood Bats*. The basic tactic is to wait until the bats leave and then seal their entrance before they return.

August

Notes

43

Orca

Called killer whales, they were regularly portrayed as the most fearsome, vicious predator in the oceans. Then in the early 1960s a few were captured and exhibited in aquariums and marine theme parks such as Marineland and Sea World. In no time they became superstars of the animal world and more were captured—a total of sixty were taken from the Pacific Northwest. Many people became fascinated with these charismatic animals, scientists included, and the more we learned about them, the more we wanted to know. The Marine Mammal Protection Act went into effect in 1972, and Ken Balcomb conducted the first census of killer whales in the Salish Sea. Ken counted only sixty-eight individual whales, recognized by their dorsal fin and saddle patch markings, and in 1976 the capture and removal of killer whales in our region stopped.

In the meantime, the killer whales in captivity played with their keepers, performed amazing stunts, displayed their intelligence and totally charmed almost everyone who saw them. The savage killer of the sea had an image change and got a new name. People began using the name of the species, from *Orcinus orca,* and now orca is a common word, at least in the Pacific Northwest. As mentioned in chapter 13, on gray whales, the change in attitude toward whales in the last two decades is nothing short of phenomenal and is certainly one of the most encouraging examples of knowledge bringing understanding and appreciation, and eventually respect and protection, for wildlife. And the orca's popularity is still growing after the movie *Free Willy* resulted in Keiko (the star) getting a new, more humane home in the Oregon Coast Aquarium.

Ken Balcomb and the Center for Whale Research are still studying the orcas of the Salish Sea, numbered ninety-four in 1994. These resident orcas, members of three pods, are the most studied whales in the world. Every individual is known, as is the family tree of each pod. Birth announcements and other news of the pods are not unusual in our newspapers, and many northwesterners are proud of our orcas as symbols of our natural heritage.

The switch to orca from killer whale favors accuracy, because orcas are technically not whales but rather the largest members of the dolphin family. This is taxonomic nit-picking, however, for both are cetaceans, as discussed in chapter 13. The "killer" part of the name, however, is quite accurate, for orcas are the top predator in all the world's oceans. They have been known to eat just about everything, including fish, seals, porpoises and even large whales, but not, interestingly enough, humans—who are their only predators. People have never hunted orcas as much as they have hunted the "true whales," but today we are the cause of a greater threat—global oceanic pollution.

Orcas are sometimes called "wolves of the sea" because they live in family packs and cooperatively hunt mammals larger than themselves. Orcas are very social mammals, living their whole lives in a matrilineal group that includes a female and her offspring, sometimes of several generations. Matrilineal groups join together to form pods. The bond between a mother and her young is strong and it is believed that most orcas rarely leave their mothers during their lives. Sometimes large pods will split to form new pods, and separate pods are known to merge for a while into a "superpod."

In the Salish Sea there are two types of orca—residents and transients. The three resident pods are large (with about twenty to forty-five members), are very stable and stay in the Salish Sea or off the west coast of Vancouver Island. Transient pods are much smaller (with two to six members), travel long distances and are much less predictable. Transient orcas eat mammals primarily, while the resident orcas feed almost entirely on fish. Another big difference between the two groups is in their differing vocalization. Orcas use two types of vocalizations— clicking sounds used for echolocation, and a variety of whistles and squeals used for communication with other members of the pod. Transients are very quiet, usually making their echolocation clicks sporadically, and rarely calling. Residents, however, are real chatterboxes, and each pod has its own distinctive dialect, with seven to seventeen discrete calls. Studying these dialects can help reveal the relationships between pods.

Washington

Hot Spots

The first whale-watching park in the nation is considered the best place to see orcas from land in the United States. **Lime Kiln Point State Park** is on the west coast of San Juan Island about 9 miles from Friday Harbor. The park has picnic tables overlooking Haro Strait, an area used regularly during the summer by all three resident pods. As usual on the West Coast, lighting is best in the morning, although whales are seen any time of day. This is another test of patience; you can see orcas three times in an hour or once in two days, so be prepared to wait. While watching for orcas, you'll also have a chance to spot Dall's and harbor porpoises and minke whales, as well as numerous marine birds. Unfortunately, the best time to see orcas is in the summer months, when the popular San Juans are overrun with visitors. Orcas are seen regularly in May and September, however, which are generally better times to visit the island. In May the wildflowers and birding are excellent.

To get to Lime Kiln Point State Park from Friday Harbor, head southwest on Spring Street and stay on it as it turns into San Juan Valley Road. Turn left on Douglas Road after passing the airport, and head south until it turns to the west and becomes Bailer Hill Road. Bailer Hill Road will then turn into West Side Road, which goes into the park. The park can also be reached from the north via Roche Harbor Road, West Valley Road and Mitchell Bay Road. Be sure to check out the birding at both American and British Camps while you are on the island.

If you do not take your car to San Juan Island, there is now public transportation available. Call San Juan Transit, 1-800-887-8387, to get the current schedule for getting to Lime Kiln Point State Park and other good spots from the ferry dock. You should seriously consider *not* taking your car on the ferry in summer in order to avoid the long waits and to save money. In Friday Harbor, be sure to visit the Whale Museum, just a couple of blocks from the ferry. The museum is open from 10 A.M. to 5 P.M. every day, June through September, and from 11 A.M. to 4 P.M. the rest of the year.

The best way to get close views of orcas is to take to the water yourself. **Sea kayaking** has become a tremendously popular activity in the San Juan Islands, and there are many companies offering rentals and tours, some specifically for viewing orcas and other wildlife. A copy of *Sea Kayaker* or *Outside* magazine is a good source for names of outfitters. Probably the surest way to see whales up close is on a whale-watching boat trip run by one of the commercial tour operators in the San Juans, Victoria or Vancouver. You can get a list of operators that follow approved guidelines for observing whales without negative impact from the Whale Museum.

The San Juans are very popular for sailing, and those who spend much time cruising the islands often get close views of orcas. And for those who can't get to sea any other way, there are always the **ferries.** It is possible to see orcas from any of the ferries plying the waters of the Salish Sea, but your chances are best from the San Juan Island Ferry. Remember, it's much cheaper and easier to ride the ferries as a foot passenger than to take your car. Occasionally orcas are seen from shore throughout much of the Salish Sea, even from downtown Seattle!

British Columbia

Orcas are sometimes seen from the **Victoria Breakwater** along the southeast coast of Vancouver Island at spots like **Clover Point** and the **Ogden Breakwater** (chapters 10 and 62). And of course, there is a chance of spotting them from ferries or other boats in the Strait of Georgia. But the best place *in the world* to see orcas is at the other end of the island, way up north near Port McNeil.

Johnstone Strait is really out of the range of this book but not to include it in a chapter on orcas would be gross negligence. A population of about two hundred frequent the Johnstone Strait area during the summer and into fall. A favorite spot is **Robson Bight Ecological Reserve,** where the whales like to rub themselves on shallow pebble beaches. Since this is such a sensitive site, Robson Bight is closed to entry by humans on foot or by boat. There is no good spot for observing orcas from land, although some residents are working on the idea. The only way to really see the beasts is by boat. Several tour companies run whale-watching trips during the summer and fall out of the towns of Port McNeil, Telegraph Cove and Sayward. To get the latest information on commercial whale-watching trips (booklet #12) and whatever printed information is currently available on Johnstone Strait and Robson Bight, call or write Super, Natural British Columbia (see appendix).

44

Marmots and Pikas

Summer is time for backpacking in the mountains, and journeys into the subalpine and alpine zones bring us into contact with two charming mammals that are favorites with many hikers—marmots and pikas. Marmots are the biggest squirrels in the world, and a big hoary marmot perched on a rock is about as impressive as rodents get—few are larger. Often living near marmots are the smaller pikas. A common misconception is that pikas are also rodents, sort of a North American guinea pig, but they are actually small relatives of rabbits. Both these mammals are notable because they live year-round in one of the harshest environments on earth. Much of their range is essentially uninhabitable for half the year, and surviving the winter is their greatest challenge. Interestingly, the two animals take completely different approaches in adapting to this harsh climate.

A mammal facing a harsh winter has three basic choices for survival—migrate, hibernate or accommodate. Elk are a good example of a mammal that migrates, marmots are champion hibernators and the pika accommodates with a unique behavioral adaptation it shares with humans.

Like all lagomorphs, the group of animals that includes rabbits, hares and pikas, pikas don't hibernate. They are so small that migration isn't practical. They have adapted to the harsh alpine winter by living in a microhabitat that provides excellent shelter and by storing food. Pikas live in rock slides and talus slopes that border mountain meadows. The rock piles provide excellent shelter, and the meadows provide food. Storing food is common with rodents but is not done by any of the pika's relatives, so this behavior is unusual. Some foods, like seeds, are easily stored, but the pika eats greens—grasses, sedges and herbs. How are these stored? The same way we humans store grasses and certain herbs—by drying the plants to make hay.

All summer long the busy little pika gathers its favorite food plants and lays the plants on rocks to dry in the sun. When the hay is ready, it is moved down into the pika's chambers and passageways between the rocks or piled under large overhanging boulders. When snow covers the rocks, the pika remains active, moving through its territory of tunnels under the snow and eating its hay. As you might expect for an animal that depends on a stored food supply, pikas are very territorial and defend their haystacks from others who try to raid their stores.

Marmots store food too, but in a very different way. Marmots eat like crazy all summer long and build up big fat reserves in their eventually quite rotund bodies. A big adult marmot can be 50 percent body fat at the beginning of hibernation. Then marmots do that slickest of endotherm tricks, they "go ecto" (see chapter 6). Their body temperature drops to just above freezing and their breathing, heart rate and all their metabolic processes slow dramatically. In this torpid state the marmot uses very little energy, and if it has stored enough fat it can remain in hibernation for seven, eight or even nine months. The main cause of marmot mortality is the winter death of young marmots born the previous spring. It is much more difficult for a smaller animal to conserve body heat and store enough fat to hibernate successfully, and three out of four marmots don't make it through their first winter. To help conserve heat, a colony of marmots may hibernate together in a big clump.

Marmots like living in big rocks near mountain meadows, so it is not uncommon to see marmots and pikas living close to each other. Both are diurnal and quite vocal, making them much easier to find and to watch than most other mammals. Marmots whistle and are often called "whistler," "whistle pig" or "siffleur" (French Canadian for "whistler"). The hoary marmot makes a loud, shrill, humanlike whistle that startles (or greets) many hikers in subalpine meadows. The call of the pika is also whistlelike, but is better described as a high bleat with a bit of a nasal character. It doesn't take long to tell the two apart, and they are both welcome sounds of the high country. Marmots and pikas can get used to humans and become quiet tame, making it possible for people to watch pikas making hay and marmots chowing down or basking in the sun.

Unfortunately, marmots can get *too* tame, and many are fed by hikers along busy trails. Such artificial feeding can lead to a number of problems, and park managers in Canada and the United States are constantly pleading with visitors not to feed the wildlife, including those adorable rodents. It is actually illegal in both countries to feed wildlife in national and provincial parks, but of course no one is going to get hauled off to jail for giving gorp to a chipmunk. It is up to all of us to resist the urge to feed these cute little critters.

Marmots and pikas have an interesting distribution that can only be explained by the climatic changes that took place during the last Ice Age. Pikas are found on mountaintops throughout the West from British Columbia to New Mexico. Many populations on the peaks of mountains in the Great Basin are isolated from one another by miles of desert. Biologists who study animal geography have been fascinated by the pika's distribution for years. It now seems accepted that about ten thousand years ago pikas were widely, and more evenly, distributed throughout the West south of the glaciers. As the glaciers retreated and the climate got hotter and drier, the pikas retreated northward with the glaciers, except for some populations, which retreated up the slopes to the subalpine zones in the higher mountains. Populations of pikas that didn't make it into areas with sufficient habitat became extinct. Isolated populations of an animal species are a classic setup for the evolution of new species, so scientists are now studying the genetics of these Pleistocene pockets of pikas.

Marmots are thought to have a similar history, except that the four kinds of marmots in our area (and a fifth nearby) are all now considered separate species by most biologists. The yellow-bellied marmot is by far the most widespread and abundant marmot in the West and occurs from the Cascades east in our region. It lives in a much wider range of habitats and elevations than do other marmots, in many kinds of rocky situations from near sea level to alpine areas and even around old log piles and buildings. It can be common in rimrock in the eastern part of Oregon and Washington.

The other three marmot species are all alpine specialists, living near timberline or above in northwestern mountains. The hoary marmot has the largest range of the three—from Alaska to the Cascades and Rockies in Washington, Idaho and Montana. Where the ranges of the yellow-bellied and the hoary overlap, the hoary seems to displace the yellow-bellied in the higher elevations. The Olympic marmot is found only in the Olympic Mountains, and the Vancouver marmot, probably North America's rarest mammal, is found only in a small area on Vancouver Island. The Olympic and Vancouver marmots are believed to be very closely related to the hoary marmot and to represent two island populations that became isolated by the retreat of the glaciers. Some biologists believe that all three are really one species. It is situations like this that challenge our ideas about what really constitutes a species.

Regardless of their fascinating evolutionary history, these animals are two of the most pleasant companions a hiker in the high country could have. Certainly either one would be a good candidate if one were to choose a totem of the high places, as suggested in Earl Larrison's *Mammals of the Northwest*.

Oregon

Hot Spots

The first time I was hiking in the **Columbia River Gorge** and heard a pika bleat, I couldn't believe my ears. I had never seen or heard one below 7,000 feet before, and there I was about 400 feet above sea level. What was going on? I looked around, and sure enough, the habitat looked great, a huge talus slope of big chunks of Columbia River basalt. And there it was, a pika in a classic pose on the edge of a big boulder. It gave another bleat and disappeared into the cracks in the rocks. I didn't know it then, but I had just seen one of the lowest pikas in the world! The Gorge is a slice through the Cascades (see chapter 4), and its steep cliffs are just 20 miles from the top of Mount Hood, the highest spot in Oregon. This steep and short descent from the alpine zone down has allowed pikas to colonize good habitat almost to the river. From the **Multnomah Falls** visitor area you can hike to the top of Multnomah Falls on the **Larch Mountain Trail** (#441) or to Oneonta Gorge and Horsetail Falls on the **Ak-Wanee Trail** (#400). Within the first 2 miles of both trails you traverse some big rock slides, and these have traditionally been home to pikas.

The only species of marmot in Oregon is the yellow-bellied marmot, which can be found from subalpine meadows to desert rimrock, from the Cascades to all of eastern Oregon, but it is unpredictable and just doesn't seem as conspicuous as the hoary. I have most regularly seen them in rimrock areas near good forage, specifically at **Malheur National Wildlife Refuge.**

A friendly greeter to the alpine world—a robust, hoary marmot near Mount Ranier.

Washington

Hoary marmots and pikas are frequently seen, and heard, by those hiking near or above timberline in the Washington Cascades. The **Hart's Pass** area in the North Cascades is great for finding both, and it is discussed in chapter 51. To the south, both **Mount Adams** and **Mount Rainier** have trails that circle the peaks, and it would be hard to spend much time hiking either one without seeing both animals. In Mount Rainier the eastern section of the **Wonderland Trail**, which goes through Summer Land and Ohanapecosh Park, is loaded with marmots and a smaller number of pikas but requires a backpacking trip. To see both animals on a pleasant day hike you can't beat the **Sourdough Ridge Trail** out of Sunrise. You will also see lots of mountain wildflowers and possibly mountain goats on this trail, as well as some of the most awesome scenery in the Northwest, making the Sunrise area one of the must-see places in this part of the world.

The Sourdough Ridge Trail starts between the ranger station and rest rooms at Sunrise, and there is a self-guiding brochure for the trail. The trail goes west $1^1/_2$ miles to a major trail junction just past **Frozen Lake.** Pikas can usually be seen in the section just before Frozen Lake, and marmots are often seen around the trail junction. From the trail junction, trails go to **Mount Fremont, Burroughs Mountain** and **Berkeley Park,** and both animals, as well as mountain goats, can be seen from any of these routes. The most popular area in Mount Rainier National Park is **Paradise,** where there are a number of trails and visitor services. Paradise is a good spot for marmots and is well known for its wildflowers, but it can be very crowded on summer weekends.

The Olympic marmot is found only in the Olympic Mountains and can easily be seen in **Olympic National Park. Hurricane Ridge** is a developed visitor

Marbled godwits and a willet—two of the bigget and easiest of our many shorebirds to identify.

area that is very popular, and Olympic marmots are regularly seen there. Hurricane Ridge is reached by a main park road from the park headquarters and visitor center in Port Angeles. A map of the Hurricane Ridge nature trails actually shows the location of a marmot colony on the **High Ridge Trail.** If you don't see them there, try the **Hurricane Hill Trail** or the road to **Obstruction Point.** You will likely see deer begging for food. Please remember that it is important not to feed them.

Like Sunrise, Hurricane Ridge will give you some spectacular views and has a good display of wildflowers, but don't look for pikas. Interestingly, pikas are one of the mammals that are commonly found in the Cascades but have not been able to cross the lowland barrier of the Puget Trough to reach the Olympics. It is puzzling that marmots made it to the Olympics but pikas did not.

British Columbia

The North Cascades of Washington continue into Canada's **Manning Provincial Park.** Here is another area that combines the pleasures of mountain wildflowers with the charming company of these two mountain mammals. The **Heather** and **Paintbrush Trails** in the **Blackwall Peak** area are well known for marmots and pikas as well as for the spectacular floral display. Naturalists conduct guided walks in this area in summer. The marmots here have become incorrigible beggars, and the park staff would appreciate your help in keeping these guys on a natural foods diet.

45

Fall Shorebird Migration

It's hard to get used to the idea, but fall for shorebirds starts in July, or even late June for some species. Shorebirds typically spend a very short time at their breeding grounds. In some species, the adults of one sex will actually head south soon after the eggs hatch, leaving the other parent to take care of the babies. It is common for the adults to leave before the young have fledged and for the juveniles to arrive in our area as much as a month later. For many species, these juveniles sport plumage that is distinct from the adults.

Birds migrating in fall travel at a more leisurely pace than they do during the spring. Since different age groups, and sometimes different sexes, migrate at different times, migration is spread out over a much longer period in the fall than it is in the spring. Each species has about a three-month migration period sometime between July and October. There is a lot more wandering and getting lost in the fall, especially by the inexperienced juveniles, which results in a much greater variety of species in any one area during fall migration. Fall is also the time when most rarities, like lost Asian peeps, show up along our coast. This all means that fall migration provides the most birding action.

Shorebirds do present some really tough identification problems, especially the smaller sandpipers that are often called "peeps." During fall migration, adults may be in breeding plumage, winter plumage, or somewhere in between. Add to this the juvenile plumages and the difference between sexes in some species, and it's clear why fall is by far the most challenging for shorebird identification. There is also the undeniable fact that shorebirds are a fairly homogeneous group—many of them look very much alike, especially in the nonbreeding plumages.

One almost essential aid in shorebird identification is a good spotting scope. Start in winter, when there are the fewest species around, and keep going into spring, adding new species bit by bit as they come through in breeding plumage. During May and June you can study the few breeders present, and by July, when fall migration starts, you may be ready for the onslaught. Learn the easy ones first—killdeer, black oystercatcher, American avocet—before taking on the peeps. "Take advantage of flocks" may seem like odd advice, but shorebirds are found regularly in mixed flocks, and in these situations you can best judge the size of many shorebirds, and some other characteristics, by comparing them with other birds you know that are nearby.

Read chapter 19 on spring shorebirds with this chapter and consider all the hotspots listed here as spring hotspots also. The shorebird species usually seen in the fall and not in spring are the two golden-plovers, the lesser yellowlegs and the "rare but regular" Baird's, pectoral, sharp-tailed, stilt and buff-breasted sandpipers. Red phalaropes are common fall migrants but are usually well offshore.

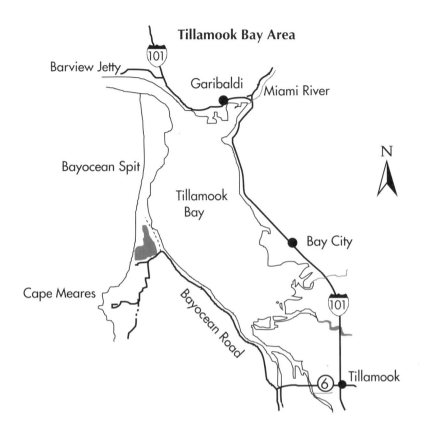

Oregon

Hot Spots

Clatsop Spit forms the southern edge of the mouth of the Columbia River and is the site of the **south jetty of the Columbia River,** well known throughout the state as *the* south jetty. During high tides many birds come to the small ponds just north and east of parking lot C at the jetty. This area is within **Fort Stevens State Park,** reached from U.S. Highway 101 between Astoria and Seaside. Follow signs to the park, and in the park follow signs to the South Jetty and parking area C. While you are here, be sure to check out the scene from the wildlife observation blind at parking lot D. This is usually good for waterfowl and other waterbirds.

Bayocean Spit separates **Tillamook Bay** from the ocean and is reached from the Three Capes Scenic Route out of Tillamook. Follow the directions to Cape Meares given in chapter 31, and before the left turn to go up the hill to the cape, turn right onto the dirt road that goes out to the spit. You will see some birds from the car as you drive in, but park in the parking area and get out of your car. The area to your east and along the shore to the south is known as "the shorebird flats" and is where you want to head, following the trail worn in the salt marsh. Rubber boots are not necessary, but watch your step—the wet mud is really slippery. The ideal timing is to get there at high tide and watch as the tide goes out. As the first mudflats are uncovered, the birds will come in to feed.

In **Coos Bay,** Oregon's largest estuary, there is a favored spot just east of the airport called **Pony Slough.** From Hwy. 101 in the town of North Bend, head west on Virginia Avenue, following signs to the airport. In about a mile, turn right and head north on a rough gravel road that will dead-end at a boat ramp in just over a mile. From here you can scan the mudflats to the east and south. The same strategy used at Bayocean Spit works here—arrive as high tide is starting to go out. The Coos Bay area (Charleston) is home to the annual **Oregon Shorebird Festival** in early September. The festival offers two days of field trips, led by experts, to the best shorebird areas nearby, including **Bandon Marsh,** which does not otherwise have easy access. Since the festival does not draw a huge crowd, this is a good way to get to know shorebirds in the field with experts. For information about the festival, write the Cape Arago Audubon Society, P.O. Box 381, North Bend, OR 97459.

Washington

Willapa Bay has been called the largest unspoiled estuary on the West Coast. The 20-mile Long Beach Peninsula separates the bay from the ocean, and at its northern tip is **Leadbetter Point.** The last 4 miles of the peninsula are in **Willapa National Wildlife Refuge** and **Leadbetter Point State Park.** This is truly one of the outstanding birding spots on the Washington coast. Directions to Leadbetter Point are in chapter 22. Remember, part of the refuge is closed to all entry from April through August to protect nesting snowy plovers. There is a sign at the trailhead indicating the closed area, but don't worry, there is still plenty open for birding. As usual, birding is best as high tide is going out. This is a good place to wear rubber boots.

Northeast of Leadbetter on the other side of Willapa Bay is the little town of **Tokeland** on the end of **Toke Point.** Tokeland is not known for large numbers of shorebirds but has historically been one of the most reliable places for some of the "big guys," such as marbled godwit, long-billed curlew and willet, which all winter here. From State Highway 105 turn south onto Tokeland Road, following the signs to Tokeland. Right away you'll come to an area where the road runs along the shoreline, and you can usually see some birds by pulling over on the roadside and looking from your car. This is Shoalwater Indian tribal land, so bird from your car to avoid trespassing.

In about $1^3/_4$ miles from Hwy. 105, Tokeland Road angles off to the left, but keep going straight on Fisher Avenue and drive a couple of blocks to where it meets 7th Street. Right at this corner there is a small parking space, and from it you can walk out onto the beach. This is the spot most frequented by the big sandpipers mentioned above.

Taking 7th, you can return to Tokeland Road and continue southeast to the **Tokeland Marina.** Look all around the shore near the public dock and the marina. There is a small jetty that you can get to by going down to the shore by the marina and walking along the shore to the jetty. Do not go into or through the RV park.

North of Willapa Bay is **Grays Harbor,** the second largest estuary in Washington. On the north side of its mouth is the **Ocean Shores Peninsula,** considered by many to be the best fall shorebird spot in the state, especially for some of the rarities, such as buff-breasted, Baird's, pectoral and sharp-tailed sandpipers. To get to Ocean Shores, take State Highway 109 along the north shore of Grays Harbor. This is also the route to Bowerman Basin, and in the spring you should try also to visit Ocean Shores when you go to Bowerman. From Hwy. 109, take State Highway 115 south; it will take you into Ocean Shores, where you will go right onto Damon Avenue, then left onto Point Brown Avenue, and then right again onto Ocean Shores Boulevard. At the corner of Ocean Shores Boulevard and Point Brown Avenue is a visitor center with maps and information.

Head south on Ocean Shores Boulevard until you get to the jetty at **Point Brown,** which is always worth checking. From Point Brown, go another three-quarters of a mile east on East Ocean Shores Boulevard to the sewage treatment plant (you can see the fence as you make a turn to the north). Park where you can find space along the road and find the trails into the **Ocean Shores (or Oyhut) Game Range** that run along the outside of the north and south sides of the fence. These trails provide access to the mudflats, salt marsh, and sand spit to the east and north of the sewage plant. The famous spot for pectoral and sharp-tailed sandpipers is northeast of the plant at the end of the inlet near the salt marsh. Ocean Shores has a wealth of other birding opportunities and a bird list of 290 species! Bob Morse has written a comprehensive fifty-page birder's guide that covers all of Ocean Shores in detail. Another spot worth checking is **Damon Point,** which has some closed areas for snowy plovers. You can usually get information about Damon Point from the visitor center. In fall there are awesome views from Damon Point with Mount Rainier rising over Grays Harbor to the east and the Olympic Mountains looming up to the north.

Dungeness National Wildlife Refuge is described in chapter 8 on winter waterfowl and is also considered an excellent spot for shorebirds. In eastern Washington the delta where the **Walla Walla River** joins the Columbia is considered excellent for fall migration. The Walla Walla River Delta is just west of the **Wallula Habitat Management Unit** described in chapter 8.

Just across U.S. Highway 12 from North Shore Road is a small, rough dirt road that goes up to the train tracks. It's probably best to park on the east side of Hwy. 12 and walk the short distance up this road. From near the tracks you can see the Columbia and part of the delta. What will be visible will vary, and a scope is necessary. Some really adventuresome birders will actually bushwhack and wade out into the delta when the river is low if there is a lot of bird activity.

British Columbia

It's back to the Delta area south of Vancouver for more fabulous birding. **Boundary Bay** and **Iona Island** are two of the hottest shorebird spots on the west coast of North America. Boundary Bay, an International Biosphere Reserve, is the stopping point for most of the world's population of western sandpipers. The highest number of wintering bird species ever recorded in Canada was in the Boundary Bay ecosystem, and all but a few of the shorebirds that occur in western North America have been seen there at one time or another. Boundary Bay is also described in chapter 1 on wintering raptors, since it also has the highest density of wintering raptors in Canada. Here are the main points for shorebirds. There are numbered streets that go south from Ladner Trunk Road or its continuation on Hornby to the dike on the north shore of Boundary Bay. The dike at the end of 112th is the best, then come 104th and 96th. At the end of each road you can park and walk on top of the dike to the east or west. A scope is essential here, as it usually is with shorebirds. It is important to come at a high tide when the birds are pushed in close to shore by the encroaching water.

Iona Island is just north of the Vancouver International Airport and is the site of a big sewage treatment plant and Iona Beach Regional Park. This is the most famous spot in western Canada for rare shorebirds such as Baird's, white-rumped, pectoral, buff-breasted and upland sandpipers, as well as ultra-rarities like the rufous-necked stint and spoonbill sandpiper. There are three main areas to bird here—the beaches and mudflats around the regional park, the rocks on the long jetty and the ponds in the treatment plant.

To get to Iona from Provincial Highway 99, take Exit 39A, and follow signs to the airport. You will end up on Sea Island Way and will cross the Fraser River on Sea Island Bridge. As soon as you cross the bridge, turn right and follow an inconspicuous sign to Iona Beach. You'll make several twists and turns on a couple of roads, but just keep following the signs to Iona Beach.

After 4 miles you'll come to Iona Island, and the first feature before you will be the sewage treatment plant. You are welcome to park in the plant's parking lot and bird the sewage ponds on foot when the office is open, weekdays from 9 A.M. to 5 P.M. Sign in just outside the main door of the plant office in the bird-sightings registration book, which you will want to check to see what has been around lately. After birding the sewage ponds on foot, get back in your car and drive to Iona Beach. You will drive alongside a huge cement effluent conduit. If you have not or could not get into the sewage ponds on foot, you can stop briefly at any point here and climb up on the conduit to overlook the ponds.

Eventually the road crosses the conduit and comes to a parking area with rest rooms at **Iona Beach Park.** The last and largest pond is outside the fenced treatment plant and just east of the parking lot. This pond is generally better for gulls and waterfowl than shorebirds, but you never know what may show up here. After checking the pond, explore the beach and the jetty. The jetty is the best place near Vancouver for the "rock pipers"—tattler, oystercatcher, turnstones. Again, shorebirding is best during the highest tides. Iona has been mentioned in several chapters because it is a great spot for wintering seabirds, waterfowl, gulls and raptors, in addition to shorebirds.

Two of the most popular spots for shorebirds on Vancouver Island are **Esquimalt** and **Witty's Lagoons,** both close to each other and to Victoria and described in chapter 8 on waterfowl. Another good spot described in chapter 3 is the **Courtenay River Estuary** between Comox and Courtenay.

46

Aquatic Rodents

Rodents are by far the most successful group of mammals on the planet, not counting the rather recent population explosion and impact of humans. Just over 40 percent of all living species of mammals are rodents, and they have adapted and diversified to become common in almost every terrestrial habitat on earth. Because they are so successful, it is no surprise that rodents are some of the most commonly seen and well known of our wild mammals. Human attitudes toward rodents are interesting in their extremes. Some are kept as pets, and many others are considered cute and lovable and appear as main characters in stories and cartoons. At the same time, wild Norway rats and house mice are despised as the most widespread and destructive mammalian vermin in the world.

Being as successful and diverse as they are, some rodents would be expected to have adapted to freshwater habitats, and indeed there are a couple of dozen semiaquatic rodents found throughout the world (no rodents are considered truly aquatic because they all must come to land to give birth). In the Northwest we have three outstanding examples of semiaquatic rodents—beavers, muskrats and nutrias. Both beavers and muskrats were originally abundant in almost all of the United States and Canada. The nutria is a recent introduction from South America.

Beavers are probably the most well known and popular rodent in America and Canada and are the most important animal in the history of European settlement of North America. The quest for beaver pelts was the greatest driving force in the early exploration of the West. Because of intensive trapping, beavers were exterminated from much of their original range but have made an impressive comeback under modern management practices. Beavers are now abundant enough in some areas to be considered pests, particularly where they dam culverts, which can result in flooded roads. With their return to a healthy population they are legally trapped, and almost five thousand are taken each year in Oregon alone.

Everyone knows about beavers as the engineers of the animal world, and it is generally accepted that no other animal, except the human, modifies its environment as much as beavers do. By damming streams, beavers create a series of wetland habitats that are home to many other animals and plants. With time, the ponds and marshes they create fill with soil and become drier, turning to meadows and eventually to the surrounding forest or woodland.

Beavers are found throughout our region, from low-elevation tidal rivers to high-mountain streams to desert canyons. Their main food is the cambium layer of trees and shrubs, and it is rare to find them where their preferred trees (aspen, alder, willow, cottonwood) are not in good supply. They have shown themselves to be quite adaptable and have resettled wetlands in many urban areas, including the Willamette River in downtown Portland. They are easiest to find on small to mid-sized streams in the Cascades and Coast Range.

Muskrats are often seen as a minibeavers, but the two are not closely related. Muskrats have a little webbing and ridges of stiff hairs on their feet for swimming instead of the completely webbed feet of beavers and nutrias. The muskrat's tail is unique and very different from the famous flat tail of the beaver. Muskrat tails are flattened on the sides, not on the top and bottom. Muskrats are only half the length and a fraction of the weight of beavers, which are the second largest rodents in the world.

Muskrats have been an important source of fur for probably as long as humans have been in North America, and for many years have been the most valuable furbearer in America. Muskrats are most often associated with cattail marshes and shallow quiet waters at low elevations. They readily use irrigation systems and other ditches, as well as reservoirs, and because of this they have become quite abundant in many agricultural areas with these features.

The history of the nutria, or coypu, is yet another tale of human folly and the disruption of a natural ecosystem. In the 1930s nutrias were imported to the United States from their native South America to be raised in captivity for their supposedly valuable pelts. The nutria craze was one of many get-rich-quick schemes desperate Americans tried during the Depression. The nutria craze peaked in the 1950s followed by a total collapse in the market. Some nutrias had been escaping captivity for years, but when the whole industry failed, thousands were turned loose. Interestingly, the two spots in North America where they became well established and have become most common are along the lower Mississippi River (Louisiana especially) and the lower Columbia River. From the lower Columbia they have spread along the coast to southern Oregon and the Fraser River.

Nutrias can now be found in almost any freshwater habitat at lower elevations on the west side of the Cascades, and are very common locally. They prefer the same habitat as muskrats, and wildlife biologists familiar with both species are convinced that nutrias displace muskrats once they move into an area.

These three rodents can be difficult to tell apart, and identification information is surprisingly scarce, so here are some tips. If you see the whole animal, identification should be easy. Beavers have a very distinctive flat tail and are clearly bigger than the biggest house cat you've ever seen. Nutrias are smaller than beavers but can be close in size. The nutria's tail is long and round with a little hair. Muskrats are significantly smaller than either beavers or nutrias, to me they always look smaller than an opossum, or about the size of a small house cat. The muskrat's laterally compressed tail (flattened from side to side) is naked, with a ridge on the top. This makes it easy when you see the whole animal, but that's rare. What you usually see is the top of a head moving through the water.

Size can be very tricky to judge, so don't use it unless the animal is really big (beaver) or really small (muskrat). I have discovered two clues to be reliable in the Northwest. First, the flattened tail of the muskrat often breaks the water as it swims. If you see what looks like a rodent head with a garter snake swimming after it, it is probably a muskrat. The second characteristic is coloring. Beavers are a solid rich dark brown, as is the head and back of a muskrat (muskrats have lighter bellies). All the nutrias I have seen have grizzled or otherwise mottled fur on their heads, particularly around the mouth and behind the ears, which seem to stick out more than a beaver's or muskrat's ears. The *lighter fur around the base of the ears* usually shows up well when nutrias are swimming.

Hot Spots

All three of these semiaquatic rodents are widespread and can be common in the right habitat, but they move around a lot and are legally trapped. Ask at local ranger districts, park visitor centers or regional offices of wildlife agencies for current information on locations. All three are most commonly seen around dawn and dusk, although some urban nutrias are quite bold and can be out almost any time. One of the best ways to see any of the three is to quietly canoe (or kayak) through good habitat early or late in the day.

Oregon

The **Ripplebrook Ranger Station** in Mount Hood National Forest is about 25 miles southeast of Estacada on State Highway 224. In the various tributaries of the Clackamas River near the ranger station there is lots of beaver activity, partly because some of the nuisance beaver trapped in the Portland area are released here. Ask at the Ripplebrook Ranger Station for suggestions and directions. The **Alder Flat Trail** just west of the ranger station goes through some nice old growth forest and circles an old beaver pond. Soon after starting, the trail forks and you'll want to go left around the southern edge of the pond to the other side, where you can see dams and the lodge. Other dams can be seen from the roads near the ranger station, and there has been lots of activity at the rifle range on Pint Creek.

The BLM has just finished developing a major interpretive trail at its **Wildwood Recreation Site,** 15 miles east of Sandy on U.S. Highway 26 to Mount Hood. The site is well marked; take the first left after you enter the area, park in the trailhead parking area and take the universally accessible **Wetlands Trail** through the marshy area south of the Salmon River. This is excellent lush low-elevation west-side coniferous forest, and there are lots of birds around the old beaver ponds. The old beaver lodges and dams are covered with plant growth now, making them hard to see in summer, but beaver are still active in the area and fresh sign may show up at any time.

Beavers and muskrats are both seen at the **McNary Wildlife Nature Area,** a rehabilitated wetland downstream of McNary Dam. From U.S. Highway 730 in Umatilla, just east of I-82, go north into the main entrance for McNary Dam. Before you get to the visitor center, turn left on to 3rd Street, following signs to the wildlife area. From the parking area at the end of Ferry Road you can explore trails on both sides. This area is also good for waterfowl in the

The lighter hair around the ears is your best clue that this is a nutria, not a muskrat or a beaver.

winter if the ponds are not frozen. A map and checklist are available at the visitor center.

Whiskey Springs Interpretive Trail in the **Rogue River National Forest** near Medford has trails, boardwalk and viewing platform in a wetland area with lots of recent beaver activity. Go 30 miles east from Medford on State Highway 140, the Lake of the Woods Highway. Just before Fish Lake, turn left to go north on Butte Falls Fish Lake Road, Forest Road 37, following signs to Willow Lake. After 8 miles turn right on Forest Road 3065 and go half a mile to the campground.

In the big east-side marshes of **Malheur National Wildlife Refuge, Summer Lake Wildlife Area** and the refuges in the **Klamath Basin,** muskrat habitat is excellent and the animals are regularly seen. In the **Upper Klamath National Wildlife Refuge** there is an established canoe trail starting at the Rocky Point Resort (which rents canoes) where you may find beavers, muskrats and river otters.

Washington

Ridgefield National Wildlife Refuge is one of the best areas for wildlife watching near Portland (see chapter 58). All three of our swimming rodents live here, but the nutria is by far the most abundant. Actually, this could be one of the densest populations of nutrias in the West. Muskrats have become very scarce here, and this has led several naturalists to suspect that nutrias displace muskrats. Chances are good you will see nutrias any time you're at Ridgefield.

Brown Creek Campground is just 15 miles off U.S. Highway 101 north of Shelton, making it a possible stop on the way up the east side of the Olympic Peninsula. Seven and three-quarters miles north of Shelton, head west on the Skokomish Valley Road—there is a big sign reading Olympic N. F., Skokomish River Rec. Area. In just over 5 miles take the right fork onto Forest Road 23 and stay on it, following the signs to Brown Creek Campground. After another 9 miles you'll turn right onto Forest Road 2353, go almost a mile to a Skokomish River bridge, then cross the bridge and immediately make a sharp right turn onto Forest Road 2340.

In half a mile you come to the small and charming Brown Creek Campground, and next to the well is the beginning of the **Beaver Pond Loop Trail, #877.** Take the trail, and when it forks, go right, continuing around the lake and hugging the shore to your left. At one point you'll come out onto Forest Road 2340-540 and pass by a horse camp. Watch for the trail to leave the road again on the left, where it is marked Skok Trail. In a short distance there is another fork; stay left to continue around the lake. Lodges are conspicuous. One nice aspect to this beaver pond is that you can camp at the campground, making it easy to look for beaver at dawn or dusk.

The **Selkirk Mountains** of northeastern Washington appear to be loaded with beaver. Two beautiful areas to see beaver and lots of other wildlife are the **Little Pend Oreille National Wildlife Refuge** and **Big Meadow Lake.**

The Little Pend Oreille (pronounced *pond-or-ray*) National Wildlife Refuge has been going through some changes as the U.S. Fish and Wildlife Service takes over management of the area from the state. It's tricky finding your way around, and there hasn't been a good map to date, but there will probably be some changes in roads and signs and a newer map should be available at some point. **McDowell Lake** has beavers and muskrats (and nesting red-necked grebes). Before you go, get the best information available for getting on the trail from campground #1 to the north end of McDowell Lake, and for getting to the overlook on the east side of the lake. Keep your eyes out for the endangered Pend Oreille white-tailed deer, as well as moose and black bear!

Big Meadow Lake is 8 miles west of Ione. Go west on Main Street through the "city center" of Ione, turn right at the train tracks and go to the stop sign. Turn left, go 2 blocks and turn left again, then go south 1 block and turn right, following the signs to Smackout Pass and Big Meadow Lake. Two miles after the pavement ends, turn left and stay on Forest Road 2695 to the lake. Big Meadow Lake has a good variety of habitats, so its wildlife is plentiful. Beavers and muskrats are regulars, and moose are becoming more common. The wooden observation tower on the **Meadow Creek Trail** gives a great overview of the area.

British Columbia

Manning Provincial Park is one of the best places in our region for summer adventures and has already been mentioned in several chapters for birding and wildflowers. There is a lot of beaver activity along the **Similkameen River** and its tributaries in the center of the park near the visitor center, and there are naturalist programs during the summer that include walks in these areas and discussions of beavers. The self-guided nature trail around **Beaver Pond** has interpretive signs and is an excellent example of an old beaver pond that is now abandoned and changing into a meadow. There is current beaver activity at **Rein Orchid** and **Twenty Minute Lakes,** both with short, easy trails around them.

47

August Shorttakes

Berries

One of the benefits of living in the Pacific Northwest is the bounty of wild berries every summer. Almost half of the bushes or shrubs found west of the Cascades have fleshy fruits, and most of these are considered edible by humans, not to mention the hundreds of animals that rely on them for food. The abundant berries were a major food resource for Native Americans, who ate them straight off the bush in season or dried them, often blended with other ingredients, to make a variety of storable foods called *pemmican.*

Two families dominate the list of choice berries in the Northwest—the rose family and the heath or heather family. The rose family includes the various types of blackberries and raspberries (including dewberry and blackcap), thimbleberry and salmonberry. Thickets of these plants are usually called "brambles," an Old English term for thorny shrubs. Two blackberries, the evergreen and the ubiquitous Himalayan, are introduced and very invasive. Most of these blackberry-type plants (genus *Rubus*) are common at low elevations and can be found just about anywhere on the west side, especially at the edges of fields and woodlands and along streams.

The other big berry family, the heath, includes all the blueberries and huckleberries (including bilberry and lingonberry) and salal, one of the most abundant plants in coastal coniferous forests. Many forest understories are dominated by members of this group, as are unforested habitats high in the mountains. Some of the mountain blueberries and huckleberries form solid thickets between about 2,000 and 4,000 feet in elevation. Two of the best-known areas for these are around **Lolo Pass** and the road to **Cloud Cap** in the **Mount Hood National Forest,** and the **Indian Heaven** berry fields on Mount Adams in **Gifford Pinchot National Forest.** The Indian Heaven fields are along Forest Road 24, but the areas to the north or east of the road are reserved as traditional berry-harvesting areas for Native Americans.

Meteor Showers

The largest meteor shower of the year is the well-known Perseid meteor shower. This is seen best around 8 P.M. between August 11 and 13, and the meteors appear to be coming from the constellation Perseus. Lucky observers with good conditions sometimes see fifty meteors an hour!

48

A Closer Look: Summer Bug Safari

The large female sank its feeding tube deep into the vessel of its food source. While she slowly sucked the life-giving nutrients, her abdomen began to ripple with contractions. Slowly, out of her reproductive opening, a new daughter started to emerge. In a few minutes her legs were wiggling in the air and then she was out, standing next to her mother. The large female repeated the process every 2 hours and was soon surrounded by a small herd of daughters, all with embryos already starting to develop in their reproductive systems. There were no males for months as females produced females that produced females, on and on, until, finally, eggs were laid that hatched into winged males and females. They mated, the females laid eggs and they all died. The entire population of this creature survived for months as fertilized eggs in suspended animation. Then their food again become available and they underwent another females-only population explosion.

A scene from *Aliens V?* Nope, just aphids on your roses. Yes, aphids give live birth to little female babies that start to eat and grow immediately and are soon reproducing themselves. No males and no fertilization are involved. This process is called *parthenogenesis* (which means "virgin birth"), and you can watch it happen in your own backyard or even right in your hand. If you want to see lots of amazing animals with almost no effort, it's easy—just step outside into your yard. Even with a modest variety of plants, you'll have dozens of fascinating insects at your fingertips. I'm still astonished that just about every time I go on a bug safari in my yard, I find yet another new insect that I've never seen before. And I still haven't figured out what some of them are! Life's never dull for naturalists on their hands and knees.

The joys of backyard bugs have been promoted by naturalists for years, and there are some great books to help you decipher the astonishing lives of insects. Two timeless classics from the 1960s that many budding entomologists have cut their teeth on are *The Strange Lives of Familiar Insects,* by Edwin Way Teale, and *Life on a Little Known Planet,* by Howard Evans. An instant classic the moment it was printed in 1983 is *A Guide to Observing Insect Lives,* by Donald Stokes, which has some of the newest details on the interesting and often bizarre life cycles and behavior of very common insects. With these books, a magnifying glass and a couple of field guides for identification, you'll be all set to make sense of the jungle out there.

On my cedar fence there are small shallow grooves between the lines of grain in the wood. It looks like someone may have taken a sharp fingernail and scraped out a very thin layer of wood. Who would do this? I wondered for years. Then one summer's day I saw yellow jackets landing on this area of the fence. I watched closely, and sure enough, the yellow jackets were chewing on the fence. Of course! Yellow jackets are members of the paper wasp family, and paper is made from wood. Since then I have seen other paper wasps chewing on my fence for the pulp to make their paper nests. Another backyard insect mystery solved.

One overwhelming fact that becomes very clear the more one studies insects is that there are a lot of them. No matter how you figure it, in total numbers, in numbers of different species or in biomass, insects rule the world. There are many more different *kinds* of insects than there are all other animals put together. This means there's no end to the fun you can have as an entomologist, amateur or otherwise.

I've been using the words "bug" and "insect" interchangeably, but just what is a bug? The term bug is about as vague as you can get. Almost any small animal, and even protozoans and bacteria, are sometimes called bugs. When most people use the word bug, however, they are usually referring to insects, and maybe spiders. Let's be precise about these beasts, because they are usually easy to tell apart.

Most of the animals called bugs are *arthropods.* Arthropods have no bones but instead have a tough, usually hard skin that supports the body. To be able to move, they have joints in this hard skin, or *exoskeleton.* It is from this characteristic that the term arthropod, or "jointed leg," comes, and the main groups of arthropods can easily be told by the number of legs they have. If it has six legs, it is an insect, and will also have three body segments and a pair of antennae. If it has eight legs, it is an arachnid, and will not have antennae. If it has more than eight legs and two pairs of antennae, it is a crustacean. There are two groups of arthropods that are long and skinny with many distinct body segments. If one of these has one pair of legs on each segment, it is a centipede, and if it has two pairs of legs on each segment, it is a millipede. Most adult insects have wings and can fly, but no other arthropods ever do.

In your backyard you have representatives of all five of these arthropod groups. Insects are by far the most numerous and are the ones you know best. The biggest and most common arachnids are the spiders. Everyone recognizes almost every spider they see as a spider, and many people know a few kinds by name, such as the black widows, jumping spiders and crab spiders. There are lots of other arachnids in your yard, but you will very rarely see them unless you're looking hard because they are so tiny. These are the mites, close relatives of ticks, and many kinds live in soil.

It comes as a shock to most people to learn that they have crustaceans in their yard, but *isopods,* variously called sow bugs, pill bugs, roly-polies or potato bugs, are actually terrestrial crustaceans. You have probably noticed a few millipedes and centipedes in your yard at some point too, since they are distinctive.

Following are some of the most common and conspicuous insects that people regularly find in their yards in the Northwest. This list may be a bit biased for the west side, but some insects may be equally common in some areas east of the Cascades.

Grasshoppers are very familiar insects but will usually be common in your yard only if you have or live near grassy fields. Their relatives, the crickets and katydids, may show up from time to time and are usually noticed later in the summer, when they start to sing. Male crickets and katydids sing by rubbing their wings together in order to attract mates. Their ears are on their legs, an arrangement humans find odd.

Earwigs are clearly unpopular insects, probably because they have little pincers that look pretty nasty, emit a foul odor when bothered (or smashed) and often show up in large numbers inside things left lying around the yard. They occasionally do eat flowers, but they are primarily predators and scavengers and are therefore beneficial. The female will guard her eggs and tend her babies for a short time, unusual behavior for an insect. The most common earwigs in our area have actually been introduced from Europe.

Leave a light on outside at night in the summer you're sure to attract some interesting insects. Various moths are common, and some interesting beetles will show up, but one of my favorites is the jewel-like green lacewing. I love the shiny, golden eyes on these delicate and beautiful creatures. Lacewings are considered beneficial because their larvae are voracious predators of aphids and indeed are often called "aphid lions."

The most famous aphid predator is, of course, the ladybug. Books always give the proper common name for these attractive beetles as "ladybird beetles," but I've never heard that name used in the West. This name, by the way, can be traced back to the Middle Ages, when these insects were associated with the Virgin Mary. I guess she didn't like aphids. Ladybugs gobble up large numbers of aphids as larvae and as adults. They also like to eat scale insects, nasty pests of citrus trees. So ladybugs are very beneficial from an agricultural standpoint and can even be bought at nurseries in the spring for release into your own yard.

Beetles are the largest group of insects, which means there are *lots* of beetles. One big family that has lots of gardener's helpers is the predaceous ground beetle family. There are probably six hundred or so ground beetle species in the Northwest, and most individuals can be recognized as members of this family by the flattened edges on their squarish thoraxes. These guys are usually nocturnal but are easy to find hiding under rocks and logs or hanging out at the compost pile. The adults and larvae are major predators of many types of caterpillars, including many of the worst pest species. Two genera of the big ones, *Calosoma* and *Scaphinotus,* are famous as the slug- and snail-killers of the Northwest.

There really is almost no end to the insects and other arthropods around your home. Start looking in natural habitats and you'll find even more. My favorite type of bug hunt is looking through streams and ponds for aquatic beasties. It's a whole new world. Happy hunting.

September

Notes

49

Pelagic Birding

I thought people only turned green when they were seasick in cartoons. But there he was, a seasick birder, and his face was actually a pale waxy green. I was on a pelagic birding trip off the Oregon coast and had already joined many of my fellow passengers at the rail for a little chat with Neptune. Of course, it was also raining, which seemed odd, because we were sure it was cold enough to snow. "Yeah, it just doesn't get any better than this" came the sarcastic comment from one of the cold, wet birders huddling under the tiny wheelhouse overhang, which afforded little protection since the boat's motion drove the rain horizontally into our faces. Why were we putting ourselves through this torture?

"Shearwater! Black-vented! Maybe. Coming at eleven o'clock," shouted our leader. The deck was immediately transformed into a beehive of activity and the boat leaned as a wave of people hit the port rail. This was it, the reason all these people were putting themselves through the rigors of a pelagic birding trip. Nobody on the boat, including the guides, had ever seen a black-vented shearwater before, and many of us didn't even know such a thing existed. All eyes were glued on the small dark bird as it flew quickly by the boat and was gone. "Did anyone see if its vent was black?" asked one of the superbirders on the trip. "Its vent? I couldn't even tell if it had a *head!*" came the reply from a neophyte to the wonders of pelagic birding. So was it a black-vented or an even more rare Manx shearwater? No one will ever know, for both are fabulously rare in our region and almost impossible to tell apart.

Such are the joys and demands of pelagic birding. After an exhausting and challenging 8-hour day, we had a trip list of twenty-nine species, a fraction of what would be expected from a hard day of birding almost anywhere on land. But a third of those species were brand new "life birds" for half the people on the trip, and we all knew that this was the only way we would ever see many of these birds. This tale illustrates the essential characteristics of pelagic birding—hard work for few, but big rewards.

Pelagic birding is definitely birding on the edge. It's birding on the edge of the ocean and it's birding on the frontier of our knowledge of birds. Of course, conditions are not always unpleasant on all boat trips. I've been on trips in California when the sun was shining, the sea was like glass, and people were wearing T-shirts, but in the Northwest you've got to be prepared for the worst.

What's all the hubbub about pelagic birds? Why bother? Well, because they're there. In every serious birder's life the point comes when you just have to put to sea because there is a group of birds that you will only see by boat—unless you spend hundreds of hours perched on rocky headlands during fall and winter storms. These are the pelagic birds, and they remain some of the most mysterious birds in the world. Pelagic means living on the open ocean and any pelagic animal—bird, fish or mammal—is hard to study because it roams over vast expanses of ocean. Many marine animals are actually coastal, coming out of the water regularly throughout the year for various purposes. Truly pelagic animals, on the other hand, spend their entire lives on and in the open oceans.

Some marine mammals, like cetaceans, never have to come onto land. One group of marine reptiles, the sea snakes, are similar to mammals in that they do not lay eggs, thus completely freeing themselves from the land also. But bird and reptile eggs drown, so all birds and sea turtles have to come to land to lay their eggs, regardless of how pelagic they are the rest of the year. Some travel fantastic distances as they roam the oceans. The short-tailed shearwater, for example, nests in Tasmania and winters (during our summer) near Alaska, traveling 20,000 miles every year!

Like the word "seabird," the term "pelagic bird" is not precise, resulting in some variations in use. Always called pelagic, and in fact the most pelagic of all birds, are the tubenoses, of the order Procellariiformes. There is no regularly used common name for this group because most people will never see them. The only tubenoses most people have ever even heard of are albatrosses, sometimes called gooney birds in old travelogs and nature shows. The tubenoses include the albatrosses, shearwaters, petrels, storm-petrels and the fulmar.

By far the most common and abundant tubenose is the sooty shearwater, seen on just about every boat trip off our coast and often seen from shore. In late summer and early fall, hundreds of thousands of sootys migrate up the Pacific Coast. Sometimes huge flocks will pass by shore close enough to be seen with the naked eye for hours at a time. For most people, such a sighting will be the greatest number of animals of one species seen at one time in their lives! It is now thought that sooty shearwaters are one of the most abundant birds in the world, with estimates of up to a *billion* individuals worldwide. Any time in August or September when you are at the coast, scan the ocean with binoculars or a scope just outside of where the farthest waves are forming. With patience and practice you can almost always find sootys zipping around out there, looking like giant sea swifts with their long, stiff, arched wings.

No other tubenose is remotely close to the sooty shearwater in numbers. The others regularly seen on pelagic-birding boat trips are: black-footed albatross; northern fulmar; pink-footed, flesh-footed, short-tailed and Buller's shearwaters and fork-tailed storm-petrel.

The other group of birds almost always described as pelagic is the family of alcids or auks. These are discussed in chapter 31. The species commonly seen on boat trips are: common murre; pigeon guillemot; rhinoceros and Cassin's auklets; tufted puffin and, less commonly, marbled and ancient murrelets. The tubenoses and the alcids are clearly the largest groups of pelagic birds in North America. However, there are other birds belonging to different families that are usually included in lists of pelagic birds, even though they may spend more time on land or actually be more coastal than these two hard-core pelagic groups.

In the gull and tern family are several species that we see almost exclusively offshore while they are migrating or wintering here. Pomarine and parasitic jaegers are seen quite regularly; the long-tailed jaeger is much less common and irregular. Black-legged kittiwakes, Sabine's gulls and Arctic terns are regular and fairly common migrants, and many of the kittiwakes stay for the winter. The red phalarope is the most pelagic of all shorebirds, and large numbers migrate offshore.

Of course, there are other aquatic birds commonly seen by birders on boat trips that are not usually considered pelagic. These are the cormorants, gulls, loons, grebes and sea ducks. Any time you're at sea, watch for marine mammals. Pelagic birders in the Northwest see harbor and fur seals; Steller's and California sea lions; orcas; harbor and Dall's porpoises; Pacific white-sided and northern right whale dolphins; gray whales; and occasionally humpback and minke whales; and elephant seals.

A pelagic birding trip requires a lot more preparation than does your average birding trip. The biggest problem, of course, is the small matter of a boat. If you own a seaworthy boat or have a friend who does, you can be very independent about your birding. Very few birders fall into this category, however, and the rest of us have two options—sign up for organized pelagic birding trips or arrange to go on fishing charters. You have a lot more flexibility using fishing charters, which go out almost every weekend day. The chambers of commerce of most coastal towns can provide a list of local charter operators and may actually know the names of those specializing in whale- and bird-watching trips. The vast majority of birders do not find an average charter satisfactory, however, because the purpose of the trip is not birding and there are rarely other people on the boat who have any knowledge of, or interest in, pelagic birds. It is much more satisfying to go on a trip whose goal, or rather obsession, is finding and identifying pelagic birds. These organized trips will have knowledgeable leaders, as well as hotshot birders, who can help with the challenging task of identifying gray birds whizzing by through bouncing rain-spotted binoculars. Another way to see some pelagic birds, and lots of coastal species, is from ferries.

Organized trips will require registration in advance, usually way in advance, because space is limited. You will have to meet at the boat very early in the morning, and this often means staying in a nearby motel the night before. Trips usually last 8 to 12 hours. You must be well prepared! Be sure you have all the clothing necessary to keep warm and dry under any weather conditions you may encounter (it's hard to overdress). Be especially prepared for wind, and wear your "grippiest" shoes. Bring all the food and drink you will need for the duration of the trip—keeping in mind that most people eat lightly to avoid seasickness. Leave your scope on shore—it's useless on a boat. Bone up on your seabird identification, because many of your sightings will be brief and under poor conditions.

Seasickness deserves some special attention because it is the biggest problem facing many pelagic birders and can really ruin a trip. There is some seasickness lore passed down over the years that many people believe can help. Common sense tells you to get plenty of sleep, and don't drink alcohol the night before or the day of the trip. Eat a light breakfast and have lots of little snacks during the day that are high in carbohydrates and low in fats. Drink plenty of liquids. Most people find they do best if they stay standing up and active on the open deck in the fresh air. Lying down inside seems to make things worse. If you get woozy, keep your eyes on the horizon.

There are several medications available for motion sickness. Many people have good results with meclizine (available as a generic or under the brand name Bonine), which doesn't make them as sleepy as do most other over-the-counter medications. Take your first dose an hour before departure. What seems to be the ultimate remedy for many, and is now all the rage, is "the patch," a small adhesive disk placed behind the ear that delivers scopolamine transdermally over three days. The brand name is Transderm Scop, and it is available by prescription only. There are some possible side effects that you should discuss with your doctor, and it is important to follow the directions carefully. In order for the patch to work properly, put it on the night before the trip. With any seasickness medication, and with the patch especially, it is important to test it out well in advance of your actual trip to find out if you have any side effects.

Many who desire a more natural alternative to the standard medicines have success with ginger, an ancient herbal remedy for nausea and upset stomach (there really was a reason why your mother gave you ginger ale when your tummy was upset). People will eat gingersnaps or candy, drink ginger ale and even take capsules of powdered ginger. There is some scientific evidence that ginger is effective, but even if it isn't, a box of gingersnaps makes a fine snack. Another alternative is acupressure wrist bracelets, which have not been found effective in any scientific tests but which some people swear by.

Fall is the traditional time for most pelagic trips, and October is still considered the best month for the biggest variety of birds. In recent years birders have wanted to get more data on pelagics throughout the year, and some trips are now available almost every month except for December and June. The ferries, however, sail every day, and provide a taste of pelagic birding at low cost (and high comfort).

Hot Spots

Following are the most regularly run pelagic birding trips from year to year. Schedules are always changing, so you must contact individual operators to get the latest information. There are other trips run by local Audubon Society chapters, museums and natural history associations, but they are not as predictable and can be hard to locate. The best single source for information on pelagic trips in North America each year is the January issue of *Winging It,* the newsletter of the American Birding Association.

Oregon

The Portland Audubon Society conducts six to ten trips a year, mainly from the end of July through October. They depart from Garibaldi or from Ilwaco in Washington. The cost is $60 to $150. Write: Pelagic Trips, Portland Audubon Society, 5151 NW Cornell Road, Portland, OR 97210; (503) 292-6855, fax (503) 292-1021.

Washington

Terry Wahl, one of Washington's top birders and coauthor of the essential *A Guide to Bird Finding in Washington,* has been running trips out of Westport for many years. There are twelve to fifteen trips a year, most from July through October. The cost is $80 to $200. Write: Westport Seabirds, c/o Terry Wahl, 3041 Eldridge, Bellingham, WA 98225; (206) 733-8255.

British Columbia

The only regularly occurring trips in British Columbia are those run by Michael Shepard, out of The Field Naturalist nature store in Victoria. Trips leave from Ucluelet and vary quite a bit from year to year. There is always a trip on the second weekend in October, the Canadian Thanksgiving weekend. Contact Michael at The Field Naturalist, 1126 Blanshard Street, Victoria, British Columbia, V8W 2H6; (604) 388-4174.

Ferries

All our regularly occurring seabirds (loons, grebes, cormorants, waterfowl, gulls, terns and alcids) can be seen from the ferries that ply the Salish Sea. Some of the tubenoses and jaegers are also possibilities on some trips. Ferry schedules change during the year, so it is always important to get the current schedule for the times you are considering. Ferries are listed in the appendix.

The *M.V. Coho* goes back and forth between Port Angeles, Washington, and Victoria, British Columbia, with two departures a day from each city in October and November. The hour and a half crossing of the Strait of Juan de Fuca is by far your best chance to see truly pelagic birds from a ferry. Sooty and short-tailed shearwaters, northern fulmars and forked-tailed storm-petrels occur most frequently, making this ferry ride a miniature pelagic trip. The Tsawwassen–Swartz Bay Ferry and San Juan Islands Ferry are considered the best all-around ferry rides for wildlife and will usually have plenty of seabirds, but it is very rare to see the truly pelagic birds on these routes. Always be on guard, however—you never know what might show up.

50

Ancient Forests

Often called the crowning glory of a land filled with superlatives, the ancient forests of the Pacific Northwest are certainly one of our greatest natural, and national, treasures. The unique climate west of the Coast Ranges, Cascades and Coast Mountains from northern California to southeastern Alaska has created the greatest coniferous forests in the world. The factors encouraging these lush forests are moderate temperatures and lots of rain—the heaviest precipitation in North America. This combination sounds great for any plant, but most of the rain falls during the coldest part of the year, and there is a significant summer drought. These are tough conditions for broad-leaved trees. Conifers, however, with their needles, or scalelike leaves, can thrive in this environment and indeed, it is here that they reach their greatest glory.

So how great is great? About half of the twenty-five tallest species of trees in the world grow in this forest. For every genus of coniferous tree represented in the Pacific Northwest forest, the largest species in that genus is found here (except for the junipers). In all of eastern North America only one tree gets over 200 feet high, while in our forests *thirteen* different species regularly grow to over 200 feet, the tallest reaching almost 400 feet! The redwoods are, of course, the most famous of these Pacific giants and just range into the southwestern corner of Oregon from their stronghold in northern California. Close behind the redwoods in height and mass are Douglas fir, Sitka spruce, western red cedar, western hemlock, grand fir, Pacific silver fir, Port Orford cedar, sugar pine and ponderosa pine.

Biomass is a term for the total amount of all the living and once-living material in a particular area and is sometimes used to compare the "productivity" of two areas. We frequently hear about the diversity, productivity and importance of tropical rain forests, but the biomass of the richest tropical rain forests is about 180 tons per acre, while the biomass of the average Pacific Northwest old growth coniferous forest is around 400 tons per acre. The biomass of old growth redwood forests can reach over 1,500 tons per acre, the highest biomass of any ecosystem on earth!

This great forest developed after the last Ice Age and for ten thousand years covered a 2,000-mile stretch of land with an almost unbroken blanket of giant conifers. Native Americans used the western red cedar extensively, but their impact on this primeval forest was minuscule. Things changed dramatically in a geological wink of an eye when the new Americans and Canadians started to settle the West. With their advanced technologies and insatiable demands for building materials and fuel, they made short work of what was treated as an inexhaustible resource. Now in the United States only about 10 percent of this original, ancient or old growth forest is left, and in Canada maybe as much as 40 percent remains. This is a much greater percentage of habitat loss than the often-deplored loss of wetlands in the United States or the current destruction of tropical rain forests. One major reason this loss seemed to go on for so long before being noticed was that few people were aware of the differences between the old growth forests being cut down and the younger forests that replaced them. An old growth or ancient forest is a special type of forest very different from the new forest that replaces it. There are several

The ancient forests of the Northwest are more threatened than tropical rain forests.

characteristics or components that make a forest "old growth." As the name implies, there must be old trees. For the primary species in these forests—Douglas fir, Sitka spruce, western hemlock and western red cedar—"old" starts around two hundred years, and four hundred to five hundred years is considered a good, healthy middle age. But the big guys aren't the only trees living in an old growth forest. Indeed, one of the most important characteristics of old growth is the presence of trees of all ages and of a variety of species, creating a multilayered canopy. And where the ancient giants have finally fallen, they have made openings in the canopy, letting light into the forest. This unevenness or diversity is one of the glaring differences between an ancient forest and a new forest planted in its place.

When these giants die, they are as important to the forest as when they lived. A standing dead tree is called a *snag,* and as many animals use snags as use living trees. Studies in Oregon have found sixty species of birds and mammals that use snags regularly for food, shelter or both. Snags can remain standing and serve the forest for one hundred years. A fallen tree is just as important as a living tree or snag, and big fallen logs may last as long as four hundred years on the forest floor. As many as 130 species of vertebrates may utilize a fallen log as it slowly rots, returning nutrients to the soil and to other plants. A very common sight in the Northwest is the "nurse log"—an old log with a garden of plants, especially young hemlocks, growing on it. Fallen logs are giant sponges, serving as reservoirs of water for plants and animals during the summer drought.

Fallen logs in streams create the pools, falls and riffles that are habitat for many aquatic animals. They shade the stream and help keep the water temperature low, resulting in the higher oxygen content needed by trout and salmon. Fallen logs and all organic debris on the ground play an absolutely critical role in maintaining the quality of watersheds by preventing soil erosion, abating floods and acting as filters to keep silt out of streams. It is for all these reasons that ancient forests create the greatest rivers and streams for salmon, and why logging kills fish. The presence of many snags and fallen logs is an essential characteristic of old growth forests.

Scientists have only recently begun to understand the extreme complexity of ancient forest ecosystems. *Lobaria,* a lichen, by fixing nitrogen from the air, and thereby making it eventually available to other plants, plays a critical role in the forest's nitrogen cycle. Tiny rodents called voles spread spores of fungi in their droppings that are essential for establishing symbiotic mycorrhizae in the roots of plants, greatly enhancing root function. Many animals utilize old growth forests, and some are completely dependent upon this specific type of habitat.

Not many birds have made the cover of *Time,* but the spotted owl's appearance in 1990 made it by far the best-known denizen of the ancient forest. The marbled murrelet is the next best known, old-growth-dependent species. The little voles so characteristic of old growth (red tree, California red-back and Pacific) don't make exciting copy, so we don't hear a lot about them, or about unpopular animals like salamanders, but they are all unique species that play important roles in the ancient forest ecosystem. The majority of animals found in old growth forests are also found in other forest types, but old growth is their preferred habitat and the one in which they do best. Some of the other animals most closely associated with our ancient forests are Roosevelt elk, American marten, Sitka black-tailed deer, chickaree or Douglas squirrel, seven bat species, bald eagle, osprey, pileated woodpecker, Vaux's swift, brown creeper, Townsend's and hermit warblers, red crossbill, pine grosbeak, tailed frog, Olympic salamander, Pacific giant salamander, Del Norte and slender salamanders.

The controversy over the fate of the few remaining ancient forest fragments has been the hottest environmental issue in the region for over a decade, and no resolution is at hand. The forces of commerce and the "Wise Use" movement, well represented in the Congress elected in 1994, present the greatest threat to the protection of wildlife and natural habitats in twenty-five years. It is more important than ever that those who treasure these increasingly rare and threatened resources make their voices heard at every opportunity.

Oregon

A small but nice sample of ancient forest very close to Portland is in **Oxbow Regional Park,** at the eastern edge of the greater metro area on the Sandy River. From Greshem, take Division Street east 5 miles then angle to the right onto Oxbow Drive and take it 2 miles to the junction with Oxbow Parkway. Turn left and take Oxbow Parkway into the park; the route is well marked. At the entrance station (there is a fee) you can get a park map. The old growth forest is south of the road near trail markers D and E and is shown on the map. Oxbow Park is also the site of a Salmon Festival in October.

Another nice example of old growth with easy access is the **Salmon River Trail** in **Mount Hood National Forest.** About 18 miles east of Sandy and past the traffic signal in Welches, turn right off U.S. Highway 26 onto Salmon River Road, Forest Road 2618. Go south just about 5 miles to the Green Canyon Campground, and just after the campground, before the road crosses the Salmon River on a bridge, you will see a parking area on the left with a trailhead for the Salmon River Trail, #742.

Trail #742 heads south and immediately goes up a steep hill for a short haul, then levels out and is easy going from then on. Although the trail is high on the canyon wall, you can look right into the middle of some huge old maples that are totally fuzzy with moss and ferns, and you'll actually have a chance to get a good look at some of the birds that usually stay high in the trees. The trail drops to the river, and across a small side channel there is a river bench with a very scenic old growth grove. The trail continues upstream into the wilderness area and continues to be very beautiful, but the forest does get a bit younger.

Some of the biggest and most accessible old growth Douglas firs and western hemlocks in the **Columbia Gorge National Scenic Area** are in the **Multnomah Basin,** the area between Multnomah Falls and Larch Mountain (which has no larches, by the way). There are lots of trails in this area and you can make many different loops by combining sections of various trails, but a good map is essential: *50 Old-Growth Day Hikes in the Mount Hood National Forest* is excellent. The most big trees seen per calories expended are probably on the Upper Multnomah Loop that starts on Larch Mountain and goes on Trail #441 to #444 to #424, then back to the start on the road.

Two classic examples of western Cascade ancient forest are among the many described in *50 Old-Growth Day Hikes in the Willamette National Forest.* **Opal Creek** is probably the most famous unprotected ancient forest site in Oregon, and timber sales are still planned despite the intensive efforts of conservationists to save the area. This is a moderately strenuous hike into a controversial area where trails are changing, so it would be wise to get the latest information available on trails and access, starting with the Detroit Ranger District at (503) 854-3366. *A Walking Guide to Oregon's Ancient Forests,* by Wendell Wood, had the best information at the time this was written.

To reach Opal Creek from I-5 near Salem, take the North Santiam Highway (State Highway 22) 25 miles east and turn right (north) onto North Fork Road, which follows the Little North Santiam River. There is a flashing yellow light at this turn and a sign for the Elkhorn Recreation Area. Head northeast on North Fork Road, and in about 15 miles it enters the Willamette National Forest and becomes Forest Road 2207. In just over a mile go left onto Forest Road 2209 and travel another 5 miles until you reach a locked gate. Park near the gate (never block a gate!) and continue up the road, following the Little North Santiam River. In a mile and a half you'll be in old growth, and at 2 miles there should be a bridge over the river and onto the new Opal Creek Trail. Plans are for this trail to go to Opal Creek, cross it, then go up the east side of Opal Creek to Opal Lake. Until the bridge over Opal Creek is completed, crossing Opal Creek in high water would be difficult and is discouraged.

The **Shale Ridge Trail** (#3567) is easy to find and hike and goes through some of the best ancient forest in the southern end of **Willamette National Forest.** The trailhead is near Milepost 30, about midpoint on the **Aufderheide National Scenic Byway,** which is Forest Road 19 between State Highways 58 and 126 and is described in chapter 55. In the first 2 miles the trail goes through several groves with some very large Douglas firs, and then enters a fantastic forest of huge western red cedars.

Oregon's Coast Range has been so heavily logged that only a few tiny remnants of the once solid ancient forest remain. One of the few places to see old growth Sitka spruce forest is in **Oswald West State Park,** named after Oregon's governor from 1911 to 1915. Oswald deserves our eternal gratitude for making all of Oregon's beaches public, one of Oregon's greatest claims to fame, and this state park is a fitting tribute. A section of the Oregon Coast Trail goes the length of the park, which is basically between Arch Cape and Neahkahnie Mountain.

In the middle of the park are several parking areas. From the main parking area east of U.S. Highway 101, the one with the rest rooms, a wonderful trail goes through a great Sitka spruce forest to **Short Sands Beach** in Smuggler's Cove, one of the most beautiful little coves on the coast. Short Sands Creek is famous for its dippers, the beach is famous for its surfers and the charming walk-in campground is famous for its little wheelbarrows for hauling your stuff to the campsite. The segment of the **Oregon Coast Trail** that goes north from the Short Sands area to Cape Falcon and eventually Arch Cape goes through some more fabulous Sitka spruce forest.

Many Oregonians have heard that redwoods, the ultimate ancient forest tree, grow in Oregon, but few have seen them. Small wonder, since almost all have been cut down. Very few redwoods remain in Oregon, but to the astonishment of the general public and the dismay of conservationists, only two small stands of redwoods in the state are formally protected. The easiest way to see some of Oregon's giant redwoods is on the **Redwood Nature Trail** in the **Siskiyou National Forest** adjacent to **Loeb State Park,** about 9 miles northeast of Brookings on North Bank Chetco River Road.

For a different mix of old growth species typical of southwestern Oregon with its heavy California influence, try the **Big Tree Trail** in **Oregon Caves National Monument.** You'll see giant white firs, incense cedars and the rare Port Orford cedar, as well as one of the contenders for the biggest Douglas fir in Oregon! The trails are also good for wildflowers and begin at monument headquarters. Oregon Caves is at the end of State Highway 46, 20 miles from Cave Junction.

The Northwest's east-side ancient forests are not as well known or protected as are the west-side ancient forests. The **Metolius River Trail** in **Deschutes National Forest** goes through an excellent example of old growth ponderosa pine forest. A 9-mile stretch of this trail runs along the west side of the Metolius from Lower Canyon Creek Campground to Candle Creek Campground and can also be accessed from the Wizard Falls Fish Hatchery just south of the trail's midpoint. The southern section from the hatchery to Lower Canyon Creek Campground is considered the most scenic. Be sure to visit the fish-viewing platform at the bridge in Camp Sherman and the head of the Metolius Springs, 2 miles south, when you're in the area. The Camp Sherman–Metolius River area is reached by Forest Road 14, about 9 miles west of Sisters on Hwy. 20/126.

In the **Fremont National Forest** are the last two large unroaded stands of old growth ponderosa pine in Lake County. Intermingled with these magnificent "yellow bellies" (a nickname for the big old ponderosas) are some old growth white fir, western white pine, western juniper and some beautiful meadows and aspen groves. These two areas are **Dead Horse Rim** and **Coleman Rim,** northeast and southeast respectively, from **Gearhart Mountain Wildlife Area.** Both are fairly large, with several areas to explore, and trails that aren't on the forest service map, so it would be best to use Wendell Wood's *Walking Guide to Oregon's Ancient Forests* for details.

Washington

The ultimate temperate rain forest in the lower 48 is found in the **Hoh, Quinault** and **Queets river valleys** in **Olympic National Park.** Hiking up the Queets is difficult because you have to ford the river, but there are outstanding trails in the Hoh and Quinault rain forests. The **Hall of Mosses Trail** in the **Hoh Rain Forest** has the classic scene of bigleaf maples draped with mosses that you often see in photographs, but the Quinault Valley is equally impressive. Either one is a must-see for anyone visiting the Pacific Northwest. The **Quinault Loop Trail,** near Quinault Lodge, and the **North Fork Quinault** and **Enchanted Valley Trails** are all fantastic hikes and are well marked.

Some of the finest ancient forests in the Cascades are preserved in **Mount Rainier National Park.** The **Grove of the Patriarchs Trail** at Ohanapecosh, in the park's southeast corner, is a self-guided nature trail through classic old growth with trees five hundred to one thousand years old. In the opposite corner of the park the **Carbon River Rain Forest Trail** is a bit wetter and is less visited, offering a better chance for some solitude among the giants. While visiting Mount Rainier, be on the lookout for mountain goats, marmots and pikas, and spectacular mountain wildflower displays in July and August.

A small but excellent example of Cascade ancient forest, and one convenient to the Emerald City megalopolis, is the **Asahel Curtis Nature Trail** near **Snoqualmie Pass.** This has got to be the last old growth stand in the I-90 corridor and makes a great stop any time you're passing through or going to nearby Gold Creek, with its migrating salmon, beaver and possibly mountain goats. This is a great drive in October, when fall colors are peaking and the salmon are running. The Asahel Curtis Trail has interpretive signs and is an easy hike for all ages. From I-90 take the Asahel Curtis/Denny Creek Exit, #47, turn right at the first stop sign, then left at the second stop sign and drive to the end of Forest Road 55 and park. Pick up the trail (which actually starts at the picnic area) just east of the parking lot.

National wildlife refuges are rarely known for their forests, but a unique ancient forest is protected in **Willapa National Wildlife Refuge.** Long Island, the largest estuarine island on the Pacific Coast, is in the southern end of Willapa Bay, and on the southern end of this island is the 274-acre **Long Island Cedar Grove.** It is estimated that there have not been any major changes to this grove in four thousand years! This grove has codominant western hemlock and western red cedar trees five hundred and one thousand years old, respectively. You can only get to the island by private boat, so access is dependent on the tides. A boat launch is available near refuge headquarters on Hwy. 101. There are five primitive campsites on the island, but water may not be available during the driest months. It is important to check with refuge staff before planning an overnight trip.

British Columbia

West Vancouver's **Lighthouse Park** is an almost-wilderness park of 185 acres within half an hour of downtown Vancouver. The heavily forested park on Point Atkinson is almost all original ancient forest. The park is reached by driving west on Marine Drive for about 5 miles from the Lions Gate Bridge and turning left onto Beacon Lane at the large wooden sign for the park. There are many trails crisscrossing the park, and finding your way can be confusing. Start at the gate at the end of the parking area and head east toward the park's summit. From here make a clockwise loop east, then south, then west, intersecting the road to the lighthouse. From here you can go south on the road to the lighthouse, with its scenic views of Burrard Inlet, or make another clockwise loop, this time to the west, then back north to the parking area.

It seems that the best examples of ancient forest still standing in southwestern British Columbia are on Vancouver Island. The **Rain Forest Trail** in the Long Beach Unit of **Pacific Rim National Park** is actually two short loop trails in lush temperate rain forest that looks like the perfect home for ewoks or gnomes. Most of the trails are on boardwalks that wind over the forest floor and let you appreciate how dense the vegetation really is. The well-marked parking area is off Provincial Highway 4 just about 4 miles north of the main visitor center at Wickaninnish. Loop A is on the north side of the highway, Loop B starts in the parking lot and both are under a mile long. The trails go through similar habitat and have interpretive signs, but each area has its own character and the signs cover different topics.

For an "instant" ancient forest experience, stop at **MacMillian Provincial Park,** usually called the **Cathedral Grove,** which is right on Hwy. 4 between Combs and Port Alberni. Park on the highway and step right into old growth forest on either side of the road; the biggest trees are south of the highway. You can hear traffic from the highway, and this well-used area is obviously not a wilderness, but the trees are impressive, there are lots of snags loaded with old woodpecker nests and it certainly makes a great break on the way to the west coast.

Carmanah Pacific Provincial Park was established in 1990 just in time to stop the logging of one the most spectacular stands of Sitka spruce remaining in Canada and home to the world's tallest known Sitka spruce (312 feet high). The planned logging of adjacent old growth forests continues to be a raging issue. Carmanah Pacific Provincial Park is a wilderness park, and there are no facilities or services within about 20 miles and travel is on dirt logging roads, so be prepared and have a good map. There are several approaches to the park, but they all eventually lead to the Caycuse River Bridge near the tiny settlement of Didtidaht Reserve (with the nearest emergency telephone) and just south of Nitinat Junction. After crossing the Caycuse River Bridge, turn right onto the Rosander Mainline and head south, then east, about 17 miles to the park entrance. The park brochure, available from British Columbia Parks offices in Victoria or North Vancouver, has good directions and maps and is invaluable if you're planning a visit.

51

Raptor Migration

In the first *Seasonal Guide to the Natural Year,* Scott Weidensaul tells it straight when he writes, "The autumn hawk flight is the mid-Atlantic region's greatest wildlife spectacle." The Hawk Mountain Sanctuary in Pennsylvania could easily be the most famous bird-watching site in North America. Like the search for the Northwest Passage, western birders have been on a quest for the "Hawk Mountain of the West" for decades. Although there is no place in the West to compare with the hawk-watching sites near the East Coast, some spots have been found that do have big concentrations of migrating raptors in the fall.

Unfortunately, none of the contenders for the title of Hawk Mountain of the West is in our region. The hottest spot in the West is atop the Goshute Mountains in northeastern Nevada, near the Great Salt Lake. The next busiest raptor spot is Marin County, just north of San Francisco.

What makes a "hawk mountain?" Hawk-watching sites are places where two things happen—the hawks from a large area are concentrated, and people can get close enough to see them. Most hot hawk-watching spots are on mountains, because this gets the people up closer to the birds. But the topography of the mountain may also be the reason for the concentration of birds over that particular spot. When wind hits mountains, air is deflected upward, and it is these steady updrafts that the hawks seek in order to conserve energy by soaring, which is flying without wing-flapping. Soaring provides a tremendous advantage to birds, especially during long flights, but it only works when the air the bird is flying in is going up. This happens in two situations. One is the upward deflection of wind already mentioned. The second is when air gets heated and rises, creating a *thermal.* Skillful soarers can remain aloft for hours without flapping their wings if conditions are right.

Migrating hawks commonly follow mountain ridges, because when the wind blows properly, there is an almost continual updraft off the ridges that allows them to soar for long distances. Some of the best hawk-watching sites are on such ridges at points where the birds get closest to the land and are funneled into a smaller area when the ridge narrows or even ends. This is one of the reasons why the Goshutes are great. Good hawk-watching sites are sometimes a corridor of good habitat near or in a large area of bad habitat, and this is the second reason birds fly over the Goshutes, to avoid the Great Salt Lake Desert.

A common place where thermals become important is around a large body of water. Because land near the water will almost always get hotter than the water during the day, thermals rise over the land. If hawks have to cross a particularly large body of water, they can save a tremendous amount of energy if there is a point of land near a good crossing with strong thermals. The birds can catch the thermals, ride them as high as they can, then soar across the open water, slowly losing altitude but greatly reducing the amount of time they will have to actively flap. This is the situation in Marin County, where the hawks pile up over the Marin Headlands in preparation for soaring over the Golden Gate or San Francisco Bay. The best hawk mountain in our region is also a headland near a major water barrier.

Since the Pacific Northwest is relatively mild in climate, there simply are not as many birds passing through our region during migration as there are in the East. In fact, many raptors from farther north stop to spend the winter here, and many don't leave. In our region the most common migrating raptors are the two smallest accipiters—the sharp-shinned and Cooper's hawks—the ubiquitous red-tailed hawk, turkey vultures and golden eagles. Also regular are osprey, bald eagles, northern harrier, American kestrels, merlin and peregrine falcons. In addition, areas east of the Cascades will occasionally have Swainson's hawks and prairie falcons. Much less likely but showing up in small numbers are rough-legged hawks, northern goshawks and, at Beechey Head, broad-winged hawks.

Hawk-watching in the Northwest can be very pleasant because some of our nicest weather is in September and early October, and the best watching is usually in the middle of the day, making for a more leisurely schedule than does catching the dawn chorus in spring. Since they are usually up on high points of land, hawk-watching spots provide fabulous scenic vistas. The best conditions are clear with moderate winds from the west or southwest, and especially before a storm front coming from the north. Be sure to dress warmly. Scopes are not very convenient for watching flying hawks, and because hiking is involved at most of our spots, think about leaving them behind (but not in your car at a trailhead). Binoculars with a wide field of view are a real advantage when trying to find birds in the air, so many people find compact models unsatisfactory in this situation.

All the hawk-watching sites in the Northwest are relatively new, so we know little about the timing of different species and the best conditions for seeing large numbers. Generally the best period is mid-September to mid-October. You may be able to make a significant contribution to our knowledge of raptors by recording your observations of fall hawk migration and making contact with HawkWatch International to let them know what you have seen. Contact Hawkwatch International if you are interested in finding out more about raptor migrations in the West or want to help with counts.

Oregon

Hot Spots

To date, the best spot that HawkWatch International has found in Oregon is **Bonney Butte**, near the Badger Creek Wilderness in **Mount Hood National Forest**. Access is reasonable (a high-clearance vehicle is desirable), and there are campgrounds nearby. The biggest days so far have included around 150 birds. To get to Bonney Butte, head east from Government Camp on U.S. Highway 26 to State Highway 35 and take Hwy. 35 east $4^1/_2$ miles to the White River East Sno Park. Go south on Forest Road 48, also called White River Road, which has signs for Rock Creek

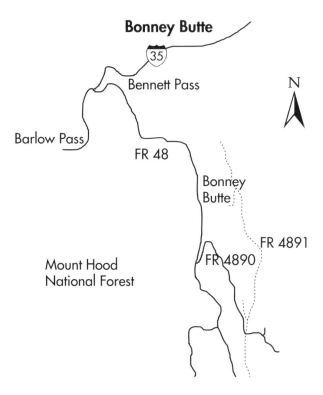

Reservoir and Wamic. In 7 miles turn left onto Forest Road 4890, which is paved and has a sign on it after you turn. Go $3^3/_4$ miles and you'll come to a well-marked intersection with Forest Road 4891.

Following the signs to Bonney Meadows, go north on the rough, bumpy dirt Forest Road 4891 4 miles until you get to the campground. Any car with average to higher clearance should be able to make it with care. The road to the top of Bonney Butte starts just a quarter of a mile north of the campground. I recommend parking at the campground and hiking the 1 mile to the top. Views are awesome—reach out and touch Mount Hood.

Washington

The road to **Hart's Pass** and **Slate Peak** is the highest in the state of Washington and provides a fairly convenient, and very dramatic, route for exploring the subalpine zone. The road is steep and narrow with turnouts, but it is well-maintained gravel. In summer this area is great for mountain flowers, high-mountain birds, pikas and marmots, and provides access to the Pacific Crest Trail and the Pasaytan Wilderness Area. If you drive the North Cascades Highway in the fall, include a good part of a day for a trip to the top on this road. A big day for hawks here is about eighty birds.

From State Highway 20, 16 miles northwest of Winthrop, follow signs to Mazama, which mainly consists of the Mazama Store and the Mazama Country

Inn (which is highly recommended). From the Mazama Store take Mazama Road northwest, following the signs to Hart's Pass, about 20 miles away. At Hart's Pass there is a sign for Slate Peak, the best hawk-watching site, another 3 miles away.

Washington's other regularly used hawk-watching site is **Red Top Mountain** in the **Wenatchee National Forest** between Wenatchee and Ellensburg. Take U.S. Highway 97 south from U.S. Highway 2 between Leavenworth and Wenatchee for 29 miles. Just before you come to the Mineral Springs Resort, turn right onto Forest Road 9738 and follow the signs to Red Top Mountain. The route is well marked, so just keep following the signs. In a little over 2 miles you'll take a left fork onto Forest Road 9702, and in 7 miles you'll be in the parking area at the top.

From here it's a little over a half-mile hike to the old lookout on the peak. The trail is steep and slippery, with loose rock near the top. Watch your footing and take the most gradual trail to the top, avoiding shortcuts. Here is another spectacular panorama, with the Stuart Range in the Alpine Lakes Wilderness right in front of you to the northeast and Mount Rainier looming up in the southwest. This is currently the hawk-watching site where you have the best chance of seeing prairie falcons and Swainson's hawks. About as many birds are seen here as at Hart's Pass.

HawkWatch International has just started using **Diamond Head**, just 9 miles east of Red Top, and they believe it has the potential for more migrants—they have had some days of 120 birds. Just about 8 miles north of the Mineral Springs Resort mentioned above, right at the marked boundary line between Chelan and Kittitas Counties, go right on the unmarked dirt road, which is Forest Road 9716. After $2^7/_{10}$ miles turn left onto Forest Road 9712 and drive $1^3/_5$ miles to where you pass the intersection with Forest Road 3530. Just 30 yards past this intersection, take the unnamed road north to the southern end of Diamond Head. Walk to the widest part of the ridge and watch to the north.

British Columbia

There is only one place in the Northwest that can truly make a claim to be a Hawk Mountain of the West, and it's on the southern tip of Vancouver Island. This spot doesn't seem to have an official or consistently used name yet, so you may hear it called "Beechey Head," "East Sooke Park" or "Hawk Ridge." It is in **East Sooke Regional Park** and is a rocky hilltop lookout above Beechey Head, so these names all make sense. This is a relatively new sight, first discovered by local birders in 1990.

Beechey Head provides a classic example of a place where migrating birds bunch up as they gain altitude over the last suitable point of land before trying to cross a major water barrier, in this case the 10-mile-wide Strait of Juan de Fuca. Thermals rise as the land heats, and the birds soar to high altitudes before heading south and starting a long glide to the Olympic Peninsula. In March the same thing happens in the opposite direction, with birds piling up over Cape Flattery before heading north.

Currently, fourteen species of diurnal raptors have been seen from this point, all the species that would be considered "normal" for southwestern British Columbia, plus rough-legged hawks and at least one broad-winged hawk every year! Record daily highs for the most abundant species are 1,000 turkey vultures, 101 red-tailed hawks and 56 sharp-shinned hawks. Other migrating birds are seen, and the Beechey Head lookout appears to be on a main migration route for band-tailed pigeons and Vaux's swifts as well. Since this site is so new to birders, it carries the excitement of the unknown and the possibility that you too could be the one to discover something new.

The best observation time seems to be the last week in September and the first week in October. The broad-winged hawks have been seen during a rather narrow window of time, September 20–29. A visit would be worthwhile on any good day in September or October, even though it might not be the day of peak numbers or rarities. The best time is between 10 A.M. and 2 P.M. on clear days without significant wind from the southwest.

Take Trans-Canada Highway 1 west from Victoria, then take the Sooke-Colwood Exit for Highways 1A and 14, using this point as zero miles. Head south on Sooke Road, also called the Island Highway, Highway 14 and Highway 1A at this point. In about $1^1/_2$ miles, Highway 1A will take off to your right. Stay on Highway 14 (Sooke Road), pass some huge gravel pits and in 3 miles turn left onto Metchosin Road. You will pass Witty's Lagoon Regional Park, a good spot for shorebirds and waterfowl during migration and winter and almost always worth a stop if time allows. At $8^1/_3$ miles turn right onto Happy Valley Road, following signs to Becher Bay. In just half a mile turn left onto Rocky Point Road, where you again will see a sign for Becher Bay.

In $3^1/_3$ miles you'll come to a major fork—go to the right onto East Sooke Road, and in just over 5 miles turn left onto Becher Bay Road. There is a small sign for East Sooke Regional Park, which is at the end of the road in 1 mile. The hike to the lookout is about 1 mile from the parking area, and the signs were quite confusing when I was there, so follow these directions carefully.

Once you have parked, walk back to the entrance road, Becher Bay Road, and then south (through the locked gate) on the wide dirt path that would be the continuation of Becher Bay Road if it went straight. Go straight on this trail; if you come to an unsigned fork, stay to the right or in the forest. You will come to a sign reading Beechey Hd. Trail and Coast Trail Straight Ahead, which is correct. Do not take the trail on the right to Babbington Hill. You will come to a key sign that will show Cabin Point to the right, which you want to take. *Do not* go to Coast Trail, Lookout or Petroglyphs at this junction. Pass the second sign indicating Babbington Hill to the right, and at this point go straight, which *this* sign says is to Coast Trail, which you didn't take before. From this point on follow the signs to Lookout, which means going left at the next fork and then following the last sign up the hill to the right.

When you get up on top of the lookout you will have a truly awesome view, especially since you waited for a clear day to make the trip. You'll be drawn to look south at the fabulous scenery, but for birds watch to the north— they will come down the ridge and rise overhead on thermals.

52

Swift Roosts

Swifts are one of those plain little birds that, if you know them well, you notice constantly in summer. To me, swifts are one of the sounds of summer in Portland. But if you don't know swifts, and that means being able to recognize their high-pitched "chittering" calls overhead, you have no idea that they exist. Since swifts spend all their waking hours flying, usually quite high, only bird-watchers and others who spend a lot of time looking up at the sky see them. There is one time, however, when they are so noticeable that they end up in newspapers and on television news. This is in September, when they form large communal roosts in chimneys.

The swift in question is the Vaux's swift, smallest of North American swifts. Swifts are among the world's fastest birds and are constantly zipping through the air catching insects. Vaux's swifts are present in small numbers in almost all older forests throughout the Northwest during their short summer stay. They are regularly seen over parts of some towns, either over water or areas with lots of trees, including old neighborhoods with old street trees. They are only in our area from the second half of April to October, making their visit to the Northwest for breeding one of the shortest of all migrating birds. They spend the rest of the year in the Tropics, from central Mexico to northern South America.

Before migrating south in the fall, these speedy little birds start gathering together in huge numbers in communal roosts at night in preparation for migrating south together. Many birds migrate in large groups for protection from predators, and this may be true for swifts. Group migrations also help young birds learn routes and feeding stops from the old-timers. Swifts may also conserve energy by roosting in groups, because all those hot little bodies grouped together in a chimney would reduce heat loss by individuals. *Roosting* is the term describing when birds are sleeping or resting for an extended period, almost always at night, for most birds are strongly diurnal.

By "large communal roosts," I mean thousands of birds at one time. Roosts of two thousand to four thousand birds are not uncommon, and some have been estimated at forty thousand birds! To see that many birds close together at one time is definitely a wildlife spectacle, and when it happens the news usually spreads quickly through the birding community and sometimes makes it into the general news media. Sometimes a roost will become a cultural event, with hundreds of people arriving ahead of time with lawn chairs, and even vendors selling snacks.

What people are gathering to watch is the swifts' descent into the chimney for the night. This happens right around sunset, so the time varies daily, and the period during the month when the swifts use the chimney will vary from year to year. Arrive at least half an hour before sunset to select the best viewing site, trade bird stories with other wildlife watchers and generally get into the mood.

At first you'll see just a few individual birds zipping around, and then small groups may start to form. Gradually, more and more birds will start coming in, and they will start flying together more and more. Then the flocks will get larger and start joining together until there are one or two huge flocks swirling in big circles over the area. The birds may disperse suddenly and then reform. Eventually there will be one huge "tornado" of swifts circling over the chimney, swooping closer and closer.

Rather suddenly the birds will start dropping into the chimney. To me it looks like the chimney has become a giant vacuum cleaner and is sucking the birds out of the air. Others have described the sight as looking like a black cloud of smoke going back down into the chimney. What is amazing is how quickly all the birds are gone and the sky is suddenly empty and quiet. If you are at a roost with a crowd, expect applause after the last swift has disappeared.

The swifts cling onto the sides of the chimney with their tiny feet (and big claws) and hang there closely packed together, looking like feathery shingles. They sleep in this position all night and leave at dawn (when there are never groups of people standing around watching). This may go on for several weeks, and then the number of birds will start to diminish until they are all gone.

By now you should have asked yourself, What did these birds do before there were chimneys? In times past, the vast forests of the Northwest were full of old dead trees (called snags), some of which were hollowed out at the top from decay or fire. Some of these big natural chimneys were the sites of communal roosts. Swifts also nest inside hollow trees, but as individual pairs, not in groups. As the forests were cut down, the swifts were forced to try to find other spots for nesting and roosting. At the same time chimneys started to appear, and slowly these birds have adapted and learned to use chimneys, and a few similar structures, as substitute hollow snags. Most authors describe the Vaux's swifts' use of chimneys as a recent development. The bird's close relative, the chimney swift of the eastern United States, has been regularly using chimneys for a longer period of time, presumably because settlers started altering the landscape and building chimneys there earlier.

Vaux's swifts have also started using chimneys for nesting. The peak of their nesting season is in July, and if you hear little cheeping noises coming from your chimney during this month, you've got swifts nesting in there. Close the damper so they won't get into your house, and for goodness sakes don't build a fire! If a baby swift happens to fall into your fireplace, there is probably nothing you can do to help it unless there is a wildlife rehabilitation center in your town that will take and care for it. Don't worry about the swifts moving in; in a month at most they'll be completely gone. Their delicate little nest of sticks and dried saliva will quickly fall apart or go up in flames with your first fire, so don't worry about it blocking your chimney. If you are so blessed as to have your chimney chosen for a communal roost (it does happen), you will need to have the fireplace and chimney thoroughly cleaned after they are gone. You may consider covering your chimney with a screen if you don't want a repeat performance the next year, or you can decide to leave your chimney as a swift-roosting refuge.

Wildlife observation sites are all unpredictable to some degree, but fall swift roosts may be the most unpredictable in this book. Roosting chimneys may get capped, screened or completely destroyed, and the swifts may stop using a particular chimney for no apparent reason. The best way to find current swift roosts is to contact a local birding group or natural history club, usually a chapter of the Audubon Society in the United States.

Notable swift roosts will often be mentioned on rare bird alerts, so it's always worth giving these a call in September. The roosts below have been very active for many years—I hope they will still be hopping by the time you read this.

Oregon

Hot Spots

Chapman School is located in northwest Portland near the intersection of NW 27th and Raleigh. There is a big unused brick chimney at the back of the school, the side facing 27th. This has been quite a festive scene the last few years after getting television coverage. Estimates have run as high as forty thousand birds at the peak of activity.

The town of **Newberg** is about 20 miles southwest of Portland on State Highway 99E. The U.S. Post Office is downtown at 401 E. 1st Street, and the building has a chimney. This is another roost that has been on TV.

In **Roseburg** there is an old chimney on what is now the clay studio at the **Umpqua Valley Arts Center,** which used to be part of the Veteran's Hospital complex. Coming south on I-5, take the Harvard Avenue Exit (#124) and go west on Harvard to Fir Grove Park. The chimney is obvious, and you can get to it by turning right toward the Veteran's Hospital and then making a quick left in half a block. No one is sure about how long swifts have been using the chimney, but its use goes back at least seven years. Unfortunately, this chimney is showing itself to be unstable and will probably be demolished in the near future. But then again, large government agencies are not known for speedy action, so a call to the arts center might reveal the chimney is still standing: (541) 672-2532.

Washington

The little hamlet of **Klickitat** is on the Klickitat River about 12 miles upstream from the Columbia River at Lyle. Just 2 miles east of town, on State Highway 142, is a public access area for the river, and next to the parking area is an abandoned apartment building with a big old chimney. (By the way, the canyon of the Klickitat is beautiful and is the northernmost site for acorn woodpeckers, so keep your eyes peeled on your way up.) Farther upstream is the **Klickitat Wildlife Area,** and in the fall it is possible to see turkeys among the oaks.

▶ **Sumas** is on the Canadian border and is a Port of Entry. The **Historic**
▶ **Sumas Customs House,** built in 1932 and now a registered historic build-
▶ ing, is just 200 yards southeast of the current inspection station. One of the
▶ chimneys is false, added to provide symmetry. For at least thirty years (no one
▶ is sure when it started), four thousand to eight thousand swifts have been
▶ using the false chimney for roosting, both in the fall and briefly in the spring.
▶ The building has an interesting tale. A new customs building was built in
▶ 1990, and the old one was therefore slated to be demolished. There was a lot
▶ of concern for the swifts, and a strong desire by many to preserve the historic
▶ building. Eventually the building was saved, moved and renovated for com-
▶ mercial office space, but through a complex series of circumstances the building
▶ remains vacant and for sale as we go to print. Let's hope the building, and its
▶ swifts, survives another period of uncertainty.

53

September Shorttakes

Ants and Termites

Ant and termite colonies produce winged adults only once a year, and for many species this happens during September, often just after rain. When conditions are right, the air in some places is filled with thousands of flying termites or ants. The termites are more noticeable, probably because they are bigger and attract more birds, which gobble them up as fast as they can catch them. Sometimes on the coast in September you'll see lots of gulls flying in fairly small circles over a certain spot. They are eating flying termites that are swarming up out of the ground. These winged termites and ants are making their mating flights. After mating, the fertilized females go on to become the queens of new colonies.

Pelicans and Terns

As summer wanes, many brown pelicans start moving north up the coast from their breeding grounds in California and Mexico. Some pelicans arrive earlier in the summer, but most don't show up until the end of breeding season. They always come as far as Oregon, and many can usually be seen as far north as Tillamook Bay. How far north they travel each year varies with weather and ocean conditions. During strong El Niño years they have gone as far as Vancouver Island. Elegant terns breed on islands off the Baja Peninsula and also wander north in the fall after breeding. They were never recorded in our region until 1983, the year of a dramatic El Niño effect, when they were even seen off the coast of Washington. Be on the lookout for unusual terns when you see lots of pelicans or migrating common terns (which occur regularly in September) along the coast.

Woolly Bears

Those big fuzzy caterpillars that you start noticing this month are woolly bears. You see them a lot in fall because they are big and because they are roaming around looking for a place to hibernate. Woolly bears are the larvae of the Isabella moth, one of the plainest of the usually colorful tiger moths. You may see the adult around lights on summer nights. And no, you can't predict the weather from the width of the colored bands of hairs.

Harvest Moon

Don't forget the Harvest Moon, the full moon nearest the autumnal equinox and the full moon that stays low in the sky the longest, making it a perfect backdrop for scenes of harvested corn, migrating geese and other autumn motifs.

A Closer Look: Bird Migration

The regular disappearance and reappearance of many kinds of birds has puzzled people since ancient times. It took a surprisingly long time for the idea of birds making long migrations to be accepted, and it has only been in the last few decades that we have really begun to understand what's going on. The term *migration* is used for the regular, extensive seasonal movements made by animals between their breeding region and their nonbreeding region, usually called their winter range. Birds are rightly famous for their amazing migrations, but they are certainly not the only animals that migrate. Some mammals, reptiles, amphibians, fish, insects, crustaceans and mollusks migrate. But birds travel some of the greatest distances and at the greatest speeds.

The distances covered by birds during migration are almost unbelievable. A round-trip migration of several thousand miles is common, even for small songbirds and some hummingbirds. The record holders are shorebirds, terns and shearwaters, some of which fly 10,000 to 15,000 miles in a big loop each year! This sounds too fantastic to be true, but if a bird flies three hundred days out of a year, it has to average 50 miles a day to make a journey that long. This may seem like a lot, but actually many songbirds fly about that much in an average day. What is really impressive is how far they go at a time. Many birds regularly fly 300 to 500 miles at a time, but some shorebirds and waterfowl have been known to go 1,500 to 2,000 miles *nonstop*. That's around 80 to 90 hours of continual flying! That's about the equivalent of a human runner doing four-minute-miles continually for four days and has been called the "greatest physiological feat of any vertebrate." Such multiday nonstops are, however, the exception and not the rule. Most birds stop regularly to rest and refuel by eating.

Why in the world would they do that? There's no question that making such long flights is dangerous in many ways. The common belief is that birds have to migrate to get away from cold weather. This is partially true, but it isn't just cold that makes birds migrate, as demonstrated by the fact that a number of birds do live year-round in some of the harshest weather imaginable. After all, birds are endotherms and have feathers, the greatest insulation around. The key to survival is food—getting enough calories to produce lots of heat internally. This becomes impossible for birds that feed in the water when the water freezes. Insects and other invertebrate life becomes extremely limited and hard to find in winter, so almost all insect eaters also have to depart. Interestingly, birds like chickadees, nuthatches and woodpeckers have adapted to eating arthropod eggs, larvae and pupae from trees and bark and are some of the common winter residents in the north.

Two-thirds of North America's birds are considered migratory, and about two hundred species winter in the American Tropics (the Neotropics). If they go down there because there is lots of food and the climate is less stressful, why don't they just stay? Why go back north? This question needs to be viewed in a different way. The traditional thinking is that "our" birds leave their "homes" up here in the northern temperate zone to escape the weather and "winter" some-place warmer, only to "return home" in the spring. Actually, many of these birds spend more time in their winter range than they do up here. Another way to look at it is that these birds are tropical birds that take a quick trip north in summer to take advantage of the long days (day length doesn't change in the Tropics) and exploit the massive explosion of insect life that makes raising their babies much easier than in the overcrowded, highly competitive tropical forest. As soon as the young are on their own (or even before, in some cases), these birds return "home" to their tropical habitats. This portrays neotropical migrants not as helpless wimps fleeing their homes until they can come back, but as bold marauders exploiting the brief but plentiful bounty to the north for as long as it pays well.

There are some other good reasons to head north besides longer working hours and tons of food. In general, the farther north you go from the Tropics, the fewer animals there are, which means there are fewer predators and less com-petition for food and space. Two other advantages might be reduced parasites in the Far North because they are wiped out each winter by the cold, and a change in diet that might provide some essential micronutrients harder to get in the Tropics. The validity of these last two factors, however, hasn't been demonstrated yet. Given this kind of view, the question might be, Why don't more birds mi-grate north? This touches on the really big question: How did all this migration business get started in the first place? And this is a question science can't answer right now.

One of the other big questions that always comes up when discussing migra-tion is, How do the birds know where to go and how do they navigate? There actually has been a lot of progress in answering these questions in the last two decades. To find their way south on their first trip, many birds follow the leader. Almost all birds migrate in flocks, often huge flocks, and the novices can just go along and learn the route. This isn't the whole story, however, because there are a number of birds where the adults leave first, before the young can even fly. Despite never having flown the route before, the vast majority of these young birds go the right way. How do they know? Exactly how this works is another mystery for science.

Bird navigation has been studied intensely, and science has learned a lot about it. Birds actually use five main techniques for heading in the right direction. The one easiest to understand is something humans use all the time—established landmarks. As they fly over the land, birds see and memorize its main features. Conveniently, many of the main geographical features in North America hap-pen to run north and south, which gives a strong indication of general direction.

This is fine and dandy, but most songbirds migrate at night and others regularly migrate when they can't see the land because of clouds or fog. What then?

Birds are excellent celestial navigators, using the sun by day and the stars by night. Since both appear to move as the earth turns, birds must have an accurate biological clock in their brains in order to compensate for the earth's rotation when taking a fix on either the sun or other stars. How can we know this is true? There have been many excellent experiments in planetariums, where scientists can manipulate the sky, that demonstrate these abilities. As amazing as this is, it still won't work if the bird can't see the sun or stars because of clouds and fog. Any more tricks?

No problem; how about the earth's magnetic field? For years scientists suspected that birds might be able to sense variations in the earth's magnetic field, which could be used for navigation, and now experiments have demonstrated that this is indeed true. It turns out that some birds are very sensitive to minor variations in magnetic fields and that minute magnetic particles in their brain may play a role in this ability. Such particles have been found in other animals, and there is now even a bit of evidence that some humans may have these magnetic particles also, which may partially explain why some people have a better sense of direction than others.

Two more senses may play a role for some birds. Birds can hear very low frequencies of sound, called infrasonic, that are undetectable to humans. Very low sounds like this are made by ocean waves, wind blowing against mountains and thunderstorms. Since birds can hear these sounds, do they use them to help find their way? Another unsolved mystery. And because most birds have a very poor, possibly nonexistent, sense of smell, it is unusual that a few are known to use smell for navigation. Storm-petrels nest on islands and can apparently smell their islands from out at sea and find their burrows by smell alone. There may be some other birds who can smell better than we think and might also use scent to some degree in finding their way.

Everyone seems to agree that any one bird will use different combinations of these techniques to find its way. Despite all our knowledge, there have been a few experiments whose results are still hard to explain. Manx shearwaters have been taken from their burrows at night in Wales, put in a lightproof box, flown to Massachusetts, 3,200 miles away, and released. In less than two weeks the birds are back in their burrows in Wales! White-crowned sparrows have been similarly kidnapped in California and released in Maryland. Some have found their way right back where they started from, but it takes them a year. Unless these birds have learned how to use our global positioning satellites, how they do this remains yet another unsolved mystery of migration.

October

Notes

55

Autumn Color in the Mountains

The changing colors of leaves in the fall must surely be one of the most powerful symbols of seasonal change, at least in the temperate zone. Even the most isolated-from-nature urban dweller knows that changing leaves means winter is on its way. Transplanted easterners may consider our colors ho-hum compared to the spectacle of the eastern hardwood forests, but I guess that's the trade-off for having the most magnificent coniferous forests in the world. Despite the abundance of evergreen conifers, we have plenty of color to get us in the mood for jack-o'-lanterns and turkeys with cranberry sauce.

Many of North America's large families of common deciduous trees are represented in the Northwest, even if they are overshadowed (literally) by the evergreens. We have maples, willows, oaks, black cottonwood, quaking aspen, Pacific dogwood, Oregon ash and, in addition to two birches, their close relatives the alders. Then there are many species of smaller fruit trees and shrubs like crabapple, chokecherry, osoberry and the huckleberries. These may not be as conspicuous, but they contribute to the colors and textures of the fall palette. Most folks would consider the maples, quaking aspens and cottonwoods the most spectacular. The vine maple, a common understory and edge species on the west side, is one of the first to change color, and has the brightest and richest reds, making it really stand out.

Both aspens and cottonwoods turn bright yellow, but it is the effect of seeing a large mass of either one that makes an impression, not just the color. Cottonwoods, the tallest and most massive broad-leaved tree in the Northwest, grow along rivers and streams, and the golden outline of cottonwoods winding through arid land is a beautiful sight east of the Cascades. Aspens are also found on the east side and stand out from their often duller surroundings. Aspen leaves range from yellow to orange even to red, but it is the striking contrast between their colored leaves and their bright white trunks that is so appealing. One characteristic of aspen is that in a particular grove, all the trees will have leaves the same color; they are unusually synchronized in their turning. This is quite different from the normal variation you see among a group of trees but makes sense when you know that the grove is actually composed of clones, all the trees having started from runners of an original tree. The whole grove is essentially one plant.

An unusual tree that adds interest and color to the coniferous forest is the western larch. Larches are the only deciduous conifers in North America. In fall the needles turn a bright yellow, and the sight of golden larches standing among their evergreen relatives is a special sight on the mountain slopes where they occur. The word "evergreen" is usually used as the equivalent of "conifer" by most folks, but the larches demonstrate that not all conifers are evergreen. Conversely, there are broad-leaved or hardwood trees that are evergreen, such as madrone, chinkapin, rhododendron and California laurel (or Oregon myrtle).

Most people know how leaves change color. Each leaf actually has several different pigments of different colors present all the time, but all the other pigments are masked by overwhelming amounts of green chlorophyll. As winter nears, the chlorophyll starts to break down and the tree starts to absorb some chlorophyll into the trunk and roots, letting the other colors show through. The proportions of the different pigments, and the amount of sugar present in the leaves, determines whether the leaf is yellow, brown, red, purple or combinations of these colors. Weather, especially nighttime temperatures, greatly affects these chemicals, resulting in the great variation from tree to tree, and from year to year in the same tree. The trees are preparing for winter, when the value of the leaves as food producers falls far short of their risk as water losers and energy consumers. The leaves become liabilities and the tree drops them.

Since weather conditions vary from year to year, so does the timing and the intensity of fall foliage colors. Interestingly, despite all our detailed knowledge of the processes at work, humans have not yet been able to accurately predict what a particular year will be like in terms of changing leaves. The first leaves start to change in September, but it is not until October that we start to see big changes in our deciduous trees. Of course, winter comes sooner at higher elevations, and the color change starts high in the mountains and works its way down as fall progresses. One of the most pleasant ways to enjoy fall colors is to take scenic drives in our spectacular mountains in October. This is great in combination with visiting ancient forests, watching migrating raptors and looking for spawning salmon. And when it comes to scenic mountains, easterners who gloat about their colorful hardwood forests can eat humble pie.

Oregon

Hot Spots

Steens Mountain rises above the surrounding Great Basin in southeastern Oregon and is one of the most dramatic fault block mountains in the West. Near the top of the mountain in the dramatic gorges carved by Pleistocene glaciers are huge groves of aspen. When they turn in the fall it is one of the most spectacular displays of fall color in our region. Unfortunately, Steens Mountain gets more than its share of strong winds, and the trick is to see the leaves after they have turned but before they have been blown off the trees. A call to the Burns BLM office might help determine the best timing. Be sure to ask for whatever maps and brochures are available on "The Steens," as it is usually called. The trees seem to be at their best during late September. Steens Mountain Loop Road heads up the mountain near Page Springs Campground, about $2^1/_2$ miles east of Frenchglen. The best aspen groves are toward the top of the mountain, above Lily Lake. Although the road is a loop, the southern half, after the trail to Wildhorse Lake, is very rough. Be sure to stop at the Kiger Gorge Viewpoint for an incredible view down a glacial cirque.

Two popular scenic loop trips in the central Cascades are the **Cascade**

Lakes Highway and the **McKenzie-Santiam Tour Loop.** Both loops are also great in June for seeing mountain birds and provide access to many popular recreation sites. The Cascade Lakes Loop starts in Bend and follows these roads in order: Century Drive, Cascade Lakes Highway, Lava Lake Road, Odell Road, Forest Road 42, South Century Drive, U.S. Highway 97. A brochure describing the route is available from the Bend Area Chamber of Commerce.

The other loop goes around Mount Washington. Starting at Sisters, go west on Highways 20 and 126 to where Hwy. 126 splits and goes south. Head south on Hwy. 126 to State Highway 242, which you take east back to Sisters. Special sights on this route include Indian Ford and Cold Springs Campgrounds for birds, Lost Lake for nesting Barrow's goldeneyes, the fish-viewing platform at Camp Sherman and the amazing Dee Wright Observatory at McKenzie Pass overlooking one of the largest, most recent lava flows in the United States.

For a drive through lush lower-elevation west-side forest, try the **Aufderheide National Scenic Byway** in **Willamette National Forest.** This is Forest Road 19 between Oakridge on State Highway 58 and near McKenzie Bridge on Hwy. 126. There is a brochure and self-guiding audiocassette available from either the Oakridge or Blue River Ranger Stations.

Washington

The North Cascades Highway, State Highway 20, goes through part of what is often called The **North Cascades Complex**—North Cascades National Park, Ross Lake and Lake Chelan National Recreation Areas and parts of Mount Baker–Snoqualmie and Okanogan National Forests. This very scenic drive offers access to many fabulous hiking trails and several wildlife-watching opportunities mentioned in this book. The drive is not necessarily better for fall colors than other mountain pass roads in the Cascades, but it is the only place I know of, in the United States, where a certain rare tree can be seen from a paved road. Just on the east side of Washington Pass you will see a few small groups of larches that stick out dramatically when they are yellow in the fall. However, these are not the common western larch but the subalpine larch.

The subalpine larch (also called alpine larch) has a very small range, growing only in the highest mountains of the interior Northwest. It grows near timberline in conditions considered too severe for the few other trees that hang on at these altitudes. **Washington Pass** and the road to **Hart's Pass** give tree enthusiasts a chance to see these rare trees without serious backpacking.

Nearby to the west is **Mount Baker,** the third-highest peak in Washington. State Highway 542 winds up the Nooksack River, then climbs the northeast side of the mountain, ending at Artists' Point at about 5,000 feet. Trails from Artists' Point to the Table Mountain and Ptarmigan Ridge areas are good places to look for white-tailed ptarmigan, as well as rosy finches, pikas, marmots and occasionally mountain goats.

Due east 150 miles from Mount Baker, Hwy. 20 goes over **Sherman Pass,** at 5,575 feet the highest road in the state kept open all winter. This section of

Hwy. 20 has been designated a National Scenic Byway, and October is when it's at its most scenic, with lots of golden western larches. There is a lot of beaver activity in Sherman Creek that you can see from the highway on the east side of the pass. Any of the valleys in eastern Washington will have beautiful displays of cottonwoods along the rivers and streams.

Although low in elevation, the **Chuckanut Drive,** State Highway 11 between Burlington and Bellingham, is a favorite for the red maples and the madrones, with their red bark and red berries. It is also known for the good restaurants on the route. There are scenic views across Samish Bay of the San Juan Islands, and Larrabee State Park is a fair spot for seeing waterbirds from the beach and forest birds on the trails.

The section of U.S. Highway 2 between **Stevens Pass** and **Leavenworth** is another excellent route convenient to the Puget megalopolis. And the timing is perfect for going to the annual Wenatchee River Salmon Festival, one of the best places to see big salmon spawning in the wild (see chapter 57). You could also drop by Red Top Mountain for some migrating raptors, and make a return loop over Snoqualmie Pass, also scenic and near Gold Creek Pond, an excellent place to see kokanee salmon spawning. All in all, another great fall trip fueled by Bavarian pastries from bakeries in Leavenworth.

Another great loop through the Cascades goes through **Mount Rainier National Park,** putting this trip off the scale of scenic wonder drives. A good place to start is at Ohanapecosh Visitor Center, where you can view exhibits on forest ecology and the history of the park. Nearby is **Grove of the Patriarchs,** an excellent example of ancient forest. From Ohanapecosh head north on State Highway 123 to Cayuse Pass, where you turn right onto State Highway 410 and go to **Chinook Pass.** Sometimes you see marmots along the side of the road between the two passes. Stay on Hwy. 410 as it follows the American River and then the Naches River toward Yakima. There are numerous campgrounds along the way, and in the area of Hells Crossing and Pine Needle Campgrounds you will see a big rock ridge north of the highway. This is Fifes Ridge, and sometimes mountain goats are seen there, but it is not as reliable as the spots described in chapter 39.

Just before you get to Naches you will come to the junction with U.S. Highway 12, often called the **White Pass Highway.** Turn right and take Hwy. 12 west to White Pass, going by Rimrock Lake, which is worth checking to see if the kokanee salmon are running. This area has lots of western larches, and there is a great scenic overlook at Clear Creek Falls, just east of Dog Lake. Just before you get to White Pass you will get some awesome views of The Big One, Mount Rainier. There are even some turnouts convenient for taking photos. Once you come to Hwy. 123 you have just about completed the loop and can go north back into Mount Rainier National Park or head west to Packwood for pie and coffee and then take Hwy. 12 to I-5. This loop is in the best area in the Northwest for seeing mountain goats, so be sure to read chapter 39 and consider a trip to Timberwolf Mountain as part of this trip, since fall is really as good as any time to see those woolly spirits of the high mountains.

56

Arrival of the Geese

The most dramatic and romantic harbinger of fall is the arrival of big flocks of honking geese. I think the first wild goose calls you hear in the fall cause the release of an "autumn hormone" that makes your arms start moving like they're raking leaves and makes you smell imaginary smoke from a fireplace. We are lucky to live in the flyway or winter home of hundreds of thousands of geese, giving us a spectacular display every fall when the first big flocks start coming in.

This is one of six chapters on waterfowl, the group of birds that has been the most intimately connected with people down through the centuries. Here we will discuss our region's geese, except for the brant, which has its own chapter (22), and the emperor goose, a rare and irregular winter visitor. The other regularly occurring geese in the Northwest are the Canada, the lesser snow, the greater white-fronted and Ross's goose.

All geese share certain characteristics similar to swans but different from most ducks. In all our geese the males and females look alike and can only be told apart by their behavior, including the calls they make. All make honking sounds, but there are some subtle differences between them that experienced birders use for identification. Geese mate for life and share care of the young and are very territorial about their nest sites. In size, geese are intermediate between the ducks and the swans. Geese spend more time on land than either swans or ducks and eat a lot of plant material, including grass. The majority of geese in the Pacific Northwest are migrants passing through on their way from northern breeding grounds to more southerly winter ranges. However, many thousands do stop in our region to spend the winter, and some of the migrants may stop for a month or more at a time on their way through.

Canada geese are the most abundant geese in the Pacific Northwest and North America as a whole. Tens of thousands winter here, and they are the only goose that breeds in our region, mainly east of the Cascades. You will often hear Canada geese give a definite two part *honk, honk* call, with the second honk higher in pitch than the first. This two-part call is actually done by a pair of geese singing a closely timed duet!

Snow geese are the most spectacular bird to see during migration because they usually travel in huge flocks of nothing but white geese. Snow geese nest from the Canadian border north, and most fly through our region on the way to California. However, significant numbers, tens of thousands, remain in the Northwest all winter. In British Columbia and Washington snow geese tend to stay on the west side, while in Oregon they are more common east of the Cascades.

Thousands of snow geese arrive at Reifel Refuge near Vancouver, British Columbia, in late October.

White-fronted geese nest in the Far North, all breeding in areas above 60° latitude. They are the first geese to arrive here in fall. They tend not to be noticed as much as other geese because they remain aloft flying all day and land to rest at night. They are also easy to overlook because their color and markings blend in well with plowed fields, which is where you often find them. Like snow geese, white-fronted geese move through the Northwest on their way to California, with a few staying behind for the winter, many fewer than the number of wintering snows. In general, they come down the coast of Washington until they get near the Columbia River, then most go over the Cascades and down the east side. They are uncommon in British Columbia.

Compared to the others, the population of Ross's geese is very small indeed: There are only thirty thousand to forty thousand in the world. Ross's geese look like small snow geese and present an identification challenge. In Oregon these two white geese are sometimes found together, which is ideal for learning to tell them apart. A significant proportion of the world's Ross's geese migrate through Oregon to California, but only a few ever remain in the state for winter. They are usually seen only in eastern Oregon.

Migrating geese will start arriving in September with the first white-fronted geese and will slowly build in numbers until the population of migrating and wintering geese hits its peak, sometime in November. The timing of peak migration differs from species to species and is affected by weather. It is very common for northwesterners to notice large numbers of geese just before waterfowl hunting starts in mid-October. This makes early October the best time to get out and see the fall movements of geese before hunting season spooks the birds and causes closures and restrictions in refuges. Once goose hunting has started, many people like to wait until the waterfowl seasons are over in January before heading out to see flocks of wintering waterfowl.

Hot Spots

It's been mentioned before that the national wildlife refuge system in the United States was established mainly to protect good habitat for waterfowl usually during migration and winter. This means that just about any refuge will be a good spot for waterfowl, including geese. Canada geese should be easy to see at any of the spots mentioned in chapters 8 and 15 and will be common at all the places described below.

Oregon

Oregon presents the best opportunities for seeing the greatest numbers of all four goose species. Three eastern Oregon areas have some of the greatest concentrations of white-fronted, snow and Ross's geese in the West—**Klamath Basin, Harney Basin** and **Summer Lake.** Klamath Basin, which actually has six national wildlife refuges and the state's Klamath Wildlife Area, is truly one of the West's finest places for waterbirds and raptors and is discussed in chapter 7. The best areas in the basin for geese are **Lower Klamath** and **Tule Lake National Wildlife Refuges** and **Klamath Wildlife Area.** The largest concentrations of white-fronted geese in North America are here in late October and early November. These three areas are the only places in our region where you can regularly see Ross's geese.

Harney Basin is home to **Malheur National Wildlife Refuge,** which deserves, and gets, its own chapter (26), and the fields south of **Burns,** described in chapter 15. Smaller than these first two areas but just about as exciting is **Summer Lake Wildlife Area,** described in chapter 3. North of these three superstar hotspots are **Umatilla** and **Cold Springs National Wildlife Refuges,** both covered in chapter 8. Birds often travel back and forth between these two refuges, which are only about 20 miles apart, so it's good to check both in the same day. These two never have as many geese as the eastern Oregon refuges above but usually have some white-fronted and snow geese all winter.

In the Willamette Valley there are four areas that are major wintering sites for Canada geese and are regularly used as stopping places by white-fronted and snow geese. The three national wildlife refuges—**William Finley, Ankeny,** and **Baskett Slough**—are all managed together, primarily as wintering habitat for the dusky Canada goose. Maps to all three areas are in one brochure available from the Willamette Valley National Wildlife Refuges office (see appendix). Geese are best seen by car from the roads going through the refuges because trails are closed during the winter and the geese are easily frightened by people on foot. **Sauvie Island Wildlife Area,** near Portland, is the fourth area and is discussed in chapter 58.

Washington

Washington rarely has any Ross's geese, and white-fronted geese are uncommon and fairly restricted to the southwestern part of the state, **Willapa Bay** in particular (chapter 22). Washington does, however, play host to one of the Northwest's best-known populations of snow geese. **Western Skagit County** is one of the best areas in the state for winter birding. The delta of the Skagit River is a big favorite with waterfowl, and the state has established the **Skagit Wildlife Area** to protect some of this prime habitat for the twenty-five thousand or so snow geese that winter there. The geese start arriving in October, but usually hunting season starts before large numbers are present. Hunting is pretty intense here, so most consider the best birding to be after the season ends, from mid-January through March. To check on hunting and to get information on the Skagit Wildlife Area, contact the regional office of Washington's Department of Fish and Wildlife in Mill Creek (see appendix).

To visit the Skagit Wildlife Area, exit I-5 at the Conway Exit 221, about 5 miles south of Mount Vernon. Go northwest through Conway and continue west on Fir Island Road. In a little under 2 miles from I-5, turn left on Wiley Road and go about three-quarters of a mile to the wildlife area headquarters, where there is a large bulletin board with maps and information. If you are lucky you may find a staff person there—he or she will know where snow geese were last seen. There are trails at headquarters that go out onto the dikes for a couple of miles. After you have looked around the headquarters area, go back to Fir Island Road and turn left to go west again. Fir Island Road will make a big curve and head north, but you continue straight (west) on Maupin Road. Just before Maupin takes a right turn there is a little dirt road on your left that goes to a small parking area at the dike. This is called Jensen Access; take this road and park at the dike. Be very quiet and sneak up onto the dike, peering carefully over the top. There may be thousands of waterfowl on the shore or in the bay just on the other side.

After checking out Jensen Access, get back on Maupin and go west, then north as it turns, to Rawlins Road. Turn left and head west on Rawlins until it ends at the dike. Sneak up on the dike again for another look into Skagit Bay. You may want to hike along the top of the dike back to the southeast for better looks at birds. Over 100,000 ducks have been seen in Skagit Bay at a time! Viewing is best at high tide. Geese are often in the farm fields on Fir Island or in the area commonly called the Skagit Flats. Using a good map, you can navigate around Fir Island, then go north on Fir Island Road and Chilberg Road–Best Road to drive the roads near the intersection of Calhoun and Bradshaw Roads. The brochure and map *Skagit County Bird Watching Guide,* produced by the Washington Department of Fish and Wildlife, is excellent for this area.

British Columbia

As with Washington, white-fronted geese are pretty scarce, and Ross's geese are almost unheard of in British Columbia. Snow geese are a different matter entirely, and of course there are the ever-abundant Canada geese and huge flocks of brant in the spring. All these geese can be found, in the delta of the Fraser River, the winter waterfowl Mecca of Canada. Certainly one of the best spots in the whole Delta area is **Reifel Refuge** on Westham Island.

The George C. Reifel Migratory Bird Sanctuary, usually shortened to Reifel Refuge, is the most famous place in the Pacific Northwest for snow geese. About forty thousand snows spend at least part of the winter here. Their arrival in huge flocks in late October or early November is simply breathtaking. One reason this area is so well known for its snow geese is the annual Snow Goose Festival, which takes place in early November. This is a great time if you like festival-type events but, to be honest, is not the best time to see wildlife because all the people and hubbub frighten many of the animals. Any other time is good for seeing the geese from their arrival in October until some time in January, when a lot of them actually go down to the Skagit River Delta. There is never hunting in the refuge. It is best to come during high tide, when the geese are closest to shore or inland. As always before any big trip, it's a good idea to call the sanctuary to make sure the geese are in and to find out if they are hanging out in places where it is reasonably easy to see them (see appendix).

Reifel Refuge is easy to find—there are lots of signs. Ladner Trunk Road goes due west through the town of Ladner, where it becomes 47th A Avenue in the center of town. Head west on 47th A Avenue and it will then turn into River Road West, which you stay on until you come to Westham Island Road. Turn right, following signs to the refuge, and drive through Westham Island. The farm fields are often full of geese and tundra and trumpeter swans during late fall and winter. About 7 miles from Ladner you'll come to the refuge visitor area, where there is parking, a book and nature store, rest rooms, the sanctuary office and the manager's residence. The visitor center is open from 9 A.M. to 4 P.M. every day. There is a small fee for visiting the refuge. At the visitor center you can get all the information you need about the refuge and what birds are being seen where. Allow plenty of time to visit Reifel—it would be easy for an avid birder to spend the better part of a nice day here. And remember, Reifel is just one of many fabulous spots to bird during the winter in the Delta area.

57

Fall Salmon Runs

Fall is the time when the largest numbers of Pacific salmon return to spawn, and this seasonal spectacle is considered one of the greatest in the natural world. The return of the salmon was one of the most important annual events in the lives of the Native Americans living in the Northwest, not only because it was their single greatest source of food but also because it was a sign that things were right in the world.

The Pacific salmon fisheries of the Northwest were among the greatest fisheries on earth, and the Fraser and Columbia Rivers were two of the greatest salmon producers in the world. Such a bountiful resource was quickly exploited by settlers, and the Columbia suffered the most. The fish were caught in every way imaginable, but the great fish wheels were the most effective. One fish wheel in 1882 took 6,400 large chinook out of the river in one day!

Overharvesting can be a relatively easy problem to correct, however, and with the banning of fish wheels and other regulations in the early part of this century it appeared that the Columbia River salmon might be able to recover. But then came the big dams on the Columbia and its biggest tributary, the Snake River.

The Army Corps of Engineers, the Bureau of Reclamation, Idaho Power and several public utility districts in Washington built a system of dams that have been the single greatest cause of the dramatic collapse of the Columbia River Basin salmon fishery. At present there are sixty-six major multipurpose dams on the Columbia and its main tributaries. It has been estimated that historically the Columbia River system had an annual run of salmon between 11 million and 16 million. Estimates for the 1995 run are around 500,000, and most of those are hatchery fish. Some runs of Snake River salmon have been classified as endangered and other runs will no doubt follow.

Overharvesting and dams are not the only causes of the salmon decline in the Columbia, and in some rivers dams are not a factor in such declines. The other major players in this situation have been habitat destruction and pollution. Habitat destruction has occurred in many ways. Urbanization has destroyed many streams outright and contributed greatly to pollution. Logging practices have significantly affected fish in many areas, mainly by destroying riparian vegetation and by causing increased erosion into streams, thus silting up spawning areas.

Agricultural practices have caused many problems. Overgrazing increases erosion by the removal of bankside vegetation and the trampling of stream banks by livestock. Unscreened irrigation ditches and pipes have sucked many salmon to their deaths, and irrigation has left some streams with too little, or no, water. Pesticide and fertilizer runoff from agricultural lands is a major source of water pollution. Fish hatcheries, which once were seen as the solution to the dams, have caused problems of their own by replacing the wild native stocks with hatchery fish that are not as well adapted to survive and reproduce in the wild. Hatchery programs are controversial, but research is underway on techniques that can produce fish better able to survive in the wild.

There is much to be done if we are going to attempt the recovery of the Northwest's salmon. In the U.S., recovery programs are required by law for those runs that become classified under the Endangered Species Act. We will have to make some changes in our lifestyle if salmon recovery is going to have a chance. At a minimum, we will have to use less electricity and pay more for what we do use. The salmon issue is as complex as the relationships between salmon and their ecosystem and will be the single biggest environmental issue of the 1990s in the Northwest.

Oregon

Hot Spots

The **Salmon Festival in Oxbow Regional Park** had over ten thousand attendees in 1995, its twelfth year. The festival is the second weekend in October, Saturday and Sunday, from 10:30 A.M. to 5:00 P.M. (Directions to Oxbow Park are in chapter 61.) There is an entrance fee for each car ($6 in 1995). Pick up a map at the entrance showing where activities take place, or get information in advance by contacting Metro Regional Parks and Greenspaces (see appendix). If you go to Oxbow some other time to look for salmon on your own, the best places are in the Sandy River next to group picnic area D, and in the stretch between trail markers M and K, near group camping area 3.

Another place near Portland to see spawning salmon is the **Clackamas River** near **Ripplebrook Ranger Station**. Spring chinook spawn from mid-September to mid-October—the last week in September is usually the peak. Take State Highway 224 southeast from Estacada to the Ripplebrook Ranger Station, which is worth a stop to get the latest information on salmon and other wildlife-watching news. From the ranger station continue east on Hwy. 224 half a mile until it crosses a bridge and splits into Forest Road 57 and Forest Road 46. Turn right onto FR 46 and go just about $2\frac{1}{2}$ miles to a turnout on your right (which should have a sign). Park here and walk west to the edge of the bluff to view the river. Another access that offers hiking along the river through some ancient forest is to drive another half-mile to the Riverside Campground and take the **Riverside Trail** downstream (north). In 4 miles you reach Rainbow Campground near Ripplebrook. Fish watchers have seen as many as a hundred fish at a time along this stretch of the Clackamas.

There are fish going up **Deadline Falls** on the **North Umpqua River** in autumn. (See chapter 40). The best fall viewing, however, switches to **Marster's Bridge** and **Soda Springs**. About 50 miles east of Roseburg, State Highway 138 crosses the North Umpqua at Marster's Bridge. Park near the bridge and look downstream from the north bank for spawning chinook.

For Soda Springs, drive east another 5 miles, then turn left (north) for Soda Springs Reservoir and take another left onto Soda Springs Road, heading for the transfer station. In just under a mile cross a bridge and park on the other side. Walk along the banks looking for fish and redds (salmon nests). The peak of spawning is usually within the last week of September and the first week in October.

Washington

The grandmama of all salmon festivals is **Issaquah Salmon Days,** which celebrated its twenty-fifth anniversary in 1994 and has attendance figures in the 200,000 range! The original impetus for this cultural phenomenon is the return of chinook salmon to Issaquah Creek and the hatchery. The **Issaquah Salmon Hatchery** has been operating in the middle of town since 1936 and has some great interpretive signs, making it an excellent visitor facility. In addition to seeing fish at the hatchery, huge chinooks are easily seen in Issaquah Creek from several places in town. Issaquah Salmon Days are always the first full weekend in October, if you like festivals, but of course the fish are there before and after.

The **Wenatchee River Salmon Festival** is a newcomer but is growing fast. The festival takes place in and around Leavenworth. Most activities are at the Leavenworth National Fish Hatchery (see chapter 40), and the salmon viewing is up the Wenatchee River from town. The festival is the second weekend in October. For festival information, contact the Leavenworth Chamber of Commerce or the Salmon Festival Director at Leavenworth National Fish Hatchery. To see spawning wild summer chinook anytime between mid-September and mid-October, drive up **Tumwater Canyon** on U.S. Highway 2 from Leavenworth. Look for good turnouts where you can park and scan the river from the roadside anywhere along the first 3 miles upstream from Icicle Road, the road to the fish hatchery. Another good spot is the **Swift Water Picnic Area,** $6^1/_2$ miles up the canyon.

Some sockeye have become landlocked and can no longer return to the sea. These fish are called kokanee salmon and are just as colorful as regular sockeye. There are two well-known places in Washington to see kokanee spawn—**Gold Creek Pond** and **Rimrock Lake.** Gold Creek Pond is a wonderful example of a restoration project for wildlife habitat. The area around Gold Creek was used as a gravel quarry for the construction of I-90 and a wasteland was left behind. Years later, in a massive cooperative effort involving state and federal agencies and volunteers, the area was rehabilitated to provide wildlife habitat and a universally accessible interpretive trail. Now there's a nice spot right off I-90 near Snoqualmie Pass where you can possibly see beaver, mountain goats, Canada geese and spawning kokanee salmon.

Just east of Snoqualmie Pass take Exit 54, the Hyak–Gold Creek Exit, and follow the signs to Gold Creek. You'll parallel the interstate on the north side, heading east on a frontage road for about a mile, then will see a brown binocular sign, where you turn left. Follow the road as it curves to the left and in half a mile you'll come to the parking area. Paved trails lead to the pond and other spots to see salmon in the spawning channel. Watch the distant mountainsides for mountain goats. I-90 makes a great drive for fall colors, and you can stop at Asahel Curtis Nature Trail for an ancient forest hike (chapter 50).

U.S. Highway 12 is a great auto route for fall colors, and **Rimrock Lake** is a great stop for viewing a big kokanee run. The kokanee swim up the tributary streams that flow into the lake in October, and the easiest place to see them is the short section of the North Fork Teiton River that runs between Clear Lake and Rimrock Lake. From Hwy. 12 about three-quarters of a mile west of Indian Creek Campground, head south, following the signs for Clear Lake or Tieton Road. In less than half a mile go left to Clear Lake Campground, and just after you pass the North Clear Lake CG sign turn left again onto a campground loop road. Go to the end of the campground loop and park at or near the last site, then make your way down the informal trails to the north bank of the river.

Chinook and coho come right into Capitol Lake and up the Deschutes River in Olympia and can be seen in **Tumwater Falls Park.** Coming into Olympia from the south, take Exit 103 for the Deschutes Parkway and turn right into the park's parking lot just a few blocks after exiting. Coming from the north, take Exit 103 for Second Avenue, which you take south a few blocks to Custer Way. Turn left onto Custer Way (at the fire station) and immediately turn right onto Boston Street after you cross the river. Take Boston back over the river until it ends at Deschutes Parkway at the Falls Terrace Restaurant. Turn left onto Deschutes Parkway and immediately turn left again into the park parking lot. From trails along the river and a footbridge you can see fish in the river. You can also see adults being held in the Washington Department of Fish and Wildlife facility near the parking lot and can see artificial spawning at certain times during the run (usually Monday, Wednesday and Friday; 9 A.M. to 12 P.M.).

British Columbia

On Vancouver Island, **Goldstream Provincial Park** provides one of the most spectacular salmon runs with convenient access and viewing. From mid-October into mid-December, thousands of mainly chum salmon, with some coho and chinook, spawn naturally right in the Goldstream River, where they can easily be seen from the trails. The Freeman King Visitor Center, open every day during the run, has exhibits, programs, printed information and staff on hand to answer questions and give directions to the best viewing spots. Goldstream Provincial Park is 10 miles northwest of Victoria on Trans-Canada Highway 1. Park in the main parking and picnic area near the north end of the park and take the Lower Goldstream Trail to the visitor center. The eggs and the carcasses of spawned-out salmon provide a rich bounty for a number of predators and scavengers including gulls, bald eagles and dippers during the day and raccoons, river otters, mink and even black bear at night.

Stamp Falls Provincial Park is described in chapter 40 and has a large chinook run in September and October. Nearby is **Robertson Creek Hatchery,** reached by taking Great Central Lake Road north from Provincial Highway 4 about 6 miles west of Port Alberni. Large numbers of big chinook can be seen in the lagoon near the hatchery and through underwater windows in the fishways.

About 60 miles east of Vancouver two tributaries of the Fraser River provide great viewing of wild fish in natural settings and in hatchery operations. The Harrison River flows down from the north to join the Fraser near the small town of Harrison Mills. **Weaver Creek Spawning Channel** has been developed as a major spawning site for the most colorful of the salmon, sockeye. The spawning period is brief, with peak numbers between October 10 and 25. The nearby **Chehalis Hatchery** is a good example of a large hatchery with chum, coho and chinook present in October. Coming from Vancouver on Provincial Highway 7, turn left onto Morris Valley Road at the Sasquatch Inn and go north about 6 miles. The hatchery will be on your right. For Weaver Creek, take Morris Road north from Hwy. 7 as before, but in just 100 yards take the right fork in the road and follow signs another 8 miles to the spawning channel. Bald eagles know about the Harrison River also, and hundreds gather here later in the winter.

The **Chilliwack River** flows west from Chilliwack Lake on the U.S. border. Before it gets to the Fraser, however, it gets a new name, the **Vedder River.** The point where this identity crisis takes place is south of the town of Chilliwack, where Vedder Road crosses the river at Vedder Crossing. Just before the bridge crosses the river, on the right-hand side as you're headed south, is a small parking area for a new trail that has just been developed. The trail goes along the top of the dike along the north bank of the Vedder River, and from the trail you can see chum, coho and chinook salmon in the river.

From the trail's parking area, drive east on the north side of the what is named here the Chilliwack River, and you can find pullouts in which to park and scan the river from the roadside. When the road crosses the Chilliwack River, take a right over another bridge and there is a small park where Tamihi Creek joins the Chilliwack that has good viewing. Continue on the main road going east along the south shore of the Chilliwack and you'll come to the **Chilliwack Hatchery** at Slesse Creek. From the hatchery you can see fish in the Slesse and Chilliwack—in the entrance channel into the hatchery and in holding tanks.

A more natural and low-key experience than the big hatcheries that is only half as far from Vancouver can be found at **Kanaka Creek Regional Park** and the **Bell-Irving Hatchery.** From Haney, head east on the Dewdney Trunk Road and turn right (south) onto 256th Street at the school. Drive into the park and cross the creek to the hatchery. You can see fish in the tanks at the hatchery, and from the hatchery you can hike down the trail to the "fish fence" and see chum salmon in Kanaka Creek.

58

Sandhill Cranes

Cranes have always made a big impression on people. They are among the tallest birds in the world, and with their upright posture they have an air of nobility. They also have powerful voices that can be heard for distances of a mile or more, the result of a special coiled trachea that has been likened to a French horn. On top of this, they all have very elaborate, dramatic courtship displays that are usually referred to as dances, and indeed have inspired human dances. Cranes are represented in ancient Egyptian wall paintings and have popped up frequently over the centuries in a variety of art forms from different cultures. It is not uncommon for cranes to be powerful symbols in the mythology of people who live near them, especially in Asia.

Two characteristics of cranes that have led to their high status among humans are their longevity and their fidelity. Cranes can live a long time for a bird, over forty years, and as a result are prominent symbols of long life in China and Japan. Cranes mate for life and are almost always seen in pairs when not in a flock, so it is no surprise that they are also symbols of a happy marriage. In fact, they serve as examples that fidelity and a happy marriage *lead* to a long life. In the past thirty years they have taken on a new meaning because of Kawabata Yasunari's book, *A Thousand Cranes,* the heartbreaking story of Sadako Sasaki, a Japanese girl who died from leukemia caused by the atomic bombing of Hiroshima. Every year Japanese children make thousands of origami cranes in memory of Sadako and as a demonstration for world peace.

North America has two cranes, the whooping crane and the sandhill crane. Whooping cranes are one of Canada's and America's rarest birds and one of our most famous endangered species. As far as we know, whoopers have never occurred in the Pacific Northwest. Sandhill cranes have always been much more numerous than whoopers, and despite population reductions from habitat loss are now locally common in many western states and are still abundant in much of their breeding range in Canada and Alaska. They occur regularly in our region. There is a breeding population of about two thousand sandhills east of the Cascades, the majority in southeastern Oregon. A small number usually overwinter in the western lowlands, but the biggest numbers are seen during migration as birds that breed in Canada and Alaska travel to and from California.

Fall crane migration starts in September, peaking in October in Oregon. As expected, birds arrive earlier farther north. By November most have left, and the only regularly wintering population is the one hundred or so birds that stay in the Sauvie Island–Ridgefield area near Portland. As is typical for many birds, the spring migration is more condensed, with the most arrivals in March in Oregon and spreading into April farther north. There are thousands migrating on both sides of the Cascades, but the biggest numbers are in the east, where the migrants mix with the breeding population.

Sandhill cranes can easily be mistaken for great blue herons, and the much more common great blue is frequently called a crane. Both herons and cranes are also called storks, because of the familiarity with the old European folktale of storks bringing babies.

A great blue heron and a sandhill crane do look a lot alike, but there are several easy ways to tell them apart. The easiest to remember is the basis for the idiom "crane your neck." Cranes almost always stick their necks out straight. This is especially apparent when they are flying with their long necks out in front and their long legs out in back. Herons usually hold their necks at least partially folded into an S shape. This is really obvious when they fly and hold their heads folded all the way back over their bodies. Another good clue is the monochrome coloring of cranes. Sandhills vary from grayish to brownish (the young are brown), but they are basically one color. Great blue herons are blue-gray and have white and black on them. These other colors are most apparent on adults in breeding plumage, when they also have plumes on their heads. Another interesting field mark for cranes is the rear end, which looks like a bustle!

Cranes nest in shallow marshes and well-flooded fields and hunt for food in almost any open grassy habitat, from marsh to flooded pasture to dry grain field. They are omnivorous and opportunistic (the two go together) and eat lots of plant material in the winter. They are very gregarious, except when paired off to breed, and it is unusual to see one crane by itself. You have a good chance of seeing some of their courtship dance early in the morning in the spring, even among the migrating birds.

Oregon

Hot Spots

Sauvie Island, the large island at the confluence of the Willamette and Columbia Rivers, is the most famous crane spot west of the Cascades. Upwards of 2,500 lesser sandhills can be on the island at a time during the peak in October. Some birds may arrive as early as the end of August, and most years about one hundred stay through winter until the spring migration, when they rejoin their buddies for the trip north. Fewer stop in March, and for a shorter time than in the fall.

Sauvie Island is about half private farmland and half state land managed by the Oregon Department of Fish and Wildlife as the **Sauvie Island Wildlife Area.** It is probably the single most popular birding area near Portland because it is has good habitat, is close to town and has a great variety of bird life—about 250 species visit the island at some time during the year! A parking permit is required at all times to park in the wildlife area. Permits can be purchased at the small store near the east end of the bridge to the island. Much of the wildlife area is closed, except for hunting, during the waterfowl season, which is generally mid-October to mid-January. There are some-

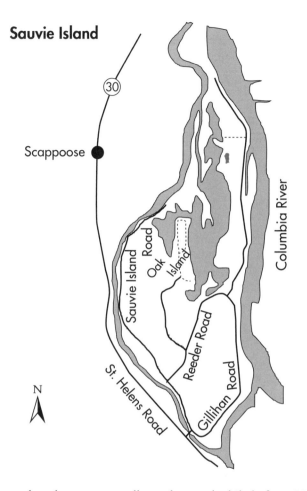

Sauvie Island

Scappoose

Columbia River

Sauvie Island Road

Oak Road

Island

Reeder Road

Gillihan Road

St. Helens Road

N

times other closures, so a call may be worthwhile before visiting. However, some of the best birding is from the public roads through the private farm-land, where many birds can be seen from the car. Many people like the pe-riod right after hunting season ends for the best winter birding on Sauvie.

To get to Sauvie Island, go ten miles northwest of downtown Portland on U.S. Highway 30 toward Astoria. Watch for signs for the bridge, and cross over it and onto the island. There is a dirt parking area on the east, or island end of the bridge, where groups often meet. If you go north from the bridge on Sauvie Island Road past Reeder Road, you will come to the wildlife area headquarters, where you can usually get maps and information on current closures. Cranes are often seen from the paved portion of Sauvie Island Road in the fields near the county line (there is a sign for Columbia County on the road). The best place to look is usually along the road to Oak Island. Oak Island itself is usually closed during the hunting season, but the private land just before the state land is very good for cranes and waterfowl. Throughout the winter Sauvie Island is an excellent place to view waterfowl (lots of Canada geese), raptors, gulls and wintering sparrows. In addition to driving north on Sauvie Island and Oak Island Roads, make the Reeder Road-Gillihan Road-Sauvie Island Road loop around the southern end of the island.

The breeding greater sandhill cranes in Oregon are concentrated around the Burns-Malheur area. The fields and pastures south of **Burns** and the marshes at **Malheur National Wildlife Refuge** (chapters 15 and 26) host about three thousand cranes during October but have over twice that many in April. Other good locations on the east side are **Summer Lake Wildlife Area** (chapter 3) and the **Warner Valley** near Hart Mountain (chapter 61).

Washington

Ridgefield National Wildlife Refuge is just across the Columbia River from Sauvie Island, and the two can be considered as one area. The birds certainly don't think twice about flying back and forth between the two, so when the closures are getting you down on Sauvie, or things are just too slow from hunting and other human activities, zip on over to Ridgefield. The whole northern section, the **Carty Unit,** never has hunting and is always open for birding, and the **River S Unit** is open for birding on no-hunt days. Be sure to call the refuge for hunting day schedules from October through January (see appendix).

To get to the refuge, take the Ridgefield Exit (14) about 12 miles north of the Columbia River and head west on State Highway 501. As you come into the town of Ridgefield you'll see that the north-south cross streets are numbered. To get to the River S Unit, the area with the most wetlands and most waterbirds, but also the area with hunting closures, turn left and head south on South 9th Street. In a few blocks 9th turns into Hillhurst as it climbs the hill south of town. In just under a mile you'll see a dirt road to the right with a refuge sign. Take this road, which becomes the auto-tour road through the River S Unit. Drive this road to its end, birding from the car when possible but getting out when needed and especially at the observation blind, a short walk from a small parking area. Cranes could be out in the fields anywhere but are often near the southeastern side of Rest Lake, opposite the blind.

Ridgefield is also a great place for waterfowl, including swans, which will be starting to come in with the cranes and will build in numbers into the winter. Ridgefield is also known for wintering bald eagles, and from the end of waterfowl hunting season (mid-January) through March is simply a great winter birding spot, and very convenient from the Portland metro area.

The Carty Unit of Ridgefield National Wildlife Refuge has a good trail through a nice mix of habitats, including oak woodlands, which means a diversity of birds but not the big numbers of waterbirds seen at the River S Unit. Back on the main road in Ridgefield (Hwy. 501), go west until the road ends at Main Street. Go north on Main Street just over a mile and you will see the parking area for the Carty Unit on your left. The 2-mile **Oak to**

Ridgefield National Wildlife Refuge

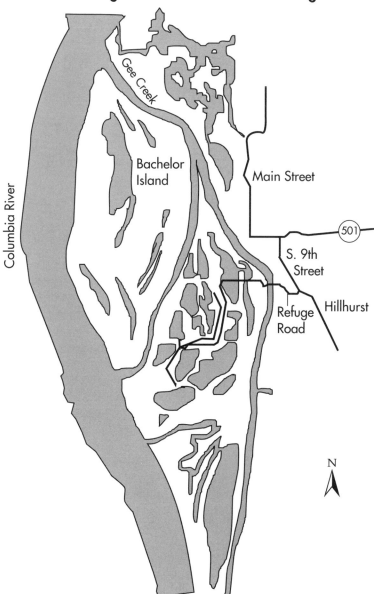

Wetlands Wildlife Trail starts on the other side of the bridge over the train tracks and goes through some very pleasant terrain that can have some excellent wildflower displays in the spring.

Two major stopping areas for cranes migrating through eastern Washington are the mosaic of wetlands and fields around **Potholes Reservoir** and the area west of **Banks Lake. Columbia National Wildlife Refuge** and the fields to the west of the refuge and north of State Highway 26 usually have good numbers of cranes during March. This is a spectacular area for spring water-fowl migration and is discussed in chapter 15. Be sure to check on closure dates in the refuge when planning a trip.

If you drew a line between the two small towns of Mansfield and Coulee City, the midpoint of that line would be in an area called **St. Andrews.** St. Andrews is well known for large flocks of sandhills in March and is also good for raptors, including long-eared owls in riparian areas. Drive St. Andrews South Road north from U.S. Highway 2, about 6 miles west of Coulee City, to Buckeye Road. Take Buckeye east to State Highway 17 (Leahy Road) and head north toward Leahy. Explore any of the basic grid of farm roads in the area that look interesting.

British Columbia

The vast majority of the migrant and breeding sandhill cranes in British Columbia pass well to the east of our area in the Okanagan (spelled Okanogan in the United States). A small number pass through the Delta area, where a few sometimes winter. There is a very small (three to five pairs) breeding population of greater sandhill cranes in the Pitt Wildlife Management Area, usually called just **Pitt Meadows.** Birds may be seen here almost any time of year, but since they breed here, April through June should be best. The best description of this area, which is rich in other species, is in *A Bird Watching Guide to the Vancouver Area.*

To get to Pitt Meadows, take Provincial Highway 7, the Lougheed High-way, southeast from Port Moody. Within a half-mile after crossing the Pitt River, turn left at the signal for Dewdney Trunk Road and go east $1^2/_5$ miles to a T junction with Harris Road, which is not marked. Turn left and go north on Harris 2 miles and turn right onto McNeill Road which will take you east. McNeill twists around a bit, and in $2^1/_2$ miles you'll come to an intersection, with Neaves Road south of the intersection and Rennie Road north of the intersection. You want to turn left onto Rennie and go north.

In another $2^1/_2$ miles you'll come to a big power line. This is where to start searching seriously for cranes, if you haven't seen them already. Park as best you can along the road and scan carefully in all directions. After looking from this spot, proceed by creeping along on Rennie Road going north, which eventually angles northeast and ends at the Pitt River. Try driving open side roads or walking the tops of dikes that head east from Rennie Road. Pitt Meadows is also famous for osprey and other raptors and as a nesting site for gray catbirds, eastern kingbirds and American redstarts.

59

October Shorttakes

Fungi Fun

When the rain starts in earnest in October, the Pacific Northwest becomes a fungus festival with thousands of different kinds of mushrooms, particularly in the wet forests west of the Cascades. There are many fungus fans in the Northwest, and many cities have a mycological society, or mushroom club with field trips, programs and sometimes classes. The Puget Sound Mycological Society in Seattle has a permanent number: (206) 522-6031. Many mycological societies put on mushroom shows in October on a Saturday or a Sunday. These shows are listed in local newspapers, and attending a mushroom show is an easy way to find out what's going on with fungi in your area. At this time the following cities have been regularly holding October mushroom shows: Portland, Eugene at Mount Pisgah Arboretum, Lincoln City and Medford in Oregon, Seattle (two-day show), Tacoma, Olympia, Everett, Bellingham and Bremerton in Washington; Vancouver and Victoria in British Columbia.

Spiders

Fall is spider time. All those babies that hatched out in the spring have been porking up all summer and are now noticeable as they weave webs all over your yard. Most dramatic are the large members of the orb-weaver family, usually called garden spiders or argiopes. These are the spiders that weave the classic big circular webs and then usually hang upside down in the middle. Spiders are tough to tell apart, and the only reasonable book for amateurs is the classic Golden guide, *Spiders and their Kin,* from 1968.

Another fabulous spider event that takes place in the fall is "ballooning." Young spiders climb to the top of a plant, stick their abdomens into the air, and shoot out a strand of silk. When the silk is long enough to catch the wind and lift the spider, it lets go and wanders off, drifting over the countryside to a new home. This is the way most spiders disperse, and it is extremely effective; ballooning spiders are seen on high mountains and remote islands, although most travel short distances. Where millions of spiders have landed, the ground or vegetation can become covered with masses of threads, and this is called *gossamer.* A field of dry grass covered with gossamer reflecting the sunlight of a bright fall day is one of the most beautiful and ethereal sights I've ever seen.

60

A Closer Look:
National Wildlife Refuges

It happens every time I take a birding class on our first field trip to a national wildlife refuge. At some point I mention that during hunting season some areas are closed to bird-watching because of hunting. "What, hunting? On a wildlife refuge? How can that be?" There are always people who are surprised, and often almost outraged, to learn that there is hunting on a wildlife refuge. Part of the confusion lies in the word "refuge," which means a protected place and in common usage is pretty much synonymous with "sanctuary." There are different kinds of refuges, however, and a National Wildlife Refuge (NWR) is a specific type of federal land managed by the U.S. Fish and Wildlife Service with definite management objectives. When considered compatible with the management goals and objectives for a NWR, regulated hunting is allowed in compliance with all other pertinent state and federal laws.

There are plenty of people with very strong feelings and opinions about hunting who believe there should not be any hunting on NWRs, and many who don't want any hunting allowed anywhere, period. How one feels about hunting in general is very personal and involves many factors, including opinions that can't be labeled right or wrong. Comments about hunting on NWRs, however, often reveal a great deal of confusion about the history and purposes of the national wildlife refuge system. Both antihunting birders and gung-ho hunters have common myths and misconceptions about the refuge system, and each other, that contribute to the confusion. A little history helps people understand what the national wildlife refuge system is all about.

From the time the first Europeans settled in North America up to the time of the American Civil War, the attitude of these settlers and their descendents can pretty well be summed up as unbridled exploitation of all natural resources, including wildlife. It wasn't until the 1870s that the earliest stages of what would be called the conservation movement began. The extinction of the passenger pigeon and near extinction of the American bison, both unbelievably abundant just a few decades earlier, were some of America's first wake-up calls to the destruction of our natural resources. Some of the earliest actions taken were the establishment of Yellowstone National Park in 1872, the passage of the first state game laws and the creation of state game departments. Early conservationists like Theodore Roosevelt, Gifford Pinchot, George Bird Grinnell and John Muir began to have an impact on other political leaders and the general public. By

World War I there was a broad-based popular conservation movement under way and a growing awareness of the impact of human activities on wildlife and nature in general.

An important landmark was the establishment of the first national wildlife refuge in 1903 by President Roosevelt. It is important to note that like most of the early conservation activists, Theodore Roosevelt was a sportsman—his interest in wildlife was connected with his love of hunting. It is important for contemporary environmentalists to recognize that throughout the history of wildlife conservation in this country, many of the most important and influential activists and groups have been hunters (and anglers) and their organizations, such as the Izaak Walton League and Ducks Unlimited. The most familiar case of sportsmen helping wildlife conservation is the Migratory Bird Hunting and Conservation Stamp, usually called the Duck Stamp. The "Duck Stamp" Act in 1934 established the process by which hunters buy the current Duck Stamp to hunt waterfowl legally in the United States, and the money goes into the Migratory Bird Conservation Fund, which is used to acquire land for national wildlife refuges.

The Duck Stamp program was extremely important for the acquisition of land in the beginning of the refuge system, and many sportsmen today proudly claim that they have paid for the national wildlife refuges. Sometimes nonhunting visitors to the refuges (nonconsumptive users) are portrayed as freeloaders or parasites, using the refuges for recreation but not paying for their purchase or upkeep. These common misconceptions are quite wrong.

There is no question that funds from Duck Stamp purchases by hunters has contributed significantly (about $90 million) to the purchase of land for the national wildlife refuges since the beginning of the program. But over time, other sources of funds for refuge acquisition have been used, and since the early 1960s Duck Stamp funds have accounted for about a fifth of the total money used to buy land. And the direct purchase of land has been one of several avenues for refuge land acquisition. Most of the land in the NWR system was already in the public domain and was essentially "reclassified." So despite the accurate claim that hunters have helped pay for the NWRs, their contributions have not been the only source of funds for refuge acquisition.

Getting the land for the refuges is one cost, but equally important is the money needed to operate, maintain and improve the refuges already in the system. Since 1961, all of the funds for refuge maintenance, administration, operations and law enforcement have come from general taxpayer receipts at the level of about $300 million a year. So all American taxpayers have helped pay for the national wildlife refuge system, whether they have ever hunted or not, even though sportsmen historically and currently have paid more, on average, than the nonhunting public.

Regardless of how much different individuals contribute, the total funding for the NWRs is not adequate. The 1992 report of the Commission on New Directions for the national wildlife refuge system said the system "suffers chronic fiscal starvation and administrative neglect." In comparing the national park system and the national forest system to the national wildlife refuge system, the Fall 1993 *Refuge Reporter* states that national park employees outnumber refuge employees by eight to one, while forest service employees outnumber refuge personnel by seven to one. If you look at the amount of funding per acre in the three systems, funding for the smaller national park system is seven times greater than for the refuges, and for the larger forest system it is four times greater. Some funds that have been collected and designated for acquisition of land for wildlife (the Land and Water Conservation Fund), have even been diverted by politicians to other purposes.

The national wildlife refuge system suffers from a lack of public awareness and of an effective group of citizen advocates. To this end, the U.S. Fish and Wildlife Service is initiating the "100 by 100" public education campaign designed with a goal of every American (100 percent) knowing something about the national wildlife refuge system by the year 2003 (the 100th anniversary of the first refuge). All of us who use and value this 91,000,000 acre system of over five hundred refuges in all fifty states needs to show our support every way we can. We especially need to let our representatives in Washington know that there is no "contract with America" directing them to give away parts of this system to greedy commercial interests.

State and provincial wildlife agencies are distinct from federal agencies and have differences in programs, funding and regulations that vary from state to state. Regardless of the level of independence, there is a great deal of communication, coordination and cooperation among state wildlife agencies and between the states and "the Feds." In general, hunters contribute a much higher proportion to state wildlife management programs then they do to federal programs, and it is here that complaints of nonconsumptive users not paying their share have more substance. In the last twenty years there has been a major change in the mission and orientation of state wildlife agencies. Today there is much more interest and emphasis on nongame species, the vast majority of wildlife in a state that is not hunted. State agencies, and the U.S. Fish and Wildlife Service, are increasingly managing wildlife with the ecosystem approach and viewing wildlife in a broader, more holistic sense.

A major reason for this shift is the decrease in hunter numbers and the dramatic increase in people interested in wildlife watching. The problem facing state agencies is that most of their funds come directly from the consumptive uses of wildlife and are therefore dedicated to the management of game species. It is currently very difficult to get funds committed to nongame wildlife management. There is currently a lot of serious consideration being given to new methods of funding nongame programs, such as special taxes on items such as binoculars and bird feeders similar to the excise taxes paid by hunters on guns and ammunition. A change must come at the federal and state levels so that all wildlife is seen as a valuable resource to all people and so that money is spent where it does the most good for the protection and management of natural habitats and for the greatest diversity of wildlife.

November

Notes

61

Pronghorn

The name "antelope" conjures up images of the African plains and animals looking like impalas or gazelles. Those are correct images, because the true antelopes, members of the Bovidae family, all live in Africa, Asia and Europe and are the animals one frequently sees in scenes of the African plains. However, we have an animal labeled with the misnomer antelope, the pronghorn. Pronghorn are not really antelopes but something much more special.

The pronghorn is the world's only living member of a family of hoofed mammals called the *Antilocapridae*. There used to be more members of this family in North America during the Ice Ages and earlier, but they are now only fossils. The Antilocapridae family is something very rare, a whole family of animals completely restricted to North America. This makes the pronghorn a truly unique animal of the American West. But whereas everyone knows about the American bison, or buffalo, pronghorn are surprisingly unknown and definitely underappreciated. They truly are a unique symbol of our American West and deserve to at least grace the back of a nickel.

One very unusual feature of pronghorn is the horn that gives them their name. They are the only animal in the world with a branched horn, for they definitely have horns and not antlers. Their horn is also unlike any other animal's in that the horny outer sheath is shed every year, leaving a bony core. Both males and females have horns, but the female's are small and inconspicuous.

I advocate increased pronghorn awareness and believe these animals should really be appreciated for the amazing creatures they are. They can make a solid claim to the title of the most highly adapted animal for running in the world. Right away most will think, Oh yeah? What about cheetahs? It is very hard to accurately measure animal speeds, and you can find a variety of top speeds given for cheetahs and pronghorn in different books. It does seem to be universally accepted, however, that cheetahs can just beat pronghorns with a top speed of possibly 70 miles per hour, while pronghorn appear to reach a maximum more around 60 miles per hour. But cheetahs can only hit their top speeds for a few seconds; they are definitely sprinters. Pronghorn, on the other hand, can maintain top speed for longer and apparently can cruise along at over 40 miles per hour for several miles. When it comes to sustained high-speed running, pronghorn are the champs.

How pronghorn can maintain such high speeds is a marvelous study in adaptation and evolution. Pronghorn anatomy and physiology have been studied quite closely, for these animals seem to represent a limit in evolution for running. Like other *ungulates,* or hoofed mammals, pronghorn have legs that are highly specialized for running. Their legs and feet are very long and thin and highly modified compared to more average mammal legs. This gives them a very long stride, the most basic requirement for a fast runner. One of the main limiting factors in how fast and how long an animal can run is its ability to get oxygen to its muscles, and this is where the pronghorn has some of its most extreme adaptations. Compared to a goat, which is about as close a living relative to the pronghorn as you can find, pronghorns have five times the lung capacity, a heart three times larger, a larger windpipe and more hemoglobin in the blood. This all goes toward making the pronghorn the super runner of the American plains.

Pronghorn, and other ungulates, developed their running abilities to escape predators on the emerging grasslands of a drying world. Their habitat has remained the prairies and sagebrush plains of the American West. They truly are animals of the wide open spaces and will not seek shelter in trees. They once ranged from Canada to Mexico in most western states in numbers estimated as high as 50 million. Like their close associate on the prairies, the American bison, pronghorn were decimated by hunters. But their numbers never got as critically low as bison, probably because they were able to retreat more to the periphery of human activity, particularly in the sparsely settled sagebrush lands of the Great Basin and Wyoming. Starting around the turn of the twentieth century, they were completely protected for about twenty-five years and then managed as a big-game species. Today there are about half a million living over much of their former range where the habitat is still suitable and human disturbance is minimal.

Because running away is their means of escaping predators, pronghorn must be able to detect predators well in advance. They usually don't have to worry about predators sneaking up on them because they stick to open spaces. Pronghorn have the keen senses of smell and hearing typical of ungulates, but they mainly depend on their exceptional eyesight to spot predators 2 or 3 miles away. Their eyes are very large and are unusually high and far back on the head. They have an interesting way of signaling one another in times of danger: When they are frightened, the white hairs on their rumps stand erect as they run away. Other pronghorn see these white patches disappearing into the distance and take off themselves. Their excellent eyesight and cautious nature can make pronghorn difficult to see except at long distances. Fortunately, some pronghorn seem to have accommodated to traffic along certain Oregon roads and so not all viewings are dots in the distance.

Pronghorn ranged historically throughout the Great Basin, and that is the part of our region where we find them most easily today, in Oregon's Great Basin country. The Great Basin does not extend into Washington and British Columbia, and there are no pronghorn in those areas, although there was an unsuccessful attempt to introduce pronghorn into eastern Washington. The only practical way to see pronghorn is to drive the roads mentioned in the areas below carefully, watching for the distinctive white-and-tan in the distance. As with many animals, some pronghorn may actually allow a vehicle to pass fairly close but will immediately run off when they see a human on foot. Stay in your car, it is your traveling observation blind.

Oregon

The sagebrush plains and grasslands of the southeastern quarter of Oregon is the heart of the Northwest's pronghorn country. You could see pronghorn almost anywhere in this area in proper habitat, but there are some particularly good places.

Not surprisingly, the best place is **Hart Mountain National Antelope Refuge**, about 45 miles northeast of the town of Lakeview. From Lakeview, go 4.5 miles north on U.S. Highway 395 to the junction with State Highway 140. Go east on Hwy. 140 toward Adel, but turn north on the Plush Cutoff after 15 miles. After 17 miles on the Plush Cutoff you'll come to the tiny hamlet of Plush (last chance for gas and a store). Continue north and east, following the signs to the refuge as the road makes a few right-hand jogs. Just outside of town you'll come to a BLM interpretive area on the Warner Basin, which is definitely worth a quick stop. Hart Mountain will have been looming in the east for some time, and it will be obvious where you're headed.

Hart Mountain is a classic fault block mountain. Layers of basalt flowed over the area, making a flat landscape. Then a major fault developed and the land east of the fault was pushed up to become Hart Mountain while the land west of the fault dropped and became the Warner Basin, filled with a huge lake during the last Ice Age but now containing a chain of shallow lakes.

You will start driving along the base of the escarpment and will come to the end of the paved road. Soon after this you will see a sign about bighorn sheep. This sign is well placed, because from that point until the road starts its steep climb up the mountain is the best place in Oregon to see bighorn sheep (see chapter 63). After looking for bighorns, continue up the mountain to the refuge headquarters. At headquarters there is a small visitor center with a rest room and information. There is a wildlife-sightings register that may give you current information on the location of pronghorn and other wildlife. If a member of the refuge staff is in the office, he or she can give you the latest tips on locating pronghorn and on road conditions.

Pronghorn are usually seen from the main road that crosses the refuge and goes through headquarters, and from the Blue Sky Road, which goes south from headquarters to **Blue Sky**, a beautiful grove of ponderosa pine and aspen. Check to see if the Blue Sky Road is open. In the past it has usually been closed from November 1 until spring, but there are plans to keep it open for more of the year in the future. To take the Blue Sky Road, start at headquarters and drive south following the signs. After 1.5 miles the road forks. The right fork goes to Hot Springs Camp and the left fork goes to Blue Sky. Watch carefully all the way along the Blue Sky Road. Blue Sky itself is a beautiful place in which to get out and walk around a bit. Go back to headquarters the way you came.

For the really adventurous there is another area that is a real hotspot for pronghorn. In the southeast corner of the refuge are a series of lakes where the largest numbers of pronghorn often congregate. The road, however, is very rough and is best done in a four-wheel-drive or high-clearance vehicle. This road, the **South Boundary Road,** takes off from the Blue Sky Road at its southernmost point. I would not take this road without a refuge map in hand and after a consultation with a refuge staff member, especially when traveling midweek and off-season. Most people get plenty of good views of pronghorn from the main roads.

Remember **Hot Springs Camp** mentioned above? After a dusty day of wildlife viewing, what could be better than a nice soak in a hot springs? South of headquarters take the right-hand fork to Hot Springs Camp, which is well marked. After $2^1/_2$ miles you'll see a light green brick structure to your right down a side road—this is the bathhouse for the hot spring. There is an obvious parking area for the roofless bathhouse, which is open to anyone. The water is not very hot (I couldn't stay for a long soak with freezing air temperatures), but it is very pleasant.

While looking for pronghorn, keep your eyes out for some of the interesting common fall and winter birds of the refuge: rough-legged hawks, northern harriers, golden eagles, horned larks, Townsend's solitaires and mountain bluebirds. You may see sage grouse in the sagebrush and chukar on rocky slopes.

By the way, the refuge staff at Hart Mountain have taken a bold step in recommending that all livestock grazing on the refuge be stopped for fifteen years to allow the habitat to recover from the negative impact of over one hundred years of livestock use. Such a recommendation can be very controversial in a rural area like Lake County, but it is necessary, and the staff should be supported for their wise decision in favor of wildlife and natural plant communities.

There are other areas in Oregon where chances of seeing pronghorn are almost as good as at Hart Mountain. **Malheur National Wildlife Refuge** and the adjacent BLM lands (see chapter 26) provide lots of good pronghorn habitat, and it is unusual to spend several days in the area and not see pronghorn. Watch for them in the sagebrush anywhere in the area, but the road from New Princeton to refuge headquarters seems better than average, especially in the spring.

62

Wintering Birds in the Salish Sea

One of the major physical features of our part of the world is the complex inland sea consisting of Puget Sound, the Strait of Georgia, the Strait of Juan de Fuca and the numerous other interconnected inlets, channels, passages, straits and bays—the area I call the Salish Sea. This dramatic feature was formed in an appropriately dramatic manner during the last Ice Age. The entire Salish Sea area, sometimes called the Puget Trough or Puget Lowland, was covered by a large lobe of the Vashon Glacier. Imagine, a solid sheet of ice at least 3,000 feet deep over what is now Seattle! The ice gouged out the land between the Cascades and the Olympics, and when the ice melted, in came the sea.

The Salish Sea today is an incredibly rich ecosystem inhabited by an estimated two thousand different species of invertebrates and at least two hundred species of fish. Such a large and varied food resource allowed the Coast Salish people to develop a very rich, elaborate cultural life and has continued to support many additional people since. This bounty provides for many other predators as well, making the Salish Sea a haven for many marine mammals and birds, despite the fact that the most heavily populated part of the Pacific Northwest is on its shores. Every winter, vast numbers of waterbirds representing ten different families converge on the Salish Sea to escape the much harsher weather in their breeding grounds. The first winter visitors start arriving during September, but numbers don't get big until November. Most of these winter visitors will remain into March, some even to April. Although many people don't think of winter as the best time for many outdoor activities, it is the best for seeing most seabirds. An excellent guide to the seabirds of the Salish Sea is the booklet *Waterbirds of the Strait of Georgia,* available from the British Columbia Waterfowl Society (see appendix).

Who are our winter seabirds? The closely related loons and grebes are very well represented here—all five of the world's loons and six grebes occur regularly. Common, Pacific, and red-throated loons are common. The yellow-billed loon is rare but is seen every year, and the Arctic loon (until recently combined with the Pacific as one species) is accidental in British Columbia. Western, red-necked and horned grebes are all common, eared and Clark's grebes are regular but in much smaller numbers. The pied-billed grebe is not usually considered a seabird, but it is a common year-round resident in fresh water.

Three of our most common seabirds are the cormorants—double-crested, Brandt's and pelagic. All three are quite common year-round, but the Brandt's does vary in some places, being a bit more prevalent in winter. Gulls are another well-represented family, with several species common year-round and others showing up during the winter (chapter 10). The waterfowl are a huge group and have the greatest number of birds, and species, in the Salish Sea in winter. The group of waterfowl most often thought of as wintering seabirds are the sea ducks—the surf, white-winged and black scoters, the harlequin duck and the oldsquaw. These should all be expected when observing wintering seabirds, but you can actually find any of the waterfowl that occur in the Northwest.

All of the alcids discussed in chapter 31 are possibilities in the winter, but the rhinoceros auklet and the tufted puffin are much more commonly seen during the breeding season, when they come to nest on islands in the Salish Sea and along our coasts. Another group of seabirds, some of which may be seen in winter, are the tubenoses featured in chapter 49. Of the tubenoses, the northern fulmar and short-tailed shearwater would be the most likely to be encountered in the winter, but neither are common within the Salish Sea. Tubenoses are much more prevalent off the open coast.

One group of birds that usually doesn't come to mind in discussions of waterbirds is the birds of prey. Several of them, however, like to eat waterbirds (and shorebirds) and show up where their potential prey gather. Bald eagles will regularly congregate during the winter around a reliable food supply, and some of these winter gatherings of eagles are quite large. Two other birds of prey that become more common along shores in winter, but in much smaller numbers than bald eagles, are the peregrine falcon and merlin. Peregrines prey on a wide range of birds and will eat alcids, ducks and shorebirds, while the much smaller merlin is pretty much restricted to shorebirds. Watch for these falcons along shore, especially near mudflats where shorebirds gather.

By Boat

Hot Spots

Those who own or have access to a boat will have many opportunities to view marine wildlife, often at close range. **Sea kayaking** has become very popular in recent years in the Salish Sea, and there are now many outfitters offering a variety of services, from basic rentals to extended guided trips. Sometimes Audubon Society chapters and other organizations arrange kayak trips that are specifically geared to wildlife watching. Unfortunately, almost no trips or rentals are available from November through March, the best time for birds, because of the usually dangerous weather and sea conditions. This may change as the sport becomes more popular, but for now it looks like October and April would be the best times for birding by sea kayak if you don't own one.

A good option for those who don't own a boat, or who aren't quite ready to hop in a kayak during the winter, is a trip on a ferry. All ferries provide some opportunities for viewing wildlife, but the **San Juan Islands Ferry,** the **Tsawwassen–Swartz Bay Ferry** and the **Port Angeles–Victoria Ferry** (see chapter 49) are generally considered the best.

The Tsawwassen to Swartz Bay Ferry goes through **Active Pass,** which can have huge numbers of seabirds at certain times. The portion of the trip be-

Salish Sea Wintering Bird Sites

tween Vancouver Island and Active Pass is also good. Opinion varies, but the best time seems to be as the high tide is going out (ebbing). To go through Active Pass at this time, take the first ferry that leaves after the time of high tide given for Point Atkinson—this time is printed in both of Vancouver's main newspapers every day. The earlier in the day you can go, the better. If you ride the ferry as a foot passenger rather than take a car, you'll have a four-hour round-trip through beautiful scenery and, with the largest ferries, in great comfort.

The **San Juan Islands Ferry** from Anacortes to Sidney, in British Columbia, is one of the best all-around ferry trips for wildlife and scenery. Unfortunately, there is only one departure daily (8 A.M. in Washington, noon in British Columbia) during the best birding months. However, a shorter trip that goes through the best areas for birds, the Anacortes-to-Friday-Harbor route, has two additional daylight departures.

From Shore

With its thousands of miles of coastline, the Salish Sea provides many excellent opportunities to see marine animals from shore; try undeveloped sections of coastline with public access. All areas below are generally best at, or just before and after, high tide. My favorite areas are **Ediz Hook** (chapter 10), **Dungeness National Wildlife Refuge** (chapter 8), **Port Townsend, Kayak Point County Park, Washington Park** (Anacortes), **Padilla Bay** (chapter 22), **Birch Bay** and **Point Roberts.**

Port Townsend, with more authentic Victorian buildings than any place north of San Francisco, is very picturesque and popular as a tourist destination. I'll bet it has one of the highest densities of bed-and-breakfasts and country inns in the states! Going in winter is great, with all the charm and no crowds. The Keystone Ferry from Port Townsend to Whidbey Island has already been mentioned (chapter 31) as a short, inexpensive ferry ride that provides good wildlife viewing. Two spots in Port Townsend that provide excellent viewing of seabirds from shore are **Point Hudson** and **Point Wilson.**

Point Hudson is in the historical district right near downtown. The area is privately owned by the Point Hudson Company, which runs a motel, marina and RV camp, but birders are welcome to park in the motel parking area and walk to the shoreline. To get there, drive northeast on Water Street, go left 2 blocks on Monroe, then turn right onto Jefferson and take it to its end at the motel.

Point Wilson is in historic **Fort Worden State Park.** Get onto Cherry Street headed north and take it into the park. Just after you enter the park, turn right onto Pershing Avenue and take it until it ends at Defense Way. You must go left on Defense, so take it until it ends at the lighthouse. The public must stay out of the lighthouse area; walk north over the dunes to the beach, and from here you can watch the channel. All the regular wintering seabirds are likely here, and there is a chance of seeing ancient murrelets. Maps of Port Townsend are available at the visitor's center as you come into town on State Highway 20.

Kayak Point Regional Park has a nice pier that affords good views of wildlife in Port Susan Bay. Although it's best for birds, some marine mammals are seen from the pier, including gray whales on occasion. Heading north from Marysville on I-5, take Exit 206 and head west on 172nd Street, which is also called Highway 531 *and* Lakewood Road. The road twists and turns a bit, but just stay on Lakewood and follow signs for Kayak Point County Park. At Goodwin Lake, do *not* take Highway 531 as it heads south. About $8^{1}/_{4}$ miles from I-5 you'll come to a stop sign at Marine Drive. Go south on Marine Drive, making a little jog that's marked, and you'll come to the park. You'll have no trouble finding your way to the waterfront and pier.

Birch Bay State Park, just south of the Canadian border, is another excellent spot that is easy to find. Take Exit 266 from I-5 and go west 7 miles on Grandview Road. Turn right onto Jackson Road, and in less than a mile turn onto the park road and drive down to the shore. Birch Bay Drive goes along the shore for a mile in the park, then continues into the cute little town of Birch Bay. There are many places in the park in which to stop and scope the waters of Birch Bay. Here I once had beautiful males of all three scoter species in one scope view.

Point Roberts is the end of the small peninsula that's the western border of Boundary Bay in British Columbia. It really should be part of Canada, but the international border happens to slice through the tip, leaving a little 4-square-mile chunk of Washington hanging out there all by itself, attached to British Columbia. Regardless of its geographical oddness, the southern tip of Point Roberts is considered one of the absolute best spots in the region for waterbirds.

From Provincial Highway 99 near Ladner, take Provincial Highway 17 south, following the signs to Point Roberts. Turn left onto 56th Street (also called Point Roberts Road) and take it south to the border, where it turns into Tyee Drive. Just keep going south and follow Tyee as it turns to the west and becomes Edwards Drive. Take Edwards to Lighthouse Park, where you can park and scope the surrounding waters. All the regulars are usually present, including numerous harlequin ducks and oldsquaw and such harder-to-find birds as black scoter and ancient murrelet. And, for a special bonus, this is considered the most consistent spot in Washington to see the elusive yellow-billed loon!

British Columbia

Roberts Bank Coalport, near Vancouver, is at the end of a long causeway that juts out into the Strait of Georgia. From Provincial Highway 17 about 3 miles south of Ladner, go west on 28th Avenue, which becomes the paved road going out onto the causeway. On the very southern edge of the causeway is a small dirt road on which you can drive and park. You can get on this road right at the beginning of the causeway and just before the terminal itself at the end, where the dirt road again joins the paved road. There is no access to the terminal at the end of the causeway, and you are not allowed to stop or park on the paved road, so do all your birding from the dirt road. Fortunately, you can get on the paved road at either end, so you don't have to go all the way out and back on the dirt road, which is a bit rough. Drive the dirt road and stop anywhere that looks interesting in order to scope the thousands of birds that will probably be just offshore.

Iona Beach Regional Park is just 5 miles north of Roberts Bank and is described in chapters 10 and 45. The south jetty at Iona is another long causeway ($2^1/_2$ miles) that sticks out into the Strait of Georgia. Cars are not allowed, but you can walk or bicycle all the way to the end. You usually don't have to go very far out before seeing a big variety of waterfowl, seabirds and gulls. In addition, the rocks of the jetty itself are good for rock-loving shorebirds such as tattlers, turnstones and surfbirds. In the fall, truly pelagic species are sometimes seen from the end of the jetty. A bicycle seems to be the ideal way to bird this jetty. While you are at Iona, be sure to check the other areas for gulls, shorebirds and raptors.

The southern end of **Vancouver Island** is surrounded by the Salish Sea and, as one would expect of an island, has many good spots for observing seabirds. The protected waters of the Strait of Georgia host huge numbers of waterbirds during winter and migration. Any of the spots described for seeing brant (chapter 22) are good bets, as are most provincial or regional parks on the coast or on the Gulf Islands. Very conveniently, some of the best spots are right in Victoria along the breakwater on the southeast corner of the city. The Scenic Marine Drive, including **Clover** and **Cattle Points,** is described in chapter 10. In addition, the **Ogden Point Breakwater,** at the mouth of Victoria Harbor gives you an opportunity to walk out into the sea a bit. This concrete pier is off Dallas Road (part of the Scenic Marine Drive) about a dozen blocks west of Beacon Hill Park.

63

Bighorn Sheep

Seeing bighorn sheep in the wild often tests one's limits of patience, eyesight, optics and determination. Unless you are seeing bighorns at a winter feeding station, the beasts will probably be far away and will blend right in with the rocky cliffs they inhabit. Often you cannot see them with the naked eye but can find them only after careful searching with binoculars. Get the best information you can on location, and be prepared to spend some time. These sheep have exceptional eyesight and will usually know you are there long before you see them. Sometimes this will cause them to start moving away, and their movement may catch your eye. The most common way to find them is to spot the white rump—in good light it will often stand out against the dark basalt typical of the Northwest. Another way to find them is to see their silhouettes on a ridge top.

Your efforts may be rewarded by the sight of one of the West's most charismatic animals. Rams have been popular macho symbols of strength, stamina and determination for centuries. Think of all the sports teams named after them. Much of this reputation is deserved, for the males engage in spectacular bouts over ewes during the winter rut. Rams charge at one another with all their might, and crash their huge horns together so hard that the sound can be heard for miles. Rams need big horns even if there are no fights, because the ewes clearly go for the guy with the biggest curls.

Bighorn sheep, also called mountain sheep, were once widespread and common throughout western North America in mountains and canyons. Now just a fraction of the original population lives in scattered, and often isolated, pockets in some of the West's most remote country. Their near elimination from the United States had three main causes. Unregulated hunting and habitat destruction are both pretty obvious and clearly played a big role in the bighorn's decline. But the third factor was more insidious and deadly—disease. Just as European people brought new diseases to America that decimated the Native Americans, European domestic sheep brought new animal diseases that spread to the nonresistant native bighorn. *Pasteurella,* scabies and lung diseases took their toll. By the 1940s bighorn sheep had been completely eliminated from Oregon and Washington.

Since bighorns are highly valued as big game and are legally classified as such, there was a great deal of interest in, and some money for, reintroducing the sheep in the Northwest. Starting in the 1950s, bighorns from Canada, which still had healthy populations, were reintroduced into parts of their former range where there were absolutely no domestic sheep. The introductions have continued and have been successful enough to support limited hunting of bighorns in both states.

There are two subspecies or races of bighorns in our region. The California bighorn originally ranged from the lava plateaus and canyons of the Great Basin up the east side of the Cascades all the way into the Okanagan region of British Columbia. Rocky Mountain bighorn sheep lived in the Rocky Mountains and their related ranges, such as the Selkirks in Washington and the Blue Mountains in southeast Washington and northeast Oregon. Wildlife managers have been careful to introduce the right subspecies into their proper historical ranges, although there are those that believe there is no real distinction between the two races.

Like all ungulates, bighorn sheep are vegetarians—grazers eating grasses and sedges. They are adaptable, however, and will eat a variety of other plants when necessary. Like their relatives the mountain goats, they live on steep rocky slopes and cliffs, using their phenomenal climbing ability to avoid most predators. Look for them in their proper habit, where they are known to occur, by carefully scanning all rock cliffs. Look particularly at the bases of cliff faces and in patches of grass. When there is snow on the ground, they will usually be found on steep or southern-facing slopes, where the snow cover is lightest.

Oregon

Hot Spots

California bighorns have been successfully reintroduced to three classic examples of Great Basin fault block mountains in Oregon—**Abert Rim, Hart Mountain** and **Steens Mountain.** Finding bighorns on Steens Mountain is difficult, but be aware that sheep are there any time you're exploring it.

Hart Mountain is within **Hart Mountain National Antelope Refuge,** which is described in chapter 61. Bighorn sheep are most commonly seen along the western escarpment, usually in the steepest spots. Coming from the tiny settlement of Plush on Hart Mountain Road, you will come to an appropriately placed sign about bighorn sheep soon after the old CCC camp. From here to where the road begins its steep ascent up the mountain is the easiest place to spot sheep, if they are there. Stop along the roadside at regular intervals and scan all the cliffs. Afternoon lighting is a tremendous advantage; in the morning you may only be able to see sheep if they are silhouetted against the sky.

The northern portion of the mountain is called **Poker Jim Ridge,** and sometimes people get good views of sheep by hiking out on this ridge from Poker Jim Road and sneaking up on the sheep from above.

It's always a good idea to talk to refuge staff for the latest information on bighorns. If no one is available at headquarters, consult the wildlife-sightings register in the visitor room. Headquarters also provides the only rest room for many miles. Hunting is finished by the middle of October, and from then until the first snow is the best time to look for sheep, as well as pronghorn. Changes in road access and campgrounds are expected in the near future, so be sure to get the latest information before heading out to this rather isolated area.

Another big fault block just west of Hart Mountain is **Abert Rim.** Five and a half miles north on U.S. Highway 395 from its junction with State Highway 31 is a wildlife viewing area with great interpretive signs. Bighorns frequent the escarpment from this wildlife viewing area to the northeast for about 5 miles. Just over 3 miles from the wildlife viewing site is a geologic marker with a pullout that is a good spot for scanning the cliffs.

Rocky Mountain bighorn sheep have been successfully introduced into the **Blue Mountains** of northeastern Oregon. The best way to see them is to call the staff of the **Wenaha Wildlife Area** (chapter 69) and find out if any have been seen lately and where they are. It is also important to check on hunting seasons (don't go when there is hunting) and find out about road conditions. One spot the sheep frequent is the cliffs above **Sawmill Flat.** From the town of Troy, take "the low bridge" over the Grande Ronde River toward Elgin and Wallowa. In just 0.2 mile, before you come to the first signed intersection, a small dirt road takes a sharp hairpin turn to the right. Take this road for just under half a mile to where it comes out into a flat open area (Sawmill Flats). Get out and scan the cliffs that rise above you to the south. Occasionally some of the sheep are actually seen down on the flats. You may also see bighorns when you're driving through other parts of the Wenaha looking for elk.

Washington

There are two good areas for seeing reintroduced California bighorns near Yakima. The **Yakima River** has carved a beautiful canyon through the basalt ridges coming off the east side of the Cascades. State Highway 821 parallels the river as it winds 20 miles through the canyon between Ellensburg and Yakima—a much preferred scenic alternative to traveling U.S. Highway 97. About 5 miles from the northern end of the canyon is the **Umtanum Recreation Site,** where there is a trail going up Umtanum Creek, considered a great area for a variety of wildlife. The best area for finding sheep is just north of Umtanum around Mileposts 18 and 19. Unfortunately, there is little room for pulling over along this stretch of road, so you have to be creative in finding a spot to park for scanning the cliffs. Just north of Milepost 18 there is just barely enough room to pull over next to the guardrail on the west side. I have seen sheep from this spot. As usual, they will probably be far away on the cliffs and hard to find. The best lighting is at midday, but this is not usually a period of much sheep activity. Overcast conditions would probably be advantageous because there wouldn't be harsh shadows or glare.

Near the **Yakima River Canyon** is a feeding station for bighorns operated by the Washington Department of Fish and Wildlife as part of the **Oak Creek Wildlife Area.** Some people don't like an artificial situation like this, but it does provide some outstanding opportunities for observation. On your way to see the elk at Oak Creek Wildlife Area (see chapter 69), stop by the **Clemen Mountain Feeding Station.** Timing is great for this because the sheep are usually fed between 10:00 and 11:00 A.M. and the elk at 1:30 P.M. About 13 miles northwest of Yakima, Hwy. 12 and Hwy. 410 split, and Hwy. 12 heads south to Oak Creek. Right at this split, on the north side of Hwy. 410 across from the weigh station, is the Old Naches Road that heads east. Go one-half mile on this road and you will come to the conspicuous Mountain Sheep Winter Feeding Station sign and parking area. Search all the cliffs surrounding the feeding station if sheep are not right there waiting for you and your camera. Call the Washington Department of Fish and Wildlife office in Yakima to make sure they are feeding the sheep and elk, because this varies a great deal with the weather. Feeding generally starts in December and continues through February.

There is another well-known sheep-feeding station tucked in the far northeastern corner of the state, this one for Rocky Mountain bighorns. Near the southern end of Sullivan Lake is **Sullivan Lake Bighorn Sheep Winter Feeding Station.** Head north from State Highway 20 on State Highway 31. Half a mile south of Ione, turn and head east on Elizabeth Avenue and follow green signs to Sullivan Lake. In a bit over 8 miles turn right onto the road to **Noisy Creek Campground.** Just after you turn onto the road for the campground, right where the message board is, there is another, smaller road going to the right. Go a few hundred yards down this road and it will make a loop. You will see a metal gate blocking the road to the feeding station. Park nearby, making sure not to block the gate and road, and walk north on the road to the feeding station. Walk along the road, following the power line, for about 300 yards, until the point where the road starts to go down to ford the creek. Angle off to the right at about 45 degrees, following a trail (probably faint) that goes to a footbridge over the creek. As you cross on the bridge be very quiet, and watch ahead to the feeding station very carefully. If you see any sheep, approach as quietly and slowly as you can until you can get a satisfactory look. If the sheep start to react to your presence—freeze (well, you may actually be feeling frozen already, but stop moving). Although the sheep are accustomed to a certain amount of human activity, this encounter will be a test of your stalking skills and patience. Call the Spokane office of the Washington Department of Fish and Wildlife to make sure the sheep are being fed and that roads are open (see appendix).

64

Harlequin Ducks

Try to find an article about harlequin ducks that doesn't use the word "turbulent." Fat chance. This duck is born to bob in the rapids of mountain streams and the churning currents around rocky ocean shores. Despite being fairly common winter visitors to the Salish Sea, harlequins are just unusual and rare enough that they are much sought by birders visiting the Northwest. They are certainly unique in appearance; even the restrained authority Frank Bellrose calls them the "most bizarrely colored waterfowl," and many consider them one of our prettiest birds.

No other duck in the Northern Hemisphere is dependent on turbulent mountain streams for part of its life. It is the unique lifestyle of the harlequin that makes it both interesting and sensitive to disturbance. It is sometimes called an "indicator species" or a "canary in the coal mine," an animal that gives early warning of disturbance to an ecosystem. There are two distinct populations of harlequin ducks—an eastern one centered around Labrador and Greenland, and a hundredfold greater population in British Columbia, the Yukon and Alaska. The eastern population has declined so much that the harlequin is listed as endangered in eastern Canada and is a candidate for listing in the United States. Oregon already classifies harlequins as a sensitive species because breeding numbers are very small in the state.

Harlequins spend most of their lives in the ocean close to rocky shores. In May they fly up into the mountains and nest on rocky shores next to the rapids of fast-moving streams. Once the female starts incubating, the male leaves and goes back to the coast, which can happen as early as the end of June. Females do not return to salt water until their young can fly in September. The majority of harlequins nest in remote areas that are free of much human activity. It is in their nesting habitat, however, where harlequins are very sensitive to disturbance. The riparian zone can easily be damaged by logging, and females can be frightened into abandoning their nests if hikers, anglers, rafters and kayakers repeatedly come too close. Since the males leave when incubation begins, there is no chance for a second brood to replace a first one lost to flooding or other causes. When human activity increases near nesting areas, harlequin numbers start dropping.

Unfortunately, these colorful ducks are also threatened in their winter range. Actually, this is a good example of how the terms "winter range" and "winter visitor" can be misleading, because harlequins are actually residents in salt water for most of the year and only leave for nesting, a very short time indeed for the males. But tradition treats the nesting range as the bird's "home," and the area where it doesn't breed as temporary winter range. Regardless of terminology,

Harlequin ducks are easy to find along the rocky shores of the Salish Sea in winter.

harlequins at sea are vulnerable to pollution. These ducks were one of the species hardest hit by the *Exxon Valdez* oil spill in 1989, and there is still almost no reproduction by harlequins in the spill area.

Since harlequins are sensitive to disturbance while nesting, they should be left alone during that time. The place to see them is in their wintering range from about September through April. Look for them close to rocky shores, especially where the water is (I have to say it) turbulent. It's fun to watch harlequins feed, because they eat almost any animal they can get down their throats, and it's often amusing to see some of their struggles with beaks full of legs and claws flailing about. They eat lots of crustaceans, including many types of crabs and barnacles, and lots of mollusks, shells and all. One animal they eat that few others do are chitons, which are extremely hard to pry off rocks. But these buoyant little sea ducks manage to do it somehow, and grind those mollusks up with everything else in their powerful gizzards. In their freshwater habitat they forage under the water for aquatic insects, swimming with both feet and wings and walking on the bottom like a dipper, a common associate in mountain streams.

The farther south you go, the less of these northern ducks there are by an order of magnitude per state. Estimates of the number of harlequins in the winter in British Columbia are in the thousands (twelve thousand), in Washington in the hundreds (three hundred to five hundred) and in Oregon in the dozens.

A closely related duck that is also unique and is sometimes found wintering with harlequins is the oldsquaw. The oldsquaw is actually the most abundant nesting duck in the high Arctic, but fewer of them get down into the Northwest, their population following the same pattern as the harlequin, only at much lower numbers. The oldsquaw is the only duck in which the male has two different bright plumages in addition to a drab eclipse plumage. Oldsquaw are also well known for being one of the noisiest ducks; they are constantly making loud calls to one another.

Oregon

Inside the mouth of Tillamook Bay just west of Garibaldi, there are some picturesque rocks just offshore that are locally called **The Three Graces,** at least that's what they're called on postcards. But to Northwest birders they are commonly known as the **Harlequin Duck Rocks,** and they deserve the name. This is probably the most reliable place in Oregon to find harlequins, or at least is the most reliable place that has reasonable access.

Going west on U.S. Highway 101 from **Garibaldi,** you will go around a corner passing the Pirate's Cove restaurant and come to a stretch of road with a big wall of riprap running along the west side. You will see the tall Three Graces in the bay. Drive past this area until you can find a good place to turn around, then head back on the other side of the road so you can safely pull over and park in the impromptu pullout area between the pavement and the train tracks. Head for the lowest spot in the riprap and either peer over it or climb up on top of the big boulders to scan the entire area, especially around any exposed rocks in the bay. In addition to harlequins, this is a great spot to see all three cormorants together, black oystercatchers and occasionally black turnstones and surfbirds, several gulls and a few alcids flying by. From June through September this is a great spot to see brown pelicans. Watch out—the train tracks are still being used. Be sure to check out Barview Jetty (chapter 9) when you are in this area.

The **south jetty of Yaquina Bay** in Newport is the other reliable spot in Oregon for the "little Italian clown" duck and is described in chapter 9. This is one of the best spots in Oregon for many types of wintering waterbirds and should always be checked when you're in the area.

Washington and British Columbia

Any rocky coastline with turbulent water in the Salish Sea is good harlequin habitat, and they are fairly common throughout the sea, although you will rarely see more than a few in one place. All the hotspots from shore in chapter 62 have great potential, except for Dungeness Spit, which is sand. Probably the best is **Point Roberts,** Washington. A good addition to this list is **Salt Creek County Park** on the Olympic Peninsula (chapter 38), which is also excellent for black oystercatchers. The **Victoria Breakwater** is also very reliable, and you can watch for rare gulls and ancient murrelets at the same time.

65

November Shorttakes

Samhain

During November we make the change from fall to winter, and it seems illogical that the official first day of winter is on the winter solstice near the end of December. Once again, the ancient Celtic calendar makes more sense, because *Samhain,* the beginning of winter, falls in the first few days of November. Samhain was a major festival, and the Druids performed sacred rights then to prepare for the coming season of darkness. In typical fashion, the early Catholic Church used Samhain as a basis for creating a Christian holy day, and the result of this unique blending survives today as Halloween in North America and *Los Dias de Muertos* in Mexico.

Banana Slugs

Banana slugs are common year-round residents in our moist forests but are only seen out and about when the humidity is high—about 100 percent does nicely. Like all mollusks, banana slugs will dry out quickly in dry air and so are usually active only during very moist nights or on rainy days. They use a lot of water to make their famous slime and must be able to soak up enough from their environment to replace the lost water if they are to be able to crawl about. Needless to say, such conditions are common much of the year west of the Cascades, and in November, when rain is common and temperatures not yet too cold, there is plenty of slug activity. Banana slugs are quite famous in the Northwest, which is very unusual for a mollusk but is as it should be for an animal that's unique yet common to the region. You can even buy a number of interesting souvenir items featuring banana slugs. Many kids know that if you lick a banana slug, your tongue will become numb. It's actually a very weird and fairly unpleasant feeling that lasts all day and is apparently the reason so few predators ever eat this slow and apparently defenseless beast. For more fascinating slug lore I recommend *The Banana Slug* by Alice Harper.

66

A Closer Look: Bird-Feeding Basics

Sitting by a picture window, feeling the glow from the hearth with a hot latté in hand and watching the juncos, siskins, song sparrows, towhees, goldfinches and house sparrows scratching around in the snowcapped feeder—a perfect winter's day in the Northwest. Colder temperatures mean more calories are needed by warm-blooded endotherms just when food is most lacking. Many birds will come to a feeder for those extra calories, allowing for some great up-close bird-watching. The level of interest in bird feeding has skyrocketed in recent years. It is now estimated that around 70 million Americans regularly feed, watch or photograph birds at or near their homes every year.

To attract birds to your yard, provide them with the basics all animals need to survive: food, water and shelter. The best way to provide these elements on a year-round basis is by managing your habitat; that is, landscape your yard for wildlife needs. The greater the diversity of plants and habitats in your yard, the more diverse will be your birdlife. Plants, and the insects they attract, will provide birds with their natural foods and provide the natural shelter they seek. In the last few years landscaping for wildlife has come to be called naturescaping. The best single source of information about attracting wildlife to your yard in our region is *Naturescaping: A Place for Wildlife,* by the Oregon Department of Fish and Wildlife; it's available from the main Portland office for $14.50 (includes postage). This chapter is limited to discussing "artificial" feeding.

There are two main types of "artificial food" to offer birds: seeds and suet. Many of our winter residents are seedeaters because this is a food source that is naturally available during the winter. By offering seeds, we are providing supplemental food very similar to the birds' natural diet. Suet is a substitute for insects, a food source that is drastically reduced during the cold winter months.

You can feed both seeds and suet year-round; however, suet will spoil much faster in warm weather and, as insects become more abundant, the birds' interest in suet wanes. Another reason for not feeding during the summer is that the variety of birds at feeders decreases significantly during the warmer months.

Many people worry that if they begin feeding birds during the winter and then stop, the birds will perish because they have become dependent on the food supply at the feeders. Opinions on this topic vary, but many believe that such interruptions in bird feeding are not usually a problem. In general, the artificial feeding of birds by people has little overall impact on bird populations.

There are three types of seed that will attract and satisfy all our local seedeating birds: sunflower, millet and cracked corn. Sunflower seeds are the most preferred food of many birds, especially finches, grosbeaks, chickadees, nuthatches, jays and even smaller woodpeckers. All types of sunflower seeds are great, but the black oil type is a highly favored seed and has become all the rage. Those birds that lack beaks adapted for opening sunflower seeds favor millet and cracked corn. There are several types of millet, the best being white proso, which is the type usually used in mixes. Birds especially fond of millet include all the sparrows, including juncos and towhees, and mourning doves. These birds will also eat cracked corn but almost always show a preference for millet.

Cracked corn deteriorates quickly in wet weather and can cause problems in some types of hopper feeders, where it easily molds and cakes, resulting in a clogged feeder. The advantages of cracked corn are that it is very inexpensive and is eaten by many birds, even if it isn't their "favorite." Larger ground-feeding birds such as quail, pheasant, dove and many waterfowl relish whole-grain corn kernels. Other foods, such as peanut pieces and niger (often called thistle) seed are highly rated for some birds, but neither is more popular than the black oil sunflower and both are more expensive than any other type of seed. For the Northwest, a basic mix of black oil sunflower and white proso millet, with a little cracked or whole-kernel corn, will keep the local birds coming to your feeders for more.

A word of warning. Almost all "wild bird food" mixes sold at supermarkets contain other seeds added as cheap filler that are either not eaten by birds or are favored by such generally unwanted guests as starlings, house sparrows and blackbirds. The most common filler is milo, a type of sorghum. It is a round reddish seed that looks like a BB pellet or radish seed. If you buy mixed seed with much milo, you're wasting your money. Quality seeds and mixes without milo or other useless fillers are available at wild bird stores and at many pet and feed stores.

Seed is best served in some type of elevated feeder. Ground-feeding birds such as juncos, towhees and sparrows will get plenty of seed spilled on the ground by other birds at the feeder. And if the feeder is big enough, sometimes called a feeding table, these ground-feeding birds will land right on the feeder. Feeders can be mounted on a pole, hung from a tree limb or roof or mounted against a window. Some newer plastic feeders can be mounted right on the window pane with suction cups! It is important that any feeder is located with enough clear space around it so that the birds can easily see if there are any cats or other predators within striking range.

Feeders need not be fancy or expensive. All that is important is that the birds can get the seed and the seed does not get too wet. Even on the rainy west side you don't need a roof on your feeder if all you do is put out a couple of handfuls of seed each day and the birds eat it all before it gets soaked. Most people, however, prefer a feeder that has some type of hopper to hold more than one day's supply of feed, and hopper feeders need a roof to keep the seed dry.

Suet, the hard fat from beef and sheep kidneys, attracts birds whose natural diet is primarily insects, particularly the sedentary eggs, larvae and pupae that are available during the winter. The fact that beef fat can serve as a substitute for insect larvae seems rather odd, but there is no doubt about the popularity of suet among chickadees, nuthatches, woodpeckers, bushtits and pine siskins.

Chunks of raw suet can be offered without any preparation. It can also be ground, melted and formed into suet cakes to fit feeders and for convenient storage. It is not necessary to add anything to suet, but many people believe that the addition of cornmeal or peanut butter or both makes the suet more attractive to a wider variety of birds. Many people believe seeds should not be added to suet because this mixes two very different types of food that are best offered at separate locations to avoid crowding and competition. Also, the greased seeds in the suet may be harder for some birds to open. It is important to note that there are some authorities who feel feeding straight peanut butter can be harmful, and that it should only be used as an additive to suet.

Suet is best offered in hanging plastic mesh bags, wire baskets or suet logs. It can also be strapped directly to trees. Do not feed suet on the ground unless you want to fill your yard with starlings!

Water is not usually a limiting factor for birds west of the Cascades. On the east side, however, the addition of water to your yard can make a big difference, and depending on your location your yard may become a true oasis, attracting many birds from a large area. A shallow birdbath, not more than 2 or 3 inches deep, will provide water for many birds and will help attract those species that do not usually come to feeders. Place rocks in the birdbath to provide places to perch at different water depths. As with feeders, there are many types of manufactured birdbaths available. It is easy, too, to make your own. Commercial birdbath heaters are available for keeping birdbaths ice-free during freezing weather. It is surprising how much some birds like to bathe, even during the coldest weather.

Few bird-feeding topics generate as much controversy as does feeding hummingbirds. Most authors encourage the planting of flowers and other plants that provide hummers with their natural foods: nectar and insects. Some people feel that the use of feeders and sugar water can harm hummingbirds. Here are some general guidelines to follow for hummingbird feeders. Use only sugar, never honey, which promotes dangerous fungus growth. Sugar should be dissolved in boiling water in a ratio of one part sugar to four or five parts water. Any unused mixture should be stored in the refrigerator. Feeders should be thoroughly cleaned in hot water weekly. There is no clear consensus whether red food coloring is potentially harmful or not. Red is attractive to hummingbirds, and red objects, such as plastic flowers on feeders, may help attract them, but it is not necessary to add red coloring to the water.

Should you leave your hummingbird feeder up all winter? There is no correct answer. There are Anna's hummingbirds in parts of the Pacific Northwest all year. These birds are here regardless of whether people are feeding them or not, and many of them will perish during the coldest weather even if extra food is available. The rufous hummingbird, our common summer resident, will migrate south on schedule regardless of the presence of feeders. The artificial feeding of hummingbirds during the winter will probably have no effect on the hummingbird population as a whole, but in some cases it may allow an individual bird to survive a bit longer than it would otherwise.

December

Notes

67

Deer

The deer family is well known throughout the world, and about forty species live from the Arctic to the Tropics. These animals have been highly revered as big-game animals by humans. After all, some of our earliest art is cave paintings of deer. The does and fawns are frequently described with some of our most endearing language, and the bucks are symbols of animal machismo at its finest.

One of the nicest things about deer is that there are still a lot of them to see. Unlike much North American wildlife, deer are more abundant now in many areas than they were before European settlement. Ironically, one of the problems sometimes facing managers of deer is overpopulation. There are several reasons for the increase in deer populations. One is the wholesale removal of their predators in most of their range. Another is the preference of deer for forest edges and successional stages of forest growth, habitats caused by some of our land uses, such as clear-cut logging. Another factor is their desirability as a game animal, resulting in sportsmen's money going into intensive management of deer populations. Also, deer have shown themselves to be more adaptable than many other hoofed mammals.

The deer family is one of the main families of ungulates, mammals with unique legs that are highly adapted for running. Ungulates have long legs to increase their stride and a simplified skeletal structure to reduce the weight of the leg so it can be moved faster by the muscles. The most striking result of this simplification and elongation in the leg and foot is that ungulates actually stand, and run, on their tippy toes, which are few in number and are capped with an incredibly large, strong toenail called a hoof. Most ungulates walk on two toes (per foot), while others, like the horse, walk on just one big toe. There are many interesting details in the evolution of ungulate anatomy that have resulted in mammals that use running fast as their main defense against predators. As discussed in the chapter on pronghorn, some ungulates have reached what may be the limit for land speed in animals.

As with most other ungulates, deer have exceptionally keen eyesight, as well as sensitive hearing and a highly developed sense of smell. The most likely situations for seeing deer are in places where the deer have become acclimated to people being nearby and do not feel threatened. As with other animals, deer may tolerate you being close while you are in your car, but as soon as you step out— off they go with a bound.

Deer are *browsers*—animals that eat the tender, most nutritious parts of trees and shrubs. This term is often used in contrast to *grazer,* an animal that eats primarily grass. Deer do eat some grass, but even when you see them out in the grassy meadow eating, they are usually picking out the more tender broad-leaved plants, like dandelions, which are called *forbs* by biologists. Logging can often be good for deer because it opens up the forest canopy, letting in more light for understory plants (browse), but what's good for deer is not necessarily good for other wildlife.

Members of the deer family are the only animals in the world with antlers. People often get antlers and horns mixed up, but the differences are very clear. Antlers are shed and regrown every year, while animals with horns have horns their whole life, which grow continually as the animal ages. Antlers are almost always found only on the male of a species. Animals with horns, however, have horns on both the male and female, although the male's horns are significantly bigger. Antlers are usually branched and horns never are, except for the pronghorn's, whose unique horn is described in chapter 61. A fundamental difference is that antlers and horns are made out of different material. An antler is bone. This bone is covered by a thin layer of skin while the antler is growing, but this skin falls off when the antler is fully grown, leaving bare bone. A horn has a bony core covered with skin, and then an outer layer of keratin, the tough protein found in fingernails.

In the Pacific Northwest we have white-tailed deer and mule deer. Each species has two subspecies, or races, found in our region; in general, one race is found on the east side and one on the west side for each species.

The white-tailed deer is the most widespread deer in North America, living in almost every state but most abundant east of the Mississippi. The mule deer is very common throughout the West. White-tailed deer prefer thick forest interspersed with some grassy openings and are often found near water. Mule deer live in a wider range of habitats and are often found in more open and drier habitats than whitetails and are more common at higher elevations. Mule deer are currently more abundant and widespread throughout our entire region than whitetails, which are localized and in smaller numbers.

White-tailed deer are recognized by their fairly big tails, which are brown on top and bright white underneath. They often flip their tails up when running away, exposing the white underside that gives them their name. A mule deer's tail is either all black on top (the black-tailed race), or light with a distinct black tip, and mule deer do not tend to flip their tails up, as white-tailed deer do. You can also tell the two species apart by their antlers. The antlers of whitetails have a main beam that sweeps forward with tines coming up from it. Mule deer have antlers that stick straight up more, and they divide evenly or fork into two main branches, which then each divide evenly again on mature bucks.

There are two types of white-tailed deer in the Northwest. A Rocky Mountain subspecies known as the Idaho white-tailed deer is most common in the Blue Mountains in northeastern Oregon and adjacent parts of Washington, and also in the Selkirk Mountains in northeastern Washington. These east-side whitetails are scattered and hard to see predictably. West of the Cascades is an endangered subspecies of deer, the Columbian white-tailed deer. This deer used to be abundant west of the Cascades from the Umpqua River to Puget Sound, but by the 1930s it was thought to be extinct. However, two small populations were discovered, one near Roseburg, Oregon, and the other in the lower Columbia River near Cathlamet, Washington. In 1972 a national wildlife refuge was established for the Columbia River population. The Roseburg population has also been protected, although not with a refuge, and both populations have grown so large that the Columbian white-tailed deer will probably be taken off the Endangered Species List in the near future.

East of the Cascades, mule deer are abundant and easily seen. Found west of the Cascades is the race of mule deer called the black-tailed deer, once considered a separate species. Black-tailed deer act a little like white-tailed deer in that they hide in thick forest more than do the "regular" mule deer, which are often seen out in the open, including in mountainous areas with steep slopes. Because mule deer live at higher elevations, they migrate more during the year because of snow conditions and food distribution. They also tend to gather more in big groups on winter ranges.

The deer breeding season, or *rut,* begins in September or October and runs through December, with November being the peak. During this time bucks travel looking for does. Sometimes bucks will fight over a doe using ritualized displays and threats and occasionally requiring battles with their antlers. Deer do not, however, gather and defend harems the way elk do.

December is a good time to see deer because many of them start to gather in winter ranges then, deer hunting seasons are usually over and the bucks still have their antlers. It is important that when viewing deer, or any other animals on their winter ranges, people are careful not to disturb them. If you frighten animals enough to cause them to run, they will expend valuable energy during a time when they can least afford it. View from a distance and stay in your car when possible.

In addition to the areas below, you are likely to see deer at any of the hotspots listed for elk in chapter 69.

Oregon

Mule deer are quite common in eastern Oregon and are regularly seen even along many of the main highways. Two areas that are particularly good are U.S. Highway 97 and State Highway 31 going south from La Pine toward Klamath Falls and Lakeview, respectively. On Hwy. 31 is **Oatman Flat Deer Viewing Area,** the most famous wintering spot for deer in the state. At Oatman Flat there is an alfalfa pasture on the west side of Hwy. 31 that is 39 miles south of La Pine and 8 miles north of Silver Lake, right where a forest service road intersects with the highway. There is a pullout with brown binocular wildlife viewing signs, but no other signs identify the spot. Numbers sometimes approach one thousand deer, according to the *Oregon Wildlife Viewing Guide!* Usually the deer are in the pasture early in the morning or around sunset, but on some winter days hundreds stay in the pasture all day long. Be sure to check out Oatman Flat when headed to or from Summer Lake Wildlife Area (chapter 3) or Hart Mountain National Wildlife Refuge (chapter 61).

South of Oatman Flat and Summer Lake, Hwy. 31 joins U.S. Highway 395 at the tiny settlement of Valley Falls. The stretch of Hwy. 395 just south of **Valley Falls** for several miles is excellent for seeing mule deer late in the day. Another general area that usually provides lots of good sightings of mule deer year-round is **Malheur National Wildlife Refuge** (chapter 26). **Wallowa Lake State Park** is well known for its semi-tame deer, which regularly come into the picnic and camping areas. Feeding wild animals is a bad idea, so please don't participate in such feeding.

Washington

The place to see Columbian white-tailed deer is, of course, the **Julia Butler Hanson National Wildlife Refuge for the Columbian White-tailed Deer.** The deer are very good at hiding in the brush, and you can drive right by and miss them if you're not watching carefully. But usually you'll see some deer right out in the open as you drive the roads through the refuge.

The refuge is easy to find and well marked. Going west on State Highway 4 toward the coast from I-5, watch for a big sign for the refuge and Steamboat Slough Road, just over a mile west of Cathlamet. Turn onto Steamboat Slough Road and slowly drive through the refuge. You will pass the refuge headquarters, where you can get a map, checklist and wildlife news if one of the staff is there. You will drive from the southern end of the refuge to the northwest end, where Steamboat Slough Road intersects Brooks Slough Road. You can turn right and drive through more of the refuge on Brooks Slough Road or go straight into the little town of Skamokawa. In either case, you end up back on Hwy. 4.

As you drive through the refuge looking for the Columbian white-tailed deer, you may also see elk, for there is a small elk herd on the refuge. Other common mammals you may see are coyote, river otter, beaver, muskrat and especially nutria. This is one of the best places in Washington to see the black-shouldered kite, and the refuge has a good variety of winter waterfowl, including tundra swans, as mentioned in chapter 3. The swans are often seen across from the barn and shop buildings on Steamboat Slough Road. J. B. Hanson is a good place to visit on your way to the Willapa Bay–Grays Harbor area.

The largest herd of mule deer in Washington winters in the **Methow Valley,** famous for its cross-country skiing, as mentioned in chapter 2. Mule deer are commonly seen in the valley during the winter by skiers and by people traveling any of the roads through the valley. The Washington Department of Fish and Wildlife owns and manages the **Methow Wildlife Area** to protect winter habitat for the deer. Area managers are concerned about the deer being disturbed in winter, so do your best not to scare them, which means you should view them from your car.

Methow Valley and Wildlife Area

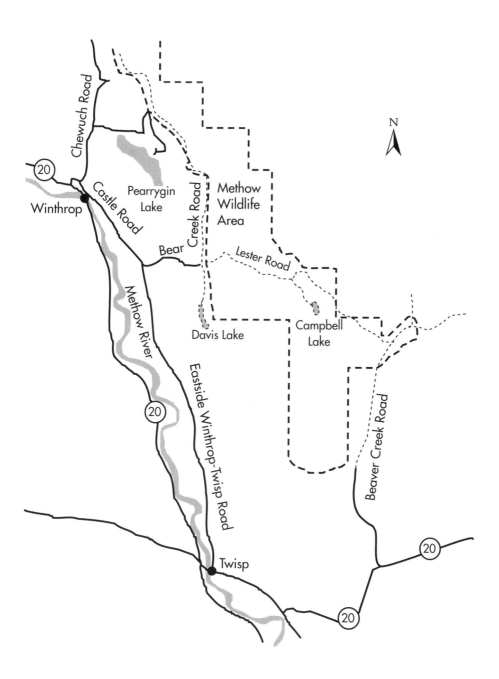

It's a bit tricky finding your way around the Methow Wildlife Area. The Okanogan National Forest map is generally the best, but the DeLorme atlas is better for the names of roads. During winter, snow closes most roads, but conditions vary and it's worth calling the Twisp Ranger District, (509) 997-2131, for latest conditions. Two roads are usually kept plowed and open—Bear Creek and Beaver Creek. The simplest access is to go about 5 miles east of Twisp on State Highway 20 and head due north on Beaver Creek Road (Forest Road 1637) as far as it is clear of snow. This will usually be about 5 miles, to the intersection with **Lester Road.** Lester Road is a narrow dirt road, steep in parts, but just fine in any vehicle when it's dry. If Lester Road is open, a great drive is to take it over the hills to Bear Creek Road. This is a scenic route through the middle of the wildlife area.

You can make a loop out of Winthrop on **Bear Creek Road** by following signs to Pearrygin Lake State Park, turning right onto Bear Creek Road a mile and a half out of Winthrop. When the road forks, go left on Bear Creek Road to the Methow Wildlife Area instead of right into the park (there are signs). Keep to the right at the next two intersections, following the signs to Davis Lake. In 4 miles from Pearrygin Lake, Bear Creek Road will become paved right where Lester Road intersects it from the east. Just follow the paved Bear Creek Road until it intersects the next paved road, which is Eastside Winthrop–Twisp Road. Turn right and you'll end up back in Winthrop; go left and you'll come to Hwy. 20 on the east edge of Twisp.

Another important winter range and a good place to observe mule deer is the **Klickitat Wildlife Area,** between the towns of Glenwood and Goldendale. About 10 miles west of Goldendale, the Glenwood Highway leaves State Highway 142 and winds for 22 miles northwest to Glenwood. The middle section of the Glenwood Highway passes through parts of the wildlife area favored by mule deer, particularly the south-facing slopes. The Klickitat is a beautiful area and includes lots of oak-pine woodlands, an uncommon habitat in Washington. It is a good wildflower area in the spring.

A good area for seeing black-tailed deer is along the recently rebuilt **Spirit Lake Highway** (State Highway 504), which goes up the North Fork of the Toutle River to Mount Saint Helens National Volcanic Monument. Late in the day deer are common along the road from about Milepost 20 until you near the Coldwater Ridge Visitor Center. This recently completed visitor center gives you one of the most spectacular scenic vistas in the Northwest and is also one of the best places to see elk in western Washington, so don't miss it.

As is often the case in national parks, the black-tailed deer at **Hurricane Ridge** in **Olympic National Park** have become very used to humans and, unfortunately, have learned that some people will feed them. When you visit Hurricane Ridge in the summer for wildflowers and marmots (chapters 37 and 44), you will most likely get some close looks at deer also. Please do not feed the deer—it causes many problems and is against park regulations.

68

Urban Wetlands

Any natural habitat remaining in an urban area is significant, but wetlands are particularly important because they provide some, if not all, of the needs of so many wildlife species. Wetlands are also important in controlling flooding and maintaining water quality. It is appropriate that they receive special protection, and landowners must get permits from the U.S. Army Corps of Engineers and other agencies to fill any wetlands. Some of the best good-news conservation stories in the Northwest are of the "Local Nature Club Saves Wetland" type. All those concerned with protecting wildlife habitat must be vigilant in watching for attempts to destroy more wetlands.

Sometimes the results can be very rewarding. For years Portland environmentalist Mike Houck envisioned an urban wildlife refuge system in the Portland metropolitan area, with wetlands and stream corridors as major components. Spearheaded at first by Mike at the Portland Audubon Society, this idea gained momentum and hundreds of active supporters, eventually evolving into the Metro Regional Parks and Greenspaces program. The Portland metro area now has one of the most outstanding systems of protected wetlands, and other natural habitats, of any city in the West. A master plan for protecting more habitat is in place, and voters approved additional funding for implementation of the plan in 1994.

Bellevue, Washington, is another city where the vision and perseverance of one individual, parks director Lee Springgate, has resulted in a park system that includes significant protected natural habitat with key wetlands as major components. The central piece to the system is the Lake to Lake Trail and Greenway, making a walking connection from Lake Washington to Lake Sammamish through the main wetlands and nature parks of the city. Only a few short links remain to complete an outstanding trail in the midst of urban/suburban development.

Many cities have a park pond or river running through part of town, but these do not always have natural habitat around them and may not be much different from the surrounding city in terms of wildlife. Fortunately this is changing, and there is much more awareness of, and concern for, natural areas that serve wildlife needs primarily, along with compatible passive recreation (hiking, birding and so on). This change is happening because citizens concerned about wildlife and natural habitat in their cities are making their interests known to city officials and are helping parks departments get the work done.

Any time of year is good for visiting urban wetlands, but there are a few reasons to go during the winter. The fewer people there are in a park, the better the chances are for seeing wildlife. Since this is the wintering range for many species of waterfowl and other waterbirds, northwestern wetlands, even in the middle of cities, can be loaded with ducks, geese and gulls and may even have a few loons, grebes and raptors that hunt around the wetlands. Larger lakes on the west side tend to have the biggest numbers and variety of waterbirds. Most of the mammal life you'll see in wetlands are active in winter and may be easier to see because of the reduced amount of vegetation. The cold-blooded animals, or ectotherms, however, will not be in evidence, so come back in the summer for frogs, garter snakes, newts and bugs.

Oregon

Hot Spots

Metro Regional Parks and Greenspaces manages a system of parks, trails and greenspaces—areas of natural habitat within the urban environment that support wildlife and give people the opportunity to get in touch with nature. In addition to managing its own parks, the Greenspaces program serves as a coordinator for similar programs of other agencies, such as the parks departments of cities, and conservation organizations like the Audubon Society and The Nature Conservancy. The best way to find out what's going on in the way of nature-related programs and activities in the metro area is to get the current issue of Metro GreenScene by contacting Metro at 600 NE Grand Avenue, Portland, OR 97232; (503) 797-1850.

The largest wetland in the metro system is **Smith and Bybee Lakes.** Plans are under way to start building an interpretive center in 1997. Until then, access is by improved universally accessible trails from a parking area on North Marine Drive. There are two wildlife viewing shelters, one for each lake. The area is loaded with waterfowl and herons, beavers and river otters are sometimes seen, and the area is one of the few where native turtles are still present.

The city of Portland has two wonderful wetland areas conveniently near each other. **Oaks Bottom Wildlife Refuge** includes a remnant of the Willamette flood plain at the base of the Sellwood Cliffs. Best access is currently from the **Oaks Bottom Trailhead** on SE Milwaukie Avenue, immediately south of McLoughlin Boulevard. From here a trail leads down to the bottoms, runs along the base of the cliffs on the east side of the wetlands and crosses to a railroad right-of-way at the northern and southern ends of the wetland. Currently, access to the railroad right-of-way is restricted, but negotiations for improving the situation are under way.

Just a mile east of Oaks Bottom is **Crystal Springs Park,** which includes Crystal Springs Lake and the Rhododendron Gardens on the east shore. Although this is landscaped park habitat, the lake is an excellent place to see a surprisingly large variety of ducks, and a few other waterbirds, at very close range. Wood ducks are particularly conspicuous in winter, to the delight of birders and nonbirders alike. This is a birding site with excellent access, because you can see almost everything from good paved trails. The parking lot for the park is on SE 28th, just north of SE Woodstock and across from Reed College. There is a small admission charge on some days. The main trail heads south from the parking lot, then crosses a wooden bridge. Explore as many of the trails that follow the lakeshore as you can, although the southern end of the lake usually has the most waterfowl.

The city of Hillsboro and the Unified Sewerage Agency jointly own and manage the **Jackson Bottom Wetland Preserve,** one of the purposes of the reserve being improvement in the quality of wastewater going into the Tualatin River. Over one hundred different birds frequent the area, and beaver, river otter, mink and raccoon may be seen. Jackson Bottom is south of downtown Hillsboro along State Highway 219, which is its western border. There is one observation platform at the northern end, just past the water treatment plant, and a second platform at the southern boundary, just before Hwy. 219 crosses the Tualatin River. The **Kingfisher Marsh Interpretive Trail** goes east into the marsh for a mile from the southern platform and provides excellent viewing.

Another good chunk of Willamette River floodplain is protected in **Minto-Brown Island Park,** just southeast of the state capitol in Salem. From downtown, take Commercial Street south and turn right onto River Road toward Independence. In about a mile turn right onto Minto Island Road and follow signs to the park. The park has a mix of sloughs and channels and riparian woodlands, and therefore has a good mix of bird species.

The **West Eugene Wetland** is a 1,500-acre area between downtown Eugene and Fern Lake Reservoir. The city is managing this complex mosaic of natural habitats and commercial property with the goal of protecting and enhancing the wetlands while allowing appropriate, planned development to continue. The booklet "West Eugene Wetland Self-Guided Tour" is available from the address in the appendix.

Washington

As mentioned earlier, the **city of Bellevue** has an exceptional system of parks, greenbelts and trails that include significant wetland acreage. The largest wetland is in **Mercer Slough Nature Park,** 320 acres that include interpretive trails, a visitor center and the slough itself, which is best viewed by canoe. If you want to canoe the slough, get the brochure "Canoeing Mercer Slough" (and other park information) from the **Winters House Visitors Center** on Bellevue Way, just north of I-90; (206) 462-2752. The park department also produces an excellent booklet *Nature Trail Guide,* which describes in detail the trails in the park system.

The **Nature Center at Snake Lake** is a 54-acre island of wildlife habitat in the midst of Tacoma. The central feature is Snake Lake, a shallow lake and swamp surrounded by dense vegetation. The lake is loaded with ducks, including plenty of wood ducks, and the thickets are bustling with songbird activity, especially in spring. About 2 miles of loop trails start at a nice visitor center. From I-5 in Tacoma, take Exit 132 and head west, toward Bremerton, on State Highway 16. After 2 miles, exit onto South 19th Street heading east. Go a couple of very long blocks, passing the big parks department head-quarters on your right, and turn right onto Tyler Street (there is a Fred Meyer's on your left at this intersection). Immediately after getting onto Tyler, make a left turn into the center's parking area on the east side of Tyler.

In Seattle, an interesting example of what may lie in store for other land-fills can be seen at the **Montlake Fill,** also called the Ecological Research Area at the University of Washington. Being used as a garbage dump has been a common fate for wetlands throughout the country. The Center for Urban Horticulture is experimenting with restoration techniques here that could someday be used throughout the country. The fill is now an odd mix of grassland, shrubland, patchy wetlands (including seasonal ponds) and the lakeshore. An amazing variety of birds has been seen here, including such uncommon ones as solitary sandpiper, northern shrike, Lapland longspur, snow bunting, Say's phoebe, yellow-headed blackbird and snowy owl. As the rainy season progresses, the seasonal wetlands get wetter and wetter, attracting more and more waterfowl and making rubber boots highly desirable in winter.

Finding Montlake Fill and a parking place are a bit tricky. Drive north of downtown Seattle on I-5 and take Exit 169 so you are going east on NE 45th Street. Drive along the north edge of the campus, go down a big hill, and turn right onto Union Bay Place (near a Baskin-Robbins), which will turn and become NE 41st Street. Drive to 36th Avenue and try to park, either on 41st Street or 36th Avenue. From here, walk over to the Center for Urban Horticulture, and at the far west end of the parking lot you will find the start of **Wahkiakum Lane,** a paved-to-gravel path heading toward the main cam-pus. You may find a trail map in a dispenser near the beginning of the trail. You can just explore on you own or take the main loop trail, which heads to the southeast just before the first big pond you come to. Following this trail you will make a clockwise loop, passing near the lakeshore where you can see scads of waterfowl, and then returning to join Wahkiakum Lane. If you have six quarters you can pay and park in the center's lot, #E-16.

Washington's second largest city, Spokane, straddles the Spokane River, and there are some sections of good riparian habitat scattered along the river in various parks. The real gem, however, is the **Little Spokane Natural Area,** which is on the northwestern outskirts of town and not really surrounded by urbanization. About $7^1/_2$ miles of the Little Spokane River are included in the natural area, and the river is ideal for canoeing. There is a good put-in spot just west of the intersection of Rutter Parkway and Waikiki Road, near the trout hatchery. The take-out spot is on Boat Launch Road, which is off State Highway 291 just a mile north of the intersection with Rutter Parkway and is well marked. You can also explore the same stretch of river by trail. **Indian Painted Rocks Trailhead** is where Rutter Parkway crosses the river, right in the middle of the natural area. There is a great blue heron rookery about a mile downstream from this trailhead, and beavers are regularly seen early or late in the day. For information contact **Riverside State Park.**

British Columbia

Burnaby Lake Regional Park and nearby **Deer Lake Park** are a wetland oasis surrounded by the greater Vancouver megalopolis. Burnaby Lake Regional Park is 740 acres and is part of the Greater Vancouver Regional District's park system. It has three entrances, but the best place to start is the **Nature House** at the Piper Avenue entrance, where there are displays, trailheads, rest rooms, an observation tower and information. The lake has a significant number of marshes along the shore, especially toward the eastern end. Deer Lake is smaller, with little marshland, and is a city park. It is, however, worth a visit when one is going to Burnaby Lake because it has some good grassland habitat, and you're almost always going to find a few bird species at one that aren't at the other.

Both parks can be reached from the Kensington Avenue Exit 33, from the Trans-Canada Highway (Hwy. 1). To reach the Nature House at Burnaby Lake, take Exit 33 and go north on Kensington Avenue. Follow signs for the Lougheed Highway east, but as soon you cross over Still Creek, turn right immediately onto Winston Street. Take Winston east to Piper Avenue and turn right, following signs for the park. To reach Deer Park, take Willingdon Avenue south, Exit 29, and go to the first traffic signals. Turn left onto Canada Way and take it east to Royal Oak Avenue. Turn right and go south on Royal Oak, cross Gilpin at a stop sign, and in a quarter-mile from the stop turn left into the parking lot.

Swan Lake Christmas Hill Nature Sanctuary in Victoria has the lake, marshes and upland habitats, including rocky outcroppings with oaks—a nice mix. It also has a visitor center and a floating-boardwalk trail. The lake gets considerably larger in winter (a familiar story) and attracts large numbers of waterfowl. Hours are generally 9 A.M. to 4 P.M. weekdays, and noon to 4 P.M. on weekends and holidays. Heading north from downtown Victoria on Blanshard Street, turn right and go west 1 block on McKenzie, then turn right again onto Rainbow Street. Go south on Rainbow a few blocks, then left on Ralph for a block, then turn right onto Swan Lake Road and go into the parking-area entrance.

69

Wintering Elk

Elk are *big*. They are often described as regal and majestic, but what it really comes down to is that these guys are big, and big is impressive. Only a few land animals in the Americas are heavier than big bull elk at half a ton, and with their huge racks of antlers they really have a lot of charisma. In the Northwest, elk are certainly one of the most popular and talked-about animals; it seems that most everyone is interested in seeing them. Among hunters, elk are a highly prized game animal, and small wonder, considering how much tasty meat one elk can provide.

The animal that we in America call the elk is called the red deer in Europe. And what Americans call a moose is what Europeans call an elk. So if you're talking to a European about elk, moose or red deer, be sure to get your species sorted out. Using scientific names is more precise; both the European red deer and our elk are subspecies, or races, of the species *Cervus elaphus*. All this, of course, is of no consequence to the elk and moose themselves, who have no trouble telling each other apart and who call each other whatever they please. This confusion over names has caused many American naturalists and sportsmen to advocate the use of the Native American name *wapiti* for our American elk. Although wapiti is used frequently, it just hasn't quite caught on with the general public.

As one can see by their antlers, elk are members of the deer family. The moose is the only other member of the deer family that is larger, and both animals have tremendous racks of antlers—elk can have antlers with a length of 5 feet and a spread even wider. That these animals grow a whole new set of antlers every year baffles many. What's the selective advantage in having to expend all that energy and consume all those nutrients every year to grow a new rack? But the calcium is used again by rodents, who quickly eat the antlers when they are shed in late winter. New antlers begin growing soon after the old set is shed.

Unlike mule and white-tailed deer, elk are mainly grazers instead of browsers, meaning they eat more grass. Elk are, however, adaptable, and they will eat a wide variety of plant foods. Like all deer and the majority of other ungulates, elk are *ruminants*—they have highly specialized digestive systems, including complex stomachs divided into chambers. Ruminants are well known for regurgitating wads of partially digested food for extra chewing, a practice commonly called "chewing the cud." These adaptations allow ruminants to get the most nutrients possible out of tough, hard-to-digest plant material, particularly grass.

Elk originally occupied a wide range of habitats in North America, from the coniferous rain forests of the Northwest to the chaparral mountains of the Southwest, and from the eastern forests to the Great Plains. Authorities now believe

Winter feeding areas provide close views of elk.

that before European contact, elk were more widespread than either species of deer and were found in every contiguous state and most Canadian provinces, and probably numbered ten million. Elk were quickly killed off by hungry settlers in most of their range and were left only in the least accessible parts of the western mountains, their stronghold today. After intensive management for most of this century, including reintroductions, elk numbers have increased, and many areas now support healthy populations.

Unlike deer, elk are herd animals, and the females spend their whole lives as part of a herd. Young males stay in the herd with their mothers for about the first year. The older males form smaller groups (bachelor herds) with other males, except preceding the rut, when they become solitary. During the rut, or breeding season, individual mature bulls attempt to gather a harem of cows that they will mate with exclusively. Competition between males is intense, and it is during this period (September and October) that the males give their famous bugling call and engage in various bluffs and battles for cows. During some of these battles the massive antlers become deadly weapons, although most disputes are settled without coming to blows. The unique sound of bugling elk has a mysterious and powerful quality and can be heard during September and October when you're in good elk habitat, such as near the hotspots below. The bulls do not bugle, however, while the animals are gathered on their winter ranges.

Most current elk populations make regular, sometimes quite long, seasonal movements in response to food availability. Typically, elk will spend the warmer months high in mountain meadows and come down into valley bottoms, where food is available, in winter. Unfortunately, almost all of the flat valley bottomlands are now managed intensively by people for agriculture or are urbanized. This tremendous loss of winter range is the biggest problem facing elk today. To compensate for this loss, federal and state wildlife agencies, and some private conservation organizations, have acquired critical winter rangeland for elk. In some cases the elk are fed on these winter ranges, not so much to keep them alive but to keep them from damaging nearby private agricultural land. These managed winter ranges provide the easiest opportunities by far for viewing elk, and that is where most of our hotspots are. December is the earliest time in which elk will start showing up in numbers on the winter ranges and feeding programs will begin, but better viewing is often in January and February.

In the Northwest we have two subspecies, or races, of elk, the Roosevelt elk, sometimes called the Olympic elk, and the Rocky Mountain elk. The Rocky Mountain elk was originally the most widespread of the elk in North America and today these animals are found east of the crest of the Cascades and in British Columbia's Coast Mountains. The Roosevelt elk is a specialized race that lives in the moist coniferous forests along the coast and in some parts of the western slope of the Cascades. Roosevelt elk are slightly larger and darker, with smaller antlers, than the Rocky Mountain elk, but it takes an expert's eye to tell them apart. In much of their range where winters are mild, Roosevelt elk do not migrate.

Oregon

Hot Spots

Oregon has the most unique elk-viewing experience in the Northwest. The Oregon Department of Fish and Wildlife manages, in different parcels, almost 10,000 acres of land near Baker City as the **Elkhorn Wildlife Area.** On the largest parcel, the **North Powder Tract,** the department started a unique service for the public in 1993. The Oregon Trail Trolley, a private concessionaire hired by the department, provides wagon rides, drawn by Percheron horses, right into the elk feeding area for unparalleled views of one to two hundred elk no farther away than 100 yards. You're almost tempted to try to pet them, but don't—they are wild elk even though they have become accustomed to the horse trolley.

The free trolley rides have been running every half hour from 11:30 A.M. until 3:00 P.M. on every Saturday and Sunday from about the middle of December through the end of February. Space on the wagon is assigned on a first-come, first-served basis when you arrive at the viewing area. Once you've signed up and been given your ticket, you will probably have to wait an hour or two, for the rides have been very popular. While you wait, you can view the elk from the road, look for other wildlife (there are lots of hawks in the area) or huddle in your car to stay warm. There are outhouses at the waiting area and sometimes snacks and drinks are available.

Finding the Elkhorn trolley rides is a piece of cake. From I-84 about halfway between Le Grande and Baker City, take Exit 285 for the little town of North Powder. North Powder has a motel, store and the North Powder Cafe, which is always open and is well known for serving vast quantities of food. Just west of I-84 take North Powder Lane west; don't get on U.S. Highway 30. Just stay on North Powder Lane going west, and follow the brown binocular wildlife viewing signs or signs for Elkhorn Wildlife Area. Go straight at the first intersection, and when you come to the fork to Tucker Flat, go left to the feeding area.

This program is experimental, so be sure to call the Oregon Trail Trolley at (541) 856-3356 or the Oregon Department of Fish and Wildlife at (541) 963-2138 or 898-2826 to be sure the trolley is running and to get the exact schedule for the current year, as well as tips on which days or times are least crowded.

Another good place for elk in northeastern Oregon is the **Wenaha Wildlife Area.** Wenaha is an excellent place to see not only Rocky Mountain elk but also mule and white-tailed deer and bighorn sheep. Wenaha has a feeding program, but the feeding areas are not open for viewing. However, it is often possible to go out with the staff to feed, or arrange other types of tours. Call the staff to find out what's possible and where the best viewing opportunities are. It is also wise to ask about road conditions. December may not be the best month to go to Wenaha, because some hunting seasons continue into the month and feeding may not be started if weather is mild.

Wenaha Wildlife Area is near the tiny town of Troy, which is on the Grande Ronde River at the bottom of a beautiful canyon and is about as out in the middle of nowhere as you can get. But this is the kind of nowhere in which you could spend months—the scenery in this corner of Oregon is truly spectacular. There is a small motel-restaurant-bar in Troy, a Shilo Inn, of all things, which is handy because the next nearest accommodations are about 50 miles away in Enterprise. To get to Troy, go north on State Highway 3 from Enterprise for about 33 miles. Just after the Rimrock Inn is the turnoff to Flora and Troy. Take this road, head west and follow signs to Troy. This road is steep and twisty and would not be fun if it were snowy or icy, so get information about road conditions before leaving. A less treacherous but longer alternative is to continue north on Hwy. 3 into Washington until you come to Grande Ronde Road and take it back upstream, along the river, to Troy.

If you have not made any arrangements with the staff and are heading out on your own, here is the best route to find elk. As you stand in "downtown" Troy you'll see two bridges that cross the Grande Ronde River. Go over the bridge farthest south or upstream, the low bridge, following the signs to Elgin and Wallowa. In just over 1/5 mile you'll come to a marked junction; turn right, following signs to Elgin and Tollgate Ranger Station. After a bit more than 2 miles you'll come to a fork in the road—go left, following the sign to Eden Bench. Just slowly cruise out this road for a while and then turn back (10 miles should be plenty), looking carefully on both sides for elk and deer. You may see them along this road as they are coming and going from the feeding areas and the river. The best bet, however, is to make arrangements with the staff to go to the feeding areas.

There is an outstanding area in which to see Roosevelt elk between Portland and the coast, the **Jewell Meadows Wildlife Area.** This is another Or-

311

egon Department of Fish and Wildlife site where winter feeding takes place. About seventy-five to two hundred elk can be seen on most days from November into April. To reach Jewell Meadows from Portland, head west on U.S. Highway 26 to Jewell Junction, just past the Elderberry Inn. Go north on Fishhawk Falls Highway (there are no signs) to Jewell. At Jewell, turn left to head west on State Highway 202. The wildlife area is along the road for several miles starting a couple of miles outside of Jewell. There are several parking areas where you can stop and get out to view elk in the meadow. The phone number for Jewell Meadows is (503) 755-2264.

Another choice spot for Roosevelt elk is the **Dean Creek Elk Viewing Area** near Reedsport. Just $3^1/_2$ miles east of Reedsport on State Highway 38 there is a big new wildlife viewing and interpretive site (with outhouses). There are other places on the south side of the road to pull over and view elk for the next 2 miles. As usual, the best viewing times are around dusk and dawn.

Washington

The Cascade Mountains around **Mount Rainier National Park** are home to the Yakima herd of Rocky Mountain elk, descendants of elk introduced here in 1913. There are two areas in the eastern foothills of the Cascades where some of these elk winter. One is **Oak Creek Wildlife Area,** managed by the Washington Department of Fish and Wildlife, and the other is the **Heart K Ranch**, recently purchased by the Rocky Mountain Elk Foundation.

The headquarters of the Oak Creek Wildlife Area has been developed into a major viewing site with a small visitor center and rest rooms. Elk are fed at this site every day at 1:30 P.M. usually beginning in December and continuing through February, but the feeding varies with the weather conditions, so it is good to call before going. To get to Oak Creek headquarters from Yakima, go west about 20 miles on U.S. Highway 12 to where Hwy. 12 and State Highway 410 split. Go south on Hwy. 12 about 2 more miles and you'll see the area well marked with signs.

After viewing elk at Oak Creek headquarters, you might want to drive up Oak Creek itself to see elk in a less artificial setting. Just south of headquarters, turn right onto Oak Creek Road and drive up this beautiful canyon as far as you like, looking for elk on the distant hillsides and also watching for the western gray squirrel, an increasingly rare mammal in Washington and most abundant in the oak woodlands of Oak Creek canyon. The number for Oak Creek Wildlife Area is (509) 653-2390, but you might have better luck calling the wildlife department regional office in Yakima at (509) 575-2740. When you are in the area, be sure to check for bighorn sheep (chapter 63).

For years, winter travelers on I-90 west of Ellensberg have sometimes been surprised, and delighted, to see elk in the big pastures just south of the freeway. A large parcel of some of the best of this winter range has been acquired by the nonprofit Rocky Mountain Elk Foundation as part of their continuing mission to benefit elk. The purchase of the Heart K Ranch is an excellent example of how private individuals, agencies and conservation organizations can work together for wildlife. To get a much better view of the elk than you do whizzing by on I-90, take the Thorpe Exit 5 miles west of Ellensburg. Go south on Thorpe Highway, away from Thorpe, for half a mile until you come to T. Cemetery Road. Go west about 4$^1/_2$ miles on T. Cemetery Road until it intersects Taneum Road. Go straight to continue west, south of the freeway, and you're now on Taneum Road. Watch the fields and hills beyond from this point until Taneum turns to dirt and becomes Forest Road 33, where you can turn around and come back.

The best time to see elk is in the evening. How many elk are in the fields in any one month will depend on snow and foraging conditions in the mountains, but December is when they usually start gathering in the fields regularly. You also have a good chance of seeing some deer and maybe coyotes.

The most reliable spot to see elk in western Washington is along the new Spirit Lake Highway (State Highway 504), which goes to the **Coldwater Ridge Visitor Center** in **Mount Saint Helens National Volcanic Monument.** This was also mentioned as a good spot to see deer in chapter 67. A drive up this road and a visit to the center are an absolute must-do in the Northwest. The 1980 eruption covered the floor of the Toutle River Valley with a massive debris slide. The Soil Conservation Service quickly seeded the area to reduce erosion, and the next year surviving Roosevelt elk returned to use the valley for winter range and to eat the new grass. Now the wintering herd has reached almost five hundred elk, and the state has established the **Mount Saint Helens Wildlife Area** to protect the herd and its habitat. Because they are often out in the open in the area devastated by the eruption, the Mount Saint Helens herd is very visible, although usually at a distance. The elk can often be seen from the Coldwater Ridge Visitor Center, and center staff sometimes have scopes set up so the public can see the elk below. There are three main viewpoints on Hwy. 504 at Mileposts 33, 37 and 41 where you can get out and search for elk in the valley below. When this book went to press, the Rocky Mountain Elk Foundation, the Weyerhaeuser Corporation and the Washington Department of Wildlife were working together on another visitor center, focused on the elk, for the **North Fork Ridge Viewpoint,** at Milepost 33.

A well-known spot for Roosevelt elk is the **Hoh Rain Forest** in **Olympic National Park.** The elk are not very visible because of the thick vegetation, and they are not gathered in big groups as they are at the areas where they are fed. But elk are common in the valley and are accustomed to people, so those hiking the trails, and especially those camping in the area, sometimes get close looks at the elk in a forest setting that is the natural home of this Pacific Northwest speciality. The Hoh is considered an excellent place to hear elk bugling during the rut. Incidentally, the Hoh Rain Forest is another of the must-see places in our region. Also, when you visit the **Julia Butler Hansen National Wildlife Refuge** to look for white-tailed deer (chapter 67), be on the lookout for the small herd of Roosevelt elk that live on the refuge.

70

Crow's Nest or Drey?

If you live in a neighborhood with lots of big deciduous trees, what do you see when you scan the bare trees in winter? You see last summer's nests, finally revealed by the loss of their shrouds of leaves. There are two fairly large nests, similar in size, that attract attention and start some folks wondering about what lives in them. Most abundant by far are the crows' nests, which have a broad upside down cone shape, are almost 2 feet wide by a foot deep and are made of small sticks. Their location makes it clear where the term "crow's nest," used on sailing ships, came from. These nests are usually toward the top center of the tree in a substantial crotch and really do remind one of the crow's nest atop the foremast of a clipper ship.

The other nest really confuses people—it looks like a soccer ball made out of leaves. It's not cup-shaped like most bird nests and doesn't even appear to have an entrance. These are the nests made by tree squirrels, and in England they are called *dreys* (or drays), a word rarely used in North America. Although they do look a bit like crows' nests, there are three easy ways to tell the two apart: dreys are mainly made out of leaves, not sticks; dreys are usually quite spherical, not conical or bowl-like and dreys are usually lower and placed more toward the trunk than crows' nests.

All of our North American tree squirrels make these leafy-ball dreys, but they are not the only nests that tree squirrels use. The preferred nest for most of the year, and especially for breeding, is a cavity in a tree, most commonly an old woodpecker nest. These cavity nests (usually called dens) are more secure from predators and bad weather than are the dreys. So during the winter most tree squirrels use them exclusively. The leafy-ball dreys, also called "summer nests," are mainly used in the warmer months but will be used year-round if weather is mild or cavities are in short supply. In many northwestern neighborhoods and parks, cavities are in limited supply because snags and dead limbs are removed, so dreys can be quite common.

Have you been squirreling money away for retirement? Have your kids been acting squirrelly lately? You know that an animal must be common if it has generated two slang terms based on its name and behaviors. Tree squirrels are one of the most familiar mammals in much of North America because they are very active and out in the open during the day all year long (they never hibernate). Some are quite adaptable and live close to people in urbanized areas, including big parks in the middle of cities. They are frequently seen when they visit feeders with seeds, either feeders designed for them or bird feeders, where they are sometimes unwelcome guests.

Tree squirrels all store large numbers of nuts, seeds or cones for the winter either by burying them or by stuffing them into hollow logs or under rocks. Squirreling away means saving for the future, but to me it also implies something sneaky going on, like hiding Halloween candy from your siblings. People often wonder if squirrels ever find the nuts they bury. There seems to be a difference of opinion about this, but it is clear that squirrels do find most of the food they have hidden, but by no means all of it. This results in tree squirrels having the reputation as the Johnny Appleseeds of the forest, inadvertently planting thousands of trees when they can't find a nut that happens to be buried in a good spot in which to sprout and grow. Squirrels, and even more so jays, answer the mystery of how trees with heavy seeds can actually spread *up* a hill. Evidence indicates that squirrels rarely remember where they have stashed their goodies. They just look in good places where any squirrel in his or her right mind would hide nuts and, lo and behold, there they are. They could be finding nuts buried by themselves or by other squirrels in the area.

Tree squirrels are territorial and will often scold and chase intruders. During the mating season, which happens twice a year, they get really wound up and chase one another all over the place. Such chases are usually males going after or fighting over a female. All this hubbub really does make the squirrels appear crazy, hence the term "squirrelly" for people (did I say teenagers?) who are whipped up and acting nutty.

Tree squirrels are common in most of the earth's forests and are distinguished from their close relatives the ground squirrels (including marmots, chipmunks and prairie dogs) by their big bushy tails. The word squirrel comes from two Greek words that mean "shadow tail," and indeed, some do use their tails as parasols to shade the body. The tail is most important, however, for insulation and for climbing and jumping. Tree squirrels are called tree squirrels because they are superbly adapted to life in the trees. They are incredible climbers and jumpers, and their tails are important for maintaining balance, for acting as a rudder when jumping and for breaking falls like a parachute. The ultimate arborial rodents are the flying squirrels, which have perfected the art of gliding flight.

There are five tree squirrels in the Northwest, not counting the northern flying squirrel, which is quite distinct. The chickaree or Douglas squirrel is abundant and could be the mascot for the coniferous forests in the western half of our region; its loud chatter is one of the signature sounds of the Pacific Northwest. Its close relative the red squirrel has the largest range of any American squirrel and is found in northeastern Oregon and Washington, most of British Columbia and, interestingly, on Vancouver Island. Both of these are small tree squirrels of coniferous forests and are not as common around human dwellings as are the big guys. Their dreys are very hard to locate because they are built in the thick foliage of evergreens.

There are three very closely related tree squirrels that are all noticeably larger than the chickaree and red squirrel and prefer habitats with more deciduous trees. The beautiful western gray squirrel is native only to the Pacific States and is found in oak woodlands and mixed pine-oak woodlands. Unfortunately, these habitats are also highly favored by humans, and western gray squirrel popula-

A typical drey of a gray fox or squirrel, which is easy to spot in the winter.

tions have declined dramatically in most of the Northwest. An additional source of trouble for the western gray squirrel has been the introduction of its two eastern relatives, the eastern gray squirrel and the biggest bruiser of them all, the fox squirrel. These squirrels are more aggressive than our western natives, which are getting pushed out of good habitat.

Western grays are not very tolerant of human disturbance, so few people will see them around their houses. The eastern gray and fox squirrel, however, are quite adaptable and are regulars on the urban wildlife scene. Hence, human development has favored fox and eastern gray squirrels, and these are the squirrels one sees in urban parks or running along telephone wires. Since these are introduced squirrels, their distribution is irregular and spotty, determined not by nature but by the whims of humans. Oregon has more fox squirrels than eastern grays, but in Washington the grays have an edge. In British Columbia there are no western gray or fox squirrels, so all the big tree squirrels you see are eastern gray squirrels. Some eastern grays are solid black, and there are a lot of these in Stanley Park in Vancouver.

There aren't any hotspots for tree squirrels and crows' nests because they are so common and widespread. Crows are found throughout our region at lower elevations, so you could see their nests almost anywhere, although their distribution is irregular east of the mountains. In just about any coniferous forest in the Northwest you will find chickarees or, as you go east and north, red squirrels. Fox squirrels are in most cities west of the Cascades in Oregon and in southeastern and northeastern Washington. The eastern gray squirrel is common in Eugene and Salem, western Washington and north into British Columbia. Look for these two in parks and neighborhoods with big old deciduous trees.

Finding western gray squirrels is, unfortunately, getting harder all the time. Western grays are now on the Threatened Species List in Washington. Look for them in the ponderosa pine forests around Bend in Oregon and in the pine-oak woodlands along the Klickitat River in Washington.

71

December Shorttakes

Steelhead

Winter steelhead start moving up streams in good numbers in December. Some runs peak this month, many others in February and a few even later in March. Steelhead are hard to see because they are more skittish than salmon and are most often moving upstream during or after winter rains when the water is cloudy. There are a few spots, however, where you might get a good look from December into February. Two natural spots in Oregon are **Deadline Falls,** discussed in chapter 57, and **Smith River Falls.** Smith River Falls is about 20 miles east of Reedsport on Smith River Road, which you turn onto from U.S. Highway 101 just north of town. Smith River Road is also Forest Road 48 for about 12 miles, then FR 48 heads north and you continue east on what is now BLM Road 36. You can actually see steelhead trying to jump the falls, but they can't make it. The Oregon Department of Fish and Wildlife installed a fish ladder, which the fish now use to get upstream, but the fish are not visible while they are in the ladder.

Cedar Creek Hatchery is one of the Oregon Department of Fish and Wildlife's oldest hatcheries and is on Three Rivers Creek just $1^1/_2$ miles southeast of Hebo on State Highway 22. From the parking area you can walk down to the creek, and just downstream of the deadline there is shallow clear water where you can usually see steelhead waiting to move up into the hatchery intake. A deadline is a cable fixed over the river downstream from a hatchery; no fishing is allowed upstream of that line. Hatchery personnel welcome visitors, and you can get excellent views of the artificial spawning process; call the hatchery to get the schedule (see appendix).

The **Aberdeen Hatchery** offers a similar situation in Washington. Two miles east of Aberdeen on U.S. Highway 12, turn north on Aberdeen Lake Road. In half a mile turn left, following the sign for Lake Aberdeen and Trout Hatchery. You'll quickly come to a fork in the road; to the right is Lake Aberdeen and to the left is the hatchery, but there is no sign. Take the left fork and park in the small parking lot at the hatchery. Check out the big sign and map, and walk between the abatement pond and the adult holding raceways to the end of the fish ladder. You can see steelhead hanging out in Van Winkle Creek below the ladder. They usually move up the ladder at night.

Bigfoot

The first serious snow in the mountains presents an excellent opportunity to see animal tracks. This may be your best chance for finding Sasquatch, also known as Bigfoot because of the large tracks this mysterious animal leaves. Sasquatch is one of the main subjects of the relatively recent science of *cryptobiology,* the study of hidden animals. As you might guess, other objects of interest in this field include the Yeti and Nessie, the famous resident of Loch Ness. The Pacific Northwest is as well known for Sasquatch as it is for salmon, spotted owls and banana slugs, so no wildlife guide for the region would be complete without some tips on finding Bigfoot. Actually, it is very hard to give specific advice, because almost all the reported sightings and discoveries of tracks have been made in chance encounters by people who were not out looking for Sasquatch. There are some areas, though, that have produced more sightings than others. The best hotspot seems to be the southern **Washington Cascades** around **Mount Rainier** and **Mount Saint Helens**. There was so much Bigfoot activity in the late sixties in this area that Skamania County passed the world's first (and presumably only) Sasquatch Protection Ordinance, making it illegal to kill a Sasquatch under penalty of fine and/or imprisonment. There have been a number of sightings in the **Oregon Cascades** and in the **Fraser River Valley** in British Columbia, but the sites are so scattered that there is no pattern to them. If you do go looking for Sasquatch, be sure to take a camera and you may see your photo in the periodicals displayed at the checkout stand in your supermarket. Or better yet, get *Harry and the Hendersons* at the video store and sit back with a bowl of popcorn on a cold winter's night and enjoy.

72

A Closer Look:
Christmas Bird Counts

It is fitting to end the year with what surely must be the biggest nonconsumptive natural history event of the year—the Christmas Bird Count. In recent years this all-volunteer bird census has involved close to 45,000 people participating in 1,700 different counts. For many birders it is the highlight of the year, and for many Audubon Society chapters it is their biggest social event. Not bad for one guy's simple suggestion at the turn of the century.

A hundred years ago many American sportsmen participated in the traditional Christmas Hunt, wherein teams of hunters went out on Christmas Day to see which team could kill the most animals. Many people were horrified at this slaughter, so when Frank Chapman, editor of *Bird-Lore* magazine (the forerunner of *Audubon*), suggested an alternative, the idea caught on. He proposed "spending a portion of Christmas Day with the birds and sending a report of the 'hunt' to *Bird-Lore* before retiring that night." Frank received the reports of twenty-five counts, almost all made by single individuals. From this humble beginning in 1900, the Christmas Bird Count (CBC to birders) has become a massive, well-organized and standardized method for counting birds in winter.

Every year, within two weeks of Christmas, volunteers record by species every individual bird they find in one day (24 hours) in a precisely defined circle 15 miles in diameter. Since the same area is counted in basically the same way at the same time every year, CBCs show general trends in winter bird populations for the areas represented by the count circles. Although this technique is sloppy by scientific standards, the results are by far the greatest body of data on winter bird populations in North America, and in many areas the CBC data is the only data on bird numbers available.

The first counts were fairly casual affairs, with a few people counting for part of the day. The number of species seen in the first years was in the twenties, but by 1911 the then seemingly unbelievable mark of one hundred species was reached in Santa Barbara, California. These days, at least fifty counts have species lists over 150 every year. This dramatic increase is a result of better coverage of more areas by increasing numbers of more skillful birders. In the 1920s the present rules for count circles and counting time were established, and in 1941 the results of the officially titled Christmas Bird Count were first published by the National Audubon Society, still the event's sponsor and organizer. The results are still published each year in a special large fall issue of *National Audubon*

Society Field Notes, called *American Birds* until 1994.

One factor that has pushed the number of species up has been friendly competition among count areas to see which could produce the highest number of species. Every year there is close competition between the coastal areas of California and Texas for the species-high for the United States. The species-high has fluctuated between 200 and 225 for two decades, but the unbeatable low remains the 1981 count at North Star Island, Alaska—a big fat zero. Brrrr!

Christmas Bird Counts are a lot of fun. There is usually a great spirit of camaraderie, a sense of purpose (often challenged by lousy weather) and a bit of friendly competition at times for who will report the big surprise at the end of the day. At the end of the count day there is almost always a big "countdown" potluck dinner where all the teams report their sightings for the day, grand totals are tallied and a few wild stories are shared. Beginners are almost always warmly received by count leaders and assigned to teams with expert birders. This is a great way to learn identification tips from the pros, and many novices have been inspired to more serious birding through a CBC.

To participate in a CBC, find out about the counts in your area from your local Audubon Society chapter, natural history society or other nature center. The National Audubon Society coordinates all the counts, and you can get the latest information on counts and on the people to contact for your area from the western regional office in Sacramento, California. The Seattle and Portland Audubon Society chapters usually have listings of counts for their respective state. For counts in British Columbia, contact the Federation of British Columbia Naturalists. Or go straight to the top by contacting the CBC Editor of *National Audubon Society Field Notes* at the National Audubon Society offices in New York City.

Counters pride themselves on going out for the count regardless of the weather, so be well prepared to be out all day. If this sounds too brutal, be aware that feeder-watchers are included, and that sometimes there are certain small areas that can be covered by one or two people just going out for part of the day. Be sure to contact the count leader in advance to see where you can best fit in. Happy Holidays and good counting!

Appendix

The following are addresses and phone numbers of various agencies, organizations and wildlife units mentioned in this book. Additional entries that may be useful to the wildlife watcher are included.

Please note that in the fall of 1996, Vancouver Island and much of British Columbia will have a new telephone area code: 250, instead of the 604 code listed in this appendix. All numbers below with a 604* will change to the new code in late 1996.

UNITED STATES FEDERAL AGENCIES

Information Centers

Nature of the Northwest Information Center
800 NE Oregon Street, Room 177
Portland, OR 97232
(503) 872-2750

(In the center's bookstore are information and maps for all national forests in Oregon and Washington, as well as United States Geological Survey [USGS], BLM and state agency maps for Oregon.)

Outdoor Recreation Information Center
U.S. Forest Service/National Park Service
915 Second Avenue, Suite 442
Seattle, WA 98174
(206) 220-7450

(In the center's bookstore are information and maps for all National Park Service and U.S. Forest Service areas in Oregon and Washington, as well as some Washington state parks.)

National Parks and Monuments (National Park Service)

Oregon

Crater Lake National Park
P.O. Box 7
Crater Lake, OR 97604
(541) 594-2211

John Day Fossil Beds National Monument
420 West Main Street

John Day, OR 97845
(541) 987-2333

Oregon Caves National Monument
19000 Caves Highway
Cave Junction, OR 97523
(541) 592-2100

Washington

Mount Rainier National Park
Tahoma Woods, Star Route
Ashford, WA 98304
(360) 569-2211

North Cascades National Park
(includes Ross Lake National Recreation Area)
2105 South Highway 20
Sedro Woolley, WA 98284
(360) 856-5700

Olympic National Park
600 East Park Avenue
Port Angeles, WA 98362
(360) 452-4501

National Forests and Ranger Districts (U.S. Forest Service)

Oregon

Columbia River Gorge National Scenic Area
902 Wasco Avenue, Suite 200
Hood River, OR 97031
(541) 386-2333

Deschutes National Forest
1645 Highway 20 East
Bend, OR 97701
(541) 388-2715

Deschutes National Forest—Lava Lands Visitor Center
58201 South Highway 97
Bend, OR 97707
(541) 593-2421

Fremont National Forest
524 North G Street
Lakeview, OR 97630
(541) 947-2151

Malheur National Forest
139 NE Dayton Street
John Day, OR 97845
(541) 575-1731

Mount Hood National Forest
2955 NW Division
Gresham, OR 97030
(503) 666-0700

Mount Hood Information Center
65000 East Highway 26
Welches, OR 97067
(503) 622-7674

Ochoco National Forest
3061 East Third Street
Prineville, OR 97754
(541) 447-6247

Pacific Northwest Region Office—U.S. Forest Service
P.O. Box 3623
Portland, OR 97208
(503) 872-2750

Rogue River National Forest
333 West Eighth Street
Medford, OR 97501
(541) 858-2200

Siskiyou National Forest
200 NE Greenfield Road
Grants Pass, OR 97526
(541) 471-6500

Siuslaw National Forest
4077 Research Way
Corvallis, OR 97333
(541) 750-7000

Siuslaw National Forest—
Cape Perpetua Visitor Center
P.O. Box 274
Yachats, OR 97498
(541) 547-3289

Siuslaw National Forest—
Oregon Dunes National Recreation Area
855 Highway Avenue
Reedsport, OR 97467
(541) 271-3611

Umatilla National Forest
2517 SW Hailey Avenue
Pendleton, OR 97801
(541) 278-3716

Umpqua National Forest
2900 Stewart Parkway
Roseburg, OR 97470
(541) 672-6601

Umpqua National Forest—
Diamond Lake Ranger District
HC-60, Box 101
Idleyld Park, OR 97447
(541) 498-2531

Wallowa-Whitman National Forest
1550 Dewey Avenue
Baker City, OR 97814
(514) 523-6391

Wallowa-Whitman National Forest—
Eagle Cap Ranger District
(includes Hells Canyon National Recreation Area and
Wallowa Mountains Visitor Center)
88401 Highway 82
Enterprise, OR 97828
(541) 426-4978

Willamette National Forest
211 East Seventh Avenue
Eugene, OR 97401
(541) 465-6522

Willamette National Forest—Detroit Ranger District
HC-73, Box 320
Mill City, OR 97360
(503) 854-3366

Winema National Forest
2819 Dahlia Street
Klamath Falls, OR 97601
(541) 883-6714

Washington

Colville National Forest
765 South Main
Colville, WA 99114
(509) 684-3711

Colville National Forest—Spokane Information Center
400 South Jefferson Street, Suite 106
Spokane, WA 99204
(509) 353-2574

Gifford Pinchot National Forest
6926 East Fourth Plain Boulevard
Vancouver, WA 98661
(360) 750-5000

Gifford Pinchot National Forest—
Mount Adams Ranger District
2455 Highway 141
Trout Lake, WA 98650
(509) 395-3400

Gifford Pinchot National Forest—
Mount Saint Helens National Volcanic Monument
42218 NE Yale Bridge Road
Amboy, WA 98601
(360) 750-3900

Gifford Pinchot National Forest—
Wind River Ranger District
MP 1.23R Hemlock Road
Carson, WA 98610
(509) 427-3200

Mount Baker–Snoqualmie National Forest
21905 64th Avenue West
Mountlake Terrace, WA 98043
(206) 775-9702

Mount Baker–Snoqualmie National Forest—
North Bend Ranger District
42404 SE North Bend Way
North Bend, WA 98045
(206) 888-1421

Okanogan National Forest
1240 South Second Avenue
Okanogan, WA 98840
(509) 826-3275

Okanogan National Forest—Twisp Ranger District
502 Glover
Twisp, WA 98856
(509) 997-2131

Olympic National Forest
1835 Black Lake Boulevard SW
Olympia, WA 98512
(360) 956-2300

Wenatchee National Forest
215 Melody Lane
Wenatchee, WA 98801
(509) 662-4335

National Wildlife Refuges and Fish Hatcheries (U.S. Fish and Wildlife Service)

Be sure to get a copy of the excellent *Visitor Directory—Pacific Region,* available from the U.S. Fish and Wildlife Service Pacific Region Office in Portland, and at many refuges.

Oregon

Hart Mountain National Antelope Refuge
P.O. Box 111
Lakeview, OR 97630
(541) 947-3315

Klamath Basin National Wildlife Refuges
Route 1, Box 74
Tulelake, CA 96134
(916) 667-2231

Malheur National Wildlife Refuge
HC-72, Box 245
Princeton, OR 97721
(541) 493-2612

Oregon Coastal National Wildlife Refuges
2030 South Marine Science Drive
Newport, OR 97365
(541) 867-4550

Pacific Region Office—U.S. Fish and Wildlife Service
911 NE 11th
Portland, OR 97232
(503) 231-6828

Umatilla National Wildlife Refuge Complex
P.O. Box 700
Umatilla, OR 97882
(541) 922-3232

Willamette Valley National Wildlife Refuges
26208 Finley Refuge Road
Corvallis, OR 97333
(541) 757-7236

Washington

Columbia National Wildlife Refuge
735 East Main Street
Othello, WA 99344
(509) 488-2668

Conboy Lake National Wildlife Refuge
100 Wildlife Refuge Road
Glenwood, WA 98619
(509) 364-3410

Julia Butler Hansen National Wildlife Refuge for the Columbia White-tailed Deer
P.O. Box 566
Cathlamet, WA 98612
(360) 795-3915

Leavenworth National Fish Hatchery
12790 Fish Hatchery Road
Leavenworth, WA 98826
(509) 548-7641

Little Pend Oreille National Wildlife Refuge
1310 Bear Creek Road
Colville, WA 99114
(509) 684-8384

Little White Salmon National Fish Hatchery
56961 SR 14
Cook, WA 98605
(509) 538 2755

McNary National Wildlife Refuge
P.O. Box 544
Burbank, WA 99323
(509) 547-4942

Nisqually National Wildlife Refuge Complex
100 Brown Farm Road
Olympia, WA 98516
(360) 753-9467
(360) 532-6237 (recorded information on Bowerman Basin)

Ridgefield National Wildlife Refuge
301 North Third
Ridgefield, WA 98642
(360) 887-4106

Turnbull National Wildlife Refuge
26010 South Smith Road
Cheney, WA 99004
(509) 235-4723

Willapa National Wildlife Refuge
HC 01, Box 910
Ilwaco, WA 98624
(360) 484-3482

Bureau of Land Management Regional Offices and BLM Outstanding Natural Areas

Oregon

Burns District Office
HC-74 12533
Highway 20 West
Hines, OR 97738
(541) 573-5241

Medford District Office
3040 Biddle Road
Medford, OR 97504
(541) 770-2200

Oregon State Office
1515 SW Fifth
Portland, OR 97201
(503) 952-6001

Roseberg District Office
777 NW Garden Valley Boulevard
Roseburg, OR 97470
(541) 440-4930

Yaquina Head Outstanding Natural Area
P.O. Box 936
Newport, OR 97365
(541) 265-2863

Washington

Spokane District
1103 North Fancher
Spokane, WA 99212
(509) 536-1200
(all Washington)

Wenatchee Resource Area, BLM
915 Walla Walla
Wenatchee, WA 98801
(509) 665-2100

National Estuarine Reserve Research System

South Slough National Estuarine Reserve
P.O. Box 5417
Charleston, OR 97420
(541) 888-5558

Padilla Bay National Estuarine Reserve
Breazeale Interpretive Center
1043 Bayview-Edison Road
Mount Vernon, WA 98273
(360) 428-1558

STATE AGENCIES

Oregon Department of Fish and Wildlife (ODFW)

Be sure to get the directory, *Visitor's Guide—Oregon's Fish Hatcheries and Wildlife Management Areas,* a comprehensive listing of all ODFW-managed areas, from the main office in Portland or from any regional office.

ODFW Main Office
P.O. Box 59
Portland, OR 97207
(503) 872-5310

ODFW Region #1, Northwest
7118 NE Vandenberg Avenue

Corvallis, OR 97330
(541) 757-4186

ODFW Region #2, Southwest
4192 North Umpqua Highway
Roseburg, OR 97470
(541) 440-3353

ODFW Region #3, Central
61374 Parrell Road
Bend, OR 97702
(541) 388-6363

ODFW Region #4, Northeast
107 20th Street
La Grande, OR 97738
(541) 963-2138

ODFW Region #5, Southeast
P.O. Box 8
Hines, OR 97738
(541) 573-6582

ODFW Region #6, Marine
Marine Science Drive, Building 3
Newport, OR 97365
(541) 867-4741

ODFW Region #7, Columbia
17330 SE Evelyn Street
Clackamas, OR 97015
(503) 657-2000

Bonneville Fish Hatchery
Star Route B, Box 12
Cascade Locks, OR 97014
(503) 374-8393

Cedar Creek Fish Hatchery
33465 Highway 22
Hebo, OR 97122
(503) 392-3485

Elkhorn Wildlife Area
61846 Powder River Lane
North Powder, OR 97867
(541) 898-2826

Jewell Meadows Wildlife Area
Elsie Route, Box 1565 (Highway 202)
Seaside, OR 97138
(503) 755-2264

Klamath Wildlife Area
1800 Miller Island Road West
Klamath Falls, OR 97603
(541) 883-5734

Sauvie Island Wildlife Area
18330 NW Sauvie Island Road

Portland, OR 97231
(503) 621-3488

Summer Lake Wildlife Area
36981 Highway 31
Summer Lake, OR 97640
(541) 943-3152

Wenaha Wildlife Area
85060 Grande Ronde Road
Enterprise, OR 97828
(541) 828-7721 or 963-2138

Washington Department of Fish and Wildlife (WDFW)

WDFW Main Office
600 Capitol Way North
Olympia, WA 98501
(360) 902-2200

WDFW Region 1
8702 North Division Street
Spokane, WA 99218
(509) 456-4082
(northeast and southeast corners)

WDFW Region 2
1550 Alder Street NW
Ephrata, WA 98823
(509) 754-4624
(Okanogan through Franklin Counties, Methow)

WDFW Region 3
1701 South 24th Avenue
Yakima, WA 98902
(509) 575-2740
(Chelan through Benton Counties, Oak Creek)

WDFW Region 4
16018 Mill Creek Boulevard
Mill Creek, WA 98012
(206) 775-1311
(Greater Puget Sound, Skagit area)

WDFW Region 5
5405 NE Hazel Dell Avenue
Vancouver, WA 98663
(360) 696-6211
(southwest, Columbia Gorge)

WDFW Region 6
48 A/B Devonshire Road
Montesano, WA 98563
(360) 249-6522
(coastal counties and Olympic Peninsula)

Aberdeen Fish Hatchery
4203 Aberdeen Lake Road

Aberdeen, WA 98520
(360) 533-1663

STATE PARKS

Oregon

Oregon Parks and Recreation Department
1115 Commercial Street NE
Salem, OR 97310
1 (800) 452-5687 (information and reservations)

Oregon State Parks
Area 1, North Coast
Ridge Road
Hammond, OR 97121
(503) 861-0863

Oregon State Parks
Area 2, North Central Coast
198 NE 123rd Street
Newport, OR 97365
(541) 265-4560

Oregon State Parks
Area 3, South Central Coast
84505 Hwy 101 South
Florence, OR 97439
(541) 997-5755

Oregon State Parks
Area 4, South Coast
365 North Fourth Street
Coos Bay, OR 97420
(541) 269-9410

Oregon State Parks
Area 5, Portland and Columbia River Gorge
3554 SE 82nd Avenue
Portland, OR 97266
(503) 731-3293

Oregon State Parks
Area 6, Willamette Valley
1115 Commercial Street, NE
Salem, OR 97310
(503) 378-5020

Oregon State Parks
Area 7, Southern Oregon
3792 North River Road
Gold Hill, OR 97525
(541) 582-1118

Oregon State Parks
Area 8, Central Oregon
20310 Empire Avenue, Suite B1
Bend, OR 97701
(541) 388-6212

Oregon State Parks
Area 9, Eastern Oregon
2034 Auburn
Baker City, OR 97814
(541) 523-2499

Silver Falls State Park
20024 Silver Falls Highway SE
Sublimity, OR 97385
(503) 873-8681

Tryon Creek State Park
11321 SW Terwilliger Boulevard
Portland, OR 97219
(503) 653-3166

Washington

Washington State Parks and Recreation Headquarters
7150 Clearwater Lane
P.O. Box 42650
Olympia, WA 98504
1 (800) 233-0321 (information)
1 (800) 452-5687 (reservations)

Winter Recreation Office
P.O. Box 42662
Olympia, WA 98504
(360) 902-8552

Washington State Parks
Southwest Region
11838 Tilley Road South
Olympia, WA 98512
(360) 753-7143

Washington State Parks
Puget Sound Region
1602 29th Street SE
Auburn, WA 98002
(206) 931-3907

Washington State Parks
Northwest Region
220 North Walnut Street
P.O. Box 487
Burlington, WA 98233
(360) 755-9231

Washington State Parks
Eastern Region
2201 North Duncan Drive
Wenatchee, WA 98801
(509) 662-0420

Riverside State Park
Spokane, WA 99205
(509) 456-3964 or 456-2729

OTHER STATE AGENCIES

Oregon

Oregon Tourism Division
775 Summer Street NE
Salem, OR 97310
(800) 547-7842
(503) 797-4990

OSU Sea Grant Program
Hatfield Marine Science Center
Newport, OR 97396
(541) 867-0100

Washington

Washington State Department of Natural Resources
Central Region—Mima Mounds Natural Area Preserve
1405 Rush Road
Chehalis, WA 98532
(360) 748-2382

Washington State Department of Natural Resources
Olympia Headquarters
1111 Washington Street SE
P.O. Box 47000
Olympia, WA 98504
(360) 902-1000

Washington State Department of Tourism
P.O. Box 42500
Olympia, WA 98504
1 (800) 544-1800
(This office produces the excellent *Washington State Field Guide* three times a year. It includes many natural events.)

Regional, County and Municipal Agencies

Oregon

City of Eugene Public Works
Information Specialist
858 Pearl Street
Eugene, OR 97401
(541) 465-2739
(West Eugene Wetlands)

Hoyt Arboretum
4000 SW Fairview Boulevard
Portland, OR 97221
(503) 228-8733

Jackson Bottom Coordinator
City of Hillsboro
123 West Main Street
Hillsboro, OR 97123
(503) 681-6206

Leach Botanical Garden
6704 SE 122nd Avenue
Portland, OR 97236
(503) 761-9503
(Portland City Park, native plants)

Metro Regional Parks and Greenspaces
600 NE Grand Avenue
Portland, OR 97232
(503) 797-1850
(This is a good place to start for any park or natural area in the Portland area. Get the latest "GreenScene" for programs.)

Portland Parks and Recreation
1120 SW Fifth, Room 1302
Portland, OR 97204
(503) 823-2223

Washington

City of Bellevue
Parks and Community Services Department
P.O. Box 90012
Bellevue, WA 98009
(206) 455-6881

Clallam County Parks
223 East Fourth Street
Port Angeles, WA 98362
(360) 452-7831
(Salt Creek County Park, 928-3441)

Nature Center at Snake Lake
1919 South Tyler
Tacoma, WA 98405
(206) 591-6439

CANADIAN FEDERAL AGENCIES

National Parks (Parks Canada)

Pacific Rim National Park
Box 280
Ucluelet, BC V0R 3A0
(604*) 726-7721

Fish Hatcheries (Fisheries and Oceans Canada)

Capilano Salmon Hatchery
4500 Capilano Road
North Vancouver, BC V7R 4L3
(604) 666-1790

Chehalis Hatchery
16250 Morris Valley Road
Harrison Mills, BC V0M 1H0
(604) 796-2281

Chilliwack Hatchery
Chilliwack, BC V2R 2P1
(604) 858-7227

Fisheries and Oceans Canada Regional Headquarters
Station 321—Public Information
555 West Hastings Street
Vancouver, BC V6B 5G3
(604) 666-6614

Robertson Creek Hatchery
Box 1100
Port Alberni, BC V9Y 7L9
(604*) 724-6521

Canadian Wildlife Service (Environment Canada— Environmental Conservation Branch)

Canadian Wildlife Service
Pacific Wildlife Research Center
5421 Robertson Road
Delta, BC V4K 3N2
(604) 666-0143

BRITISH COLUMBIA PROVINCIAL AGENCIES

Provincial Parks System (BC Parks)

BC Parks
Fraser Valley District
Cultus Lake Provincial Park
Box 301
Cultus Lake, BC V2R 5H6
(604*) 824-2300
(Manning Provincial Park)

BC Parks
Garibaldi–Sunshine Coast District
Alice Lake Provincial Park
Box 220
Brackendale, BC V0N 1HO
(604) 898-3678
(Garibaldi Provincial Park)

BC Parks
Southern Vancouver Island District
2930 Trans-Canada Highway
Victoria, BC V9B 5T9
(604*) 391-2300
(Goldstream, Botanical Beach and Carmanah Pacific Provincial Parks)

BC Parks
Strathcona District
Rathtrevor Beach Provincial Park
Box 1479
Parksville, BC V9P 2H4
(604*) 954-4600
(Rathtrevor, McMillian, Stamp Falls and Strathcona Provincial Parks)

BC Parks
Vancouver District
1610 Mount Seymour Road
North Vancouver, BC V7G 1L3
(604) 924-2200
(Cypress, Mt. Seymour, Golden Ears Provincial Parks)

Ministry of Environment, Lands and Parks— Wildlife Branch

Wildlife Branch, BC Environment
Headquarters
780 Blanshard Street
Victoria, BC V8V 1X4
(604*) 387-9717

Wildlife Branch, BC Environment
Lower Mainland Region
10334 152nd A Street
Surrey, BC V3R 7P8
(604) 582-5200

Tourism British Columbia

Super, Natural British Columbia
Parliament Buildings
Victoria, B.C. V8V 1X4
1 (800) 663-6000
(An excellent tourist information service; select the general information option for wildlife and parks when you call.)

Regional Agencies

Capital Regional District
Parks Department
490 Atkins Avenue
Victoria, BC V9B 2Z8
(604*) 478-3344

Greater Vancouver Regional District
Parks Department
4330 Kingsway
Burnaby, BC V5H 4G8
(604) 432-6350

PRIVATE, NONPROFIT CONSERVATION ORGANIZATIONS

In the United States, local chapters of the Audubon Society are usually the "nature club" of the cities in which they occur. The Portland and Seattle Audubon Society chapters are very large and active with offices that can help with questions about Audubon Society activities in their states. Both also have excellent nature bookstores. The other source for names and phone numbers of Audubon Society chapters nearest you, and for information on Christmas Bird Counts in our region, is the Western Regional Office in Sacramento, California:

National Audubon Society
Western Regional Office
555 Audubon Place
Sacramento, CA 95825
(916) 481-5332

In British Columbia there are many nature clubs, called variously field naturalists, naturalists, nature clubs or natural history societies, and all but a handful belong to the Federation of BC Naturalists. Each issue of the federation's newsletter, *BC Naturalist,* has a complete listing of all member and affiliated clubs. Contact the federation's office for a copy or more information.

Federation of BC Naturalists
321–1367 West Broadway
Vancouver, BC V6H 4A9
(604) 737-3057

Oregon

HawkWatch International Inc.
P.O. Box 660
Salt Lake City, UT 84110
1 (800) 726-4295
1 (801) 524-8511
(Call for information about activities in Oregon and Washington.)

Mount Pisgah Arboretum
33735 Seavey Loop Road
Eugene, OR 97405
(541) 747-3817

National Wildlife Federation
Pacific Northwest Office
921 SW Morrison, Suite 512
Portland, OR 97205
(503) 222-1429

Native Plant Society of Oregon
P.O. Box 902
Eugene, OR 97440

The Nature Conservancy
Oregon Field Office
1234 SE 14th
Portland, OR 97214
(503) 230-1221

Oregon Field Ornithologists
P.O. Box 10373
Eugene, OR 97440

Portland Audubon Society
5151 NW Cornell Road
Portland, OR 97210
(503) 292-6855 or 292-WILD

Sierra Club, Oregon Chapter
1413 SE Hawthorne Boulevard
Portland, OR 97214
(503) 238-0442

Xerces Society
4828 SE Hawthorne Boulevard
Portland, OR 97215
(503) 232-6639

Washington

HawkWatch International Inc.
P.O. Box 660
Salt Lake City, UT 84110
1 (800) 726-4295
1 (801) 524-8511
(Call for information about activities in Washington.)

Methow Valley Sport Trails Association
P.O. Box 147
Winthrop, WA 98862
1 (800) 682-5787 (for snow conditions, events)
(509) 996-2148 (for central lodging reservations)

The Nature Conservancy of Washington
217 Pine Street, Suite 1100
Seattle, WA 98101
(206) 343-4344

North Cascades Institute
2105 Highway 20
Sedro Woolley, WA 98284
(360) 856-5700, ext. 209
(Offers a wide variety of educational programs about nature.)

Olympic Park Institute
111 Barnes Point Road
Port Angeles, WA 98362
1-(800) 775-3720
(360) 928-3720
(Offers a wide variety of educational programs about nature.)

Port Townsend Marine Science Center
532 Battery Way
Port Townsend, WA 98368
(360) 385-5582

Rocky Mountain Elk Foundation
2291 W. Broadway
Missoula, MT 59802
(406) 523-4500

Seattle Audubon Society
8028 35th Avenue NE
Seattle, WA 98115
(206) 523-4483

Sierra Club, Cascade Chapter
8511 15th Avenue NE
Seattle, WA 98115
(206) 523-2147

Washington Native Plant Society
P.O. Box 576
Woodinville, WA 98071

Washington Ornithological Society
P.O. Box 31783
Seattle, WA 98103

The Whale Museum
P.O. Box 945
Friday Harbor, WA 98250
(360) 378-4710

British Columbia

BC Waterfowl Society
Reifel Migratory Bird Sanctuary
5191 Robertson Road
Delta, BC V4K 3N2
(604) 946-6980

Swan Lake Christmas Hill
Nature Sanctuary
3873 Swan Lake Road

Victoria, BC V8X 3W1
(604*) 479-0211

PRIVATE ORGANIZATIONS

Oregon

Bend Area Chamber of Commerce
63085 N Hwy 97
Bend, OR 97701
(541) 382-3221

Florence Area Chamber of Commerce
270 Highway 101
P.O. Box 26000
Florence, OR 97439
(503) 997-3128

Harney County Chamber of Commerce
18 West D Street
Burns, OR 97720
(503) 573-2636

Sea Lion Caves
91560 Highway 101
Florence, OR 97439
(503) 547-3111

Washington

Westport Chamber of Commerce
P.O. Box 306
Westport, WA 98595
1-(800) 345-6223 from the U.S.
(360) 268-9422 from Canada
(Call for a directory of whale-watching charters)

British Columbia

The Field Naturalist
1126 Blanshard Street
Victoria, BC V8W 2H6
(604*) 388-4174
(This book and nature store also serves as a center for southern Vancouver Island naturalist activities.)

FERRIES

These are the ferries that take cars and passengers. There are other ferries that take passengers only, but they tend to be faster—not an advantage for wildlife watching. Be sure you have the latest schedules when you travel on ferries.

The Ferry Traveller is an inexpensive booklet ($3 U.S., $3.50 Canadian) that is an excellent all-in-one guide to British Columbia and Washington ferries. For a copy, write or call: The Ferry Traveller, 301-2250 York, Vancouver, BC V6K 2S6; (604) 733-9113.

Washington

Black Ball Transport
101 East Railroad Avenue
Port Angeles, WA 98362
(360) 457-4491
(604*) 386-2202 (Victoria office)
(*M.V. Coho* between Port Angeles and Victoria)

Washington State Ferries
801 Alaskan Way
Seattle, WA 98104
(604) 464-6400 (in Seattle)
1 (800) 843-3779 (Washington state)
(604*) 381-1551 (in Victoria)

British Columbia

BC Ferries
1112 Fort Street
Victoria, BC V8V 4V2
(604*) 386-3431 (information in Victoria)
(604) 669-1211 (Vancouver)
(The new *Spirit of BC* and *Spirit of Vancouver Island* are like being on the *QEII*.)

Victoria Line
185 Dallas Road
Victoria, BC V8V 1A1
(604*) 480-5555
(Seattle to Victoria, from May to October; takes reservations)

Rare-Bird-Alert Telephone Tape Messages

Oregon: (503) 292-0661, ext. 200
Washington, statewide: (206) 933-1831
Washington, Columbia Basin: (509) 943-6957
Southeast Washington and Northeast Oregon: (208) 882-6195
Victoria: (604*) 592-3381
Vancouver: (604) 737-3074, option 4

Selected Bibliography

Allen, John E. *The Magnificent Gateway: A Layman's Guide to the Geology of the Columbia River Gorge.* 2nd ed. Portland, Ore.: Timber Press, 1984.

Arno, Stephen F., and Ramona Hammerly. *Northwest Trees.* Seattle: The Mountaineers, 1977.

Atkinson, Scott, and Fred Sharpe. *Wild Plants of the San Juan Islands.* Seattle: The Mountaineers, 1985.

Bellrose, Frank C. *Ducks, Geese and Swans of North America.* 3rd ed. Harrisburg, Pa.: Stackpole Books, 1980.

Borror, Donald J., and Richard E. White. *A Field Guide to the Insects.* Boston: Houghton Mifflin, 1970.

Burt, William H., and Richard P. Grossenheider. *A Field Guide to the Mammals.* 3rd. ed. Boston: Houghton Mifflin, 1980.

Campbell, Eileen C., R. W. Campbell, and R. T. McLaughlin. *Waterbirds of the Strait of Georgia.* Delta, B.C.: British Columbia Waterfowl Society, 1991.

Cissel, Diane, and John Cissel. *50 Old-Growth Day Hikes in the Mt. Hood National Forest.* Old Growth Day Hikes, 1993. (map with information.)

Cissel, Diane, John Cissel, and Peter Eberhardt. *50 Old-Growth Day Hikes in the Willamette National Forest.* Old Growth Day Hikes, 1991. (map with information.)

Ditmar Family. *Visitors' Guide to Ancient Forests of Western Washington.* Washington, D.C.: Wilderness Society, 1989.

Ehrlich, Paul, David Dobkin, and Darryl White. *The Birder's Handbook.* New York: Simon and Schuster, 1988.

Evanich, Joseph E., Jr. *The Birder's Guide to Oregon.* Portland, Ore.: Portland Audubon Society, 1990.

Evans, Howard E. *Life on a Little Known Planet.* New York: E. P. Dutton, 1966.

Fisheries and Oceans Canada. *Where and When to See Salmon.* Vancouver, B.C.: Fisheries and Oceans Canada.

Gilligan, Jeff, D. Rogers, M. Smith, and A. Contreras, eds. *Birds of Oregon: Status and Distribution.* McMinnville, Ore.: Cinclus Publications, 1994.

Gordon, David. *Field Guide to the Sasquatch.* Seattle: Sasquatch Books, 1992.

Gordon, David, and Chuck Flaherty. *Field Guide to the Orca.* Seattle: Sasquatch Books, 1990.

Harper, Alice B. *The Banana Slug.* Aptos, Calif.: Bay Leaves Press, 1988.

Houle, Marcy C. *Portland's Forest Park—One City's Wilderness.* Portland, Ore.: Oregon Historical Society Press, 1987.

Johnsgard, Paul A. *North American Owls.* Washington, D.C.: Smithsonian Institution Press, 1988.

Jolley, Russ. *Wildflowers of the Columbia Gorge.* Portland, Ore.: Oregon Historical Society Press, 1988.

Jones, Philip N., ed. *Columbia River Gorge: A Complete Guide.* Seattle: The Mountaineers, 1992.

Kelly, Davis, and Gary Braasch. *Secrets of the Old Growth Forest.* Layton, Utah: Gibbs Smith, 1988.

Kozloff, Eugene N. *Plants and Animals of the Pacific Northwest.* Seattle: University of Washington Press, 1976.

———. *Seashore Life of the Northern Pacific Coast.* Seattle: University of Washington Press, 1983.

Kress, Stephen W. *Bird Life: A Guide to the Behavior and Biology of Birds.* New York: Golden Press, 1991.

Larrison, Earl J. *Mammals of the Northwest.* Seattle: Seattle Audubon Society, 1976.

La Tourrette, Joe. *Washington Wildlife Viewing Guide.* Helena and Billings, Mont.: Falcon Press, 1992.

Leatherwood, Stephen, and Randall R. Reeves. *The Sierra Club Handbook of Whales and Dolphins.* San Francisco: Sierra Club Books, 1983.

Leonard, W. P., H. B. Brown, L. L. C. Jones, K. R. McAllister, and R. M. Storm. *Amphibians of Washington and Oregon.* Seattle: Seattle Audubon Society, 1993.

Levi, Herbert W., and Lorna R. Levi. *Spiders and Their Kin.* New York: Golden Press, 1968.

Lewis, Mark G., and Fred A. Sharpe. *Birding in the San Juan Islands.* Seattle: The Mountaineers, 1987.

MacClintock, Dorcas. *Squirrels of North America.* New York: Van Nostrand Reinhold, 1970.

Mathews, Daniel. *Cascade-Olympic Natural History.* Portland, Ore.: Raven Editions/Portland Audubon Society, 1988.

McCrae, Jean, and Laimons Osis. *Plants and Animals of Oregon's Rocky Intertidal Habitat.* Portland, Ore.:

Oregon Department of Fish and Wildlife, 1994.

Morse, Bob. *A Birder's Guide to Ocean Shores, Washington*, 1994. Order from Bob Morse, 1515 Lakemoor Loop, Olympia, WA 98512.

National Geographic Society. *Field Guide to the Birds of North America*. 2nd. ed. Washington, D.C.: National Geographic Society, 1987.

Nehls, Harry B. *Familiar Birds of the Northwest*. 3rd ed. Portland, Ore.: Portland Audubon Society, 1989.

Netboy, Anthony. *The Columbia River Salmon and Steelhead Trout*. Seattle: University of Washington Press, 1980.

Niehaus, Theodore, and Charles Ripper. *A Field Guide to Pacific States Wildflowers*. Boston: Houghton Mifflin, 1976.

Norse, Elliott. *Ancient Forests of the Pacific Northwest*. Washington, D.C.: Island Press, 1990.

Nussbaum, Ronald A., E. D. Brodie, and R. M. Storm. *Amphibians and Reptiles of the Pacific Northwest*. Moscow, Idaho: University of Idaho Press, 1983.

Oceanic Society. *Field Guide to the Gray Whale*. Seattle: Sasquatch Books, 1989.

Paulson, Dennis. *Shorebirds of the Pacific Northwest*. Seattle: University of Washington Press, 1993.

Peterson, Roger T. *A Field Guide to Western Birds*. 3rd ed., Boston: Houghton Mifflin, 1990.

Pojar, Jim, and Andy MacKinnon. *Plants of the Pacific Northwest Coast*. Edmonton, Alb.: Lone Pine, 1994.

Pyle, Robert M., and Jon Pelham. *The Butterflies of Cascadia*. Seattle: Seattle Audubon Society, in press.

Ricketts, Edward F., and Jack Calvin. *Between Pacific Tides*. 4th ed. Stanford, Calif.: Stanford University Press, 1968.

Russo, Ron, and Pam Olhausen. *Pacific Intertidal Life: a Guide to Organisms of Rocky Reefs and Tide Pools of the Pacific Coast*. Rochester, N.Y.: Nature Study Guild Publishers, 1981.

Steelquist, Robert. *Field Guide to the Pacific Salmon*. Seattle: Sasquatch Books, 1992.

Stokes, Donald. *A Guide to Bird Behavior*. Vol. 1. Boston: Little, Brown, 1979.

———. *A Guide to Observing Insect Lives*. Boston: Little, Brown, 1983.

Stokes, Donald, and Lillian Stokes. *A Guide to Bird Behavior*. Vol. 2 and 3. Boston: Little, Brown, 1983 and 1989.

Stoltmann, Randy. *Hiking Guide to the Big Trees of Southwestern British Columbia*. 2nd ed. Vancouver, B.C.: Western Canada Wilderness Committee, 1991.

Sullivan, Timothy. *Oregon Coast Recreational Atlas*. Corvallis, Ore.: E&S Geographic and Information Services, 1991.

Sutton, Patricia, and Clay Sutton. *How to Spot an Owl*. Shelburne, Vt.: Chapters Publishing, 1994.

Taylor, Keith. *A Birders Guide to British Columbia*. Victoria, B.C.: Keith Taylor Birdfinding Guides, 1993.

———. *A Birders Guide to Vancouver Island*. Victoria, B.C.: Keith Taylor Birdfinding Guides, 1990.

Taylor, Ronald J. *Sagebrush Country: A Wildflower Sanctuary*. Missoula, Mont.: Mountain Press, 1992.

Teale, Edwin W. *The Strange Lives of Familiar Insects*. New York: Dodd, Mead, 1962.

Terres, John K. *The Audubon Society Encyclopedia of North American Birds*. New York: Alfred A. Knopf, 1980.

Tuttle, Merlin. *America's Neighborhood Bats*. Austin, Tex.: University of Texas, 1988.

Vancouver Natural History Society. *A Bird Watching Guide to the Vancouver Area*. Vancouver, B.C.: Cavendish Books, 1993.

Wahl, Terence, and Dennis Paulson. *A Guide to Bird Finding in Washington*. Bellingham, Wash.: T. Wahl, 1977.

Wareham, Bill. *British Columbia Wildlife Viewing Guide*. Edmonton, Alb.: Lone Pine, 1991.

Weston, Jim, and David Stirling. *The Naturalist's Guide to the Victoria Region*. Victoria, B.C.: Victoria Natural History Society, 1986.

Whittlesey, Rhoda. *Familiar Friends: Northwest Plants*. Portland, Ore.: Rose Press, 1985.

Wood, Wendell. *A Walking Guide to Oregon's Ancient Forests*. Portland, Ore.: Oregon Natural Resources Council, 1991.

Yates, Steve. *Marine Wildlife of Puget Sound, the San Juans, and the Strait of Georgia*. Old Saybrook, Conn.: Globe Pequot Press, 1988.

———. *Orcas, Eagles and Kings: Georgia Strait and Puget Sound*. Portland, Ore.: Primavera Press/Sasquatch Books, 1992.

Zim, Herbert S., and Clarence Cottam. *Insects*. New York: Golden Press, 1987.

Index

Numbers in *Italics* are photographs or maps.

About the Author

James Luther Davis has always been fascinated with nature, starting his studies as a young lad chasing lizards in the Sonoran Desert near Tucson. Schooling took him to various spots in California and to Colorado State University, where he received his master's degree in zoology. After several more years in California as a teacher of junior and senior high school science, and stints as the "Zoomobile Guy" at two zoos, he and his wife moved to Portland, Oregon, his mother's hometown. James was education director of the Portland Audubon Society for nine years and continues to lead natural history tours and to conduct other programs for Portland Audubon while also teaching at Marylhurst College. When not pursuing natural history, James can often be found playing in The Jitters, a Portland rock and roll band. James, his wife Lani, and daughter Risa, love living in Portland.